To my teachers:
My public management colleagues
and the participants in the
Kennedy School's executive programs

CONTENTS

ACKNOWLEDGMENTS

For the last two decades, faculty and students at Harvard's Kennedy School of Government have engaged in an intensive conversation about how to produce excellence in public management. It has been my privilege to serve as amanuensis to that ongoing dialogue. It is only for that reason that this book appears under my name. The true authors of the ideas recorded and organized in this book are listed below.

I am most indebted to Richard Neustadt and Graham Allison, who set me to the task of learning about public sector management almost twenty years ago. They started me on a journey that has been longer than either they or I intended, but the task has been far more complicated and absorbing than I first imagined. At the outset, I benefited enormously from the counsel of a distinguished group of fellow travelers that included Joseph L. Bower, Charles J. Christensen, Philip B. Heymann, Stephen V. Hitchner, and Laurence E. Lynn, Jr. They taught me about the difference between "implementing" and "managing" and that between "policies" and "organizations." They were soon joined by a wonderful group of reflective practitioners: Manuel Carballo, Hale Champion, Gordon Chase, Richard Darman, and Harry Weiner, who set standards for clarity and relevance in our intellectual work. I also learned a great deal from Colyer Crum and George Lodge at the Harvard Business School, with whom I had the pleasure of teaching an executive program for public sector managers.

As the Kennedy School's own teaching and research program in public management gathered steam (thanks to the leadership provided by Dean Graham Allison, Executive Dean Hale Champion, and Associate Dean Peter Zimmerman and a generous grant from the Alfred P. Sloan Foundation), a very creative group of faculty members, both academics and practitioners, gathered at the school to do research, design curriculum, and teach our students in both degree and executive programs. On the political management side, that group included Nancy Altman, Richard Darman, Michael Dukakis, Ronnie Heifetz, Susan Irving, Martin Linsky, Jonathan Moore, Gary Orren, Roger Porter, Robert Reich, James K. Sebenius, Larry Smith, and Greg Treverton. On the operational management side, the group included Mary Jo Bane, Michael Barzelay, Walter Broadnax, Olivia Golden, Steve Kelman, Dutch Leonard, Robert Leone, Michael O'Hare, and Steve Rosenthal. On the role of analysis in guiding public managers, H. James Brown, Tony Gomez-Ibanez, Marc Roberts, and James Verdier played key roles. Michael Nacht and Peter Zimmerman animated the group that stayed focused on strategy in the public sector.

The work on political management got a major boost from a faculty seminar we ran (with the aid of the Sloan Foundation Grant) entitled "Managing the Policy Development Process." That seminar involved Hale Champion, Richard Darman, Richard Neustadt, Roger Porter, and Greg Treverton. Robert Zoellick ably served as rapporteur. This work was also aided by the development of the concepts of public deliberation and leadership by Robert Reich and Ronnie Heifetz, respectively, and by Robert Reich's determined and effective efforts to get us all to produce a book, *The Power of Public Ideas*. James Sebenius's leadership in the field of negotiation analysis stimulated us further. Work with Marty Linsky and Larry Smith in a defense policy seminar focused on political management was also extremely valuable.

The work on operational management was boosted significantly by a grant from the Ford Foundation to conduct research on innovation as part of the program "Innovation in State and Local Government." Alan Altshuler, Michael Barzelay, Walter Broadnax, Dutch Leonard, Robert Leone, Michael O'Hare, and Marc Zegans have been particularly important in this venture. A little bit later, a grant from Frank Weil, along with able assistance from Mark Abramson and the Council for Excellence in Government, supported research and a conference on the important differences between innovating in the public and private sectors.

I am grateful to Howard Husock, whose leadership of the Kennedy School's Case Program has provided a great deal of grist for my particular mills, and who generously granted permission for me to use cases that his program had developed.

In addition, I am indebted to colleagues outside of the Kennedy School whose work has challenged me, and whose advice I have sought often, namely, Eugene Bardach, Robert Behn, and Marty Levin.

More recently still, I have learned a great deal from a new group of faculty members who have brought their particular perspectives to our enterprise: Arthur Applbaum, Robert Blackwell, Robin Ely, Jane Fountain, Olivia Golden, Linda Kaboolian, Chris Letts, Marc Lindenberg, Jan Shubert, Malcolm Sparrow, Michael Watkins, and Philip Zelikow.

I am also grateful to those who read drafts of this book at different stages and gave invaluable guidance. In addition to many of my aforementioned colleagues at the Kennedy School, I thank Edward Banfield, Derek Bok, Winthrop Knowlton, Theodore Leavitt, and Ray Vernon. Three wonderful junior colleagues, David Kennedy, Zachary Tumin, and Marc Zegans, became important professional colleagues while reviewing the manuscript. And two "commonwealth colleagues," John Alford and Greg Parston, kept encouraging and challenging me to make this book relevant to managerial developments and contexts in their countries—Australia and Great Britain, respectively. Two of the best reflective practitioners I know, Judy Pinke and Ellen Schall, also gave me encouragement and advice.

As the long gestation of the book indicates, getting these ideas on paper has been no easy task. At two critical times, I received just the support I needed from Linda Kaboolian and Aida Donald. And at one moment when I thought all was lost, I received invaluable editorial assistance from my cousin Curtis Church. Throughout the long process of writing and rewriting this book, I was supported admirably by my faculty assistants, Flo Chen, Kincade Dunn, and Janet Fletcher.

This was the crucible in which the ideas presented in this book were forged. To all these people I owe my heartfelt thanks.

INTRODUCTION

My colleague Graham Allison once explained why books need introductions. "Well, you wrote the book by throwing clumps of mud against a barn wall. The introduction draws a red circle around the clumps to show you hit the target!" So, that's the point of this introduction: to describe the target I was trying to hit. I also describe the materials I used to construct the argument and the tests one could use to decide whether I have really hit the target.

PURPOSES

The aim of this book is quite specific: to lay out a structure of practical reasoning to guide managers of public enterprises.[1] It presents a general answer to the question of what public managers should think and do to exploit the particular circumstances they find themselves in to create public value.

To achieve this purpose, the book develops several different kinds of ideas. First, it sets out a *philosophy* of public management—an idea of what we citizens should expect of public managers, the ethical responsibilities they assume in taking office, and what constitutes virtue in the execution of their offices. Second, it sets out *diagnostic frameworks* to guide managers in analyzing the settings in which they operate and gauging the potential for effective action. Third, it identifies particular kinds of *interventions* managers can make to exploit the potential of their political and organizational settings for creating public value.

The specificity of my purpose means that there are many important things that this book does *not* do. It does not, for example, explain why public sector organizations behave the way they do,[2] or why managers behave as they do.[3] It does not explain the behavior of organizations because it focuses on managers, not organizations. It does not explain why managers behave the way they do because it details what managers *should* think and do. In short, I develop a normative (rather than positive) theory of managerial (rather than organizational) behavior.

But who precisely are the public managers to whom this book is addressed? The answer, unfortunately, is not immediately obvious. American constitutions divide rather than concentrate public authority.[4] The result is that many officials gain effective influence over governmental operations and can, therefore, reasonably claim the mantle of public manager.

Elected chief executives—presidents, governors, and mayors, for example—could be seen as public managers.[5] They are constitutionally responsible for the execution of laws and the deployment of public resources. Alternatively, the officials whom elected executives appoint to lead their line agencies—those called administrators, commissioners, and directors—could be viewed as public managers.[6] Sometimes, these political executives assign policy staffs to assume project management responsibility for implementing specific policy initiatives.[7] Insofar as they do implement policy, these staffs could be considered public managers. Or, public managers could be the senior civil servants who support the political executives and their staffs. Some work in offices of administration and management, designing, maintaining, and operating the finance and personnel systems that guide and account for the performance of public organizations.[8] Others with deep substantive knowledge of (and long experience with) specific operating programs fill line positions in public organizations. Because all these officials have handholds on lines of public authority, they all qualify as public managers.

Farther from the lines of direct authority (but conceivably no less influential) are officials who occupy powerful oversight positions. For example, although contrary to conventional views, one could consider legislators and staffs on key legislative oversight committees as important managers of public enterprises.[9] This claim seems particularly credible when legislative committees seek to micromanage public sector operations by imposing specific restrictions on operational programs. A different kind of oversight comes from judges who are generally authorized to ensure that individual rights are protected in governmental operations. Indeed, in some cases where public managers have violated individual rights in schools, prisons, mental hospitals, or housing authorities, judges have become directly involved in managing them.[10]

Even those who lead interest groups could be viewed as important public entrepreneurs or managers since they often initiate or halt public sector enterprises.[11] Finally, some private sector managers become public managers because they produce primarily for government. Indeed, as the movement for increased privatization of public sector production takes hold, more and more "public managers" will work for the "private sector."[12]

While many officials can qualify as public managers, only a few are both held accountable for public sector performance and given direct authority over public resources. Generally, these few belong to the first group of officials I described—those politically elected or appointed officials in executive branch agencies, along with the senior civil servants who aid them. It is primarily to these officials—at all levels of government—that this book is most specifically directed.

Yet, because I am interested in the overall function of public management as well as the performance of individual managers, I want to include the others—the overseers and lobbyists—as well. What these other officials expect or demand from public managers, and how they think about and perform their own jobs, has an important effect on both the context within which public managers work and their success in achieving their objectives. So, while I address primarily those who hold line management positions in executive branch or independent agencies, I speak as well to the others who define the context for managerial action.

Note that in focusing my attention on what managers should think and do, I do not intend to take a position on whether improving managerial performance is the only or the best way to improve public sector performance.[13] I take it for granted that many factors other than managerial behavior contribute to the success of public enterprises. Indeed, it is plausible to me that the specific actions of managers may account for very little of the variance in results obtained. I also take it for granted that institutional structures and processes shape what managers think and influence what they can do. I recognize that one can view managerial performance as a *dependent* variable and institutional structures as the *independent* variable. In short, I take no position on the important question of whether "institutional reform" or "improved management" is the best way to go in improving public sector performance.

Having said this, however, I wish to give two reasons why I have chosen to write on improving management rather than institutional reform. First, my own particular position at Harvard's Kennedy School of Government has given me a comparative advantage in developing ideas about improved management. Each year, the Kennedy School welcomes hundreds of practicing public managers to its classrooms. They are eager for general knowledge about governmental institutions but particularly hungry for ideas about how to do better in their jobs. Given their eagerness, it seemed a waste of talent and energy, as well as a dereliction of duty, not to focus attention on developing ideas that would be most valuable to them.

Second, I continue to believe that improving managerial thought and practice *is* an important route to improving the performance of public sector organizations. After all, large institutional reform does not do away with managers; it simply redefines their positions and responsibilities. What the managers do with their new positions will often decisively affect how successful the institutional reform turns out to be. For example, the ideas of decentralization and "total quality management" often depend crucially on the performance of lower level managers suddenly charged with new responsibilities.[14]

Moreover, one of the most important "institutions" that needs to be reformed is our current, conventionally held views of what public managers could and should do on our behalf.[15] Indeed, if we could change only that particular institution, I think we would discover that many existing institutions could be made to perform better. For these reasons, then, we must continue to focus some of our attention on improving management as well reforming institutions.

The advice in this book is intended to be general enough to be applicable to a wide range of managerial positions in the public sector while specific enough to require managers to make only a small intellectual leap from the ideas presented here to the concrete, particular situations they face. That is what makes it a book about management in general, rather than a book about managing a particular kind of agency, or executing a particular managerial function, or dealing with a particular kind of managerial problem.

The book does not claim to be culturally neutral or truly independent of historical context. Indeed, its premises and illustrations are grounded in the context of American government in the last quarter of the twentieth century. Whether it has implications for the way that managers should think and act in other countries or in other times, I cannot now say.[16] So far, at least, I am primarily a student of late-twentieth-century public administration. It is those who practice this craft that I primarily seek to aid.

SOURCES AND METHODS

The ultimate proof of the pudding is in the eating, and I don't want to delay the meal much longer. Still, a cautious diner might want to know something of the pudding's ingredients before taking the first bite. To meet this reasonable demand, I offer the following list of ingredients.

The book is based on academic literatures that seem relevant to understanding the context, purposes, and techniques of public sector executives. These include literatures within political science, economics, organizational theory, public administration, administrative law, and business management. Perhaps no one (and certainly not I) can really hope to master these diverse literatures and distill from them the key points they offer for the development of a normative theory of public management. Still, I have been able to scan them and learn some of the most important things that each had to contribute to this intellectual task.

The political science literature revealed a great deal about the characteristics of the settings in which public managers now operate: the political context that surrounds public-policy-making and implementation;[17] the nature and behavior of legislative institutions;[18] how the press behaves and how its behavior affects the conduct of government;[19] and what motivates and shapes the behavior of elected chief executives.[20]

The economics literature not only contained an implicit theory defining the proper role of government in the society,[21] but also proposed some valuable methods for evaluating proposed and ongoing governmental activities.[22] Moreover, it suggested how owners and overseers of operations might structure incentives for managers who are supposed to act on their behalf,[23] and how complex negotiations might be analyzed and carried out.[24]

The organizational theory literature provided different images of organizations that clarified why public and private sector organizations behave the way they do.[25] It also helped explain why organizations have difficulties in adopting and sustaining innovation and why managers face obstacles as they seek to improve their performance.[26]

The literature on public administration supplied a rich, well-developed theory of public management in a democracy.[27] It contributed a philosophy of public management animated by the goal of ensuring effective democratic control over public sector organizations and the achievement of both consistency and effectiveness in public sector operations.[28] It also described the important instruments of managerial influence and how they might best be wielded to produce efficiency and effectiveness.[29] In addition, it presented several important studies of what public sector managers actually did and how public sector organizations did or did not produce consistency in their operations or adapt to changing circumstances.[30]

The literature on administrative law set out a normative conception of how public decisions involving the use of public resources should be made to ensure fairness and emphasized the continuing importance of ensuring equity and due process in public sector decision-making as well as efficiency and effectiveness.[31] This literature also examined key case studies of agencies involved in the adjudication of specific cases.[32]

Finally, the literature on private sector management offered a different, and in some ways competitive, picture of the context, philosophy, and instruments of management and organizational leadership.[33] It focused attention on the dynamics of the marketplace rather than the stability of governmental mandates;[34] on how to stimulate innovation and change in new missions rather than on how to increase efficiency in old operations;[35] and on the role of imagination and enterprise among managers as well as technical competence and dutifulness.[36]

Of these literatures, the one closest to the task at hand, of course, is that on public administration. This literature provides a treasure trove and a crucial starting point for any effort to give guidance to public sector executives. I have borrowed from it quite liberally.

At the same time, I have focused particular emphasis on two questions that, though not at the center of the classic literature, did seem much on the mind of practicing public executives. First, how should managers cope with inconsistent, fickle political mandates? Second, how can they best experiment, innovate, and reposition public organizations in their changing environments?[37]

To reach these questions my Kennedy School colleagues and I added a new ingredient to the mix: the operational experiences of practicing public executives. We tapped into that experience in three different ways. First, we wrote cases describing the problems that managers faced, the calculations they made, the interventions they chose, and (as best we could see) the results of the interventions. Indeed, over the last decade, the Kennedy School's Case Program has written and published more than six hundred cases describing managerial problems and interventions.[38]

Second, each year we encountered several hundred practicing managers in the Kennedy School's teaching programs—primarily in our executive programs. Because we taught these executives through interactive case discussions, over the years we learned how they would analyze and act in these cases as well as how the protagonists did. This meant that we often learned as much about management from them as they did from us. As one distinguished colleague explained, "They aren't just students, they're data and teachers as well!"[39]

Third, we invited distinguished practitioners to join the Kennedy School faculty to ensure close, continuing contact with those whose accomplishments indicated that they knew how to size up and exploit opportunities to create public value.[40] They, like the students in our programs, brought the perspectives and wisdom of emerging "best practice" into our midst for explication and examination.

Having written the cases and heard them discussed by our students and practitioner colleagues, we came to understand them: how the situation portrayed by the case was best analyzed, what possible interventions existed, what their prospects for success were. By repeating this process for many cases, we gradually learned how to generalize and abstract from the particular cases and how to form our generalizations into coherent intellectual forms. It is these forms that I have tried to record in this book.

I must acknowledge one more ingredient: the special set of influences that operated within the Kennedy School as an institution. It is fair to say that the view of management developed at the Kennedy School reflected our own intellectual traditions as well as the requirements of the outside world. More specifically, our views of management were shaped by the emphasis that the school gave to the use of special analytic tools drawn from economics, operations research, and statistics to analyze the substantive value of proposed or implemented public policies.

What was exciting about the study of public policy (as opposed to the study of public administration) was that it focused attention on the ends of government as well as the means. It also focused on new ideas and innovations in government rather than on routine maintenance of governmental organizations. What admitted one to these conversations was the mastery of the difficult analytic techniques that enabled one to challenge political judgments with an alternative way to gauge the public value of proposed or existing governmental enterprises.[41]

Given this culture, it is hardly surprising that the view of management we ultimately developed would be one that sought to understand how specific policy decisions were made and implemented rather than one that focused on organizational maintenance or the refinement of administrative control systems (which had long been the focus of public administration). Indeed, for a long time the idea of effective implementation of particular policies (rather than the successful management of public sector organizations) was taken as the central subject of public management.[42] This conception of management as policy implementation eventually faded because, in focusing on policy rather than organizations, it left out important questions about how public sector organizations should be developed and used. It was silent, for example, on the issue of how that portion of an organization's assets that were not engaged in a particular new policy initiative should be used. And it seemed to be indifferent to the effect that a new policy implementation effort would have on the overall performance and position of an organization.[43]

Ultimately, then, the concerns that the field of public administration had long championed, which focused on the effective administration and development of public sector *organizations,* had to be rediscovered and successfully integrated with public policy's concerns for *policies.* The natural synthesis of these two traditions was to conceive of public organizations as relatively flexible instruments to be used in achieving changing public purposes. The public purposes would develop as a consequence of both changes in political aspirations and demands and shifting problems in the world. By seeing things in this light, Kennedy School faculty would also be responding to two trends: political science observations about the inconsistent and shifting political contexts surrounding public sector organizations; and the obvious need for government to innovate as it first expanded and then contracted its horizons.[44] This view of management would also be supported by a strong resonance between its conception of public sector management and emerging ideas about private sector management.[45]

It thus may have been culturally inevitable that someone at the Kennedy School would develop an idea of "strategic management" in the public sector that put a great deal of emphasis on purposefulness, on responses to changing political mandates, and on adaptive and flexible organizations. And it may be that the appeal of such ideas owes more to their fit with cultural trends and organizational aspirations of the Kennedy School than to their truth and utility outside the cultural context in which they were developed.

TESTS

Precisely because the ideas in this book emerge from a particular cultural context, it is important to consider how they might be tested. In principle, it is not difficult to see what the test should be: offered as advice to managers, the ideas would have to be tested *in use* by managers.[46] Essentially, managers who understood and used these ideas to define their roles, diagnose their situations, and design their interventions would be expected to do better than those who did not rely on these techniques. In practice, however, it is hard to conduct such tests. To begin with, how do we define what it means for managers to "do better"?

One definition of success emphasizes the personal success of the managers themselves: managers succeed if they enhance their personal reputations and advance their own careers. If a manager's reputation for success were properly earned, individual success would be a fine operational measure of managerial success. We cannot be sure, however, that the tests used to establish reputations reliably indicate real managerial performance. We have all seen managers whom we consider more skilled in burnishing their reputations than in achieving the real substantive results that should be the basis for their reputation.

A second definition of success, then, would focus on whether managers succeed in building large, durable, and strong organizations.[47] Such a definition has the virtue of focusing on managerial accomplishment rather than reputation. And it seems consistent with a common notion of what constitutes successful management in the private sector.[48]

Yet a little reflection (combined with several notorious examples of public sector empire builders) indicates the inappropriateness of this definition when applied to public sector managers.[49] Ensuring the survival of public sector organizations is all too easy to achieve.[50] The challenge, instead, is to make them efficient, to reduce costs, and to adapt to changing political demands or new substantive tasks. It is particularly difficult to be able to reclaim resources from them when the need for them has passed. Thus, in the public sector, the increased strength or size of an organization is as likely to indicate a problem as an accomplishment.

A third definition of success in public management would measure personal efficacy in achieving preferred policy outcomes: managers succeed if they have their preferred policy objectives adopted and implemented. This definition has the benefit of rewarding managerial effort that goes beyond the goal of building or maintaining organizations to the goal of achieving some substantive purpose. But it, too, has flaws. It places too much emphasis on the particular things that the managers themselves want. It is by no means clear that public managers are supposed to achieve their preferred policy objectives. Arguably, they are in their positions to act for *society,* not their own idiosyncratic views of what society needs.[51]

Of course, managers will have to take individual positions on important policy questions. But the point is that the power and legitimacy of the policy position they adopt depends more on the extent to which their position reflects and accommodates the views of others in their political environment than on their own personal endorsement of the position. The image of success in public management as achieving one's own policy objectives leaves managers too little scope to learn what others want and too much freedom to dominate the process with idiosyncratic views of the public interest.

The definition that remains equates managerial success in the public sector with initiating and reshaping public sector enterprises in ways that increase their value to the public in both the short and the long run. This is the definition I prefer. Sometimes this means increasing efficiency, effectiveness, or fairness in currently defined missions. Other times it means introducing programs that respond to a new political aspiration or meet a new need in the organization's task environment. Still other times it means recasting the mission of the organization and repositioning it in its political and task environment so that its old capabilities can be used more responsively and effectively. On occasion it means reducing the claims that government organizations make on taxpayers and reclaiming the resources now committed to the organizations for alternative public or private uses. This is clearly the proper conceptual definition of managerial success: to increase the public value produced by public sector organizations in both the short and the long run. Indeed, the idea that public managers should produce value-creating organizations matches the criteria of success used in the private sector.[52]

But how do we operationalize this definition? We have nothing analogous to the private sector's history of profitability to measure past performance; nor can we use a stock price or similar mechanism to gauge expected value in the future. So, even though the conceptual definition of success for public managers is clear, how to measure it is not. We have no way to conduct a rigorous test of what managerial practices are better than others.

Moreover, it is almost as difficult to define what it means "to do" as what it means "to do better." After all, the ideas presented here are designed to help managers *think* about doing. The actual *doing* then has to be done. Much of the effectiveness of managerial interventions may depend on small details of execution as well as on conception. In this sense, this book gets to only part of the complex process of managerial thought and action.

Finally, it goes without saying that changes in organizational performance can rarely be definitively attributed to particular managerial interventions. Often, so many factors contribute to an organization's performance that we cannot attribute any observed success to specific managerial interventions. Indeed, many of the ideas suggested in this book focus managerial attention on orchestrating the forces and pressures that already exist to help them achieve their purposes. Insofar as this advice is taken and actually works, the distinction between the influence of managerial action on the one hand and external forces on the other becomes blurred. Those who are inclined to think that managerial action matters a great deal will impute great acumen to the managers who stimulate, align themselves with, or use outside pressures. Those who are more skeptical of the importance of management will see the manager riding a wave of outside pressure, succeeding without really having to do anything.

Since it is difficult to conduct a rigorous test of the ideas presented here, I suggest two simpler ways to test their plausibility and utility. First, the ideas should be "grounded" in the sense that they identify a recognizable class of problems and accurately identify many of the things that would, as a strictly logical matter, have to be considered if the problems are to be solved. This test is appropriate precisely because the intellectual construct that is being presented is an idea about how one might think—not an empirical proposition about how one variable is related to another.

Second, the ideas should be "useful" in the sense that they help those practitioners actually facing the problems to distribute their attention across the world in ways that alert them to important and relevant facts about their current situation, help stimulate their imaginations about how they might proceed, and offer some rudimentary guides to distinguish better ideas from worse. This is an appropriate test because it serves the purpose that the ideas are meant to serve.

To a degree, I have subjected the ideas in this book to both the rigorous and the less rigorous tests. The closest I have come to the rigorous test is to compare "successful" managers to "unsuccessful" managers, and then to compare what the "successful" managers seem to think and do with what the "unsuccessful" managers seem to think and do. I present both successful and unsuccessful managers, although my theory takes into account many more cases than I discuss here. The evidence clearly establishes three things: (1) the crucial importance of remaining purposeful; (2) the necessity of recognizing "political management" as a key function in public sector management; and (3) the need to recast our images of operational management to focus more attention on stimulating innovations of various kinds. Yet, I have not been entirely rigorous in either the sampling effort or the data collection and cannot claim the power that would come from that degree of rigor.

In the less rigorous test I have relied for evidence on feedback from practicing public managers who have been exposed to these ideas. Their testimony has been favorable and encouraging.

Still, in the end, I do not think I have proven anything. What I have done is nominate, for further consideration and testing, a complex set of ideas about how public managers should orient themselves to their jobs, diagnose their situations, and design their interventions. The methods I present differ from those many public managers now employ and from the ways they are taught and encouraged to think and act. This new approach is plausibly better adapted to the reality of the situations they now confront than what they have relied on in the past. And it may help them succeed in helping society by keeping their attention focused on the problem of defining and producing public value with the resources entrusted to them. That, at least, is my fervent hope.

CHAPTER 1

MANAGERIAL IMAGINATION

The town librarian was concerned.[1] Each day, at about 3:00 P.M., eddies of schoolchildren washed into the library's reading rooms. At about 5:00 the tide of children began to ebb. By 6:00 the library was quiet once again. An informal survey revealed what was happening: the library was being used as a day-care center for latchkey children. How should the librarian respond?

THE TOWN LIBRARIAN
AND THE LATCHKEY CHILDREN

Her first instinct was to discourage the emerging practice. After all, the influx disrupted the library. The reading rooms, quiet and spacious most of the day, became noisy and crowded. Books, particularly the fragile paperbacks, stacked after careless use in untidy heaps on library tables, slid to the floor with spines cracking. Tired assistants faced mountains of reshelving before they could leave for the day. The constant traffic to the bathrooms kept the janitor busy with special efforts to keep them neat, clean, and well stocked.

Besides, it just wasn't the town library's job to care for latchkey children. That task should be done by the parents, or perhaps other day-care providers, certainly not by the library. Perhaps a letter to the local newspaper reminding citizens about the proper use of a library would set things right. If that failed, new rules limiting children's access to the library would have to be established.

Then, she had a more entrepreneurial idea: perhaps the latchkey children could be used to claim more funds for the library from the town's tight budget.[2] She could argue that the new demands from latchkey children required additional resources. Additional staff would be needed to keep the children from disrupting other library users. Overtime funds would be necessary to pay assistants and janitors for tidying the library at the end of the day. Perhaps the library itself would have to be redesigned to create elementary and junior high school reading rooms. Indeed, now that she thought of it, the reconstruction work might be used to justify repainting the interior of the entire library—an objective she had had for many years. But all this would cost money, and a statewide tax revolt had left the town with sharply limited funds.

As the forbidding prospect of seeking funds from the town's Budget Committee came clearly into view, the librarian had a different idea: perhaps a program for the latchkey children could be financed by charging their parents for the costs of the new program.[3] Some practical problems loomed, however. For example, how much should she charge for the service?[4] She could fairly easily record the direct costs associated with providing the program and find a price that would cover these direct costs. But she was unsure how to account for indirect costs such as the managerial costs of organizing the activity, the depreciation of the building, and so on. If she included too few of these indirect costs in the price of the program, then the public as a whole would be unwittingly subsidizing the working parents. If she included too many, the town would be unwittingly taking advantage of working parents to help support their library.

She also thought that the town's citizens and their representatives might have views about whether it was appropriate for her to use the facilities of the library for a program of this type, and she could not be sure what those views would be. If she set up a fee-for-service program, would the town's residents admire her entrepreneurial energies or worry that she was becoming too independent?[5] Similarly, would they see serving the latchkey children as a worthy cause or as a service to a narrow and not particularly deserving group? She would clearly have to go back to the Town Meeting for guidance.[6]

Given the difficulties of charging clients for the service, the librarian had still another idea: perhaps the new service could be "financed" through volunteer effort.[7] Maybe the parents of the children could be organized to assume some of the responsibilities of supervising and cleaning up after the children. Maybe they could even be enticed to help the librarian make the changes in the physical configuration of the library—to accommodate the new function more easily and to maintain an appropriate separation between the elderly people who used the library for reading and meeting and the children who used the library for the same purposes but more actively and noisily. The community spirit evident in such activities might overwhelm public concerns about the propriety of using the library to care for latchkey children and the complaints of some that public resources were being used to subsidize relatively narrow and unworthy interests.

Mobilizing a volunteer effort would be a complex undertaking, however. The librarian was unfamiliar with such enterprises. Indeed, all the things she had so far considered seemed difficult and unfamiliar since they involved her in outside political activity. Making a budget presentation to the town's Budget Committee and writing a letter about the problem to the newspaper were one thing; setting up a financially self-sustaining program and mobilizing a large group of volunteers were quite another.

Then, a last idea occurred to her: perhaps the problem could be solved by finding an answer within her own organization. A little rescheduling might ensure that there would be adequate staff to supervise the children, perhaps even to provide reading enrichment programs. Maybe some things could be rearranged in the library to create a special room for the program. Perhaps movies could sometimes be shown in this special room as part of the after-school program.

In fact, the more the librarian thought about it, the more it seemed that caring for these children in the library might be well within the current mission of her organization. It might give her and her assistant librarians a chance to encourage reading and a love for books that would last all the children's lives. Moreover, it seemed to her that the claims that these children and their parents made on the library were as proper as those made by the many others who used the library in different ways: the high school students who came in the evenings to complete research projects and gossip with one another, the elderly people who came to read newspapers and magazines during the day and to talk with their friends, even the do-it-yourselfers who came in to learn how to complete the project on which they had embarked without a clear plan.

As the librarian began to think about how her organization might respond to the new demands presented by the latchkey children, she also began seeing her organization in a new light.[8] Her professional training and that of her staff had prepared them to view the library as a place where books were kept and made available to the public. To fulfill this function, an elaborate system of inventorying and recording the location of books had been developed. An equally elaborate system to monitor which citizens had borrowed which books, and to impose fines on those who kept books too long, had also been built. This was the core function of the library and the task with which the professional staff identified most strongly.

Over time, however, the functions of the library seemed to expand in response to citizen needs and the capacities of the library itself. Once the library had a system for inventorying books, it seemed entirely appropriate to use that system to manage a collection of records, compact discs, and videotapes as well. (Of course, the lending system for videos had to be changed a little to avoid competing with local commercial ventures.) The physical facility in which the books were kept had been enlarged and made more attractive to encourage reading at the library as well as at home. Heat was provided in the winter, and air conditioning in the summer, for the comfort of the staff and those who wished to use the library. Study carrels had been built for students. A children's room had been created with books and toys for toddlers. Increasingly, the library was being used to hold amateur chamber music concerts and meetings of craft societies as well as book review clubs.

As a result, the library had become something more than simply a place where books were kept. It was now a kind of indoor park used by many citizens for varied purposes. Who was to say that care for latchkey children was not a proper or valuable function for the library to provide if the librarian could think of a way to do so economically, effectively, and fairly, and with little cost to other functions of the library that had the sanction of tradition?

PUBLIC MANAGERS AND PUBLIC MANAGEMENT

The town librarian is a public manager. What makes her such is that a bundle of public assets has been entrusted to her stewardship. She is responsible for deploying those assets for the benefit of the town and its citizens. Presumably, one of her tasks as a manager is to find the most valuable use of those resources.[9] The particular question before her is whether it would be valuable to respond to the new demands being made on her organization to care for the latchkey children and, if so, how.

An Important Doctrine

In the United States public administrators have relied on a traditional doctrine describing how they ought to think about and do their jobs.[10]

The doctrine has been designed primarily to limit the prospect of self-interested or misguided bureaucrats aggrandizing themselves or leading the society toward some idiosyncratic or ill-considered conception of the public interest. It aims at keeping public sector managers firmly under democratic control.[11]

In this doctrine the purposes of a public enterprise such as a library are assumed to have been set out clearly in statutes enacted by legislative bodies or in formal policy declarations signed by elected chief executives.[12] As the hard-won results of sustained democratic debates, these formal mandates legitimate public enterprises: they authoritatively declare that the particular enterprises so established are in the public interest and can therefore properly claim social resources.[13] They also offer concrete operational guidance to managers by indicating what particular purposes are to be advanced by the particular public enterprises and what particular means may be used.[14] Taken together, the mandated purposes and means define the terms in which managers will be held accountable.[15]

For their parts, public managers are expected to be faithful agents of these mandates. Their duty is to achieve the mandated purposes as efficiently and as effectively as possible.[16] They are assumed to have substantive expertise in the field in which they work—to know the principal operational programs that can be used to produce desired results and to know what constitutes quality and effectiveness in their operations.[17] They are also expected to be administratively competent— to be skilled in devising the organizational structures and arrangements that can guide the organization to perform efficiently and effectively and in accounting for the financial and human resources entrusted to them so that it can be proven that public resources are not being stolen, wasted, or misused.[18]

This doctrine produces a characteristic mindset among public sector managers: the mindset of administrators or bureaucrats rather than of entrepreneurs, leaders, or executives.[19] Their orientation is *downward,* toward the reliable control of organizational operations rather than either *outward*, toward the achievement of valuable results, or *upward,* toward renegotiated policy mandates. Instead of viewing their task as initiating or facilitating change, they tend to see it as maintaining a long-term institutional perspective in the face of fickle political whims. Their principal managerial objective is to perfect their organizations' operations in traditional roles, not to search for innovations that can change their role or increase their value to the polity.

It is this view of public sector management that produces the librarian's first instinctive response to the latchkey children: a resounding, bureaucratic "no." Indeed, viewed from the traditional perspective, her clear duty is not to respond to this new demand but to do the opposite: to do what she can to resist the new, unauthorized abuse of the public library.

Moreover, many of her staff, influenced by their past professional training to think about libraries in particular terms, would agree with this conclusion. So would many citizens who see the library through the same traditional lenses and would quickly conclude that the library should be quiet and not used for babysitting by negligent parents.

A Modest Challenge to the Prevailing Doctrine

What is interesting and important about this town librarian, however, is that she goes beyond this instinctive reaction. Her second reaction—to use the issue of the latchkey children to gain additional financing for the library—reflects a common, if often covert, response of public managers.[20] (Indeed, it is precisely this response that makes taxpayers so determined to keep the managers under tight control.)

Reflecting the winds of change in managerial thought now sweeping over the public as well as the private sector, the librarian's managerial imagination strays beyond her traditional mandate and beyond her instinct for bureaucratic entrepreneurship.[21] She steps outside the conventional restrictions on her job in imagining what could be done.

Instead of viewing the new demands being made on the library as a problem, she sees them as an opportunity. She senses that there may be some value to be created for at least some of the town's citizens by allowing, or even encouraging, the latchkey children to use the library. She begins thinking about how the achievement of that value might be financed, authorized, and produced.

In these respects the public librarian begins thinking as society expects private sector executives to think. She focuses on the question of whether the bundle of assets and capabilities represented by the library can be used to create additional value for the town. She does not assume that her resources are immutably fixed, or that her mission is narrowly and inflexibly inscribed in stone, or that her organization is capable of producing only what it is now producing. Instead, she uses her imagination to think of how she might reposition and adapt her organization to accommodate the new demands of the latchkey children. In short, she is thinking like a leader or entrepreneur.

To many, such thoughts in the minds of public managers are troublesome and ought to be discouraged, particularly if, as in this case, the manager is a professional civil servant rather than an elected or appointed political executive.[22] Citizens take a particularly dim view of initiatives undertaken by bureaucrats because they suspect civil servants of being self-serving or of pursuing their own idiosyncratic ideas of the public interest.[23] They also resent the fact that civil service systems insulate the bureaucrats to some degree from direct public accountability. Because citizens can hold elected and appointed public officials accountable at the ballot box, they ordinarily grant these officials wider leeway to initiate new public enterprises. But citizens view the initiatives of even elected and appointed officials with a jaundiced eye, for their entrepreneurship often seems focused on winning votes by satisfying special interests rather than on finding and producing something publicly valuable.[24]

To the extent these observations are true, they underscore an obvious but often overlooked social fact: society has much different expectations of its public than of its private managers. We are inclined to view imagination and initiative among (unelected) public sector executives as dangerous and contrary to the public interest, while we perceive exactly the same qualities among private sector executives as not only tolerable but ultimately conducive to society's economic welfare.

No doubt, many reasons exist for these contrary expectations. Because the political mechanisms that oversee public enterprises are arguably more vulnerable to managerial influence and deception than the financial mechanisms that control private sector enterprises, public managers may have to be reined in more tightly than private sector managers.[25] Because the decisions of public managers bind all citizens, their initiatives must be reviewed far more closely than the decisions of private sector managers, whose decisions are taken for the benefit of only a few (voluntary) principals.[26] Because the results of managerial decisions are more subjective and (often) slower to appear in the public sector than in the private, the public sector cannot rely as heavily as the private sector does on holding managers accountable after the fact for their performance.[27] And so on.

But these different expectations have an important consequence not widely acknowledged or discussed. By discouraging thoughts such as those the librarian is having, and the actions that could follow from her thoughts, society denies its public sector the key ingredient on which its private sector specifically relies to remain responsive, dynamic, and value creating: namely, the adaptability and efficiency that come from using the imaginations of people called managers to combine what they can sense of public demands with access to resources and control over operational capacity to produce value.

Of course, society may actually be benefiting from the imagination and industry of public sector managers who have long chafed under these restrictions and found ways to circumvent them to society's benefit.[28] But the point is that society has gotten this benefit undeservedly: it has not organized its relations with public managers to demand, expect, reward, or value such efforts. Inevitably, then, society gets fewer such contributions than it would if it organized itself to expect or demand or simply allow them.

Strategic Management in the Public Sector

There is a different and more useful way to think about the role of public sector managers: one that is closer (but by no means identical) to the image society has of managers in the private sector. In this view public managers are seen as explorers who, with others, seek to discover, define, and produce public value. Instead of simply devising the means for achieving mandated purposes, they become important agents in helping to discover and define what would be valuable to do. Instead of being responsible only for guaranteeing continuity, they become important innovators in changing what public organizations do and how they do it.

In short, in this view, public managers become strategists rather than technicians.[29] They look *out* to the value of what they are producing as well as *down* to the efficacy and propriety of their means. They engage the politics surrounding their organization to help define public value as well as engineer how their organizations operate. They anticipate a world of political conflict and changing technologies that requires them to reengineer their organizations often instead of expecting a stable harmony that allows them to perfect their current operations.[30] In such a world the librarian's ruminations about how to use the library to meet the needs of latchkey children would be viewed as a potentially valuable asset rather than as the dangerous thoughts of an empire-building bureaucrat.

The principal reason to worry about this alternative conception, of course, is that it threatens precisely what the familiar, traditional conception was designed to avoid—namely, the domination of the democratic political process by self-serving or misguided bureaucrats.[31] The traditional view has the problem, however, of not only suppressing some potentially useful contributions by public sector managers but also failing to deliver on its promise to protect the political process from bureaucratic influence in the first place.

Indeed, almost as soon as the traditional doctrine was developed it began to be undermined by determined scholarship showing that maintaining a rigorous distinction between policy and administration was both theoretically and practically impossible.[32] In theory, the orthodox view discouraged bureaucrats from exercising much imagination about the proper purposes of government and prevented them from taking any responsibility for defining them. In practice, the doctrines could not prevent unelected public managers from doing both. Resourceful public officials, with agendas of their own, routinely found covert ways to shape the government's conceptions of the public interest.[33] Moreover, the covert nature of their influence turned out to be particularly pernicious because it frustrated accountability and turned those involved into corrupted cynics.[34]

An alternative approach to controlling managerial influence would be to recognize its potential utility, as well as inevitability, and to provide more formal channels through which managerial ideas about opportunities to create public value could be properly expressed. It would also be important to teach public managers how to search for and define public value more properly and effectively than they now do. Such efforts would help society make a virtue of necessity. They would allow society to have the benefit of the experience and imagination of public sector managers without having to yield to their particular conceptions of the public interest. And it is this piece of work that has not yet been done. Having forever undermined the traditional doctrines of public administration, we have not yet carefully constructed an alternative idea about how public managers should think and act.

AN ALTERNATIVE APPROACH TO PUBLIC ADMINISTRATION

That is the basic purpose of this book: to work out a conception of how public managers like the town librarian could become more helpful to society in searching out and exploiting opportunities to create public value. It is predicated on the judgment that society needs value-seeking imaginations (and associated technical skills) from its public sector executives no less than from its private sector managers.[35] To develop such a conception, I take the following steps.

In Chapter 2, I discuss the aim of managerial work in the public sector. I argue that managers should seek "to produce public value." Because that is an abstract concept, I then offer some ideas about how managers should reckon the public value of the enterprises they lead.

This, it predictably turns out, is no small task. There are many different standards for measuring public value, and none alone is up to the task. For example, both democratic theory and practical concerns would focus attention on how satisfied elected overseers of the enterprise seemed to be with the organization's performance. Alternatively, using the techniques of program evaluation, a manager could determine whether, and how efficiently, the organization achieved its (politically mandated but analytically defined) substantive purposes.[36] Or, using the techniques of benefit-cost analysis, we could estimate how much value individual beneficiaries of the enterprise gained relative to the price that those who supported the enterprise had to pay.[37] Finally, capitalizing on some loose analogies with private sector management, and aligning ourselves with the current enthusiasm for "customer-driven government," we could estimate the value of the organization by gauging the satisfaction of those who interacted with the organization as clients or customers.[38]

Arguably, each of these standards has some basis for helping managers (and the rest of us citizens) determine the value of public enterprises. But the different standards are not necessarily consistent with one another, and each of these methods has its own weaknesses.

Despite the difficulties, some important observations can be made to orient public managers toward their task. Not the least of these is that it is always worth asking the question. Indeed, continually questioning the value of public enterprises is one of the things that can help managers become purposeful and creative in their work for our collective benefit.

Because public managers must ultimately act on some theory of public value, Chapter 3 develops a practical method for envisioning value in particular circumstances. The method adapts the concept of corporate strategy from the private sector to the special circumstances of the public sector.[39] I argue that a useful, conditional conception of public value can be envisioned by public managers if they integrate: (1) substantive judgments of what would be valuable and effective; (2) a diagnosis of political expectations; and (3) hard-headed calculations of what is operationally feasible.[40] In short, in envisioning public value, managers must find a way to integrate politics, substance, and administration.

A strategic triangle can help us conceptualize this basic argument. This image focuses managerial attention on the three key questions managers must answer in testing the adequacy of their vision of organizational purpose: whether the purpose is publicly valuable, whether it will be politically and legally supported, and whether it is administratively and operationally feasible.

The triangle also serves as a device for reminding managers of the key functions and tasks that they will have to perform to help them define and realize their vision. Specifically, it highlights three different aspects of their job: (1) judging the value of their imagined purpose; (2) managing upward, toward politics, to invest their purpose with legitimacy and support; and (3) managing downward, toward improving the organization's capabilities for achieving the desired purposes. These, in turn, become the focus of subsequent chapters in the book.

Chapters 4 and 5 explore the function and techniques of political management—the part of strategic management that is concerned with managing upward, toward politics. In Chapter 4, I explain why political management is an important part of a public manager's job and how to diagnose political environments. Managers must mobilize support and resources for the organizations they lead while enlisting the aid of others beyond their organizational boundaries who can help them achieve the substantive results for which they are held accountable.[41] In Chapter 5, I characterize five different approaches to the tasks of political management including entrepreneurial advocacy,[42] the management of policy development,[43] negotiation,[44] public deliberation and leadership,[45] and public sector marketing.[46] Because the political management function is the part of the manager's job that is most threatening to democratic values, I give special attention to the question of what is proper, as well as to what is effective.[47]

Chapters 6 and 7 focus on the parts of strategic management that are concerned with managing downward, toward one's organization. Chapter 6 presents a framework to be used in analyzing the "products" produced by public sector organizations, the production process that the organization is relying on, and the ways in which that process is being shaped and guided by the organization's administrative systems.[48] Because the concept of strategic management assumes a changing political and task environment, I emphasize the techniques that managers use to innovate and to encourage continued innovation in their organizations.[49] Thus, Chapter 7 explores the techniques that managers use to introduce strategically important innovations into their organizations.

Finally, in Chapter 8, I return to the questions raised in this first chapter: namely, what sort of consciousness or temperament is required of public sector managers if they are to be successful in managing both effectively and democratically? I contend that public managers must make ethical commitments and cultivate psychological stances if they are to succeed (or gain virtue) as public managers.[50]

Before we get to matters of technique and finally virtue, however, we must consider the crucial matter of public value, the topic of the next chapter.

PART I

ENVISIONING PUBLIC VALUE

CHAPTER 2

DEFINING PUBLIC VALUE

On the day he was appointed, the sanitation commissioner drove through the city.[1] Everywhere he saw signs of public and private neglect. Trash barrels left too long at the curb were now overflowing. Back alleys hid huge, overflowing bins that had never made it to the curbs. Emptied bins were ringed by trash spilled during the emptying. In the poorer sections of town, rats scurried among the cans.

Perhaps because he was newly appointed, the commissioner felt his public accountability quite keenly. The city spent a great deal of money each year to sustain the organization's activities. Hundreds of employees earned their pay and made their careers in his organization, and scores of trucks were garaged, maintained, and deployed under his supervision. Most important, millions of people relied on his organization to keep the city clean and healthy.

Happily, as he drove through the city, he saw evidence of his organization at work. Huge trucks, painted in distinctive colors, rumbled by, trailed by sanitation workers who tipped garbage pails into their gaping maws. Street-cleaning machines trundled along the gutters in the wake of the tow trucks that removed illegally parked cars from their path. An occasional street sweeper appeared with broom and dustbin, emptying the cans that had been set out to hold the public's litter.

Still, he could not help thinking that his organization could do more. As the newly appointed commissioner, he wanted to make a difference. He wanted his organization to have an impact on the conditions he could see around him. He wanted to create value for the citizens of the city. But how?

The question seemed particularly urgent because the newly elected mayor had asked him to define and set out his management objectives for the Department of Sanitation. As part of that strategic plan, the mayor wanted to know whether it would be advisable to privatize some or all of the operations of the Department of Sanitation.

THE AIM OF MANAGERIAL WORK

The sanitation commissioner is a manager at work. The question is: At work on what? What is the point of his efforts?

We know the aim of managerial work in the private sector: to make money for the shareholders of the firm.[2] Moreover, we know the ways in which that goal can be achieved: by producing products (including services) that can be sold to customers at prices that earn revenues above the costs of production.[3] And we know how managerial accomplishments can be gauged: through financial measures of profit and loss and changes in the firm's stock price.[4] If private managers can conceive and make products that earn profits, and if the companies they lead can do this continually over time, then a strong presumption is established that the managers have created value.[5]

In the public sector, the overall aim of managerial work seems less clear; what managers need to do to produce value far more ambiguous; and how to measure whether value has been created far more difficult. Yet, to develop a theory of how public managers should behave, one must resolve these basic issues. Without knowing the point of managerial work, we cannot determine whether any particular managerial action is good or bad. Public management is, after all, a normative as well as technical enterprise.

As a starting point, let me propose a simple idea: the aim of managerial work in the public sector is to create *public* value just as the aim of managerial work in the private sector is to create *private* value.

This simple idea is often greeted with indignation—even outrage. A liberal society like ours tends to view government as an "unproductive sector." In this view government cannot create value. At best, it is a necessary evil: a kind of referee that sets out the rules within which a civil society and a market economy can operate successfully, or an institution that fills in some of the gaps in free market capitalism. While such activities may be necessary, they can hardly be viewed as value creating.

Government as a Value-Creating Sector

But this view denies a reality that public managers experience daily. From their perspective it is government, acting through its managers, that shields the country from foreign enemies, keeps the streets safe and clean, educates the children, and insulates citizens from many man-made and natural disasters that have impoverished the lives of previous human generations. To them it seems obvious that government creates value for the society. That is the whole point of their work.

Of course, this account is not entirely satisfactory; it looks only at the benefits of governmental activity, not at the costs. In reality public managers cannot produce the desirable results without using resources that have value in alternative uses. To keep the streets clean; to insulate the disadvantaged from the ravages of poverty, ignorance, and joblessness; even to collect the taxes that society has agreed are owed, public managers must have money to purchase equipment, pay their workers, and provide mandated benefits to clients. The money they use is raised through the coercive power of taxation. That money is lost to other uses—principally, private consumption. That loss must be laid against the putative benefits of public enterprises.

Moreover, to achieve their goals, public managers often use a resource other than money: they use the authority of the state to compel individuals to contribute directly to the achievement of public objectives.[6] Litterers are fined to help keep the cities clean; welfare recipients are sometimes obliged to find work; and every citizen is made to feel the weight of the obligation to pay taxes to help the society achieve its collective goals.[7]

In a society that celebrates private consumption more than the achievement of collective goals, values individual liberty greatly, and sees private entrepreneurship as a far more important engine of social and economic development than governmental effort, the resources required by public managers are only grudgingly surrendered. So, it is not enough to say that public managers create results that are valued; they must be able to show that the results obtained are worth the cost of private consumption and unrestrained liberty forgone in producing the desirable results. Only then can we be sure that some public value has been created.

The Political Marketplace: "We Citizens" as a Collective Consumer

But to whom should such a demonstration be made? And how could anyone know whether the demonstration is convincing?

In the private sector these key questions are answered when individual consumers stake their hard-earned cash on the purchase of a product, and when the price paid exceeds the costs of making what is sold. These facts establish the presumptive value of the enterprise. If individuals do not value the products or service enough to pay for them, they will not buy them; and if they do not buy them, the goods will not be produced.[8]

In the public sector, however, the money used to finance value-creating enterprises is not derived from the individual, voluntary choices of consumers. It comes to public enterprises through the coercive power of taxation. It is precisely that fact that creates a problem in valuing the activities of government (at least from one point of view).[9]

The problem (from this point of view) is that the use of the state's coercive power undermines "consumer sovereignty"—the crucial link between the individual judgments of value on the one hand and control over what is to be produced on the other, which provides the normative justification for private sector enterprises.[10] The coercion blots out the opportunity for individuals to express their individual preferences and to have those preferences control what is to be produced. Because individuals do not choose individually to purchase or contribute to discrete governmental activities, we cannot be sure that they want what the government supplies. And if we cannot be sure that individuals want what the government produces, then, by some reckoning at least, we cannot be sure that the government produces anything of value.

What this account overlooks, however, is that the resources made available to public sector managers *are* made through a process of voluntary choice—namely, the process of representative government. To be sure, *individual,* voluntary choice does not control this system. But the institutions and processes of representative democracy come as close as we now can to creating the conditions under which individuals can voluntarily assemble and decide collectively what they would like to achieve together without sacrificing their individual desires. It is the only way we know how to create a "we" from a collection of free individuals.[11] That "we," in turn, can decide to make common cause, to raise resources, and to organize to achieve its goals—all the activities that go into the policy-making and implementation roles associated with government.

Indeed, it is the explicit recognition of the power of politics to establish normatively compelling collective purposes that makes legislative and political mandates central to traditional conceptions of public administration. Those legislative mandates properly guide public sector production specifically because they define collective aspirations. The collective aspirations, in turn, establish a presumption of public value as strong as the presumption of private value created by market mechanisms—at least if they can be achieved within the terms of the mandate. So, we should evaluate the efforts of public sector managers not in the economic marketplace of individual consumers but in the political marketplace of citizens and the collective decisions of representative democratic institutions.[12]

Precisely to make such demonstrations the sanitation commissioner prepares a plan to present to the newly elected mayor. In doing so, he tries to satisfy representatives of the public that his organization responds to the public's aspirations. Once he presents the plan, he will be accountable for producing measures to show that the goals and objectives of the plan have, in fact, been achieved.[13]

The claim that public managers can presume that public value is created if they meet the test of the political marketplace is also often greeted by derision. We have all become painfully aware of the folly and corruption that can beset the deliberations and choices of representative democratic institutions.[14]

Practicing public managers, however, have no choice but to trust (at least to some degree) in the normative power of the preferences that emerge from the representative processes. Those choices establish the justification for managerial action in the public sector. Because public managers spend public resources in the enterprises they lead, they must act as though a coherent and normatively compelling "we" existed even if they have their doubts. Otherwise, their enterprises are ill-founded.

DIFFERENT STANDARDS FOR RECKONING PUBLIC VALUE

Reconciling the tension between the desire to have democratic politics determine what is worth producing in the public sector and the recognition that democratic politics is vulnerable to corruption of various kinds has been the persistent challenge to those who would offer a theory of public management in a democracy.[15] Over time, we have relied on different concepts as standards for defining managerial purposes.

Achieving Mandated Objectives
Efficiently and Effectively

For most of our recent history, the predominant conception has been that public managers should work to achieve the legislatively mandated goals and objectives of their organizations as efficiently and effectively as they can.[16] Thus, the sanitation commissioner's job is to clean the streets as efficiently and effectively as possible.

It is quite easy to agree with this conception. Yet, reflection reveals an important feature of this common standard that is often overlooked or taken for granted: namely, this standard establishes the preeminence of *political*—primarily legislative—processes in determining what is valuable for the public sector to produce. To those who value politics as a way of creating a collective will, and who see democratic politics as the best answer we have to the problem of reconciling individual and collective interests, it is hardly surprising that the political process would be allowed to determine what is worth producing with public resources.[17] No other procedure is consistent with the principles of democracy.

But to those who distrust the integrity or utility of political processes, the idea that public value would be defined politically is a little hard to stomach. They have seen too much corruption to trust the determination of public value to political processes. At a minimum these critics want assurances that the political process is a principled one that accepts the proper limits of governmental action or meets some minimal standards of fairness and competence in the deliberations that produce the mandates.[18] Alternatively, they would prefer some more objective ways of ascertaining the value of public sector enterprises and some platform for confronting political processes with this objective information.[19]

Politically Neutral Competence

At the turn of the century Woodrow Wilson offered a solution: separate politics from administration and perfect each activity in its own sphere.[20] Thus, public administrators were to imagine that political mandates came to them in the form of coherent, well-defined policies. As the hard-won products of intense political processes, the policies would have all the moral weight that effective democratic politics could give them.

Given this accomplishment of politics, public administrators could then safely turn their attention to finding the most efficient and effective way to achieve the mandated purposes. To meet these responsibilities, the public administrators were assumed to have knowledge about both the substance of the fields in which they were operating and the arts of administration.[21] By knowing what could be produced and how organizations could be made to produce what was desirable public administrators earned their keep.

However, this traditional conception failed to consider what would happen if the political reality fell short of the ideal. Often, political mandates came loaded down with special interests that were hard to reconcile with the desire to guard the general public interest.[22] Other times, managers received incoherent mandates: they were expected to produce several different things that were inconsistent with one another and were given no useful instructions about which goals and objectives should take precedence over others when conflicts arose.[23] Still other times, political mandates shifted in arbitrary and unpredictable ways, destroying investments and draining momentum that had previously been built up and would be needed again once the political balance was restored to its original position.[24]

Facing this political reality, even Wilsonian public administrators sometimes found it necessary to challenge the wisdom of politically expressed policy mandates. They did so on the basis of their moral obligations to defend the general public interest and preserve the continuity of important public enterprises.[25] In their minds their substantive and administrative expertise gave them the right to stand up to the misguided vagaries of politics. In the pantheon of bureaucratic heroes, the image of a civil servant who challenged badly motivated politicians to defend the long-term public interest stands right alongside the dutiful, responsive servant.

Once revealed, this sort of bureaucratic resistance to political mandates could not stand in a democracy such as ours. Indeed, a favorite target of our populist politics is the bureaucratic mandarin. As a result, much of this bureaucratic resistance went underground. It became a covert but legitimate rationale for bureaucrats of all political stripes to conduct guerrilla warfare against political demands for change on the grounds that the politicians were ill-informed, short-sighted, or badly motivated.

Analytic Techniques for Assessing Public Value

Yet politics, too, is mistrusted in our political culture, and soon a new platform for disciplining and rationalizing democratic politics emerged. This new platform was established on a new kind of expertise. Whereas the traditional theory of public administration acknowledged the substantive and administrative expertise of professionals (developed through professional experience and education), the new formulation held that special analytic techniques, drawn from the fields of economics, statistics, and operations research, could be used objectively to gauge in advance—or to learn after the fact—whether public enterprises were valuable or not.[26] The new techniques included policy analysis, program evaluation, cost-effectiveness analysis, and benefit-cost analysis. Reformers hoped that use of these techniques could infuse policy deliberations with objective facts about the extent to which proposed initiatives could be expected to work and the extent to which the costs of government efforts could be justified by general benefits to society.

There is much to be said about whether these techniques have lived up to their promise—much more than can be said here. From the perspective of someone analyzing their overall impact on policy-making, one can fairly say that the techniques are neither routinely used nor invariably powerful when they are.[27] Still, they have succeeded in changing the political discourse about governmental programs. They have increased the appetite of the political process for fact-based arguments about the extent to which government programs achieve their stated objectives or serve the general interest.[28]

In discussing the utility of these techniques to managers' efforts to define and measure the value of what they are achieving, however, three points seem key. First, for reasons that are not entirely obvious, these techniques seem to be more valuable in estimating the value of particular programs or policies than the overall value of an organization's efforts. One reason, I suspect, is that to deploy these techniques successfully, managers must have narrowly specified objectives and narrowly specified means for achieving the objectives. Specific objectives and specific means are precisely what define governmental policies and programs.

In contrast, an organization is rarely easily conceptualized as a single program or policy. Often, organizations incorporate bundles of programs and policies. The different programs and policies may have been combined to achieve some larger coherent purpose, but the achievement of that larger purpose is often exceedingly difficult to measure and even harder to attribute to the overall operations of any single organization.

It may also be important that, as already mentioned, public organizations have some kind of capital value rooted in their ability to adapt and meet new tasks and challenges. To the extent that they do, an evaluation of their performance in existing tasks and programs would not capture their full benefit to the society. In any case, use of these techniques to evaluate programs and policies has been far more common than their use in assessing the overall value produced by public organizations.

Second, we should distinguish between the use of these techniques to estimate in advance of action whether a particular governmental initiative will prove valuable or not and the use of these techniques after a program has been tried to determine whether it was successful. Policy analysis often focuses on the first, program evaluation on the second. The distinction is particularly important when one uses comparisons with private sector management to offer guidance to public sector managers about how they could better reckon the value of their enterprises.

As noted above, the private sector seems to have a far more reliable way of measuring the value of its production than the public sector. The revenues and profits earned from selling particular products and services—that is, the famed bottom line—provides a direct measure of a private sector enterprise's success. What is interesting about profitability, however, is that it measures what happened in the past. That piece of information is taken very seriously in the private sector, partly because it can be used to hold managers accountable and give them incentives for performance, but also because it gives private sector managers an advantage in thinking about the future. Indeed, many private sector firms have been advised to reduce their reliance on strategic planning efforts designed to produce more accurate predictions about the future and, instead, to rely on their ability to react quickly to the market conditions they encounter through their current operations.

Thus, the lesson from the private sector seems to be that it is extremely valuable to develop accurate information about performance in the past rather than concentrate all one's efforts on guessing about the future. To the extent this is true, it follows that public sector agencies should be focusing more on program evaluation and less on policy analysis. My impression, however, is that they do the opposite. This is unfortunate, for the inconsistent attention given to program evaluation deprives the public sector of the kind of accountability, incentives for action, and capacity to react quickly that the private sector has gained by paying close attention to its bottom line.

Third, we need to look at what sorts of preferences public enterprises are designed to satisfy. Most often, analytic techniques are presented as though they were all useful tools designed to help government learn whether its efforts are valuable or not. Among them, benefit-cost analysis is usually presented as the superior technique, the one that is most general and most reliably linked to value. The only reason not to rely on benefit-cost analyses is that they are more difficult to complete. Thus, program evaluation and cost-effectiveness analysis are presented as poor second cousins to benefit-cost analysis.

Yet I see an important conceptual distinction among the techniques and would argue that for most public purposes, program evaluation and cost-effectiveness analysis are the conceptually as well as practically superior approaches. Benefit-cost analysis, taking guidance from the principles of welfare economics, assumes that public sector activities should be valued by individuals sizing up the (positive or negative) consequences for them as individuals. In contrast, the techniques of program evaluation and cost-effectiveness analysis find their standard of value not in the way that individuals value the consequences of government policy but instead in terms of how well the program or policy achieves particular objectives set by the government itself. Thus, program evaluation measures how well the program achieves its intended purposes, and those purposes are inferred from the language of the statutes or policies that authorized it. Cost-effectiveness analysis measures how well a particular governmental effort scored with respect to a particular set of purposes that had been defined for that particular effort—probably with the help of professionals who could help government policymakers define what constituted a valuable kind of "effectiveness."

In short, both program evaluation and cost-effectiveness analysis define public value in terms of collectively defined objectives that emerge from a process of collective decision-making, whereas benefit-cost analysis defines value in terms of what individuals desire without reference to any collective decision-making process. The reliance of benefit-cost analysis on pure individual preferences is, of course, what makes it a conceptually superior approach to welfare economists. But to those who believe in the capacity of a political process to establish an articulate collective aspiration, and who believe that this is the most appropriate guide to public action, program evaluation and cost-effectiveness analysis seem the better techniques precisely because they look away from individual preferences and toward collectively established purposes.

Focusing on Customer Service and Client Satisfaction

More recently still, public administrators have developed a new conception of how to gauge the value of their enterprises: borrowing from the private sector, they have embraced the goal of customer service, and committed themselves to finding the value of their efforts in the satisfaction of their "customers."[29] This idea has some important virtues. Insofar as it encourages government managers to think about the quality of the interactions that government agencies have with citizens whom they encounter as clients, and to make those encounters more satisfactory, much good will come of adopting this perspective. We have all had our fill of rude bureaucrats and badly designed governmental operations and procedures.

Yet, this idea, too, has flaws. It is by no means clear who the customers of a government agency are. One naturally assumes that they are the *clients* of government organizations—the citizens the organization encounters at its "business end" through individual encounters or transactions.

Insofar as government provides services and benefits to citizens, that model seems to work fairly well. But government is not simply a service provider. Often it is in the business of imposing *obligations,* not providing services.[30] This is true for police departments, environmental protection agencies, commissions against discrimination, and tax collectors among others. These organizations meet individual clients not as service providers but as representatives of the state obliging clients to absorb a loss on behalf of the society at large.

Of course, it may be valuable for regulatory and law enforcement organizations to think of the citizens whom they regulate as customers and to design their "obligation encounters" with as much care as "service encounters" now are.[31] Nevertheless, it is unreasonable to imagine that regulatory and enforcement agencies find their justification in the satisfactions of those whom they compel to contribute to public purposes. More likely, the justification comes from the generally attractive consequences for others of imposing particular obligations on a few. Moreover, there may be many others than those obliged who are interested in the justice or fairness with which the obligations are imposed, the fairness they would wish for themselves if they were similarly obliged.

The point is important because it reminds us that service-providing agencies, too, are judged and evaluated by citizens as well as by those who are clients of the organization. Consider welfare departments, for example. In evaluating the performance of the welfare department, we need to know how clients feel about the services they receive. But we cannot rely on their evaluation as the only or even the most important way of judging the value of the services provided. Citizens and their representatives want to be sure that the total cost of the program remains low, that no one steals from the program (even if it costs more to prevent the stealing than would have been lost if the stealing occurred), and even that the clients experience some degree of stigmatization in enrolling in the welfare program (to mark the distinction between those who can be independent and those who must rely on the state).

In short, it is important to distinguish the evaluation that *citizens* and their representatives give to governmental activities from the evaluation that would be given by *clients.* The arrested offender is not in a particularly good position to judge the value of the police department's operations. And the welfare client might not be either. The ultimate consumer of government operations is not the individuals who are served or obliged in individual encounters (the clients of the enterprise) but citizens and their representatives in government who have more general ideas about how a police department should be organized or welfare support delivered. They decide what is worth producing in the public sector, and their values ultimately matter in judging whether a governmental program is valuable or not.

In the end none of the concepts of "politically neutral competence," "policy analysis" and "program evaluation," or "customer service" can finally banish politics from its preeminent place in defining what is valuable to produce in the public sector. Politics remains the final arbiter of public value just as private consumption decisions remain the final arbiter of private value. Public managers can proceed only by finding a way to improve politics and to make it a firmer guide as to what is publicly valuable. That is why political management must be part of our conception of what public managers should do.[32]

To see how these general considerations might affect the perceptions and calculations of public sector managers, let us return to the problem faced by the sanitation commissioner at the beginning of the chapter. How ought he to think about the question of what value he is creating, for whom, and how?

MUNICIPAL SANITATION: AN EXAMPLE

The sanitation commissioner has inherited a public enterprise. Assets (in the form of tax dollars, public authority, buildings, trucks, and the cumulative experience of his organization) have been entrusted to him to accomplish more or less well-defined public purposes. It is his responsibility for the deployment of these publicly provided assets that makes him a public manager. At the time he takes office, the assets are not entirely fungible; they are already committed to particular modes of operation determined by the organization's traditions, standard operating procedures, and technologies.[33]

The current operations produce a particular set of consequences. Citizen groups, the media, city councillors, and the mayor cluster around the enterprise, continually offering advice about how the assets should be redeployed—including the recommendation that the resources be returned to private individuals or spent to support private enterprise rather than public bureaucracies.[34]

Partly because the purposes are defined generally rather than specifically, partly because overseers of the enterprise disagree about what should be done, and partly because the managers themselves are viewed as experts in defining and solving the problems that the society faces, the sanitation commissioner has some discretion in both proposing and deciding how the assets should be deployed.[35] His problem, then, is to judge in what particular ways the assets entrusted to him could be redeployed to increase the value of the enterprise for which he is (temporarily) responsible.[36]

The Product of Garbage Collection

At the outset, simple inspection of departmental operations seems to reveal what value is being produced: the department makes the city's houses, streets, and alleyways cleaner than they otherwise would be. But this observation triggers another question: why are such consequences *valuable?* Once this question arises, the analysis departs from observations of physical events and enters the realm of assertion about what citizens do (or perhaps should) value.

Note that this issue would not come up if garbage collection services were sold in the market. Then, the value that citizens attached to clean streets would be manifest in their willingness to buy the service. It is only when tax dollars finance the activity that the manager responsible for deploying this asset must give a general, politically acceptable answer to the question of why the service is valuable. The public financing of the activity breaks the link between individual desires (expressed through an individual's willingness to spend his or her own money) and the product that is delivered. It not only raises doubts about individual citizens' desires for the service (and therefore its value), but also makes it necessary to explain the value of the enterprise in terms that would be satisfactory to the community as a whole (not just to the beneficiaries of the service).

The necessity of giving a general, politically acceptable answer—of acting as though there were a collective consumer with well-defined preferences for social conditions brought about by public enterprises—is the central intellectual problem in defining the value of governmental activities. However difficult the dilemma on a theoretical level, as a practical matter, the political system resolves this issue every day by authorizing public managers to spend public resources.

The authorizations are usually justified by an account—or a story—of the value of the enterprises.[37] To be useful, the account must appeal not just to individuals in their role as clients and beneficiaries of clean streets but, in addition, to the community at large—more precisely, to individuals in their role as citizens of a society and to their representatives in political institutions. Of course, the story does not have to be repeated or sold daily. Once established, tradition will carry it on. But there must be a story to be recalled if the occasion should arise to reconsider or reauthorize the enterprise.

In the case of garbage collection, one account is the claim that clean cities are more aesthetically appealing than dirty ones. Since citizens feel better about clean cities, public value is created by making them cleaner.

Stated so directly, the proposition sounds strange, for it suggests that the government taxes the citizenry to produce cleanliness. Yet, there is nothing particularly compelling about the value of cleanliness. Indeed, it seems a little embarrassing for a liberal society to insist on the virtue of cleanliness and tax its citizens to accomplish that goal. It is tempting, then, to search for a more powerful public value—a better story—than mere cleanliness to establish the value of the enterprise.

A stronger justification is the claim that sanitation departments protect public health. In this conception collecting garbage has value principally as it produces a chain of consequences that protects citizens from epidemics.[38] Keeping organic wastes off the streets reduces the rate at which dangerous bacteria are produced (to say nothing of rats, which are aesthetic negatives and health risks in themselves). This routine in turn reduces the likelihood of an epidemic.

Note that this account introduces a new problem: namely, the empirical issue of whether garbage collection does, in fact, prevent epidemics. The problem—that the value of a public enterprise lies down a long and uncertain causal chain from the point of governmental intervention—is common in public sector enterprises. To the extent that we are uncertain about the causal connection between governmental outputs (picking up garbage) and desired social outcomes (reduced mortality and morbidity), the power of this second account is weakened.[39] But often the importance of the objective will justify the enterprise even in situations where its actual performance is quite uncertain.

The two different frames for viewing garbage collection—producing an aesthetic amenity or guarding the public's health—establish quite different contexts in the public's mind for evaluating both the level and the distribution of the publicly supplied services. In the case of producing an amenity, the public sector activity seems discretionary. There is less urgency about providing the service, and, importantly, less concern about its distribution. In the case of guarding public health, however, the public effort seems essential. More will be spent to produce the necessary protection because the stakes are much higher. There will also be more concern about the distribution of the services. The argument may well be made that everyone has a "right" to be protected from health threats.

Many of our political decisions revolve around this question of whether a particular thing will be treated as an amenity to be purchased by individuals as they choose or as a right that will be guaranteed by the broader society.[40] That debate embodies a discussion about the extent to which particular conditions in the society will be taken as a matter of public rather than private concern: in effect, a discussion about the boundaries of the public sector. When particular goods and services are established as matters of right and powerfully linked to notions of justice and fairness, the boundary of the public sector is expanded to include the obligation to produce a certain quantity and distribution of those goods and services. When particular goods and services are left as things that society considers valuable but not closely linked to conceptions of justice and fairness, the boundary of the public sector is narrowed.

The Costs of Garbage Collection

The value of clean streets and alleys becomes an issue not only because there are alternative ways of organizing the effort but also because costs are incurred in making them clean: resources that could be used for other purposes are committed to the enterprise of garbage collection. If there were no costs, minimal benefits would be enough to justify the enterprise. Because substantial costs are incurred, the crucial issue becomes whether the value that is produced outweighs the costs of production.

Garbage collection incurs essentially two types of costs. The most obvious is the budgetary cost of providing the service. Money is taken from private consumption to finance public efforts to keep the streets clean. The amount used is reflected in budgets and accounting systems. It varies, depending on how clean the streets are kept and what particular methods are used to keep them clean.

A second cost is somewhat less obvious: public authority is engaged as well as public money. We usually associate the use of governmental authority only with enforcement or regulatory agencies. But garbage collection, too, involves governmental authority. At a minimum, governmental authority is used to raise the tax revenues that finance the service.

It is also used in another important way. Whenever a valuable service is publicly provided, private efforts to purchase or provide the service tend to atrophy. In the case of garbage collection, when government collects the garbage, the citizens will do less on their own. They will stop buying garbage collection from private providers. They might even stop sweeping the sidewalks in front of their stores.

To the extent that private efforts cease, cities will be less clean than if the efforts had continued. A benefit will have been produced—namely, increased leisure or more disposable income for those who were spending their time and money for private garbage collection. But the city will not be as clean. In the extreme, private efforts to keep the city clean could collapse to such a degree that the city would end up even dirtier than before.

To prevent this from happening, the government spends moral authority to create informal or formal obligations on citizens to help keep the cities clean.[41] Informally, the government could sponsor public service programs to establish a social norm favoring responsible cleanliness over thoughtless littering.[42] For example, the Sanitation Department might finance publicity campaigns to discourage littering or arrange to place trash receptacles throughout the city.[43] Such programs aim to facilitate voluntary efforts and eliminate any excuses for "irresponsibility."

A more coercive (and therefore more expensive) effort to sustain private cleanup efforts includes ordinances prohibiting littering and formal requirements that citizens sweep their sidewalks. Backing up these obligations with fines and aggressive enforcement gives them real teeth.

We do not ordinarily think of the use of public authority as coming in degrees: it either obtains or it does not. But, like money, public authority may be used more or less intensively in an enterprise. The degree of authority might be reflected in the size of the burden imposed on citizens, or the magnitude of the punishment for noncompliance, or even the intrusiveness of the measures used to enforce compliance.[44]

It could also be measured by the elaborateness of the procedures required to establish or impose the authority: the more elaborate the required procedures, the more significant the authority engaged. To prohibit littering, or to require citizens to keep their sidewalks clean, for example, would require formal legislative or regulatory action. Typically, such actions require extensive public deliberation. Moreover, implementing the regulations by fining citizens who did not live up to their obligation typically requires formal court action against violators. What happens in these procedures is that individual citizens are persuaded to part with some of their freedom in the interest of accomplishing a public purpose. Thus, these procedures can be seen as devices for rationing governmental authority to ensure that it is used sparingly and only where appropriate and valuable.[45]

To produce public sector garbage collection, then, two resources are used: money raised through taxation and moral obligation or state authority to sustain private contributions to the solution of a public problem. In a liberal democratic society, both are in short supply. Thus, the benefits of municipal garbage collection must be large enough to outweigh these costs.

Justifications for Public Intervention

As a matter of political philosophy, most members of a liberal society generally prefer to leave the organization of its productive enterprises to markets and private institutions rather than to public mandates and governmental bureaucracies. Consequently, for a public enterprise to be judged worthwhile, it must pass a test beyond the mere demonstration that the value of its products exceeds the value of the resources used in producing the results: it must explain why the enterprise should be public rather than private.[46]

This preference stems from three ideological pillars that define a proper ordering of institutions in a liberal society: first, deep respect for the power of markets to ensure that productive activities respond to individual desires; second, a belief that private institutions are better able to cultivate and exploit individual initiative and are therefore more adaptable and efficient than public bureaucracies; third, confidence that private institutions become an important bulwark of freedom against the power of government.

To a degree, the sanitation commissioner could treat these ideas as mere abstractions that have little to do with the day-to-day running of the organization he leads. Alternatively, he could think of them as important philosophical principles that he endorses and seeks to realize in his organization's operations. Or, he could recognize that, even if these principles are not important to him, they might be important to the citizens and representatives who superintend his enterprise, and that their concerns about these matters should be accommodated.

Indeed, this last perspective would come quite naturally as these ideas gained concrete political force in his city's political processes, or as cities around the country began privatizing their sanitation departments. To satisfy those interested in ensuring proper institutional relations in a liberal society, then, a manager of a public enterprise must show that there is some special reason why government, and its authority, should be used to finance and supply the service.

In general, two different justifications for public intervention carry weight. One is that there is a technical problem in the organization of a market to supply the good in question—some reason why free exchanges among producers and consumers will not result in the proper level of production.[47] Government must intervene to correct the defect in the market.

A second justification is that there is some crucial issue of justice or fairness at stake in the provision of the service—some right or claim of an individual against the society that others agree must be honored.[48] Government must intervene to ensure that the claim is honored—not only for the current individual who has a claim but generally for all.

Note that the first justification leaves undisturbed the primacy of individual preferences as the arbiter of social value. Ideally, both the quantity and the distribution of a particular good will be determined solely by individual preferences.

The second justification, by contrast, substitutes a different standard for establishing social value. A collective judgment is made about the value of the proposed public enterprise. Citizens acting through politics, rather than consumers acting through markets, establish both the level and the distribution of production. It is the combined preferences of citizens for an aggregate social condition that must be satisfied.

These different justifications correspond more or less closely to the two different frames for establishing the value of garbage collection: the production of tidiness and the production of public health. In one frame, public sector garbage collection provides an amenity much like any other consumer good—a tidy urban environment. One thinks principally in terms of technical problems in the organization of markets as the justification for public sector intervention.

In the second frame, public collection produces something more fundamental—the protection of public health. Here one thinks more in terms of guaranteeing a socially valuable condition, fairly distributing its benefits and accepting some social obligation to help meet the required condition.

These distinct frames express the different statuses that the two values—cleanliness and health—have in our politics. Tidiness is an amenity rather than a necessity; therefore, its production and distribution can be comfortably left to markets unless some technical problem makes this impossible. Health makes a claim as a "primary good" with strong connections to common aspirations; therefore, its production and distribution become an appropriate focus of a society acting through government to assure justice.[49]

Within the frame of efficiently producing and distributing an amenity to those who really value it, public intervention is justified by three specific arguments. First, substantial economies of scale in garbage collection could justify public intervention.[50] This occurs either because the technology of garbage collection shows declining costs across the relevant range of production, or because the value associated with garbage collection is concentrated in the last few increments of performance, when the municipal environment is transformed from a bit untidy to pristine, or from pretty safe to entirely safe.

To take advantage of these economies of scale without leaving the citizens vulnerable to exploitation by a private monopoly, the society has two choices: it can establish a regulatory agency to oversee the natural monopoly that will arise in the private sector, or it can choose to supply the service itself. In the case of garbage collection, the society has often decided to have the government supply the service itself.

Second, although clean streets, fragrant air, and the absence of vermin in alleyways are all things citizens value, they are currently unowned and unpriced.[51] As a result, individual citizens have no incentive to "produce" these goods by disposing of their garbage somewhere other than in the common streets and alleyways.

To deal with this problem, the society might reasonably decide to assert common ownership of these public spaces. Having asserted ownership, it could then either establish a market for the use of these spaces by charging citizens for the privilege of dumping, or, relying on its authority, it can require private citizens to keep these areas clean on pain of both fines and the stigmatization of violating public ordinances.[52] Alternatively, the society might simply decide to supply the service itself through governmental operations and make it unnecessary for citizens to litter. In the case of garbage collection, the society has often relied on a mix of these approaches, with an emphasis on public sector provision.

Third, because the aesthetic and health benefits of collecting garbage are generally available to all citizens of the city, it is hard to exclude citizens from enjoying these benefits even if they refuse to pay for them.[53] Thus all citizens have an incentive to conceal their true interests in having clean streets. If they don't contribute to the cleanup, maybe someone else will, and they can enjoy the benefit without having to do the work. Or, even if they are willing to make the appropriate contribution, they might be reluctant to do so for fear that they would be exploited and thought foolish by their more cynical fellow citizens. In either case the city will end up dirtier than individual citizens would desire because everyone would hang back from making the appropriate contributions. To avoid this result, the society can oblige everyone to make financial and other contributions to the solution of what is, in the end, a common problem.

All these justifications for public intervention begin with the assumption that individual preferences properly establish the value of such efforts but that some technical problems in the organization of markets for the service justify public intervention. As noted above, however, one can consider garbage collection from an entirely different perspective. Instead of viewing the problem as one of organizing efficiently to meet individual desires for clean streets and alleyways, one can see the issue as a case of fairly distributing the benefits and burdens of meeting a public health need that has been recognized by individuals in the society as a collective aspiration and responsibility.

This language, and the analytic frame it invokes, changes a great deal in our view of the public value of garbage collection. Instead of seeing the value of the effort in terms of its impact on the desire of individual consumers for cleanliness and health, the value seems to be established exogenously by a public health imperative. Sanitary streets are a public necessity! Citizens have a right to be protected! Such pronouncements replace—even "trump"—individual preferences in establishing the value of the enterprise.[54]

Often it seems that such statements are exogenously established. They come from outside the ordinary machinery of either markets or politics. A distinguished public health physician establishes the view by warning of an imminent epidemic. Or, an advocate for the poor dramatizes the inequality of the existing distribution of sanitation services through pictures of rat-infested tenements. It is as though some objective reality, or some commonly shared moral aspiration, compels everyone in the society to agree that garbage collection is a public necessity. In effect, these assertions take people out of their mode as individual consumers and ask them to respond as citizens of a community facing a common problem or obliged by a common moral aspiration.

As a practical matter, however, such assertions can never be compelling if they stand alone as mere assertions. To have standing in the community—to have power to establish, sustain, and guide the public enterprise of garbage collection—they must meet a political test. These claims must command the assent of individual citizens and gain the authorization of representative institutions. Only then can such statements really begin to function as substitutes for the expression of individual preferences.

Once a collective assertion has been made about the value of garbage collection, the issue of production and distribution becomes one of fairness in distributing the benefits and allocating the burdens rather than one of efficiency.[55] As noted above, the issue of fairness arises because public authority is engaged. In a liberal democracy authority is collectively owned.[56] As a normative principle, it should never be used in any degree unless a representative body has sanctioned its use.[57] Moreover, it must be deployed generally and for the good of all.[58] These political principles governing the behavior of our governmental institutions are as fundamental to our understanding of our society as the preference for markets and private enterprise.

In the context of garbage collection these principles mean that those who own authority (namely, the citizens and those who represent them) must be satisfied that the public authority is being used well on their behalf. Using authority well means that the enterprise operates fairly (in the sense that similarly situated people are treated alike),[59] and that those subjected to the exertion of authority are able to ascertain that its use is justified in their individual case.[60] Note that fairness is a separate quality of a social enterprise—not necessarily linked to efficiency and not necessarily compensated or replaced by effectiveness. Although an individual transaction can be more or less fair, fairness is also, and perhaps more fundamentally, a feature of the aggregate operations of a public enterprise. Moreover, it is a quality that has value to citizens in their role as citizens authorizing a collective enterprise, rather than as individual clients and beneficiaries enjoying the service for themselves. (It may also be an important part of the experience of those clients who are obliged rather than served and thus an important part of what determines their willingness to comply. Ultimately, fairness may influence the economic efficiency of obliging organizations.)

Viewed from this vantage point, public sector garbage collection is justified by a shared social aspiration for a healthy (and clean) environment and by the necessity of fairly distributing the benefits and burdens of producing that result through a governmental enterprise. Its value registers partly in terms of the satisfactions of individuals who now enjoy clean streets (balanced by the pain of paying taxes and accepting obligations to assist in the garbage collection enterprise), and partly in terms of the satisfactions of citizens who have seen a collective need, fashioned a public response to that need, and thereby participated in the construction of a community (balanced by worries on their part that they have threatened a proper ordering of social institutions by making something public that might more usefully have remained private).

These views are often considered separate and inconsistent. One sees the problem either from the perspective of efficient production and distribution or from the perspective of justice and a fair distribution of burdens and benefits. My view, however, is that public managers must always see public sector enterprises from *both* perspectives. They cannot shrug off the question of efficient production and delivery of a service. Nor can they ignore the question of a fair distribution of privileges and burdens. Once public authority is engaged, issues of fairness are always present. And public authority is *always* engaged when tax dollars are being spent.

The Value of the Authorizing Process

The fact that public authority is always engaged in public sector enterprises changes who must be satisfied with the performance of an enterprise and what characteristics constitute a satisfactory performance. Because authority is engaged, and authority can only be spent by citizens and their representatives, its use must be guided by *political* agreements rather than by individual market transactions. Individual citizens thinking about what is good for the society (rather than just what is good for themselves as clients) must be satisfied with the conduct of the public enterprise as well as the clients who are directly affected by the enterprise; so must those in representative institutions who authorize the enterprise.

Consensus rarely arises in political discussions of the value of public sector enterprises. More often, debate ensues over whether and how the enterprise should be conducted. In an important sense this political dialogue is to public sector enterprises what the market is to private efforts—the place where consumers with money to spend decide what they want to buy. But three differences apply: (1) these consumers are spending their freedom as well as their money by authorizing the government to act on their behalf; (2) they are buying the product for everyone's benefit according to a political view of what is desirable for the society as a whole; and (3) they are buying whole enterprises rather than individual products of the enterprise. In short, what citizens (as opposed to clients) want is their particular conception of a fair and efficient garbage collection effort.

These apparently abstract issues often become quite concrete in the politics surrounding a sanitation department. The most common issue concerns the proper distribution of the available service across geographic areas, ethnic groups, social classes, and members of political parties.[61] Distribution provokes political debate not only because there are competing interests but also because there are quite different principles which might reasonably be used to decide how to distribute the services.

When one thinks about the distribution of the service in terms of market efficiency or welfare maximization, one is tempted by a principle that directs garbage collection efforts to areas where they will do the most good, that is, where the efforts will produce the largest gains in terms of aesthetics and public health outcomes per unit of effort expended.[62] An alternative concept would be to allocate public services toward those areas that already do a lot privately, partly as an incentive to maintain (or increase) private contributions and partly because the elevated levels of private effort indicate a stronger desire for cleanliness and therefore a more valuable place to spend public cleanup resources.[63]

When one thinks of distributing the benefits of the enterprise in terms of meeting social needs, quite different principles become salient. One is to allocate garbage collection efforts to those areas most in need.[64] This approach will establish a minimum level of cleanliness throughout the city. A second principle, linked closely to fairness, is to supply the same amount of public effort to all areas of the city and let the differences in actual levels of cleanliness reflect differences in private desires and capabilities to keep the areas clean.[65]

In the end none of these principles can stand as the proper basis for allocating services, though at any given moment each will have its advocate. Instead, as a practical matter, the distributional issue is resolved by a continuing political and administrative process that holds these competing principles in tension and adapts to changes in political demands or policy fashion.

Issues of administrative efficiency and program effectiveness are usually debated in terms of effectiveness and costs rather than fairness and justice. Rarely do these concerns arise as a result of reports issued by government agencies revealing shortfalls in performance. Instead, they arise from external sources: some dramatic (but temporary) performance failure such as an inability to clear the streets after an unexpected snowfall; or a newspaper story about corruption, waste, and inefficiency in a sanitation department; or the initiation of a broad effort to increase productivity by an incoming administration; or the initiation of a new project by a new commissioner (for example, a rat extermination program in vacant lots); or the encouragement of block parties to clean up a neighborhood.[66] Such debates about performance will generally be resolved by reports, studies, and the creation of new policies and procedures designed to rectify the problem.

The political debates surrounding the fairness and efficiency of garbage collection are important for at least two reasons. First, they renew the authorization of the enterprise, which maintains the flow of resources that the organization deploys to keep the streets clean. Second, they provide a continuing occasion for the society to reconsider the question of whether the resources committed to the enterprise are being used well. Like the annual meetings with stockholders in the private sector, the irregular but frequent meetings of the sanitation commissioner with public interest groups, the media, and elected representatives of the people give the commissioner an opportunity to account for his enterprise and to use that account to sustain old—and attract new—investment.

This ongoing political process authorizing the garbage collection efforts to continue (perhaps on some new terms) can have many different attributes. It can be more or less open, more or less fair, more or less well-informed about past performance and future opportunities, and more or less reasonable in its decisions. The particular qualities of this authorizing process are important since it is this process that links the enterprise of garbage collection to those who consume the enterprise as an institution of a well-ordered society.[67]

Since the process can satisfy or disappoint citizens who desire a fair, efficient, and effective public sanitation effort, and since their satisfaction is an important part of the success or failure of a public enterprise, one must view that political process as creating a kind of value. If the ongoing process of authorization is managed well, if citizens feel that their common aspirations are satisfied through a process of consultation and review, the enterprise will be more valuable than if they are not. And this aspect of public value exists independently of the difference between the value of cleanliness and the cost of the resources used to produce it.

The Capital Value of the Institution

There is one last thing to observe about garbage collection. Typically an existing organization—generally, a municipal sanitation department—carries out the activity. Over time that organization develops significant expertise in collecting the garbage.[68] It has operating procedures that accomplish the extraordinary task of gathering workers and equipment from all over a city and sending them out to collect the garbage. It sustains a staff of employees who know where they should go and what they should do to produce this result. It utilizes some accounting systems to show the managers and overseers of the enterprise how much it costs to collect the garbage and how much of the budget has already been spent. And it employs some managers who make sure that everyone in the organization plays his or her assigned role. All this operational capability represents an investment that the society has made in the municipal sanitation department.

Many would say that this cumulative experience and operating capability is an important asset that should be protected, or at least not casually abandoned. Those who express this view see in the competence of public sector organizations a broad, long-term perspective that is useful in balancing the narrow, short-term perspective of political representatives.[69]

To a degree, this view has merit. There *is* value in the cumulative experience of the organization. It would be very costly to have to replace it. And even though much of the productivity gains associated with its accumulating experience have probably been appropriated by its managers in terms of organizational slack that reduces their uncertainty and increases their ability to respond to crises (and by its workers in the form of less pressure in the job), the organization is still likely to be much more productive in its current activities than any alternative.[70]

The problem is that respect for institutional continuity can become an excuse for resisting change. Even something as apparently routine as garbage collection is not static. The world changes. Neighborhoods gain or lose population. Private efforts wax and wane. New technologies for picking up the garbage become available. New problems (such as toxic wastes) make new claims on the organization's sorting and disposal capabilities. New labor contracts change staffing patterns. All these changes affect the basic operations of garbage collection.

In addition, the political demands on the Sanitation Department might change. Perhaps a scandal will force important changes in the geographic allocation of services or the level of supervision. Or, the Sanitation Department might suddenly be directed to become an employer and route of upward mobility for ghetto teenagers rather than simply an agency that picks up the garbage. Alternatively, the sanitation commissioner might see an opportunity to use his force of street cleaners as a device for encouraging the development of block groups that could restore pride and stimulate investment in declining city neighborhoods.

The point is that the organization's value is not necessarily limited to its operating value in its current mission. It also has a kind of capital value rooted in both its ability to adapt its specific methods to new aspects of garbage collection and its ability to produce new things potentially valuable to the society. To the extent that the organization can exploit opportunities to perform its traditional mission more efficiently or more fairly, to the extent that it can adapt to changing circumstances, and to the extent that an organization can exploit its distinctive competence to produce other things that would be valuable to citizens, the enterprise will be more valuable than it seems from observing its current performance. Indeed, it is precisely the *adaptability* of organizations that determines the long-run value of private sector firms.[71] Perhaps the same should be true of public sector firms.[72]

TOWARD A MANAGERIAL VIEW OF PUBLIC VALUE

What does this particular discussion of the public value of garbage collection tell us more generally about how public managers and all the rest of us citizens who rely on them should analyze the value of public sector enterprises? Six points seem key.

First, an axiom: value is rooted in the desires and perceptions of individuals—not necessarily in physical transformations, and not in abstractions called societies. Consequently, public sector managers must satisfy some kinds of desires and operate in accord with some kinds of perceptions.

Second, there are different kinds of desires to be satisfied. Some are for goods and services that can be produced and distributed through markets. These are the focus of private management and need not concern us. Others are for things produced by public organizations and are (more or less imperfect) reflections of the desires that citizens express through the institutions of representative government. Citizens' aspirations, expressed through representative government, are the central concerns of public managers.

At first glance, citizens' aspirations seem to be of two types. One type concerns collective things that are individually desired and consumed but cannot be provided through market mechanisms because the product cannot be divided up and sold to individual consumers. A second type involves political aspirations that attach to aggregate social conditions such as a proper distribution of rights and responsibilities between public and private organizations, a fair distribution of economic opportunities or social obligations, and a suitable desire to economize on the use of tax monies invested in public sector organizations.

In practice, these two different kinds of desires collapse into one for a very important reason: whenever public authority is invoked to solve the technical problems in the market, the enterprise takes on public characteristics. Every time the organization deploys public authority directly to oblige individuals to contribute to the public good, or uses money raised through the coercive power of taxation to pursue a purpose that has been authorized by citizens and representative government, the value of that enterprise must be judged against citizens' expectations for justice and fairness as well as efficiency and effectiveness. Once the public starts producing something with public resources raised through state authority, it can no longer be viewed independently of citizens' political preferences and desires. The capacity of a public enterprise to satisfy these preferences is, therefore, an important part of its value-creating capabilities.

Third, it follows that managers of public sector enterprises can create value (in the sense of satisfying the desires of citizens and clients) through two different activities directed at two different markets. The most obvious way is to deploy the money and authority entrusted to them to produce things of value to particular clients and beneficiaries: they can establish clean parks to be used by families; they can provide treatment to heroin addicts; they can deploy military forces to make individuals secure and confident in the future. We can call this creating value through public sector production, even though what is being produced and valued is not always a physical product or service consumed by individual beneficiaries.

Public managers can also create value by establishing and operating an institution that meets citizens' (and their representatives') desires for properly ordered and productive public institutions. They satisfy these desires when they represent the past and future performance of their organization to citizens and representatives for continued authorization through established mechanisms of accountability. We might think of this activity as helping to define rather than create public value. But this activity also creates value since it satisfies the desires of citizens for a well-ordered society in which fair, efficient, and accountable public enterprises exist. The demands of citizens, rather than of clients or beneficiaries, are being met.

This dual nature of public sector value creation might seem odd. But an approximate analogue exists in the private sector. Private sector managers have two different groups they must satisfy: they must produce a product or service that customers will buy at a price that pays for the costs of production; and they must sell their ongoing capacity to produce valuable products to their shareholders and creditors. A similar situation confronts public managers: they must produce something whose benefits to specific clients outweigh the costs of production; and they must do so in a way that assures citizens and their representatives that something of value has been produced. In short, in both cases, both customers and owners must be satisfied with what the manager does.

Fourth, since governmental activities always engage political authority, the relative importance of these two different parts of management shifts. Because authority is involved, the importance of reassuring the "owners" that their resources are being used well gains relative to satisfying the "clients" or "beneficiaries" of the program. Moreover, it becomes important to give the "productive" side of the enterprise some qualities that are different from the maximum satisfaction of the beneficiaries of the program. The production and distribution of the organization's products must be fair as well as efficient. These operations must economize on the use of authority as well as on the use of money.

Fifth, what citizens and their representatives (as opposed to clients and beneficiaries of programs) "buy" from public managers is an account of the public enterprise—a story contained in a policy. In this sense, a policy is to the public sector manager what a prospectus is to a private entrepreneur. Viewed from the manager's side of this transaction, the manager receives an authorization to use resources to accomplish public purposes through specified means. Viewed from the citizen side of this transaction, the authorization is the purchase of an aggregate enterprise that promises to create value. It is a collective, political agreement to meet a problem (or exploit an opportunity) in a particular way. Politics is the answer that a liberal democratic society has given to the (analytically unresolvable) question of what things should be produced for collective purposes with public resources.

We know, of course, that it is treacherous to view political agreements as accurate reflections of the public will or the public interest. Political decision-making is vulnerable to many different kinds of corruption— the most important being the triumph of special interests over the general.[73] It is also vulnerable to many kinds of irrationalities including shortsightedness, an unwillingness to make painful trade-offs, and an inability to deal appropriately with risk.[74] These well-known difficulties can and do affect the moral claims of political decision-making on the conduct of government in the eyes of both citizens and managers. But imperfect political agreements entitle citizens and managers to do no more than to challenge their wisdom—not to disregard them or ignore their great moral weight.

If public managers are to create value over the long run, then, an important part of their job consists of strengthening the policies that are sold to their authorizers. Specifically, the policies that guide an organization's activities must reflect the proper interests and concerns of the citizens and their representatives; the story about the value to be produced must be rooted in accurate reasoning and real experience; and the real operating experience of the organization must be available to the political overseers through the development of appropriate accounting systems that measure the performance and costs of the organization's performance. It is here that the analytic techniques of policy analysis, program evaluation, cost-effectiveness analysis, and benefit-cost analysis make their major contributions.[75] Otherwise, the strengths of the political process will not be exploited, the knowledge and experience of the operating managers will not be utilized, and the acknowledged weaknesses of the process will not be challenged.

Sixth, the world in which a public manager operates will change. Citizens' aspirations will change, as will methods for accomplishing old tasks. So might the organization's task environment shift: new problems may crop up to which the organization may propose a useful solution, much as the problem of latchkey children arose as a problem for public libraries to solve. It is not enough, then, that managers simply maintain the continuity of their organizations, or even that the organizations become efficient in current tasks. It is also important that the enterprise be adaptable to new purposes and that it be innovative and experimental.

This, then, is the aim of managerial work in the public sector. Like private sector managers, managers in the public sector must work hard at the task of defining publicly valuable enterprises as well as producing that value. Moreover, they must be prepared to adapt and reposition their organizations in their political and task environments in addition to simply ensuring their continuity.

Unfortunately, this advice is far too general and abstract to be of much use to public managers. It orients them to the overall purpose of managing in the public sector, and to some general problems that must be confronted, but it does not give them particular advice about how to develop a sufficiently concrete definition of public value to guide their own and their organizations' efforts; nor does it tell them how they could engage their political and organizational environments to define and produce public value.

Developing more specific techniques for envisioning public value, mobilizing and learning from politics, and reengineering organizations is the principal aim of the remainder of this book. In Chapter 3, I introduce some real public sector executives who long ago saw and responded to these needs, particularly by using specific techniques for "envisioning public value," and in doing so, set a standard for today's public executives. In subsequent chapters, I describe other managers who can teach us about good (and bad) techniques for engaging the political environment and for guiding their organizations toward improved performance.

CHAPTER 3

ORGANIZATIONAL STRATEGY IN THE PUBLIC SECTOR

Public managers create public value. The problem is that they cannot know for sure what that is.[1] Even if they could be sure today, they would have to doubt tomorrow, for by then the political aspirations and public needs that give point to their efforts might well have changed.[2]

Despite the ambiguity, managers need an account of the value their organizations produce. Each day, their organizations' operations consume public resources. Each day, these operations produce real consequences for society—intended or not. If the managers cannot account for the value of these efforts with both a story and demonstrated accomplishments, then the legitimacy of their enterprise is undermined and, with that, their capacity to lead.[3]

Nor are their responsibilities limited to current operations. Some resources used today will not be valuable until tomorrow. Investments in new equipment, new knowledge, and new human capabilities, for example, are necessitated by the prospect of change and justified by the expectation that they will improve future performance. Even if no *explicit* investments are made, current operations will affect future performance, for today's experiences shape the culture and capabilities of tomorrow's organization. Public managers, then, are obliged to hold a vision of public value, good for today and into the future.

To see this abstract problem in concrete terms, consider the situations confronting William Ruckelshaus, on being appointed administrator of the U.S. Environmental Protection Agency (EPA), and Jerome Miller, on being appointed commissioner of the Massachusetts Department of Youth Services (DYS).

WILLIAM RUCKELSHAUS AND THE ENVIRONMENTAL PROTECTION AGENCY

In the late 1960s a powerful environmental movement swept onto the American political landscape.[4] Oil slicks befouled the oceans, strip-mining scarred the hills, clear-cutting denuded the forests, smog choked the cities. Ordinary citizens, mobilized by personal, concrete experience with these problems (as well as by increasing media attention) swelled the ranks of established environmental organizations and became a powerful political lobby demanding governmental action to clean up the environment.[5]

Sensing an important political opportunity, Senator Edmund Muskie, the leading Democratic presidential candidate, championed the cause of environmental protection from his position as chairman of the Senate Public Works Committee. Spurred by his leadership, Congress passed laws mandating more aggressive pollution control efforts. President Nixon responded with an executive order establishing a single organization to coordinate the nation's response to environmental pollution— the U.S. Environmental Protection Agency. Society, acting through its elected representatives, had apparently resolved to make more extensive use of public money and authority to stimulate private efforts to clean and protect the environment.

Politically, despite the apparent widespread enthusiasm for environmental protection, much remained unsettled. No one had determined, for example, what price society as a whole would be willing to pay for environmental cleanup. Starting the cleanup was easy, for its costs were then obscured. However, as soon as the effort grew expensive (either in diminished economic growth, as companies were forced to adjust their activities to produce less pollution, or in increased taxes, as local governments had to adjust their sanitation policies to minimize pollution), various groups began to challenge the program.

The politics surrounding environmental legislation and the continuing oversight of the new agency reflected the different interests in environmental protection. "Environmentalists" judged the social value of an environmental program to be very high and the costs relatively low. They pressed for aggressive cleanup. "Polluters" (primarily industry groups and municipalities) were more skeptical about the social benefits and saw the steep costs much more clearly. They resisted the rush to clean up. The public enthusiasm for environmental protection temporarily eclipsed the power of the polluters, establishing a particular precarious balance of competing interests.

The balance remained precarious at least partly because the particular values animating the environmental movement remained somewhat confused. United on the goal of environmental cleanup, groups behind the movement put forth divergent justifications.[6] Some sought to preserve the beauty and aesthetic quality of the environment. Others responded to the threats to human health. Still others wanted to maintain a natural order safe from human exploitation. Such differences were not crucial in the beginning when all could make common cause. But the different values threaded faultlines through the basic political coalition supporting environmental protection. These could break into open fissures if the price of environmental protection rose or some environmental policies favored one goal over another.

Substantively, the principal threats to the environment remained obscure. The basic science establishing the links between environmental pollutants and health damage to humans was weak. So was the engineering knowledge required for eliminating or dispersing pollutants from various industrial processes. And, despite a decade of federal efforts, the basic systems for monitoring environmental conditions and sources of pollution were far from comprehensive or precise. As a result, the EPA confronted an uncertain task: no one knew what the principal threats to the environment were, where they were located, or how they could be combatted.

Operationally, the fledgling organization was unformed and untested. Two large ongoing programs—one focused on water pollution, the other on air—had been transferred intact from other agencies and provided the nucleus of the new agency. But the new EPA incorporated fragments of other organizations as well. These had to be integrated—operationally and culturally. Even worse, the water and air programs were far from fully operational. Neither had yet established a comprehensive framework of standards necessary to form the basis of particular obligations on polluters. And the organization as a whole had some gaping weaknesses—principally in the areas of enforcement and science.

As a public manager, entrusted with the money and authority that flowed through the newly created EPA, Ruckelshaus faced the challenge of setting a course of action, a vision for the agency. That vision had to embody a conception of public value that the EPA could create for the society.

JEROME MILLER AND THE DEPARTMENT OF YOUTH SERVICES

In the spring of 1968 a riot broke out in the Bridgewater Home for Boys, a Massachusetts institution for delinquent youth.[7] The disturbance occurred in the midst of a swirling political debate about the best way to manage youthful offenders.

Previously, youth advocacy groups had criticized the Massachusetts Department of Youth Services for confining children in remote institutions rather than rehabilitating them in programs that maintained some close connection with the families and communities from which they came. In the critics' view, the remote institutions failed not only because they were inappropriately punitive for children whose criminal offenses were often minor, but also because they seemed to increase the likelihood that children would continue to commit crimes. In short, the institutions were both unjust and ineffective.[8]

The critics found a sympathetic ear in Governor Francis Sargent and his secretary for human services, Peter Goldmark. These two had launched a wide-ranging effort to improve the quality of human services by deinstitutionalizing as many of the state's clients as possible. The reforms advocated for juvenile justice fitted neatly into this more general scheme. The leader of the Massachusetts House of Representatives, Thomas McGee, also saw merit in the critics' claims.

The movement to reform the state's response to youthful offenders reached in the Massachusetts legislature, which passed a bill giving the Massachusetts DYS a new mandate. The name of the organization was changed, new programs authorized, and new funds appropriated. Jerome Miller, a professor from the University of Michigan without prior managerial experience, was appointed to implement the new legislation.

As in the case of Ruckelshaus and the EPA, it seemed as though the political system had delivered a new mandate. But, as in the case of Ruckelshaus and the EPA, exactly what was to be produced and how it was to be produced remained unclear.

Substantively, society seemed to be searching for a new balance between its short-run interests in preventing additional crimes by placing youthful offenders in secure confinement and its long-run interests in interrupting the processes leading delinquent children into criminal careers. Originally, these two purposes had been integrated in a vision of reform schools.[9] These institutions were to satisfy both objectives by providing extensive rehabilitative services to the young offenders while they remained under close state supervision.

But time had been unkind to this vision. Critics of the program contended that the flow of rehabilitative services tended to dry up in a system geared toward confinement. The institutions inevitably became "warehouses" rather than rehabilitative communities.[10] They also argued that rehabilitation would fail without efforts to reintegrate the young offenders into their communities and families.[11] But such efforts required aftercare services, and these, too, challenged an organization devoted to controlling children in institutions. Finally, critics believed that separating youthful offenders from the rest of society, and mixing less delinquent kids with more serious delinquents, effectively transformed the institutions into schools for crime that propelled children toward rather than away from a life of crime.[12]

Although these criticisms were compelling, no clear alternatives were available. The critics pointed toward increased rehabilitative efforts and more aftercare as crucial reforms. But they also seemed to harbor the conviction that institutions contained many children who did not need to be there at all. For these kids they recommended some form of alternative placements, including less supervision and much more effective integration in the community.

These ideas met resistance from those who doubted that the alternative placements would provide enough supervision to ensure that the kids committed no additional crimes. Others predicted that the alternative placements would not be tough enough to deter juvenile offenders from committing future crimes or to satisfy victims of juvenile crimes that justice had been done.

Indeed, although much of the debate about juvenile justice focused on "what would work," it also touched on a different question: how could the system *justly* deal with children who had committed crimes? Some deemed it just that children be held accountable for their crimes and worried that the punishments meted out in the juvenile court did not establish appropriate accountability. Others thought that justice for children required acknowledging that children were less morally accountable for their crimes than adults, and that society had an obligation to do a great deal more than it was now doing to foster their healthy development.[13]

These substantive questions about what would work and what would be just remained unresolved. Nonetheless, in the new legislation for

DYS, priorities clearly shifted. The legislature and the governor both seemed to be claiming that public value lay in the direction of taking more risks to enhance the social development of children even if, in the short run, that effort came at the expense of increased juvenile crime. Moreover, these new goals could be achieved through programs such as halfway houses and intensive supervision within a community.

But the bill neither firmly established nor unambiguously stated these goals. Just as it was unclear how long the political forces favoring environmental cleanup would dominate those that wanted to avoid the costs of the effort, so it was unclear how long the forces favoring youth development would dominate those favoring crime control. Just as it was unknown how best to combat environmental threats, so it was unknown how best to reduce recidivism among youthful offenders.

Operationally, like Ruckelshaus, Miller headed an organization ill-suited to his purposes. But, unlike Ruckelshaus, who had inherited an inchoate, unformed organization with disparate parts and huge gaps, Miller inherited an organization whose resources were entirely committed to doing one particular thing: namely, running penal institutions. Virtually all of his budget went to support these institutions. And all his key managers led these institutions. Whereas Ruckelshaus faced the problem of organizing what was disorganized and chaotic, Miller faced the problem of finding room for an entirely new set of activities.

Like Ruckelshaus, Miller had to define a pathway to the future for the organization he led—some way to define and meet the political aspirations implicit in a new mandate using the assets of the organization that he inherited.

MANAGERIAL DISCRETION AND LEADERSHIP IN THE PUBLIC SECTOR

What is striking about these cases is the fundamental ambiguity that Ruckelshaus and Miller faced in leading their organizations. Importantly, the ambiguity concerned *ends* as well as means. Ruckelshaus was not clearly instructed about how the costs of environmental cleanup should be traded off against the benefits of a prettier, safer, or more pristine environment. Nor was Miller told how he should balance short-run crime control against the uncertain prospects of rehabilitation.[14]

But they also encountered important uncertainties about *means.* At the outset Ruckelshaus did not know what kind of program could be implemented to reduce environmental hazards at low cost. Miller could not be sure that alternative placements would be effective in controlling crime in the short or long run.

With the ambiguity about purposes and means comes some degree of discretion and, with that, an opportunity for leadership. Society *needs* leadership from these managers to help it learn what is both desirable and possible to do in public domains for which these managers are temporarily responsible.[15]

Of course, it is easy to exaggerate the degree of discretion that public managers possess.[16] Close, continuing oversight by elected executives, legislatures, the media, and interest groups sharply limits their discretion.[17] The managers are also held in check by the limited capabilities of the organizations they lead and the restricted opportunities to innovate and experiment.[18] Taken together, these political and organizational constraints often leave relatively little room for maneuver.

Still, in most cases, there is more discretion than most public managers (and their overseers) acknowledge.[19] Nearly always, the politics surrounding a public enterprise are sufficiently contentious to suggest several different plausible and sustainable conceptions of public value.[20] Similarly, there are usually enough criticisms of the efficacy of current operations and enough proposals for improvement that enterprising public sector executives can find some room for innovation and experimentation.[21]

On occasion, public executives are given very wide latitude, indeed. This often occurs when a new problem has arisen or past approaches to a problem have become widely discredited. At such times society becomes far more willing to accept leadership from its managers and to entertain a broader set of possible actions.

Indeed, it seems that just such occasions set the context for Ruckelshaus and Miller. In the case of Ruckelshaus, a new problem appeared, without a clear solution. In the case of Miller, previous approaches to a chronic social problem were declared bankrupt, and new aspirations capitalized his enterprise with broad grants of authority and money.[22] The managerial task facing both Ruckelshaus and Miller, then, was to chart a path for their enterprises and to make the most of their respective opportunities.

DEFINING MISSION AND GOALS IN THE PRIVATE SECTOR

Private sector executives face the same challenge. They, too, must chart the course of their enterprises.[23] As I suggested in Chapter 1, society looks to them for this kind of leadership with much less reluctance than it looks to public executives. Private sector executives commonly respond by setting out strategic goals and developing operational plans for their organizations.[24] Perhaps the techniques they use for setting goals could be useful to public sector executives as well.

Initially, such techniques might seem to have limited applicability to public sector contexts.[25] After all, there is widespread agreement about the goal of private sector enterprises: to maximize the long-term wealth of their shareholders.[26] No such consensus exists about the goals of libraries, municipal sanitation departments, environmental protection agencies, and juvenile correctional facilities.

Private sector executives also gain enormously from measurement systems that tell them relatively promptly and accurately whether their planned course of action has succeeded or not. If they make money, they have a strong indication that they have created value.[27] That is the message the bottom line conveys. For their part, public sector executives may have to wait longer for program evaluations or benefit-cost analyses to be completed.[28] Moreover, even when completed, such efforts produce much less compelling information about the ultimate value of public sector efforts, for the debate continues about the proper goals of the enterprise.[29]

These features of private sector management clearly *do* ease the difficulty of setting and maintaining the direction of private sector organizations. They *may* make the techniques of private sector executives less relevant to public sector executives. But it is easy to exaggerate the significance of these differences.

After all, the concept of "maximizing long-term shareholder wealth" is, fundamentally, an abstraction. It is as abstract as the concept of "public value." By itself, it cannot resolve the complex, concrete issue of what particular products a private sector company should seek to produce and what particular investments in new plant and equipment should be made now to ready the organization to achieve the abstract goal of maximizing shareholder wealth.

To guide a company's efforts, business plans must be reasonably concrete. They must set out particular products, particular marketing plans, and particular financial arrangements.[30] Inevitably, such plans are shot through with uncertainties. No one can be sure about consumer tastes, new technological possibilities, or the future price of capital. The uncertainties leave plenty of room for debate about whether a particular plan offered by management is the best plan to maximize long-term shareholder wealth—perhaps as much room as exists in determining the best course to protect the environment or prevent juvenile delinquency.

Of course, the ability of private sector managers to determine relatively quickly and accurately whether the particular path they have chosen is a promising one compensates to some degree for the uncertainty in formulating the plan. Real experience, accurately encoded in financial returns, offers a quick thumbs-up or -down on the real value of what was originally a theoretical plan.

In judging the advantage this gives to private sector executives, however, we must remember that the bottom line measures only *past* performance, not future production. All important business planning decisions are about the future, not the past.[31] Somewhat surprisingly, then, when private and public sector managers confront the future, they often find themselves in the same leaky boat: their conceptions of value must be grounded in a *theory* of value rather than in demonstrated performance.

The Concept of Corporate Strategy

To deal with the uncertainty about what path to take to produce value for shareholders, private sector executives and those academics who work with them have developed and relied on the concept of "corporate strategy."[32] Initially, no small degree of mysticism surrounded this concept. It was much easier to describe a corporate strategy in operation and explain why it seemed to be successful than to set out the methodology to create one for the future. Later, analysts made some progress in developing more rigorous methods for investigating the strategic opportunities of particular firms in particular industries.[33] Most important for my purposes here, private sector executives have found the concept useful in guiding their organizations to sustained, value-creating performances.[34]

Perhaps the single most valuable feature of this concept is that it encourages chief executives to see their organization in a wider, longer-term, and more abstract context than is possible without its aid. Specifically, use of the concept directs the attention of chief executives away from the problem of producing today's products. Instead, it focuses their attention on the external market environments in which their organizations operate, especially on customers and competitors, and on the future.[35]

Customers are important for an obvious reason: in the end, if a private sector enterprise is to be successful, it must produce something that customers want. It is all very well for entrepreneurs to have a hunch about what customers want; it is far better to know from the customers themselves what they desire. It is also important to recognize that consumers could change their minds about what they consider valuable not only through the provision of abstract information about products but also through experience. Thus, marketing, understood as both a search for what consumers value and a device for building ongoing relationships with customers, became a key element of any well-conceived corporate strategy.[36]

Competitors are important for an equally obvious reason: it does little good to have a desirable product if one's competitors have a better one. Moreover, even if a manager had a breakthrough in a product or a production technology that gave her a competitive advantage, she must assume that her competitors will eventually be able to do the same. Consequently, in assessing their competitive advantage, managers must ask not just how large it is but also how long it will last.[37]

Once private sector executives began thinking about their market environments and how advantages within that environment tended to erode over time, they naturally looked at change and uncertainty as well, for if anything seemed clear in that environment, it was that the environment would change. Consumer tastes would change. So would technology. And so would the price of capital. These changes could improve or weaken a firm's competitive position.[38]

In addition to great uncertainty about these factors, there was plenty of room for strategic interaction among the competing firms.[39] If a competitor moved one way, the best moves for one's own firm would be quite different than if the competitor had moved a different way. And everyone's moves would be influenced by what one did with one's own firm.[40]

Faced with such uncertainties, private sector executives were encouraged to think in terms of "positioning" their firms in their environment rather than advancing down some determinant path toward wealth maximization. Their task was not simply to continue to refine their specialized capabilities for producing their current products; it was also to become diversified for the future and agile in adapting to new opportunities.[41] Current production only answered yesterday's problem and provided a base for the future. It did not guarantee a successful future.

Thus, the concept of corporate strategy impelled executives not only to look outside their organization at the external market environment but also to think dynamically and strategically: they had to think about how their market environments were likely to change; how their organizations were then positioned to exploit predictable opportunities or respond to predictable threats; and what investments, undertaken then, would strengthen their position in the future.

Distinctive Competence

The challenge of positioning their firms in dynamic competitive markets also caused private sector executives to analyze their own organizations in somewhat different terms. They looked for their own "distinctive competence."[42]

Initially, the concept of "distinctive competence" seemed to return executive attention to the present and the firm's current operations. It did not seem to concern the market environment or the future. It focused on what the organization currently knew how to do. In application, however, identifying the distinctive competence of an organization required the manager to identify an abstraction—a set of *general* capabilities the organization possessed that might indicate what position the firm could occupy in its current product markets or, indeed, in other product markets it might begin operating in.

Thus, for example, one electronic appliance firm identified its distinctive competence as "putting motors in folded metal boxes."[43] On the one hand, this phrase described a manufacturing capability rather than a product and thus seemed concrete. On the other hand, it was an abstraction that not only covered many different products produced by the firm but also suggested some new products. Furthermore, it identified the distinctive competencies of the firm compared to others in the same industry. Thus, it became possible for a manager to think: "This is what we know how to do in general. I wonder how many valuable products we could create with this set of general capabilities."

By thinking about organizations in terms of customers, competitors, and distinctive competence, private sector executives found it possible to draw back from the compelling day-to-day tasks of producing and delivering their current products and to think about their enterprises both in a wider context and in somewhat more abstract terms.[44] That stance turned out to be helpful because it allowed managers to identify threats and opportunities in their environments that would otherwise have been missed. It also helped them become more imaginative and more accurate in analyzing the varied routes they could take to maximizing shareholder wealth in the complex competitive environments in which they found themselves.

Strategy in Diversified Conglomerates

These original concepts were most appropriate for single product firms or for firms whose product lines clustered within a particular industry.

As firms changed into multiproduct conglomerates, and as the financial profiles of enterprises began to contribute to high rates of return as much as desirable new products or low-cost technologies, the concept of strategy underwent important adaptations.[45]

First, many different things within an enterprise began to acquire strategic significance. A strategic asset did not have to be a product or a technology. It could be key personnel, a strong relationship with suppliers, or a particularly valuable manufacturing location offering both transportation and tax advantages.[46] Even a license from a regulatory agency could qualify. In short, as strategic analyses became more sophisticated, they revealed the strategic value of many different features of a given enterprise.

Second, instead of viewing the firm as a single business, managers came to see the firm as a portfolio of different businesses.[47] The portfolio of businesses might turn out to produce some cost or marketing advantages to particular businesses within the family as a result of complementarities in financial transactions, production, distribution, or marketing.

But even if the portfolio did not really have any of these technological possibilities, it would still have an advantage insofar as diversification of products and industries spread a particular firm's risk. If an enterprise had products in several different industries, it was less vulnerable to occasional downturns in a particular industry and better able to take advantage of rapid growth in new sectors.[48] Diversification had its price in that the central focus of the organization might be lost and, with that, some of its productive capacity. But for many firms, the financial advantages of a diverse portfolio of products more than compensated for the loss of focus and expertise.

Thus, strategy shifted its focus to the relative strength of a firm's different products in different markets and analyzed how returns from one product would finance the development and inevitable risks of a newer product. It emphasized the problems of distributing risks and managing transitions from one portfolio of products to another, rather than finding a particular market niche in which to hole up.

Strategy as a Sustainable Deal

More recently still, the concept of corporate strategy seems to be going through another revision—this time to deal with powerful challenges to corporate governance and management. One of these challenges has come from the increasing power of outside agents other than the shareholders and the customers to make effective claims on the corporation's assets and activities.

In the past the principal group with whom management had to contend in defining the overall purposes of the firm was labor.[49] Indeed, until recently, labor has been quite effective in making claims on organizations for such things as increased pay, safer working conditions, more reliable pensions, and so on.

More recently, others have joined labor in making effective claims on private enterprise. Government, for example, now wants more from corporations than mere tax revenues. It seeks to use corporations as agents for social objectives ranging from environmental protection to affirmative action.[50] Even more recently, local communities have managed to make some claims on corporations sensitive to their image as a good corporate citizen.[51] The cumulative pressure from these various groups has gradually shifted the effective focus of a corporation from maximizing shareholder wealth to accomplishing that goal subject to an increasing number of social constraints—constraints that on occasion seem more important than the original goal itself.[52]

Predictably, these changes have stimulated another important change. Increasingly, companies find themselves vulnerable to hostile takeover attempts by entrepreneurs who claim to see some unexploited economic value in the enterprise and offer to buy control of the firm at prices far above market values.[53] Their willingness to pay the higher price testifies to their confidence that the assets of the firm could be used more intensively, or more productively, or with greater loyalty to the shareholders' interests. The shareholders are inclined to go along. Consequently, management has become concerned about warding off such takeover attempts.

These challenges to corporate governance have forced private sector managers to abandon the illusion that the authority to set the course of the company's future development has been delegated irrevocably to them. Their purposes and plans, once routinely approved in annual shareholder meetings, are now often contested by truculent shareholders, aggressive corporate raiders, determined government regulators, and angry local communities. As one business school professor put it, "We used to think that setting the strategy of the firm was the prerogative of the chief executive officer. Now we see that a successful strategy is simply a sustainable deal among a variety of stakeholders that includes the shareholders, the creditors, the customers, the employees, the suppliers, the government, and the local community."[54]

In sum, the concept of strategy in the private sector has helped private sector executives analyze opportunities for positioning and using their enterprises in an increasingly complex and dynamic world. By focusing attention on environmental threats and opportunities, and by encouraging them to see their organizations in terms of their particular distinctive competencies and the strategically important assets they control, the concept has aided private sector executives in formulating concrete business plans. Increasingly, they are also encouraged to negotiate their plans with all those who have a stake in the enterprise.

DEFINING MISSION AND GOALS IN THE PUBLIC SECTOR

Our question is whether these concepts can be usefully adapted for use by public sector executives. At the outset, the differences between the two sectors may seem crippling. For example, the focus on competitors seems out of place, since many government organizations consider themselves monopolies.[55] Similarly, the notion that government agencies might offer a portfolio of products with each one supporting another in financial terms also seems a little bizarre.[56]

Yet the concept of corporate strategy applies meaningfully to public sector executives. For example, the notion that the organization might have a distinctive competence wider than its current use is consistent with viewing the library in Chapter 1 as a kind of indoor park that could be used to provide day-care as well as a place to read and distribute books. The proposition that public sector executives should connect their performance to the aspirations of citizens, overseers, and clients fits the argument developed about public value in Chapter 2. And finally, the idea that organizations need to be positioned in an uncertain, dynamic market, and that a successful organizational strategy must embody a sustainable deal among stakeholders, captures the dilemma of Ruckelshaus and Miller far more clearly than the idea that they have a well-defined mandate to achieve. Corporate strategy may even help public sector executives accommodate themselves to a reality they have long fought—namely, that their mandate for action is both ambiguous and vulnerable to change, and that an efficient response to that reality may require organizations to be adaptive and flexible rather than rigidly focused on achieving a clearly defined objective.

The Strategic Triangle

For the last several years the public management faculty of the Kennedy School of Government has worked with a rudimentary concept of organizational strategy adapted for the public sector.[57] In this conception, an organizational strategy is a concept that simultaneously: (1) declares the overall mission or purpose of an organization (cast in terms of important public values); (2) offers an account of the sources of support and legitimacy that will be tapped to sustain society's commitment to the enterprise; and (3) explains how the enterprise will have to be organized and operated to achieve the declared objectives.

In developing a strategy for a public sector organization, a manager must bring these elements into coherent alignment by meeting three broad tests. First, the strategy must be *substantively valuable* in the sense that the organization produces things of value to overseers, clients, and beneficiaries at low cost in terms of money and authority.

Second, it must be *legitimate and politically sustainable.* That is, the enterprise must be able to continually attract both authority and money from the political authorizing environment to which it is ultimately accountable.

Third, it must be *operationally and administratively feasible* in that the authorized, valuable activities can actually be accomplished by the existing organization with help from others who can be induced to contribute to the organization's goal.

These tests are powerful because they identify the necessary conditions for the production of value in the public sector.[58] To verify their necessity, imagine what happens to managers and their organizations if any one of these three conditions is missing.

If managers have an attractive purpose broadly supported by the political environment but lack the operational capacity to achieve it, the strategic vision must fail. Either the goal will be rejected as unfeasible or the political world will find a different institutional vehicle for accomplishing it.

If managers have a substantively valuable goal that is administratively and operationally feasible but cannot attract political support, then that enterprise, too, will fail. The want of capital and resources will doom it.

If managers conceive of some organizational activities that can command political support and are administratively feasible but lack any substantive significance, then, over the long run that strategy will fail—not necessarily because the organization will be diminished, but simply because its operations will be wasteful and someone will eventually get around to blowing the whistle.

Finally and most painfully, if managers have substantively valuable ideas but are unable to attract political support or administer them feasibly, then those ideas must fail as strategic conceptions. Such ideas are "academic" in the worst sense of the word.

The Utility of the Framework

This framework, like the concepts of corporate strategy in the private sector, helps public sector executives draw back from the task of presiding over and maintaining their organizations, while refocusing their attention on the question of whether their political or task environments now either require or allow them to change their organizational purposes in the interest of creating additional public value. It helps them maintain a sense of purposefulness that allows them to challenge and lead their organizations toward the production of greater public value.[59] (It is important to keep in mind that a manager might increase public value by downsizing the organizations's operations and returning money to private consumption. In the public sector as in the private, *growth* is not always desirable. Indeed, one of the persistent values in our political environment is the desire to keep the public sector as small as possible.)

More particularly, use of the concept encourages public sector managers to: scan their authorizing environments for potential changes in the collective, political aspirations that guide their operations; search their substantive task environments for emergent problems to which their organizations might contribute some part of the solution; and review the operations of their own and other organizations in search of new programs or technologies that their organizations could use to improve performance in existing (or conceivably new) missions.

Taken together, analysis of the external demands and of the internal capabilities helps managers understand why their organizations function as they do and the extent to which managers can count on smooth sailing in the future. If citizens and their representatives are demanding what the organizations are happily producing, managers might well rest easy. If, however, important inconsistencies exist between what citizens and their overseers desire and what the organizations supply, then the executives have to realign their mandates and their organizations.[60]

Even the absence of trouble between mandates and operational capabilities does not necessarily imply that all is well. Managers, guided by the strategic triangle, have to consider the possibility that while citizens and overseers seem happy, somehow the organization still fails to produce anything of value.[61] They have to check intermittently to find out if the assumptions they and citizens make about the ultimate effectiveness of their enterprises are, in fact, true. That is the challenge implied by defining the concept of public value somewhat independently of the political support and legitimacy of the organization, and by suggesting that analytic techniques such as program evaluation and benefit-cost analysis have an important role to play in helping managers locate and recognize the creation of public value.

They also have to consider the possibility that things change—that new political demands will emerge, or that new technological possibilities will appear. To the extent that these changes redefine what is valuable for their organizations to do, managers have to be alert and respond with suitable adjustments.

In short, the concept focuses managerial attention *outward,* to the value of the organization's production, *upward,* toward the political definition of value, and *downward* and *inward,* to the organization's current performance.[62] To the extent that this review reveals important incongruities in the position of the organization, then the manager of that organization would be encouraged to rethink his or her basic strategy until it was once more properly aligned.[63]

Analytic Techniques for Strategic Planning

Each point of the triangle provides a different vantage point for considering the question of what would be valuable (and feasible) to do. More important, each point engages a different set of analytic methodologies for answering the basic question symbolized by that point on the triangle.

For example, in asking whether a particular organizational goal is substantively valuable, managers are encouraged to raise normative questions about the value of their efforts and to bring to bear the analytic apparatus that can help them answer those questions. The technical apparatus of program evaluation and benefit-cost analysis can be wheeled out to help make this important determination.[64] Managers can also apply philosophical and legal analyses of social justice, fundamental fairness, and any individual rights that might be affected by an organization's operations.[65]

In asking whether a goal is politically sustainable, one invites an analysis of the politics surrounding the organization.[66] This could include an analysis of the important values that are at stake in the organization's operations, the interests of those legislators who oversee the organization's operations, the claims pressed by interest groups, or the bits of conventional wisdom that now justify and guide the organization's activities.[67]

In asking whether a particular goal is organizationally doable, one can rely on the techniques of feasibility assessment and implementation analysis.[68] These techniques draw on what is known about the ways in which, and the rates at which, organizations can change their activities.[69]

In sum, thinking strategically in the public sector requires managers to assign equal importance to substance, politics, and organizational implementation. Currently, these elements remain disconnected. Some, such as academic experts and policy analysts, specialize in substance.[70] Others, such as political appointees or the directors of legislative affairs offices, specialize in politics.[71] Still others, such as those who direct offices of administration and management, specialize in administrative feasibility. Thus, thinking strategically means integrating these diverse perspectives. If any perspective is left out, some important consideration in choosing a value-creating path will be lost.

A Contrast to Classic Traditions of Public Administration

The strategic triangle is designed to influence how managers distribute their attention, thought, and action across their operational environments. It can be particularly helpful to them in performing the crucially important task of defining their organization's overall mission and goals. To deepen understanding of the strategic concept and further evaluate its utility, compare its recommended focus to the orientation commonly associated with the classic tradition of public administration.[72]

Perhaps the most notable difference is that the classic tradition of public administration does not focus a manager's attention on questions of purpose and value or on the development of legitimacy and support. The classic tradition assumes that these questions have been answered in the development of the organization's legislative or policy mandate.[73] The policy mandate simultaneously defines the organization's purpose and creates a normative presumption that such a purpose would be publicly valuable to pursue. The mandate also explicitly provides the organization with the resources—the money and public authority—it needs to achieve its purpose. Finally, it authorizes the managers to deploy those resources to achieve the mandated goals.

Given that the questions of resources, authorization, and value have all been resolved in the establishment of a policy mandate, managers must pursue the downward- and inward-looking tasks of deploying available resources to achieve the mandated objectives as efficiently and effectively as possible.[74] In accomplishing this goal, managers rely on their administrative expertise in wielding the instruments of internal managerial influence: organizational design, budgeting, human resource development, and management control.[75] To the extent that managers look upward and outward, they do so primarily to ensure that they operate within the framework of mandated objectives, that is, to ensure that they are properly accountable.[76] The definition (and redefinition) of purpose is left to policymakers.

In contrast, the strategic triangle rests on the assumption that public managers should define an organization's overall purpose and mission. It also reminds them to develop conceptions of valuable purposes from sources beyond the boundaries of their own administrative expertise. They are encouraged to use analytic techniques to scan their task environments and evaluate their own performance as the basis for forming independent views of the value of planned or past activities.

Managers should interact with the political system not simply through the medium of their mandated purposes but instead through more continuous and interactive dialogue. They should look behind the mandate to see how different political aspirations have been reflected in the mandate that seeks to guide them, and how the balance of political forces seems to be changing over time.[77] They should engage political overseers in deliberation to improve their judgment about what the political system would regard as valuable.[78] Moreover, they should adopt this stance toward politics not only at those rare times when legislation affecting their organization is being considered but routinely.

Even more radical is the idea that managers' knowledge of the distinctive competence of their organization—combined with what they are learning through their current operations about the needs of their clients and potential users—might suggest potentially valuable new activities for them to initiate. Thus, for example, the librarian in Chapter 1 considers whether and how to accommodate the needs of the latchkey children. At first blush, such an initiative seems beyond her mission and difficult to accomplish—therefore something to be resisted. On reflection, however, the idea might well be within her mission; it requires a distinctive competence her organization has developed. In short, she senses that there is a valuable new use for her organization. Like private sector managers who seek niches in their environments that they are well positioned to fill, so strategically oriented public sector managers might spot new opportunities for their organizations to meet emergent political demands or to respond to new needs that were not previously recognized.

Thus, this strategic conception seeks to incorporate the techniques of political analysis and policy analysis as well as administrative and organizational analysis in the required repertoires of public sector managers. In doing so, the concept of strategic management in the public sector seems to elevate public sector executives from the role of technicians, choosing from well-known administrative methods to accomplish purposes defined elsewhere, to the role of strategists, scanning their political and task environments for opportunities to use their organizations to create public value.[79] It also changes their administrative job from assuring continuity and efficiency in current tasks to one of improvising the transition from current to future performance. Like private sector executives, public sector executives serve to position the organization they lead to create public value, not simply to deploy resources to accomplish mandated purposes.

Now, such a broad invitation may pose hazards for democratic governance. It may be dangerous to encourage public sector executives to use their imaginations to search for public value. In gauging this risk, however, we must keep in mind that the primary change being recommended is *in the thoughts and actions of managers,* not in the existing institutional arrangements that hold them accountable.[80] In action, managers will still be bound by the tight process of oversight that now constrains them and by the rigidities of the bureaucracies that they seek to lead. The only new action I propose is that managers feel authorized to search their environments with purposeful, value-seeking imaginations and then to act on any opportunity they see through interactions with their political authorizing environments and innovations within their own organizations. If they succeed in finding and exploiting opportunities to create value, it will be because they earn their success in the tough institutional environments in which they find themselves, not because their world has become less demanding.

To see how this concept works in practice, and the sorts of choices a manager faces in committing himself and his organization to a particular strategy, let us return to the examples of Ruckleshaus and Miller.

THE MISSION OF THE EPA: POLLUTION ABATEMENT

Ruckelshaus, challenged to establish a direction for the fledgling Environmental Protection Agency, defined its mission as "pollution abatement."[81] This overall concept, and the more particular substantive, political, and administrative actions it entailed, turned out to function well as a strategic vision for the emerging organization.

Pollution Abatement as a Corporate Strategy

In committing the EPA to the goal of pollution abatement, Ruckelshaus made an important substantive statement about what public value he was to produce. More precisely, he signaled how he should strike the balance between society's desires to have an attractive, safe, and pristine environment, on the one hand, and its desires to enjoy economic growth, low taxes, and limited government intrusion into the operations of the market economy, on the other. In Ruckelshaus's view, public value lay in the direction of a more aggressive environmental cleanup rather than a continuation of the status quo. An important question, of course, is on what basis he decided this crucial matter.

One answer is that he formed this view in response to the politics of the issue. The concern of many Americans for preserving the quality of the environment seemed to persuade him that tilting toward environmental cleanup was not only politically feasible but also, and partly for this reason, normatively desirable.

A second answer is that actual objective conditions indicated that the quality of the environment was worsening, and worsening in ways that affected all the important ultimate values in this domain—aesthetics, health, and preservation. It is important to recall, however, that no one knew systematically at this stage whether environmental quality was deteriorating or not, or what the important consequences of any deterioration would be, or how the environmental degradation could best be reversed. Data monitoring the state of the environment, or the costs and effectiveness of interventions to reduce pollution, were simply not then available to answer these questions on a hard scientific basis. Some would argue, then, that the prudent course for Ruckelshaus would have been to wait until more evidence became available before launching the country on an expensive path toward environmental cleanup. That was certainly the course preferred by President Nixon and his staff.

Yet, Ruckelshaus decided to commit the EPA and the country to beginning the process of environmental cleanup. One justification for such a decision would be a judgment that the best way for society to learn about both the costs and the benefits of environmental protection would be to try it for a while and see what happened. Without doing something to avoid pollution or to clean up the accumulated harms, society would have no way of knowing much about either the benefits or the costs of the environmental cleanup.

Ruckelshaus himself summarized his judgment about the value of environmental protection. "There was enormous legitimacy to the issue itself," he said.[82] Both the politics and the objective circumstances as best he could then see them encouraged action to clean up the environment.

In terms of its ability to *sustain political support,* the concept of "pollution abatement" nicely balanced the competing political values that held the new agency in their grip. On the one hand, the phrase suggested a commitment to action rather than further study; that was what "abatement" meant. For environmentalists, this stance represented an important gain over past policies and therefore attracted some of their grudging support. On the other hand, the phrase left it unclear exactly how far Ruckelshaus meant to go in his cleanup efforts. Pollution was to be abated, not eliminated. It also seemed to indicate that the process would be deliberate. Polluters would have time to adapt to their new responsibilities. These features gratified those who, at least in the first instance, would have to pay for the costs of the cleanup.

In terms of its *operational feasibility,* the phrase, again, had some attractive features. It identified the key operational work that the organization had to do: namely, find some way to motivate polluters to reduce the pollutants they were putting into the air and water. And it was formulated in a way that allowed Ruckelshaus to begin making progress almost immediately without revising the organization's accepted operational objectives. As one participant in a Kennedy School executive program explained, "Ruckelshaus has found an organizational goal that is immediately achievable, but never attainable, and therefore continually challenging."

Thus, committing the EPA to the goal of pollution abatement met the conditions of a successful corporate strategy. It identified a purpose that was plausibly of public value, calculated in both political and substantive terms. It attracted enough political legitimacy and support to ensure that the EPA could remain as a going concern. And it defined an operational task that was challenging but not hopelessly beyond the organization's capacity to accomplish.

Implementing Strategy I: Maintaining Legitimacy

To make the goal of pollution abatement more than an empty slogan, however, Ruckelshaus had to take specific, concrete political, substantive, and administrative actions that reflected his commitment to this goal and shaped his organization's ability to act on it. In the *political* domain, this required him to prod and equip the EPA to act like an alert, forceful agency capable of responding to environmental crises with novel uses of governmental powers. Thus, for the first year, whenever an environmental crisis occurred, the EPA would respond—even if only to give a comment or announce a study. Moreover, the EPA initiated suits against a half-dozen large polluters—including both private sector corporations and municipal sanitation departments. These particular actions satisfied political overseers that the agency's commitment to abate pollution was real, not just rhetorical.

It also required him to show some degree of independence from the Nixon White House, for Nixon was widely (and accurately) viewed as skeptical of the value of the environmental crusade. When Ruckelshaus's independent stance and greater enthusiasm for environmental cleanup threatened his working relations with the White House staff, Ruckelshaus argued that his activist stance neutralized a potentially powerful political challenge from Senator Muskie. This argument kept him tolerably well aligned with one of his most important overseers.

In addition, throughout the period, Ruckelshaus kept lines of communication (and potential influence) open to key representatives who wanted to prevent the environmental movement from striking too hard or too suddenly at the economic interests of their constituencies. To be able to support Ruckelshaus, they needed confidence that they could shape the form and pace of governmental regulation to ensure a smooth (and minimally disruptive) adaptation. Thus, Ruckelshaus hired a special consultant to keep him abreast of the concerns of the agricultural interests represented by Congressman Jamie Whitten, the chairman of the House Appropriation Subcommittee to which Ruckelshaus was accountable. Taken together, these actions sustained a political coalition in support of Ruckelshaus, the EPA, and pollution abatement.

Implementing Strategy II:
Substantive Policy Decisions

Substantively, Ruckelshaus gave impetus to his overall strategy by deciding several particular policy issues in ways that reflected both his determination to move toward environmental cleanup and his openness to negotiating on the pace and form of the cleanup. Confronted with the question of whether to ban DDT—a pesticide made infamous by Rachel Carson—Ruckelshaus opted for an outright ban. It would have been hard to do otherwise and still be seen as someone bent on environmental cleanup. (It also helped that more effective and safer pesticides had been created since Carson's first warnings.)

Confronted with the question of whether to set air quality standards immediately even though the existing science was insufficient to show a certain or exact relationship between air pollution from cars and bad health consequences, Ruckelshaus decided to set the standards on the basis of only a single empirical study. Apparently, he believed that it was more important to get started on environmental cleanup than to get the standards exactly right at the beginning.

Confronted with the question of whether to impose penalties on automobile manufacturers producing vehicles that failed to meet environmental standards, Ruckelshaus imposed fines on trucks, not cars. This policy got the attention of the automakers without disastrously crippling them. In each of these cases, Ruckelshaus took a firm action that set the stage for further work to go forward in cleaning up the environment but did not inflict large economic losses.

Implementing Strategy III:
Building Operational Capacities

Operationally, Ruckelshaus's key decisions focused on the overall structure of the organization and the people to be appointed as subordinate managers in the structure he created. An Office of Management and Budget (OMB) Task Force advised him to adopt a standard functional organization then common to many federal organizations, that is, to appoint assistant administrators for Administration and Management, for Science and Technology, for Monitoring and Surveillance, and for Enforcement.[83] Others, eager to focus the organization on ultimate goals and objectives, recommended organizing on the basis of programs. The programs, in turn, could be defined in terms of either the media to be cleaned or the pollutant to be attacked. They proposed to have assistant administrators for Air Pollution, for Water Pollution, for Solid Waste, for Noise Pollution, and so on.

In the end Ruckelshaus followed neither recommendation. He opted for a mixed structure featuring assistant administrators for Administration, for Enforcement, for Air Programs, for Water Programs, and for Science. One could see this arrangement as nothing more than a compromise between two plausible plans. A different interpretation, however, is that this structure followed a logic dictated by an image of the EPA's *development over time* rather than by an effort to leap directly to the optimal long-run arrangements.

In the short run Ruckelshaus needed to develop some organizational capacity to take action against flagrant polluters: a powerful Office of Enforcement. This capability was central to his strategic vision for three reasons.

First, establishing such an office would powerfully and concretely embody his commitment to pollution abatement. To the extent that he had calculated correctly about the balance of political forces, creating such an office would establish his credibility and allow him to continue to operate with a reasonable amount of support and enthusiasm from his political overseers.

Second, the commitment to action reflected in the establishment of this office and backed up by continuing political support would not only give him some freedom and discretion in the short run, but would also produce a potential supply of additional money and authority over the long run. He needed this material to build the EPA's real operational capabilities in the future. He understood the difference between undertaking merely symbolic, immediate actions and building the EPA over time into an organization that could attack pollution operationally on a very broad front and on a very large scale. For that, he would need a continuing flow of money and authority long into the future, which could be used as investment now.

Third, the symbolic actions taken against polluters would help strengthen the environmental movement by focusing its attention on visible targets and by giving it a potentially powerful new ally. This alliance would help sustain a flow of money and authority to the organization in the future while conceivably producing operational benefits almost instantly. The stronger the environmental movement, the more likely the polluters to begin taking action on their own to clean up the environment. The movement might succeed in educating and persuading current polluters while putting pressure on them to change. More important, it would indicate to polluters that they would eventually have to stop polluting and that they might as well get a jump on the competition and begin adapting now rather than wait for the EPA to get around to them.[84] The EPA had to rely on such effects, for it had quite limited powers to compel an immediate environmental cleanup without societal encouragement for voluntary compliance.

For both political and operational reasons, then, Ruckelshaus naturally established an Office of Enforcement reporting directly to him. Indeed, this office made the responses that established the image of the EPA in its first few years and helped sustain the political determination to attack environmental degradation.

While the Office of Enforcement was the most important short-run priority, the largest problem facing the organization in the medium term was translating its broad political and legal authority to clean up the environment into specific obligations on specific polluters. The legislation directed at cleaning up the air and water had established particular procedures for accomplishing these objectives. In the case of air, the federal government was authorized to establish ambient air quality standards, and the states were then obligated to develop state plans for pollution control capable of meeting the federally mandated standards. In the case of water pollution, the states decided on both the standard of cleanliness to be met and how the burden for cleaning the environment would be distributed across polluters. The water program also included a large federal subsidy for municipal sanitation agencies, while the air program relied only on government authority to achieve its purposes.

At the time the EPA was created, very little of this work had been completed. Yet, until it was completed, no particular polluter had any enforceable liability for cleanup or much knowledge about how to contribute to environmental protection.

To ensure that this enterprise proceeded apace, Ruckelshaus left intact the administrative units then performing these functions. He reasoned that disrupting them would slow their performance—particularly since the central staff of the EPA would be focused on enforcement efforts and administrative arrangements necessary to integrate the diverse units.

In the long run, he reasoned, the EPA's Achilles' heel was likely to be the scientific base justifying and targeting the cleanup effort. In the short run, indignation about pollution would be strong enough to maintain support for reasonably aggressive action. Enough flagrant and economically insignificant targets existed for the EPA easily to justify its overall mission or its specific conduct in targeting particular firms for cleanup efforts. As the total and marginal costs of environmental cleanup increased, however, there would be stronger demands for justifications and greater need for precision in the targeting of cleanup efforts. To maintain the legitimacy of the issue, sheer indignation would have to yield to support from science. That could only come from strengthening the EPA's scientific base. To build that capability, Ruckelshaus had to create a home that appealed to first-rate environmental scientists; he had to give them enough time not only to develop the knowledge base but also to develop the people who could create it. Organizationally, the best way to accomplish these goals was to create an Office of Science that would insulate the scientists who worked there from most short-term operational demands while keeping them focused on the EPA mission.

The Results

As a result of Ruckelshaus's strategy, the EPA and the country launched on a particular course of action: toward environmental cleanup. The air and water began to get clean at a faster rate than a less aggressive posture probably would have accomplished. The EPA itself became a powerful agency that attracted quality people and used their talents well. Ruckelshaus gained a reputation as a first-rate governmental leader and manager—much admired by the politicians who worked with him and his staff of administrators and scientists. These consequences all register on the plus side.

On the negative side, Ruckelshaus's strategy introduced some rigidities into the government's actions in dealing with environmental degradation, which became quite costly as difficulties and new threats appeared.[85] By casting the mission as pollution abatement and emphasizing enforcement as an approach, Ruckelshaus made it much harder for the organization to shift its strategy to approaches that made effective use of markets in locating places where cleanup could be undertaken inexpensively. By failing to differentiate the possible justifications for environmental cleanup (for example, aesthetics, health, or preservation), and by emphasizing conventional air and water programs, Ruckelshaus may have slowed the government's response to toxic wastes—a problem that was arguably more important and more difficult than those that commanded much of the EPA's attention.

But these negatives suggest only that no single strategy can be successful in accomplishing everything over the long run. Indeed, a strategy by definition emphasizes some purposes at the expense of others.[86] Moreover, the decision about what to emphasize is always conditioned by the time at which the decision is made. Any given strategy will probably look worse over time. The right test for a strategy, then, is not whether it solves all problems forever, but rather whether it solves the important problems for the next several years and leaves a reasonable amount of room for adjusting to issues that were not anticipated at the outset. By this test, Ruckelshaus's strategy for the EPA seems quite valuable.

The Mission of DYS: Humanizing the Treatment of Children

Challenged to lead the Massachusetts Department of Youth Services, Jerome Miller defined his mission as "humanizing the treatment of children." This goal, too, seemed to meet the conditions required for a plausibly effective corporate strategy for his organization.

Humanizing Treatment as a Corporate Strategy

Like Ruckelshaus's strategic vision, Miller's conception was designed to resonate with, and help organize the *politics* surrounding, the organization he led. He sought to capture the enthusiasm of an emerging political constituency then bidding to overturn the political agreements that had previously guided the agency's operations. But Miller arguably went further than Ruckelshaus. Instead of balancing the competing interests, Miller staked the organization on a vision closer to the aspirations of the most radical reformers. It reflected the views of reformists who spoke in terms of justice for children and rehabilitation, as opposed to expressing the values of those inclined to protect the community from juvenile crime. Its political success depended on sustaining that more extreme political constituency.

Substantively, Miller thought that such treatment would pay off not only by demonstrating in DYS operations a proper vision of what children justly deserved, but also in practical terms by reducing recidivism and saving money over the long run. Despite little actual evidence, widely endorsed theories established the plausibility of this claim.[87] In any case, compared with the expensive, unjust, and ineffective way that DYS was currently operating, almost anything could be considered an improvement—at least in Miller's mind and in the minds of his supporters.

Operationally, the concept also identified the key tasks facing the organization. The way DYS treated kids had to change—from "dehumanizing" to "humanizing" conditions. That, presumably, meant not only increasing the flow of educational and rehabilitative services to kids but also treating them with respect—perhaps even love. It might also mean keeping them in contact with their natural parents and their communities, and seeing them as children more than urban terrorists.

Miller's vision was a bold one. Whereas Ruckelshaus's strategy seemed to go right down the middle of the political conflict surrounding the organization, Miller's strategy seemed to align itself with one of the extremes. Whereas there was enough objective evidence to sustain a broad public enthusiasm for attacking environmental pollution, there was nothing but a contested sociological theory and a sense of justice to indicate the wisdom of humanizing treatment for juvenile offenders. Whereas Ruckelshaus's strategy depended on the gradual development of a new organization, Miller's seemed to require a radical reorientation of an existing organization. Clearly, Miller adopted a much riskier strategy than Ruckelshaus.

Implementing Strategy I:
Building Operational Capacities

Like Ruckelshaus, Miller had to find some concrete ways to establish his commitment to the goal of humanizing treatment in both the political and operational spheres. At first, Miller sought to implement his strategy by changing the institutions themselves. He eliminated rules governing haircuts and dress, and thereby eliminated a source of power that the custodial staff had used to enforce discipline within the institutions. He also toured the institutions, "trying to find people who shared his goals," and authorized them to initiate new programs regardless of their status in the organization's hierarchy. He drew volunteers into the institutions to run new programs for the children. Perhaps most important, he encouraged the children to speak out about the conditions and to come to him with any complaints about staff behavior. These changes had a revolutionary impact inside the institutions; they not only altered existing policies and procedures but also shattered previously fixed and established relationships between the staff and the kids.

Although these reforms created turmoil within the institutions, Miller eventually became convinced that it was impossible to make important changes in the way kids were treated within the structure of the existing institutions. DYS, he said, was "like China": it would absorb all efforts at reform and remain unchanged. Consequently, he embarked on a series of administrative reforms to create alternative placements for children outside the institutions.

His next important move was to increase spending in a little-used budgetary line for purchase of services from foster parents and other private agencies to provide supervision and care for children. In addition, Miller significantly shortened the average period of stay in the institutions. Ironically, he did not intend to take this step. He sent a memo to the heads of the various institutions establishing three months as an appropriate *minimum* stay for children in the institutions. The heads of the institutions interpreted the memorandum as establishing the *expected maximum* stay and began paroling children from the institutions.

This may not have been a wholly innocent misinterpretation, for the heads of the institutions felt threatened and attacked by Miller's ideas, and they may have hoped that community indignation unleashed by the releases would stop Miller's innovations. If that was their goal, however, they were sadly disappointed. Both they and Miller were astonished to learn that even though the population in the institutions began to decline, no one seemed to be complaining. Miller decided to continue and accelerate the initiative.

In a dramatic gesture symbolizing his determination to deinstitutionalize the juvenile population, Miller ordered the Bridgewater institution closed when a riot occurred there during a tour by the governor's wife. He then promptly and ostentatiously bulldozed the empty structure.

As a final key step toward the goal of establishing an administrative and operational basis for supervising children outside the context of the institutions, Miller created a regional administrative network within DYS to stand alongside the organizational structure based on the institutions. He assigned the regional administrative network the job of finding alternative dispositions for children entrusted to DYS. As the population within the DYS institutions shrank, the relative importance of the regional network grew, until the regional network became the heart of the organization rather than the institutions.[88]

Implementing Strategy II: Maintaining Legitimacy

Obviously, to manage these dramatic changes in the structure, conduct, and performance of DYS, Miller needed a very heavy, sustained dose of "capital." He needed financial capital to pay the sharply increased costs associated with managing the transition from a system in which delinquents were supervised in the context of institutions (which continued to claim funds) to a program that cared for them through community-based programs (which had to be built from scratch). As important, however, was the *political* capital that would allow him to pursue his controversial vision against the concerted opposition of the custodial staffs, the skepticism of the police and judges who disagreed with his approach, and the fears of citizens who once again had to face children who had committed crimes.

To shore up his mandate for humanizing the treatment of juvenile delinquents, Miller had to sustain and build support among the individuals and groups that could authorize him to take action and protect him from attacks launched by others. Close-in support came from Governor Sargent and Secretary Goldmark, who remained strongly committed to Miller's course of action. He also received unexpected support from two key members of the Massachusetts legislature who successfully fended off proposed legislative investigations of Miller's "mismanagement" of the department.

While these individuals seem to have based their support for Miller principally on their shared commitment to his cause, he turned out to be an enormously successful politician and advocate for his cause. As one observer put it, from the outset, Miller "married the media." He was extraordinarily successful in publicizing the terrible conditions then prevalent in the Massachusetts institutions, and in showing the human side of the children who had been transformed in the public mind into vicious young thugs. He promised to save the children from public neglect. Against the political power of that value at that particular time, worries about a little administrative inefficiency and small increases in the level of juvenile crime seemed inconsequential. Except for some die-hard opponents, members of print and electronic media gave Miller and his reforms consistently enthusiastic reviews.

With the powerful values he championed, and the widespread media support, Miller managed to strengthen youth advocacy groups throughout Massachusetts. These groups provided Miller with the political muscle that sustained his supporters' commitment and held his opponents at bay. Moreover, they supplied a nucleus of people who could staff the new programs Miller needed both within and outside the institutions. Initially, many of the volunteers who created programs within the institutions came from this youth advocacy movement. Later, these people began operating programs on a contract basis outside the structure of the institutions but still under the regional umbrella of the new DYS.

Finally, Miller found one other crucial financial backer and political ally—the federal government. Pressed by national trends similar to those operating in Massachusetts, the federal government had created an Office for Juvenile Justice and Delinquency Prevention (OJJDP) whose strategy for changing the nation's juvenile justice system matched Miller's. Indeed, it seemed to OJJDP that Miller's reforms led the way to substantial reform. As a result, they contributed financial support to cover the cost of the new network of services that Miller was creating and offered assurances that Miller was at the professional and technical frontiers in dealing with delinquent children.

The Substantive Value of Humanized Treatment

What nobody knew, of course, was whether the reforms that Miller championed would actually work to reduce juvenile crime. Miller was largely unconcerned about this. He argued that his reforms merely had to beat the alternative of institutionalizing kids. He was confident that his programs could do no worse than the institutions in terms of reducing youth crime in the short and long run; his programs used public money and authority less intensively than the state institutions and embodied a more attractive relationship between the society and its children. It was not only plausible but virtually certain, therefore, that his effort created more public value than the institutions had.

The Results

Miller's tenure in Massachusetts lasted three years. In that time he laid the foundations for a radically different way of supervising juvenile offenders.[89] He shifted DYS from an organization that consisted almost entirely of state-managed institutions to one that consisted almost entirely of privately run, community-based programs. The variety of forms of care and supervision for juvenile delinquents increased dramatically, raising the likelihood that a program suitable to the particular circumstances of individual kids could be found, while broadening society's capacity to learn what did and did not work. Moreover, the purchase of service arrangements provided much greater flexibility to administrators in adjusting the aggregate level and distribution of types of social control programs.

Over time the political constituency that ushered in the reforms weakened. But it was replaced by a new political constituency rooted in the private care providers nourished by Miller's reforms.[90] Gradually, some secure care was added to the portfolio of programs available to DYS to deal with children who seemed particularly dangerous. The net result was that Massachusetts enjoyed then, and still enjoys now, a much more varied portfolio of programs to be used in supervising and caring for delinquent children than any system in the country. When challenged by assertions that the transition from the old to the new system could have been made in a tidier, more efficient way, Miller simply asked how that could have been done and pointed out that nowhere else has that been accomplished.

The Managerial Utility
of Mission Statements

Ruckelshaus and Miller made a lot of the opportunities presented to them. Their articulated purposes established the frameworks that guided governmental action and justified public investment in the domains for which they were responsible. Their organizations became resourceful and powerful in accomplishing the purposes they articulated. Although the political coalitions that gave them the opportunity to act wavered a bit, and triggered countermovements, the balance of political forces never returned to the position that existed prior to their administrations. And while the evaluations of their efforts remain equivocal (as they inevitably will), most observers judge these managers to have spent the resources entrusted to them reasonably well: in all likelihood, they increased public value through improved environmental protection and decent supervision and care of juvenile delinquents.

These managers did well because they developed and used an organizational strategy similar to those used by private sector executives. They did not articulate detailed plans to describe how the organization would move from one particular position to another. Indeed, what is striking is that neither of these managers had anything like a detailed plan.[91] Much of what they did seemed improvised and opportunistic rather than planned in advance. They had a broad goal that defined the direction in which they intended to move: abating pollution for Ruckelshaus, humanizing the treatment of kids for Miller. These goals operated as strategic conceptions for Ruckelshaus and Miller because they met the necessary conditions: in setting out the concrete path that their organizations had to take to create public value, they defined conceptions that were at once substantively valuable, politically sustainable, and administratively feasible.

This interpretation places a heavy weight on phrases that might be described as mere slogans—and not particularly creative ones at that. Yet I think the particular phrases, *and the ways that the managers used them both to guide and explain their political, substantive, and managerial actions,* can bear the weight. The careful selection, repeated articulation, and consistent use of these simple concepts helps accomplish a great deal of managerial work.[92] The contributions come in three important areas.

Maintaining Managerial Focus

First, the statements of purpose help managers stay focused on the point of their efforts: managing their organizations for performance and value.[93] Every experienced manager knows how hard it is to stay focused on important managerial tasks when trivial but urgent demands divert intellectual energy and attention, and when unexpected but critical surprises occur.

The common devices advocated for dealing with these problems include more effective delegation to save the manager's time for important issues and improved planning to predict otherwise unforeseen events. But these devices are rarely successful in themselves. And even when they are successful, they depend ultimately on developing some simple, reliable analytic criterion that allows a manager to tell whether an unexpected event or a troublesome detail is or is not strategically important.[94] To stay focused on the important, then, managers need broad, consistent statements of purpose—a ready touchstone for examining their use of their own time and attention.

Identifying Key Political and Administrative Tasks

Second, by framing the general managerial task, the statements of purpose (combined with thought and analysis of the immediate context) highlight the more particular pieces of managerial work that are strategically most important to achieve: the particular sources of political support that must be nurtured to sustain the enthusiasm and legitimacy necessary to carry the enterprise forward, the key public values that must be articulated and measured to maintain continuing political support, and the key investments and innovations that must be made in operational capabilities to achieve the purposes articulated in the strategy. In short, not only does the articulation of purpose keep a manager from becoming mired in unimportant but urgent detail, or being knocked off stride by surprises, it also sets the agenda of work that managers must actively address on both the political and administrative side of their operations if their strategy is to succeed.

Thus, in describing the EPA's goal as pollution abatement, Ruckelshaus aligned himself politically with those advocating that pollution be slowed and that the polluters accept responsibility for this end. If he succeeded, it was at least partly because he made himself and the EPA an instrument of their purposes—at least enough to appease their desire for some governmental action against pollution.[95] The goal also helped identify whence the opposition would come: from among those who were being asked to abate pollution at some cost to themselves. Ruckelshaus faced the strategic challenge, then, of finding a way to prevent the opposition from growing so strong that it would frustrate his efforts to achieve some degree of environmental cleanup on behalf of those (perhaps including himself) who thought that the world would be a better place if less polluted.

Perhaps less trivially, the goal of pollution abatement identified the key operational capabilities that Ruckelshaus needed to create and deploy and gave him an entering bias on policy decisions to be made. Operationally, he had to find a way to stop specific sources of pollution. That made it important to develop political power and enforcement authority to impose cleanup obligations on the appropriate polluters. These became the central operational foci of his administration. There would have been a much different operational focus if his goal had been cost-effective environmental cleanup or guaranteeing a healthy environment.

Substantively, his policy decisions had to reflect a commitment to action to clean up the environment, even when there was some doubt about the benefits of doing so. That is why he had to ban DDT and set clean air standards even without the benefit of detailed scientific evidence.

The concept of humanizing treatment for kids provided the same kind of diagnostic frame for Miller. Once he articulated this goal, he could easily determine whom to rely on for political support and who constituted the opposition that would have to be held off or accommodated in some way. One cannot analyze the political environment for supporters or opponents until one has decided what substantive purposes one advocates.

The goal's key contribution, however, lay in helping Miller to see what was required of the organization he led and what changes would be necessary. Humanizing treatment for kids meant taking them seriously as autonomous human beings and giving them rights and powers in their relationships with the custodial staff. It necessitated supplying them with more intensive and extensive services ranging from decent food and shelter, through general education, to employment support or psychological counselling. It also required sustaining those relationships with their parents, community, and friends that were constructive or inevitable, so that the transition back to freedom in the community would be less traumatic. These considerations flowed naturally from the concept of "humanizing treatment," yet they mandated a rather extensive overhaul in the design of the facilities and programs through which kids were being supervised.

Thus, once these managers knew the basic purpose of their organization, it became possible to see which events or tasks were strategically important and which were distractions. Without having thought through what one is trying to accomplish, one is at the mercy of one's in-box. Once one has decided what is important, the work that comes through one's in-box, and the events that occur in the world, get filtered through a different evaluative screen.[96] The work becomes grist for advancing strategic purposes rather than compelling tasks that must be responded to in their own terms or ignored as outside the frame of a carefully laid out plan.

Mobilizing External and Internal Support

Third, the articulation of broad purposes often both stimulates and guides the contributions that others can and must make to the enterprise if the organization is to succeed. On the political side, if the manager's articulated mission expresses a value or a purpose that a community advocates, then the community will be inclined to give the manager its support. When Ruckelshaus started talking about pollution abatement, for example, a great many environmental activists were willing to lend him support, or tolerance, at least for a little while. Similarly, when Miller started talking about humanizing treatment for kids, youth advocacy groups commented favorably on his actions to the governor and the legislatures. Since all public enterprises need enthusiasm from some elements of the public and tolerance from others, a statement of purpose that reflects important values being pressed by active groups can do a great deal of political work for the manager: it can become the banner under which political forces are sustained or mobilized.

On the administrative side, the articulated statement of purpose resolves a dilemma for the manager's key subordinates: it tells them what sorts of projects and enterprises will be viewed favorably by the boss, and what language they should use in describing their efforts. In the best of all worlds, this clarification would make midlevel managers and supervisors in the organization who already had projects and investments in mind that were consistent with the strategy feel authorized to act on behalf of the new purposes. It would unleash a torrent of creative energy along the desired path.

In a slightly less favorable situation, more skeptical midlevel managers would simply start mouthing the new rhetoric to "game" the system.[97] Even here, however, the articulated purposes nonetheless have value. At a minimum, they define the terms of the internal competition for resources and thus begin to shape the discussions about what projects are worth doing. More interestingly, the language itself may gradually begin to influence the culture of the enterprise.[98] As people begin to use a different language to describe what they do, they tend to change what they see and do. Thus, even in a world where the midlevel managers had no ideas, or where their fondest ideas lay in some other direction, the articulation of purpose would have value because it would begin the slow process of distinguishing them in terms of their willingness to contribute to the enterprise and educating them about what was important for them to do.

For articulated purposes to attract support and effort from others, they have to look relatively firm and settled to the political advocates and to the subordinates. Ideally, they become a piece of reality to which everyone else has to adjust rather than something merely being proposed. The manager must be seen as "reality's agent" rather than simply as someone with an idiosyncratic idea.

To produce this condition, the goals must be rooted in the political and administrative reality of a given situation, the manager must be committed to them, and the manager must look like someone who is going to survive in the job. Otherwise, the goals will not be taken seriously enough for political groups to invest in them or for midlevel managers to stake their careers on them. And if no one invests in the enterprise, and no one acts to realize the vision, then it will fail.

Of course, no strategy can look firm and settled at the outset. Certainly no strategy that challenges the status quo can have the character of inevitability. Except in a crisis, at any given moment the overwhelming expectation is that what was true yesterday will be true today and tomorrow.[99] Consequently, every articulated strategy that challenges an organization will initially look artificial and suspect.

What gives a new, challenging strategy credibility is the degree to which it resonates with the views of others interested in or active in the area. If the new strategy attracts political support, if it attracts publicity, if it attracts volunteers, if budgets begin to increase, if new legislative sponsors appear, if old political opponents back off a little, then the strategy begins to have some political bite. If the manager seems committed because he or she keeps saying the same things, and his or her substantive and administrative actions have some interpretable relationship to the articulated mission, then the strategy begins to exercise some administrative torque on the organization's operations. If the manager's personal stock seems to increase as he or she pursues the strategy, then the strategy will gather momentum inside the organization as subordinates figure either that now is their chance to do what they always wanted to do or that they are going to have to adjust to the manager's terms. It is not easy to change what people take for granted, but in the end, that is what a successful strategy does: it moves politicians and midlevel managers in an organization to a different set of expectations about the purposes and capabilities of a given public enterprise.[100]

Evaluative Criteria for Organizational Strategies

There are probably many different strategies that could be successful for a public sector enterprise. Ruckelshaus might have been successful if he had announced long-term plans to study environmental hazards and to develop an organization that could coordinate the nation's response. (Indeed, that was what Nixon expected and authorized him to do.) He might also have been successful if he had immediately begun developing a strategy emphasizing the threat represented by toxic wastes. Miller might have been successful if he had concentrated on decent care for kids within the institutions or marginally increased the flow of rehabilitative services to them.

Many different strategies are feasible because at any given moment the politics of a situation can accommodate many different ideas. Moreover, the politics will change of its own accord, in response to particular events, and sometimes even in response to managerial effort. So, if one looks ahead a little bit, the range of possible, sustainable political coalitions can become very broad.

Similarly, although organizations tend to be pretty set in their ways and do the particular things they do well, there is usually some flexibility in what organizations can do. Some slack always exists for experimental purposes if the organization is so inclined. Special programs now operate or remain in the memory of those who participated in them. Conflict arises about operational philosophy within the organization. Indeed, it often seems that all the conflicts that exist in the political world about the appropriate mission or function of the organization are expressed someplace within the organization—though not necessarily in the same balance.[101] All this becomes fertile soil for developing new and different organizational capabilities.

Finally, in the substantive realm, important doubts about the value of an organization's current operations surface, as do new, plausible ideas about better ways of accomplishing old objectives or about new tasks the organization could perform that might be valuable and sustainable. In short, there is nearly always some scope for programmatic, administrative, or strategic innovations that could improve an organization's functioning.[102]

The occurrence of conflict and change within both political and organizational domains, and the existence of plausibly valuable innovations, show that there may be many possible strategic conceptions that will work. After all, managers do not need political unanimity to have a successful strategy: all they need is *enough* political support to supply the money, authority, and people required to implement the strategy. Similarly, managers do not need organizations perfectly suited to implement their desired strategy; they need organizations that can perform key tasks and absorb investments that will carry them to improved performance in executing the intended strategy. Finally, managers do not need to know for sure that some new ideas are valuable; it is often enough that the ideas seem plausible and worth experimentation.

The existence of many feasible strategies makes the task of designing and choosing a particular strategy an interesting one. If only one strategy were feasible, the task would simply be to figure out what it was. Since there are many, it becomes easier to find one that meets the minimal criteria for success but much more challenging to determine which one should be chosen. Three dimensions along which feasible strategies might vary seem particularly important.

The Right Level of Abstraction

One concerns the level of abstraction at which the strategy of the organization is defined. To see what I mean by the level of abstraction, consult the table on page 96, which sets out alternative strategies for the Environmental Protection Agency and the Department of Youth Services formulated at quite different levels of abstraction. Most people acknowledge differences in levels of abstraction at which tasks or purposes are defined. Moreover, given any two characterizations of an enterprise, they can readily say which is the more abstract. They may not realize, however, that the level of abstraction is a fairly continuous dimension and that we can develop rules for determining at what level of abstraction it is useful to discuss an organization's purpose.[103]

Generally speaking, we prefer greater specificity and concreteness in defining organizational tasks. Greater specificity helps explain more particularly what one means by a given purpose. It allows us to calculate

Alternative strategies for the EPA and DYS: Cost at different levels of abstraction

Level of abstraction	EPA	DYS
Highly abstract	"Protect the environment"	"Ensure justice for children"
	"Keep the environment healthy, clean, and beautiful"	"Humanize the treatment of children"
	"Abate pollution"	Provide care, custody, and connection to adjudicated delinquents
Relatively concrete	Keep the air and water free from toxic levels of pollution through stringent regulation of polluting industries	Provide for the care, effective supervision, and rehabilitation of adjudicated delinquents through a system that emphasizes community-based care and the referral of children to the least restrictive setting

what particular operational capabilities must be created. And it makes easier the job of devising unambiguous, objective ways of determining whether the organization has achieved its purposes. These evaluations enhance accountability of the organization to its overseers and facilitate internal management control.

In addition, increased specificity makes feasible the planning of organizational activities in greater detail. Once one has described what one means to do in detail, it becomes possible to identify the specific activities that are necessarily implied, to determine the order in which they must be done, and to determine which steps are on the "critical path" and which are not. Thus, greater specificity facilitates measurement, accountability, control, and planning of organizational activities.

These virtues of greater specificity are well known. Somewhat less widely acknowledged are the virtues of ambiguity associated with more abstract characterizations of mission and purpose.[104] One such virtue is that ambiguity and abstraction may harmonize political conflict. Significant differences in the values that various political groups place on particular aspects of performance may sometimes be submerged by finding a more abstract characterization of purpose. At the extreme, one may have to reach as high as the concepts of "public interest" or "public value." But often a lower level concept can contain a conflict that would be all too apparent if the mission were described at lower levels of abstraction. This advantage of higher levels of abstraction is usually scorned as a kind of self-deception or sign of irresolution in our politics. And so it is. But it has some important operational advantages as well.

The crucial operational weakness of specific plans is that they tend to sacrifice flexibility. They leave little room for accommodating external shocks or for improvising solutions to unexpected problems. Above all, specific plans prevent people from changing their minds about what they are trying to accomplish.

What specificity does well is ensure the reliable and efficient achievement of a well-defined objective. What specificity hampers is the invention of new techniques or changing broader goals. At the extreme, too much specificity can lead an organization to solve, efficiently and reliably, a problem that had changed or become irrelevant; or to to fail to capitalize on some unexpected opportunity; or to fall apart completely in response to some unexpected changes in its plans. Thus, a certain amount of ambiguity may leave the organization room to invent some purpose or some means superior to what could have been imagined in advance.

More abstract characterizations of purpose also have the advantage of inviting people in the organization to feel responsible for and participate in the mission of the enterprise in a different way. They are no longer cogs in a machine designed by others; they are partners in a joint operation that requires initiative and imagination as well as responsiveness and technical competence. To the extent that this new role increases the motivation of employees, and increases the number of minds working on the problem that the organization faces, it may improve performance.

If there are managerial advantages of moving to lower levels of specificity in characterizing the mission of the organization, and also advantages of moving to higher levels of abstraction, it must be true that there is an optimal level of abstraction in defining an organization's purpose that is neither too high nor too low. Of course, one might be able to solve this problem by setting out a hierarchy of goals to define the organization's mission at different levels of abstraction ranging from very high to very low.[105] This system would lend significance to the lower level objectives, by showing their relationship to the broader purposes of the organization, and concreteness and specificity to the lofty purposes, by showing the particular things that the lofty purposes entailed.

But the development of a full hierarchy of goals and objectives would leave open the question of which of these levels would be the primary focus of top managerial attention and rhetoric. To this question, I have a tentative answer: the less political conflict exists concerning an organization's mission, and the more certainty there is about the organization's basic technologies and procedures, the more concrete should be the characterization of the mission; the more political the dissension, and the greater the need for innovation, the more abstract the characterization should be. We cannot expect public sector enterprises that are the focus of intense, shifting political conflicts to be precise about what they are trying to accomplish, for the very precision will invite constant destabilizing interventions by political overseers. Nor should we require public sector enterprises that are launched on complex, new initiatives where the appropriate means for accomplishing the goals have not yet been developed to be precise and detailed about how they will operate.[106] They need room to innovate and explore the operating features of the new technologies. We should demand great specificity and concreteness only of public enterprises whose missions and technologies are settled and refined.

Of course, determining which enterprises have settled missions and fully developed techniques is partly a matter of our political and managerial imaginations. Some might look at an enterprise and see nothing but settled purpose and routine procedure; others looking at the enterprise might see an opportunity to create additional value through new procedures.[107] Whether a manager is willing to transform a situation that seems settled and routine into one that is more open and innovative is an issue of strategy that relates to the second dimension on which strategies can vary—the degree of risk they entail for the manager and the society.

To a degree, one can see these differences in the different levels of abstraction used by Ruckelshaus and Miller in guiding their respective enterprises. In both cases, a broad political movement seemed to demand change and innovation in the performance of the organizations they inherited. Beneath the surface of those movements, however, churned a great deal of unresolved political controversy. As a result, each needed a mission formulated at a level of abstraction that could appeal to the surging political movements, accommodate the persisting concerns of traditional constituents, and frame the operational requirements for innovation within their organizations. Thus, they formulated strategies at moderately high levels of abstraction. In my view, Miller's strategy encompassed a higher level of abstraction than Ruckelshaus's because Miller needed a broader political coalition and more innovation to accomplish his strategy. For this reason, Miller also exposed himself and society to greater risk than did Ruckelshaus, though both were involved in inherently risky ventures.

The Degree of Risk and Exposure

Articulating an organizational mission meant simultaneously to establish the terms on which the organization will be accountable to its political overseers and to guide the organization's operations and investments in the future is inherently risky. No one can be sure what the political environment will expect or demand from an organization in the future. No one can know for sure what is publicly valuable. And no one can be sure what an organization will be capable of doing. Thus, in stating an organizational mission one takes a gamble—even in promising more of the same, for if the organization does not change, its political or substantive task environment might.

How big a gamble a particular strategy involves can, in principle, be measured by comparing its political and operational requirements to the existing political and administrative realities. We can think about the existing situation as fixed and incapable of change. Or, we can assume that the political and administrative environment contains possibilities not yet exploited and will change rather than remain constant.

Those unexploited possibilities could be represented analytically as probability distributions (subjectively imagined). Thus, in thinking about what is politically possible, we might visualize a distribution of probabilities over different conceivable mandates for an organization. And in thinking about what is operationally possible, we could imagine a probability distribution over different operational capabilities. Scenarios at the center of these distributions would be easier to achieve than those at their ends.

The question for the strategist, then, is not only what is now at the intersection of political support, substantive value, and administrative feasibility, but whether the intersection includes conditions that are likely or quite unlikely to occur. Obviously, the more one includes relatively unlikely events in the solution represented by an articulated strategy, the more risk one takes with that strategy. If one proposes a strategy that is politically sustainable with a high probability, but operationally feasible with only a low probability, that strategy is riskier than one that is high probability in both dimensions.

Ruckelshaus's and Miller's strategies seem quite different in terms of the risk they incorporated. Ironically, neither strategy emphasized the status quo. Even though that would have been the safest strategy in operational terms, it would have been quite disastrous in political terms. The political environment was demanding a change. Hence, all of their strategic options were riskier than those that face someone taking over an organization operating in calmer political waters.

Still, they chose strategies that had much different degrees of risk associated with them. Ruckelshaus's strategy was more conservative than Miller's. In terms of political support, Ruckelshaus's goal of pollution abatement spoke more to the center of the balance of political forces than Miller's goal of humanizing treatment for kids. In operational terms, pollution abatement created fewer demands than humanizing treatment. As for substantive value, pollution abatement seemed far more likely to create it than humanizing treatment—that is, the hypotheses tying environmental degradation to aesthetic and health damages that could be reduced by eliminating pollution seemed much more firmly established than the hypotheses linking community treatment of juvenile delinquency to reduced juvenile crime. In this sense, Ruckelshaus served as "steward" of the EPA, while Miller "bet the company."

Whose Vision and Purposes?

Indeed, the boldness of Miller's strategy still offends many people, for to expose society to this degree of risk seems inappropriate in managing public sector enterprises. This observation raises the third important dimension on which public sector strategies can vary: the extent to which the strategy is understood as a statement of public purposes as opposed to an expression of the goals of the individual organizational leader.

In the end a strategy for an organization states the purposes of an organization and therefore, inevitably, proposes how important, competing social values are to balanced. When Ruckelshaus declared that the EPA would pursue pollution abatement, it became clear that, for a while at least, the definition of public value would favor environmental cleanup over unfettered economic growth. When Miller declared that under his tenure DYS would seek to humanize treatment for children, it became clear that, for a while at least, public value would favor the social development of delinquents over short-run crime control.

But who makes such statements about public value and with what kind of authorization? If these goals are understood as accurate interpretations of the balance of political forces impinging on an organization's activities (for example, if they are at the center of the aspirations announced in recent legislation), then they can be understood as having been authorized by the political process. In this respect the organizational leader merely articulates in more concrete, particular language what the contemporary political will demands.

Alternatively, they can be seen as working assumptions about what constitutes public value nominated by public managers for consideration by citizens, overseers, clients, and beneficiaries. If the assumptions incur substantial opposition or engender no particular enthusiasm, managers might well modify the strategy (although silent accord is often the best they can hope for).

A third possibility is to see the strategic statement as an expression of the manager's own, individually held conception of public value. If this happens to accord with the current political forces, then a fortunate coincidence has occurred—the right person has filled the job at the right time. If the values expressed in the individually preferred strategy are out of alignment with the political forces, however, then managers face a difficult pragmatic and moral choice. They can keep pressing for the legitimacy of the purposes for which they stand, hoping that time and operational success will widen the tolerance of the political process for them and their purposes, or they can rebalance the political forces to favor them and their efforts. Alternatively, they can resign. Or, as a final option, they can become the instruments of the political forces making claims on them and adjust their own individual views of what is desirable to reflect those claims.

Which of these paths organizational strategists take is an important normative and psychological question confronting managers. I will discuss it extensively in Chapter 8. For now, it is enough to observe that the political pressures and the limitations of organizational capacities both do and should make claims on managers' conception of what is worth doing. Managers should not be prisoners of these constraints, for there is always some room for maneuver, and they should feel the right and the obligation to contribute their own views. But the views that are worth offering are those that interpret the possibilities of a given situation. That is what it means to have a strategy as distinct from a personal conception of what constitutes public value.[108]

Note that the degree of risk associated with a particular strategy depends on whose goal is expressed in the strategy. If the manager chooses a strategy that is at the center of existing political forces, consistent with the organization's current operating capabilities, and widely viewed as substantively valuable, then there is relatively little risk, and one can view the strategy as being almost entirely produced by the situation. The manager in this case would be nothing more than an agent of the circumstances.

By contrast, if the manager adopts a strategy that challenges the existing politics, rests on a novel idea of what is substantively valuable, and depends on significant changes in the operating capabilities of his or her organization, then there is a great deal of risk. There is also a stronger tendency to identify the purpose of the organization as the manager's purpose rather than anybody else's and to query its legitimacy as well as its feasibility.

For these reasons, most public managers tend to stay well within the political, substantive, and operational mainstream.[109] They cannot operate well outside these constraints without exposing themselves to significant risks and criticisms. Still, on occasion, public managers find the courage to operate this way, pay the price, and leave behind them either disasters or remarkable achievements depending on how their gamble pays off. In this regard it is interesting that Ruckelshaus left the EPA to wide applause, and Miller resigned from DYS under fire; yet Miller probably made the greater contribution to public value because he significantly widened the political and operational space within which juvenile justice could operate. DYS became an adaptable and innovative organization able to respond to varied political demands and heterogeneous claims from its clients.

Note, finally, that how risky a particular strategy is depends not only on the degree of predictability and congruence in the existing setting but also on the skill of the manager. Some managers are much better at diagnosing and operating on their political environments than others. Some are better at envisioning and properly reckoning the substantive value of their enterprises. Some are better at using techniques of administrative influence to make their organizations perform and change. What diagnostic and managerial techniques the best public managers use to effectively engage their political environments are the subjects of Chapters 4 and 5; I discuss the techniques they use to transform their operational capabilities in Chapters 6 and 7.

PART II

BUILDING SUPPORT
AND LEGITIMACY

MOBILIZING SUPPORT, LEGITIMACY, AND COPRODUCTION: THE FUNCTIONS OF POLITICAL MANAGEMENT

Strategic management in the public sector begins by looking up toward politics. By politics, I mean not only the current expectations and aspirations of citizens and their representatives but also the older political agreements formally enshrined in the legislation that defines public managers' mandates for action.

Politics, and the laws that politics produce, deserve this pride of place for three key reasons. First, it is this realm that managers must search to discover what purposes are deemed publicly valuable and can, therefore, be practically and normatively sustained as the focus of their managerial efforts. It is in and through politics that they can discover and help shape their mandates for action. Second, political institutions grant public managers the resources they need to accomplish their operational purposes—including money and authority over their own organizations and over those beyond their organizations who can contribute to the managers' purposes. Third, it is to politics and law that public managers are both theoretically and practically accountable; their performance is graded and their reputations made within this realm.

Two cases describing managers facing decisions strategically important to their organizations but potentially beyond their own, individual power to decide help to illustrate the importance of political management as a key managerial function.

MILES MAHONEY AND PARK PLAZA

In May 1972 Governor Francis Sargent appointed Miles Mahoney commissioner of the Massachusetts Department of Community Affairs

(DCA).[1] Mahoney assumed control of an agency that had recently been recapitalized by the Massachusetts legislature. Seized with enthusiasm for rebuilding Massachusetts cities and towns, the legislature had granted the commissioner of DCA significant budgetary resources and legal powers to achieve its aims.

Specifically, DCA received public funding to maintain an expert planning staff, to conduct surveys of public housing needs, and to provide services such as day-care or rental assistance to needy citizens. At the same time, the legislature granted Mahoney broad legal powers, the most important of which authorized him to use the state's right of eminent domain to help private developers assemble parcels of land suitable for large-scale, urban redevelopment projects that would serve public as well as private purposes. Tight statutory rules limited that power by setting out the specific conditions that had to be met if the power were to be used. The legislature also authorized Mahoney to approve all locally developed subsidized housing and redevelopment plans, to provide technical assistance to local authorities, and to appoint members of the local housing and redevelopment authorities.

Mahoney thought that the legislative mandate for DCA provided an "unparalleled opportunity to integrate urban renewal, housing, social services, and planning." Yet, at the time he took office, he considered the potential of the law vastly underutilized. Indeed, to his eye, DCA's priorities (and values) seemed all wrong. DCA was doing little more than lending public auspices to advance "downtown business interests." As a result, poor communities were being destroyed to build roads, office buildings, and hotels. Even worse, the poor were excluded from participating effectively in the planning activities that were shaping their lives.

Mahoney soon developed a different vision of how DCA's assets could be deployed to produce public value. In the term developed in Chapter 3, he developed a new "strategy" for DCA.

Substantively, with that strategy he sought to slow the pace of urban development and to ensure that the displaced poor would have some suitable place to go. He demanded that appropriate relocation plans be submitted for each proposed redevelopment project. And he commissioned a study to determine the state's needs for public housing. All these changes were designed to redistribute the benefits of redevelopment from the rich to the poor.

Politically, Mahoney felt authorized to make these important policy changes because the social values animating his strategy seemed broadly consistent with the political philosophy of the Sargent administration.

Indeed, he had explicitly articulated these views in his interview for the job and so assumed that these values had earned him the job. Finally, he intended to shore up the political support for his objectives by using his formal powers to give the poor a stronger voice in the formulation of local redevelopment plans.

Operationally, he deployed his formal powers in three particular ways to achieve his substantive aims. First, he stopped the flow of technical assistance money to local redevelopment authorities and used it, instead, to build up his own staff of experts. Second, he appointed poor people to local planning boards to increase their influence and their ability to shape redevelopment projects. Third, for the first time, he began to reject locally approved plans that ignored the interests of poor citizens likely to be dislocated by the proposed projects.

These moves, all within his statutory powers, effectively shifted influence over redevelopment projects from localities to the state and from local elites to the poor. As one might have predicted, the pace of development slowed and specific development projects more attuned to the needs of the poor emerged.

Shortly after he was appointed, and while he was in the midst of developing and implementing his overall strategy for DCA, the City of Boston submitted a redevelopment plan for his approval. The plan focused on the Park Plaza Renewal Area: a prime piece of land bordered on the north by the Boston Public Garden and lying between the city's financial and retail districts. The proposed redevelopment area also included an area that had come to be known as the combat zone: blocks of peep shows, nude bars, and nightclubs, where prostitution flourished and barroom fights occurred nightly.

The plan for the area was divided into two phases. Phase one focused on the parcels of land nearest the Public Garden and called for the construction of: a 1,000-room convention hotel; an office building with 1 million square feet of leasable space; a retail arcade with 500,000 square feet of leasable space; a 3,000-car parking garage; and three residential towers containing 1,400 luxury apartments and 150 units of low- to moderate-income housing "if subsidized financing became available." Though economically profitable, these activities contained little that could be called beneficial to the public.

Phase two of the plan focused on the redevelopment of the combat zone. Arguably, some public value could be associated with the redevelopment of this blighted area. But the developers made no specific commitment to the area's renewal. It was simply listed as part of the project to be developed sometime in the future.

The plan had an additional unusual feature: it requested no public funding. The only public resource the developers sought was the power of eminent domain to assemble contiguous parcels of land. The absence of a request for public funding seemed particularly surprising since the developers had quite modest financial resources, particularly when measured against the size of the project. The developers—Mortimer Zuckerman and Edward Linde—claimed assets of about $6 million. The estimated cost of the project was $260 million.

Despite the apparent weaknesses of the plan, it soon won the approval of the mayor, the Boston City Council, and the Boston Redevelopment Authority (BRA). Moreover, the State Department of Community Affairs had never before turned down a plan submitted by the City of Boston.

To Mahoney and his staff, however, the Park Plaza plan seemed fatally flawed. Under their statute, they had to make six affirmative findings to approve a project as a redevelopment plan (and thereby authorize the use of eminent domain): (1) the project could not be accomplished by private enterprise alone; (2) the plan was consistent with the sound needs of the locality; (3) the financial plan was sound; (4) the project area was blighted; (5) the plan was sufficiently complete; and (6) the project included an acceptable plan for relocating tenants and owners.

One could reasonably argue that the BRA's support for the plan satisfied the requirement that it be "consistent with the sound needs of the locality." But it would be difficult to make any of the other required affirmative findings on the basis of facts then established.

Perhaps the most significant problem was the division of the plan into two different phases. What public interest justifications could be mustered for the project seemed to apply principally to phase two of the plan. Yet the State Department of Community Affairs could not be sure that the developers would complete that phase. Indeed, the economics of the project favored stopping after the completion of phase one.

The weak financial position of the developers created another obstacle. An issue in any circumstances, their position was particularly problematic given that the justification for public participation in the plan depended on the expensive and financially risky phase two. If the developers' financial reserves were exhausted in phase one, phase two would never happen, and the public purposes would not be fulfilled.

These concerns dissuaded Mahoney and his staff from approving the plan. Indeed, several people in his office were convinced that it would be patently illegal to do so. But Mahoney and his staff had an additional reason to be opposed.

Recall that a crucial part of Mahoney's overall strategy for DCA depended on the department's taking more initiative and exercising more influence in local redevelopment plans. At the time Mahoney took office, few precedents existed for DCA playing this role. Indeed, DCA had been widely viewed as nothing more than a rubber stamp. Nowhere was this more true than in the agency's relations with the City of Boston. DCA had never disapproved a proposed Boston plan. Yet most of the important redevelopment in the State of Massachusetts occurred in Boston. If DCA could be influential everywhere but in Boston, it would at best be doing only a small portion of its job. But if it could successfully influence Boston, not only would it extend its influence into that crucial domain, but the other localities would probably fall more quickly into line. Thus, the very weakness of the Park Plaza plan was a strategic opportunity for Mahoney—a chance to successfully oppose the City of Boston and establish the precedent of more effective state oversight of local redevelopment plans.

After conferring with Sargent and his staff and gaining their support for the decision he wanted to make, Mahoney announced his decision to disapprove the proposed Park Plaza plan. His decision was greeted with indignation by the mayor, fury by the developers, and sustained opposition by the building trades unions and local business leaders. Eventually, the newspapers joined in criticizing Mahoney's decision. The opposition became so intense that the state legislature passed "home rule" legislation stripping the DCA commissioner of his power to approve local redevelopment plans. Governor Sargent vetoed the legislation to preserve Mahoney's legal powers, but had to face a hail of hard hats thrown by angry construction workers to do so.

Eventually, a new plan for Park Plaza was submitted. Before Mahoney or his staff had seen the plan, however, the governor held a news conference and announced that, while he did not wish to prejudge the decision of Commissioner Mahoney, in his view, the plan represented a substantial improvement. He said, "Park Plaza is now, in my view, finally on the road to reality."

A strong desire to resolve the Park Plaza issue motivated the governor to speak enthusiastically. He and his staff were then preparing to announce their decision to stop highway construction in Boston. That policy would strike at the same interests that supported the Park Plaza redevelopment project, namely, the Boston construction trades. If Sargent said "no" to all future highway construction and to Park Plaza, he would face intense opposition from the building trades. If he could persuade Mahoney to say "yes" to Park Plaza, he might face less opposition to his decision to halt highway construction.

Unfortunately, a quick review of the plan by Mahoney and his staff did not lead them to the same degree of optimism that the governor felt. The review revealed nothing more than cosmetic changes in the original plan. The serious problems that had originally doomed it remained.

Mahoney confronted a dilemma. On the one hand, he could yield to the increasing political pressure and approve the plan despite his reservations. On the other, he could disapprove the plan and wonder whether his decision would be upheld. The governor could fire him and appoint someone who would approve the project. Or, the legislature could act again to strip him of his powers to approve local projects. This time, the governor might not choose to save him.

DAVID SENCER AND THE THREAT OF SWINE FLU

In January 1976 a small flu epidemic broke out among army recruits at Fort Dix, New Jersey.[2] Most victims proved to be infected with the particular flu virus that had been the dominant cause of human influenza since 1968—the Victoria flu virus. Four victims, however, were infected with something else—the swine flu virus. This virus was thought to be related to the virus that had caused the pandemic of 1918, ultimately killing some 20 million worldwide and 500,000 in the United States. One of the four infected with this new virus died.

The Center for Disease Control (CDC), an agency within the (then) U.S. Department of Health, Education, and Welfare (HEW), was the government agency responsible for protecting society from such epidemics. To accomplish this goal, CDC had its own internal staff to map the occurrence of epidemics and test viruses. In addition, it received support from a wide network of local health officials and private physicians. This network acted both as a surveillance system alerting CDC to emergent threats and as a control system to implement immunization and educational programs in response to emergent epidemics. CDC also advised private pharmaceutical companies as to which flu vaccines should be produced according to their judgment of which strains of flu threatened most urgently.

CDC learned of the flu outbreak in Fort Dix through the routine operations of its surveillance system: its labs were asked to test the cultures taken from the afflicted soldiers. The finding that a new flu virus had appeared in the human population put an important, nonroutine question before CDC, and particularly its director, Dr. David Sencer. The question was whether the outbreak of swine flu at Fort Dix signaled a serious new public health threat—one that would require "heroic" rather than "routine" efforts to manage effectively. At the least, CDC had to decide whether to join with its sister agency, the Bureau of Biologics, to advise vaccine producers to shift to vaccines against swine flu rather than the traditional strains. More significant, CDC staff had to consider whether to sound an urgent alarm and mobilize President Ford to use his powers to generate the high levels of funding and moral urgency that would be necessary to immunize the entire population against the threat of a serious swine flu epidemic.

In considering this question, Sencer could rely on expert advice. At the time of the discovery, he was preparing to meet with CDC's prestigious Advisory Council on Immunization Programs to consider the size and nature of that year's flu threat. The council included all of the country's most distinguished epidemiologists and flu experts.

The scientists came to an ominous conclusion about the threat represented by the small outbreak of swine flu. First, the Fort Dix swine flu virus was closely related to the virus that had killed millions around the world at the turn of the century. Second, because the virus had lain dormant for a generation, little natural immunity to the disease could be relied upon. Third, since serious flu epidemics had been occurring about every twenty years, the United States seemed destined for a serious flu epidemic soon. Fourth, quick calculations revealed that the capabilities of vaccine producers, physician inoculators, and willing customers would be strained to the limit to produce adequate protection by the time the next flu season rolled around. These facts counseled prompt, decisive action. As one of the members of the council noted, "Some heroic action will have to be taken by someone soon."

As in the case of Park Plaza, however, Sencer had broader institutional reasons to prefer prompt, decisive action. To Sencer, the threat of a serious swine flu epidemic created an occasion to advance the general cause of preventive medicine. In the health field generally, preventive efforts always seemed to take a backseat to the medical treatment of illness. He hoped that the prevention of swine flu would propel the general cause of preventive medicine forward. In short, Sencer had many reasons to take effective action. But how was he to mobilize the country to act?

POLITICAL MANAGEMENT: A KEY MANAGERIAL FUNCTION

Before describing these two managers' next steps (I will conclude the cases in the next chapter), I want to analyze their predicaments in detail to illuminate the challenge of political management. Initially, the cases appear to be more different than alike. One involves mere economics, the other life and death. One involves a political appointee, the other a career civil servant. Yet, on reflection, the challenges facing the two managers show some common properties.

In each case the manager must decide an important matter of public policy. Mahoney must decide whether to approve the plan for Park Plaza. Sencer must decide whether to rouse the country against the threat of swine flu.

Moreover, although each man is expert in his own domain, his expertise cannot eliminate fundamental uncertainties or the risks that those uncertainties entail. Mahoney cannot be sure that phase two of the Park Plaza project will be completed. Sencer cannot know for sure that the swine flu threat will materialize.

The choices are made even more difficult because they involve important value trade-offs. Mahoney's determination to use his office to protect the interests of poor as well as rich communities clashes with the City of Boston's more general enthusiasm for economic development. Sencer's willingness to advocate widespread vaccination in the interest of public health clashes with concerns that widespread immunization is too expensive and too risky to be justified, particularly given the uncertain threat of the swine flu epidemic. The value trade-offs ensure that any decision either manager makes will provoke political controversy.

Moreover, Mahoney and Sencer see these specific policy decisions not only as important in their own terms, but also as key to broader strategies they are pursuing. Mahoney seeks to make DCA influential in local redevelopment and to use that power to advantage the poor. Sencer hopes to strengthen the cause of immunization and preventive medicine.

Finally, and most important, while some combination of their office and personal expertise might seem to qualify them to make these decisions for society, they need more effective influence than their current positions grant them. Mahoney faces the prospect that his decision to reject the Park Plaza project will simply be overturned by the powerful political forces supporting approval of the plan. Sencer needs more visibility and clout than he can muster as director of CDC to mobilize the country to ward off a swine flu pandemic.

For both Mahoney and Sencer, the powers of their office (as shaped by their personal resources and incumbency) seem insufficient to deal with the problem they confront. They need to *supplement* their current authority and effective influence if they hope to succeed in accomplishing the purposes they judge to be publicly valuable. This task of building support and legitimacy for a policy, or of enhancing the effective claim that an official may make on the society at large, is what political management is all about. To be more precise, political management involves four elements: building (1) a climate of tolerance, active support, or ongoing operational assistance for (2) a manager, a policy, or an overall strategy among (3) those outside the scope of an official's direct authority whose (4) authorizations or operational assistance are necessary to achieve the public purposes for which the official will be held accountable. In short, political management shapes mandates for action and invests them with the political support and legitimacy that managers need to direct operations and achieve the mandated purposes. It is the challenge of performing this function well that Mahoney and Sencer face in these cases.

To get a sharper and richer sense of the nature of this distinctive managerial function, I recommend five analytic steps. First, consider why managers must devote time to engaging and influencing those beyond the scope of their direct authority. Second, explore the different kinds of managerial contexts in which political management becomes necessary, and the different forms that political management can take. Third, list more specifically the players who become the important material with which managers must work to fashion legitimacy and support for themselves, their policies, or their organizational strategies. Fourth, understand the processes by which the interests and concerns of the diverse players are combined to form powerful mandates for action. Fifth, get a sense for the dynamics of the authorizing environment and how the situation will change over time.

Taken together, these observations will help us understand the medium within which political management occurs and the potential points of leverage and intervention. Later, in Chapter 5, I discuss the specific techniques that managers might use to meet the operational challenges of political management.

Why Political Management Is Important

Political management is an important function for a very simple reason: to achieve their operational objectives, public managers must often engage actors beyond the scope of their direct authority.[3] Generally speaking, managers need these "external" actors for one (or both) of the following reasons: they need their permission to use public resources in pursuit of a given enterprise; or they need their operational assistance to help produce the results for which they are responsible.[4] Because these officials lie beyond the scope of managers' direct authority, managers cannot simply command their compliance. Instead, they must persuade them.[5] This is what makes it appropriate to see the task as *political* rather than managerial.

For clarity (if not elegance), I will refer to this collection of powerful outsiders as the "external authorizing (and coproducing) environment." It is a group of people to whom managers should (and often do) pay as much attention as their employees and subordinates.[6]

Mahoney, for example, must focus on whether the governor and the state legislature will allow him to stay in office and support his decision to disapprove Park Plaza. He can hardly take their support for granted. The legislature has already voted to strip him of his authority to review Boston's redevelopment plans. Although a gubernatorial veto averted that threat, Mahoney can no longer be sure that the governor will support him.

Mahoney must also focus on his ability to induce the City of Boston and the developers to see and respond to his vision of the public interest. He cannot, alone, produce anything of value in the City of Boston. He is utterly dependent on what the developers propose to do and what the city authorizes. Unfortunately, the plan that has been proposed and approved is their plan, not Mahoney's. It reflects their views of what is valuable, not his.

Fortunately for Mahoney, the developers and the city also need Mahoney to agree to the plan; otherwise they cannot use the state's power of eminent domain. This requirement gives Mahoney some leverage over what they propose to do. But Mahoney cannot compel the developers or the city to do any particular thing; he can only accept or reject what they propose.

If Mahoney is to be successful in shaping the Park Plaza project toward his conception of public value, he must succeed in parlaying the leverage of his office into effective influence reaching across constitutional boundaries: across the boundary that separates state from local government and the boundary that separates public from private enterprise. If he presses that advantage too far, however, he may well find himself stripped of the formal powers that gave him the leverage in the first place.

Similarly, Sencer must be concerned with ensuring an adequate supply of resources to mount an effective immunization program. For the most part, his goal requires financial rather than legal power: public funds to support the production, distribution, and marketing of the swine flu vaccine. (A hidden piece of required financial support is public indemnification of the private companies producing vaccines from civil suits arising from the casualties of the immunization program.)

Like Mahoney, however, Sencer needs more than a continuing supply of money and authority to use in managing his own agency: he also needs a general climate of social urgency to animate a national immunization program. He has to create a context within which private drug companies, local public health officials, private physicians, and vulnerable citizens will all choose to take the particular actions that can accumulate to create an effective national immunization program even though he cannot command them to do so.

When Political Management
Is Particularly Required

These examples suggest the variety of tasks subsumed under the general concept of political management. Mahoney confronts the essential political management task of reclaiming the support of his superior for a particular policy decision he wants to make. Sencer confronts the political management task of mobilizing a president, a legislature, and a country to act to guard themselves against the threat of swine flu. One can provide some order to this wide variety of tasks by describing the common contexts in which political management becomes necessary, and the general form that political management takes in these different contexts.

ROUTINE ACCOUNTABILITY

The narrowest, least challenging, and perhaps most common form of political management could be described as "routine accountability." In this context managers are challenged to sustain a flow of money and authority to their enterprises. They do so by reporting activities and accomplishments through well-defined channels of accountability, including political superiors, legislative committees, and overhead agencies.[7] As long as their reports record acceptable performance, the managers are left alone and allowed to go about their business.

AUTHORIZING CHANGE AND INNOVATION

The challenge of political management becomes more demanding in situations where managers seek to innovate.[8] Changes in an organization's operations, administrative arrangements, or missions alter the mix of public values produced by the organization. That, in turn, triggers close scrutiny from political overseers who want to be sure that the mix of values being produced fits their ideas of what constitutes public value. They also want to be sure that there are strong enough reasons to prefer a more or less untested innovation to the established practices of the organization.

Often a proposed innovation produces conflict among the organization's overseers. Sometimes the conflicts are new because the innovation introduces new issues and new players into the political process. More often, however, the proposed innovation simply rekindles older conflicts that had been temporarily set aside.

To a degree, the conflict triggered by the proposed change creates problems for managers. They must find some way to quiet it, or they will spend all their time answering questions from outraged overseers. But conflict also creates opportunities. Indeed, if no conflicts ever arose among overseers, managers would have little opportunity for leadership. They would be forced to do whatever their overseers agreed they must. When overseers disagree among themselves, however, managers can play an important role in brokering agreements or harmonizing the conflict.[9] They do so by negotiating new terms of accountability for themselves, their policies, or their organizations.

Managers can also unsettle the balance of political forces in their authorizing environments by finding and developing latent political constituencies. Mahoney, for example, has proposed a new strategy for DCA—one that does less for downtown business interests and more for poor city dwellers. For this new strategy to succeed, however, he must find political support as well as legal backing. One solution would be to persuade Governor Sargent or his legislative overseers that they should hold him accountable for satisfying the interests of ghetto dwellers rather than the aspirations of local merchants and their political allies. Another, more satisfactory solution might be to develop a new constituency among the poor urban residents whose interests had been neglected or among those who would be sympathetic to their plight. If such a constituency cannot be activated, Mahoney's strategic innovation will eventually fail. That is why political management is key to a strategic manager's success.

ACHIEVING INTERAGENCY COORDINATION

The task of political management changes again when managers are crucially dependent on agencies and people outside their direct control to help them produce results for which they are accountable.[10] In a common scenario, managers of one agency depend on other government agencies to help them achieve their purposes. For example, Sencer must rely on what his peer agency, the Bureau of Biologics, recommends to the vaccine companies. If they do not recommend the production of vaccine effective against swine flu, his hopes for immunizing the entire country are essentially dashed.

This case gets simpler when both agencies have a common superior. In such cases managers can appeal to that higher authority to direct the other agency to contribute to the first agency's objectives. Indeed, the common superior may even have established routine policy-making processes to identify and act on such needs.[11]

This seems to be the case for CDC and the Bureau of Biologics: both Sencer and Harry M. Meyer, the head of the bureau, report to Theodore Cooper, the assistant secretary of health at HEW. Although this situation should, in principle, be fairly easy to handle, experience teaches that these simple mechanisms do not always achieve interagency coordination. The common superior cannot always be reached; and even if he or she can, the superior's effective control over the other agency is sometimes in doubt.[12]

In cases requiring interagency coordination without any immediate, common superior, managers must find other ways to induce the other agency to cooperate. That is not too difficult if there are ongoing collaborative relations between the agencies, for the ongoing relationship will create many opportunities for side payments and informal agreements to arise.[13] It is much harder if the relationship is intensely competitive or nonexistent.[14] In these cases managers will be forced to find a way to exert indirect pressure on the agency or to reach the remote superior. To accomplish both these objectives, a crisis can be created to generate pressures for cooperation and place the matter higher on the remote superior's agenda.[15]

MOBILIZING DECENTRALIZED COPRODUCTION

The challenges of political management change again if the productive capacity needed by managers to accomplish their purposes is widely decentralized among agencies and private individuals. In these cases managers cannot get leverage over the productive capacity they need simply by persuading the appropriate executive to issue the appropriate orders. They must, instead, find some way to reach thousands, perhaps millions, of decentralized decision-makers. Sencer, for example, must convince millions of Americans to take a risky flu shot in the face of an epidemic that has not yet arrived.[16]

The political management of decentralized decision-makers differs markedly from the kind of political management we associate with bureaucratic advocacy and entrepreneurship. Such situations force managers to seek wide authority to regulate the conduct of the decentralized groups and to make that authority real and effective through a general process of political mobilization. It becomes essential to find ways to engage loose networks of professions, interest groups, political associations, and the media in efforts to coproduce the managers' goals. These loosely coupled networks of organizations substitute in mass power for the (relative) precision and reliability of bureaucratic organizations responding to authoritative commands in the achievement of operational purposes.

Note, also, that at this far extreme of political management, the meaning of authorization has changed in an important way. The authorization is no longer a narrow grant of resources to a well-defined agency assigned to deploy the resources to produce a particular result. Instead, it has become a broad social authorization—perhaps even an obligation—distributed across the citizenry to act on behalf of public purposes.[17]

If Sencer can mobilize national political leaders to promote a vast immunization campaign, he might succeed in creating a context in which each citizen helps remind others that it is their duty to be immunized, and thereby may succeed in immunizing a large portion of the population—something that could not be achieved simply by expanding his bureaucracy, or even by the passage of laws requiring citizens to receive immunizations.

WHO IS IMPORTANT IN POLITICAL MANAGEMENT

As suggested above, the people who become the focus of political management vary greatly, depending on managers' specific purposes at particular times. Sometimes managers concentrate on retaining the support of their immediate superiors; other times they aim to mobilize the productive capacity of millions of citizens. Despite the variety, it is possible to identify and describe the kinds of actors that inhabit the authorizing and coproducing environment.

Political Superiors, Legislative Overseers, and Overhead Agencies

At the core of political management—the actors who are always present and must always be attended to—are those who appoint managers to their offices, establish the terms of their accountability, and supply them with resources. The single most important figures in this context are the managers' immediate superiors—usually political executives. Thus, Mahoney must gauge and seek to sustain Governor Sargent's commitment to Mahoney's preferred form of urban redevelopment, while Sencer has to consider Secretary Cooper's position on the value of general immunization programs and President Ford's willingness to lend his auspices to a national immunization campaign.

Indeed, many public managers view their immediate superior as the *only* relevant piece of the authorizing environment. This view is advanced most determinedly by political superiors who would like to gain effective control over what their subordinate managers do.[18]

But this view does not square with either the practical or constitutional reality of managers' lives. Public managers are practically, legally, and ethically accountable to many officials other than their immediate political superior.[19] They are accountable to legislative oversight committees in many instances. Indeed, the authorizing and appropriating legislation recommended by oversight committees to the legislature as a whole generally defines public managers' most fundamental terms of accountability.

The strong line of accountability that runs out to the legislature as well as up the bureaucratic chain of command is most apparent in the Park Plaza case. The legislature gave Mahoney, not Governor Sargent, the power to approve urban redevelopment projects for the state. Only Mahoney's signature will grant the developers the power of eminent domain. The legislature's control over Mahoney's actions is also evident in their capacity to strip Mahoney of his powers if, in their collective judgment, Mahoney fails to use them wisely.

Beyond specific statutes, however, legislative committees often influence an organization's operations through oversight hearings or through requests to fix specific problems that have come to a legislator's attention.[20] Such informal demands have less power in shaping an organization's efforts than the broader enabling statutes, but even these informal, particularistic demands can be ignored only at a price.

Finally, overhead agencies such as Civil Service Commissions and budget agencies also exercise enormous control over an organization's purposes by determining the allocation of fiscal and human resources to the organization's varied tasks.[21] Public managers are generally legally obligated to follow the rules promulgated by these agencies even if political superiors order them not to. In this respect, they embody at least as much power as political bosses in the chain of command.

Once one has identified political bosses, legislative overseers, and overhead agencies as important objects of political management, an obvious extension includes those who influence this first group of principals.[22] Thus, aides to political superiors or legislative committees become key elements of managers' authorizing environments. The extension applies to the political parties, interest groups, and professional associations whose judgments of and support for managers' bosses, legislative overseers, or overhead agencies carry weight.[23]

Mahoney, for example, would be wise to think of the governor's staff as well as the governor himself as an important part of his authorizing environment. He would also be wise to consider whether the chief counsel's office might be persuaded to write an opinion on the legality of the proposed plan for Park Plaza. Sencer knows that the assistant secretary of health, his immediate superior, will be influenced by the opinion of experts in flu epidemiology from the medical profession.

The Media

Somewhat farther afield (and much riskier to engage) lie the media. An important debate continues about the role that the "gentlemen of the press" actually play in shaping government policy.[24] On the one hand, practitioners of government argue that the media wield overwhelming influence. The press determines which issues will come to the public's attention. And the intense media pressure profoundly shapes the processes of deliberation. To guard against "leaks," fewer people are consulted than might be optimal for wise policy-making. To guard against preemptive mobilizations of opposing forces, fewer policy options are considered.

On the other hand, representatives of the media make several arguments: they merely report the news, they don't make it. Their reporting may mobilize others to act, which may inconvenience public officials, but a free press is supposed to cover newsworthy issues. Forcing the government to be open about contemplated actions, and explaining why the proposed actions are valuable, is a necessary part of democratic governance. In these respects, the press strengthens rather than weakens governmental policy-making.

The evidence on this matter remains unclear. There are notorious cases in which it seems obvious that the press has had impact on governmental decision-making.[25] Yet, it is easier to show an effect on the *timing* and *process* of decision-making than on the ultimate *results*.[26]

Nonetheless, because the media often *are* important in shaping the context in which political decisions are made and citizens mobilized to act, many public managers seek to engage the press through more or less formal press strategies.[27] Sometimes their efforts are covert: those who are dissatisfied with the likely result of an existing decision-making process leak information about the process, or the decision that is about to be made, in hopes of changing both the process and the ultimate decision. Other times an explicit press strategy forms part of a calculated campaign by one or more political managers to shape the public's perception of an issue or to mobilize others to act.[28] Whatever the actual results of press coverage, and whatever the tactics used, public managers generally agree that the media inevitably play a major role in the authorizing and coproducing environment and, consequently, become a focus of political management.

In the particular cases considered here, the media participate in shaping Mahoney's and Sencer's prospects. In Mahoney's case the unified support of both Boston newspapers for proceeding with the Park Plaza project has put enormous pressure on the governor and Mahoney to approve the plan. The media have cast the Park Plaza issue as one of economic development and local self-determination. None of the values that Mahoney seeks to defend by disapproving the plan count for much with the local media. He thus faces an uphill fight in winning public support for his position.

Media pressures will also influence the timing of Mahoney's decision. He might prefer to delay the decision long enough to build a constituency for his position or to negotiate a better deal with the developers. But his options for doing so are limited by the press's treatment of the governor's announcement (that "Park Plaza is finally the road to success") as an important story. Reporters will hotly pursue follow-up stories, including what Mahoney thinks of the new plan, when a formal decision will be announced, and what the developers think of Mahoney's response. Inevitably Mahoney will face reporters at every turn asking about his decision.

In the Sencer case journalists will also play a major role. The way that the media frame the issue will either help or hinder any initiative Sencer takes to mobilize the president, the wider government, the network of state public health agencies, and the people themselves to respond to the swine flu epidemic. If the media treat the threat as an important problem—comparable to the epidemic of 1918—Sencer will find the ground prepared for launching a major mobilization. If, however, the media minimize the threat, or search for political motivations President Ford might have for exaggerating the threat, Sencer will find his mobilization effort far more difficult.

It also goes without saying that should Sencer succeed in persuading the government that a major response should be made to the swine flu epidemic, the media will become crucially important in getting the message out to the rest of the country. Most citizens will learn about the threat from TV or newspapers, and they will make their decisions to get a flu shot or not on the basis of what they see or read. Consequently, Sencer must consider how the media will handle any new information about whether the threat is real and whether the vaccines are safe. For it is certain that, in such a massive immunization program, some people who are inoculated will get sick or die shortly thereafter even if the flu shots themselves are entirely safe.

Interest Groups

Citizens' associations and interest groups figure in the authorizing environment as well.[29] Sometimes such groups are organized to advance the economic interests of their members.[30] Because Mahoney's decisions will affect organized labor and the construction industry, he must deal with them. Sencer must cope with the economic interests of pharmaceutical companies.

Other times interest groups are organized to advance the political aspirations and public values of interest group members.[31] Mahoney might be aided by environmental interest groups if he can persuade them that the Park Plaza project threatens the cherished Boston Public Garden, or by groups advocating the interests of the poor if he can persuade them that the project would harm poor residents. Sencer might find that he has to fend off attacks by groups opposed to the state encouraging the mass immunization of children because such a use of government power is inconsistent with their religious or political beliefs.

Finally, since not all potential interests in the society are organized, some potential or latent interest groups could always be mobilized.[32] The mobilization could result from the actions of a determined advocate. Or, it could occur spontaneously as objective events made it transparently clear to many citizens simultaneously that some important public value was worth urgently pursuing. Just such mechanisms were important in creating the strategic opportunities that Ruckelshaus and Miller exploited.

Again, an important debate continues about the proper role of these groups in democratic governance. The early critiques of interest group influence focused on the power that economic interests and particular business firms had over governmental policy.[33] These concerns have faded a bit with the passage of labor relations laws, the establishment of regulatory agencies, and the recent appearance of public interest groups—including those concerned about the environment, consumers, tax limitation, and youth advocacy. Somewhat unexpectedly, the general concerns of citizens do seem to find organized vehicles for expression.[34]

The worry has shifted now to concerns over the stubborn refusal of the special interest groups to compromise by taking losses in their preferred values for other values of merit.[35] The rigidity and relentlessness of environmental advocates, right-to-life organizations, and the National Rifle Association are legendary. Such rigidity often leads either to policy stalemates or to wild swings in public policy as the balance of power shifts among competing groups.

Groups organized around specific substantive issues also tend to reorient our politics.[36] They undermine political parties by siphoning off money and volunteer effort that used to go to support broader causes. They shift political activity from legislative arenas to bureaucratic arenas because that is where many specific substantive issues are resolved. And they change the language of politics from discussions of broad purposes and principles to the language of substantive expertise. In short, although it has always been difficult to maintain a political focus on broad issues facing the country against the tug of narrow economic and geographically specialized issues, these traditional splintering forces have now been strengthened by the additional dividing effect of "single interest groups." This development has adversely affected the coherence of electoral mandates and the relative influence of elected (as opposed to appointed or career) officials.

From a managerial perspective, however, what is important about these groups is that they exist in the managers' external environments commenting on their actions and making claims on their organizations. They are active, vocal, and knowledgeable. They also have established relations at different levels of the authorizing environment and often reach deeply into the managers' organizations.[37] Their determination, knowledge, and established relations make them powerful obstacles to building support and legitimacy for policies they oppose.

Yet managers must acknowledge that interest group networks can enhance as well as constrain their efforts to achieve objectives.[38] Whether interest groups help or hurt public managers depends crucially on how closely aligned their objectives are. If the interest group's purposes and values closely match the managers', the groups can be activated and used—often by doing nothing more complicated than giving speeches that reflect concerns for their favored values. If not, the managers must find ways of reducing the groups' influence so that a policy-making process or an organization can be freed to move in a different direction.

To free their organizations from the influence of external groups and substitute their own purposes, managers commonly rely on the tactic of breaking off relationships with the offending group and refusing to involve the group's representatives in policy deliberations. Alternatively, they can simply remove those employees who seem to be closely aligned with the outside groups. Sometimes such tactics are successful. But they often fail because they misconstrue the nature of the problem.

The existence of a single interest group frequently signals the existence of an important public value that citizens think should be protected. To the extent that this continues to be true, the groups will survive and keep replenishing themselves. They will find new channels for expressing their demands, and new agents within the organization who will champion their point of view. Political interests and forces are a lot like energy in physics: they are impossible to destroy; they can only by deflected or transformed.

Three approaches are possible: (1) finding a countervailing power; (2) channeling the forces along a path that is more tolerable to the manager; and (3) discovering some way of dissipating the source of the energy. To the extent that the organization's responsiveness is part of what fuels the political group, resisting the organization's demands may ultimately be effective. To the extent that the political force has its own vitality, however, resistance will do little more than discredit the organization and the manager who remains stubbornly opposed.

This basic logic seems quite obvious in Mahoney's case. A great deal of political momentum has been channeled into the Park Plaza project. When Mahoney refused to respond to it, the political energy flowed through a different channel in the legislature. The legislature reacted by voting to strip Mahoney of his power. When it failed there, it began buffeting the governor, weakening his steadfast support of Mahoney. Mahoney's power to make the decision he feels he is morally and legally bound to make has become enfeebled.

Sencer is in a quite different and happier situation. The professional network of flu experts and local health officials are lined up to move with

Sencer's ambitions. Those political forces that could become a constraint if opposed are likely to become instead an enormous asset.

Courts

Courts may also be important elements of the authorizing environment. They sometimes interfere directly in agency operations by telling the agency that a decision it made was inappropriate and must be reconsidered and changed, or by ruling that an agency's action was wrong and the party adversely affected must be compensated.[39] In some extreme cases, when an agency is viewed as systematically denying citizens constitutional or even legislatively established rights, courts may enter into a long-term oversight relationship with the agency to see that it complies with constitutional standards or may even force the agency into receivership.[40]

The courts derive such powers from their role as interpreters of what the constitutions and laws of the country and the states require of public sector organizations and managers.[41] Interestingly, one can view constitutional and statutory provisions as devices that *ration* the state's authority to use public authority and money in public enterprises. When a plausible case is made in court by a citizen that the state used its authority and resources in an unjustified, injurious manner, the agency will be forced to adjust its operations.

The courts are potentially important actors in the Park Plaza case in that Mahoney might be able to ask the governor's chief counsel to issue an opinion that the Park Plaza project as now proposed would be illegal under the terms of the statute. Alternatively, Mahoney could approve the project and arrange to be sued by a disgruntled property owner forced to sell his or her property under the power of eminent domain, on the grounds that Mahoney acted illegally in approving the project.

The courts are potentially important in the swine flu case because they provide a vehicle for those who might suffer adverse consequences of their immunization to press their claims on the government. Indeed, it is the anticipation of such claims that mobilizes private drug companies who will produce the vaccine to seek legislation indemnifying them from having to pay these claims and diverting the claims, instead, to the U.S. government.

In general, the courts do not have to act directly on agencies to assure compliance with the law. They exert influence directly on agencies through legal counsels lodged in general counsels' offices, whose job it is to explain to agency managers what they may or may not do.[42] Insofar as they are accurate predictors of what the courts would do, and insofar as their counsel is heeded in the decisions and actions of government agencies, the courts' influence is felt without having to take direct action.

COMBINING DIVERSE INTERESTS AND VALUES

The interests, demands, and expectations of those who inhabit public managers' external authorizing and coproducing environment constitute the essential material the managers must use to fashion powerful and effective mandates. As important, however, is the way that these interests are combined: through formal decision-making processes or through settled agreements captured in the conventional wisdom about how best to deal with certain problems.

Decision-Making Process

If the appropriate officials agree to a decision through an appropriate process, the decision will have more legitimacy than if the decisions are made by those with suspect qualifications through truncated or flimsy procedures.[43] The greater the legitimacy behind a decision, the harder it is to ignore or reverse and the stronger the mandate.

To a great extent, formal documents such as statutes, administrative regulations, and formal job descriptions set out who is to be included in a decision and what steps must be taken. Mahoney's decision on the Park Plaza project, for example, is quite formally structured. A statute gives him as commissioner of DCA the formal authority to approve or disapprove the project. As a matter of law, the governor has no role in this decision. The law also specifies that the issue cannot come to Mahoney for decision until a plan has been approved by the local community. Finally, the law requires that once the decision is before him, he must evaluate the plan according to the criteria set out in the statute. That evaluation should be done by competent professionals in his organization. If he strays from that process by involving the governor or his aides, or by meeting behind the scenes with the developers, the process could be viewed as improperly "politicized" and therefore less legitimate.

Decision-making procedures may be sanctioned by tradition and convention or simply by efficacy alone, however. Roger Porter reports, for example, that, as President Ford's Economic Policy Board became successful in dealing with economic policy issues, it tended to draw additional issues into its network, since it was the forum where officials with issues that needed presidential decisions could come to get the issues resolved.[44] Apparently, a positive feedback cycle works in the development of policy-making processes: those that have worked well in the past will be used again, and for an increasingly varied workload. Those that have failed will be ignored even if they are formally mandated.

A process may also be created and sustained by nothing more than the stature of those who participate: the higher the ranks of those involved in a decision, the more compelling the decision tends to be. Presidents, simply by their formal position, can enhance the legitimacy and power of almost any decision they enter.[45] But their reputation and competence matter. An accomplished and popular president can bestow greater legitimacy than one who is less esteemed.[46] An effective working team of people with stature and experience seems to lend a great deal of legitimacy to choices that are made.[47]

This point is clearly in Sencer's mind as he thinks about the challenge of mobilizing the country to respond to the threat of an epidemic of swine flu. He needs the president's stature not only to ensure the supply of money and authority to operate the program but also to create a context in which thousands of physicians and millions of citizens will meet to give and get shots.

Formal legitimacy, past effectiveness, and powerful participants tend to establish the working legitimacy of a decision-making process. But the legitimacy and power of a decision-making process can also be influenced by the extent to which it does or does not have some abstract qualities that the public at large associates with a "good" or "proper" decision-making process. These expectations are closely tied to the public's commitment to broader process values such as: political representativeness; effective use of relevant expertise; respect for precedent; definitiveness and clarity in decisions; transparency and openness in deliberations; responsiveness to accumulated experience; and so on.[48]

These process values are often implicitly treated as required features of decision-making. If policy-making processes lack one or more of these qualities, they are viewed as fatally flawed.[49] Alternatively, these features could be viewed as separate qualities that a particular decision process could have more or less of. From this perspective the overall legitimacy of a decision-making process would not be "appropriate" or "inappropriate," but "better" or "worse" as a function of the presence or absence of the different attractive qualities.

Taking this alternative view reveals that some tensions arise in pursuing the different procedural virtues. "Political representativeness," for instance, is often perceived as inconsistent with the maximum utilization of expertise. Respect for precedent and continuity often clashes with responsiveness to new circumstances, whether those circumstances involve new information or emergent values that had previously been neglected. The desire to achieve definitiveness and clarity in decisions often conflicts with the virtues of future adaptability and the creation of useful working relations among people with slightly different perspectives and purposes.[50]

The presence of these (more or less) inconsistent process values in the evaluation of decision-making processes means that any given decision process is vulnerable to criticism from one vantage point or another. If our expectation is that a process will have *all* these virtues (in addition to a tradition of working well), then any process is vulnerable once a political actor chooses to make it so. This vulnerability, along with competition among different decision-making processes, limits the effective reach and useful working life of any given process. The careful legal and professional assessment of Park Plaza that Mahoney undertook at the outset became vulnerable to the criticism that it failed to respect the right of the citizens of Boston and their representatives to decide the matter. This criticism fueled the passage of the home rule amendment.

Being aware of the aforementioned virtues of decision-making processes provides managers with a template to use in assessing the strength or weakness of any particular process and in identifying what weaknesses must be shored up to smooth the process.

Public Ideas and Conventional Wisdom

The interests of the varied players in the authorizing environment may also be combined to produce a mandate through the existence of common understandings about the nature of a problem and the best way to deal with it.[51] Conventional wisdom plays an important role in legitimizing a policy idea or condemning it to irrelevance. To take one example, the concept of alcoholism elevated the importance of alcohol treatment and deemphasized the importance of controls on supply.[52] The widespread conviction that "rehabilitation never works" has had a profound effect or our understanding of the goals of imprisonment.[53]

Where these powerful, commonly accepted ideas come from, and what sustains them, remain unclear. Often interpretations of historical experience play a key role: historical interpretations of the "failure" of prohibition were consistent with (and therefore supported) the modern conception that the alcohol problem lay with the drinker rather than the alcohol;[54] the disastrous negotiations between Chamberlain and Hitler at Munich created the conventional wisdom that a country should never try to appease a totalitarian regime.[55] These "lessons of history" become powerful axioms that cannot be contested without an individual risking his or her own reputation for knowledge and sophistication.[56] Thus, for example, analogies to the pandemic of 1918 were crucial in creating the context for decision-making about swine flu.

Other times the public ideas that help create the context for policy-making come from professionals and experts with knowledge in a certain area. Although the debate about the effectiveness of rehabilitation in prison owes a great deal to fundamental ideological views about human nature, it was also fueled by expert criminologists and penologists who first insisted on the potential of rehabilitation and then had to back off as empirical studies consistently revealed that recidivism most commonly resulted.[57] But this dialogue among the experts took place over a generation, and it decisively tipped only when the evidence became overwhelming and the issue received extensive outside attention. Similarly, the cumulative weight of expert criticisms of urban redevelopment projects during the sixties set the scene for Mahoney's new strategy for DCA and his rejection of the Park Plaza proposal.[58]

Like interest groups, managers must either contend with public ideas or use them. They are forces making claims on policy by implicitly setting standards that the policy must meet. If the manager's preferred policy is consistent with what everyone believes to be true, the policy will be more legitimate than if it opposes the conventional wisdom. If a policy goes against common sense, then the manager will have to find some way of challenging common sense. This is difficult at best. At the least, it takes time. Even overwhelming empirical evidence demonstrating the inaccuracy of a conventional view cannot change the view quickly; the change will occur slowly with many fits and starts.

Alternatively, the manager can attach his or her preferred idea to a different piece of conventional wisdom than the one now dominating discussion. Since there are often many bits of conventional wisdom lying around a policy area, the easier route to dislodging a current piece might be to take advantage of an alternative.

At any rate, ideas, like structures and processes, have standing in the authorizing environment independent of the people who now occupy positions in that environment. Indeed, many of the people now in the authorizing environment achieved their favored positions by aligning themselves with the ideas that were, or became, the dominant conventional wisdom.

THE DYNAMICS OF THE AUTHORIZING ENVIRONMENT

At any given moment, the authorizing environments guiding and sustaining public managers have a distinct configuration: they sustain the managers' efforts in a particular form, at a particular scale, and on particular objectives. Up until the time that the governor announced his support for the new plan, Mahoney's authorizing environment sustained a mandate to reject the Park Plaza proposal and to pursue the strategy of making community development more responsive to the poor. Similarly, until the time that Sencer learned of the outbreak of swine flu at Fort Dix, his authorizing environment mandated that he produce routine flu vaccination programs directed at less dangerous strains of flu. It may have seemed to the managers that these mandates, held in place by a particular configuration of their authorizing environment, would stay in place forever.

What the cases reveal, however, is that the demands and expectations of the authorizing environment can and do change—sometimes rapidly. Mahoney's mandate changes suddenly when the governor announces publicly that, in his view, the Park Plaza plan is "finally on the road to reality." At that moment, the ground shifts under Mahoney's feet, and what was once a relatively firm mandate supporting Mahoney's rejection of the plan erodes badly.

Of course, the suddenness of the change can be exaggerated. A wise political manager would have realized that the government's apparently solid front against the Park Plaza project actually concealed a seething political conflict. For a while, Mahoney could sustain a mandate for his preferred outcome on the basis of arguments that the plan was both unwise and illegal. Over time, however, the political forces favoring the plan succeeded in persuading others of the virtues of the plan. That support, combined with Mahoney's apparent inability to reach a satisfactory compromise, eventually turned the governor against him. Clearly, mandates for action are hostage to the ebb and flow of political controversy and the rebalancing of political forces.

Sencer's case reveals a different source of instability in mandates: namely, changes in the objective conditions of the world. The outbreak of swine flu at Fort Dix, interpreted by experts, changes the image of the world to which government must respond. That change, in turn, requires

Sencer to alert those in his authorizing environment to the new reality to which they must adapt and to enlist their aid in helping the society respond.

In general, then, mandates for action change. The political coalitions that once sustained a policy or an organizational strategy often erode as political power ebbs and flows, and as political actors take up different issues. Groups whose interests were initially ignored may gather strength. New groups with interests in the way the government operates may suddenly come into being. Both may change the political balance in the authorizing environment and, with that, the mandate for action.

Similarly, experience accumulates with particular policies and organizational strategies, and that experience more or less quickly, and more or less accurately, begins to influence the judgments about their adequacy. As the conventional wisdom about good or effective policies changes, mandates for actions change.

Thus, just as private sector managers cannot rely on their markets to remain stable, public managers cannot rely on their political markets to remain constant. They must be prepared to adapt to changes in political aspirations or to the substantive challenges they face in their task environments.

Of course, one could easily exaggerate how much mandates for public action shift. Most public sector organizations stay in the same basic business for a long time. Both the Massachusetts Department of Community Affairs and the Centers for Disease Control will remain in business indefinitely taking actions to promote community development and stem epidemics. They will neither disappear nor radically change their mission.

One could also say that the demands remain constant in the sense that they always focus on the same dimensions of public sector performance. Mahoney and DCA may forever be twisted on a rack of conflicting values that includes the encouragement of economic development, the protection of the interests of poor people who may be adversely affected by the developments, and the proper degree of autonomy to give to local governments in making these complex value choices. Sencer and CDC may forever oscillate between the aggressive pursuit of public health immunization objectives at the expense of government money and the protection of individual choices regarding health care decisions.[59]

But the relative emphasis to be given to these large values, and the specific ways they are applied in individual cases, may be subject to important changes as a result of changing political tides. In this sense political trends affect what public sector managers are expected to produce. And it is for this reason that successful strategic managers must begin with political management.

THE CHALLENGE OF POLITICAL MANAGEMENT

To many public managers, the political environment surrounding their operations is a dangerous place. It is a complex world filled with actors more powerful than they—where unresolved conflicts and unpredictable changes transform once valued enterprises into monuments of folly, and where once shiny professional reputations become tarnished. All other things being equal, they would prefer to avoid any engagement. Indeed, they are among the last and most enthusiastic supporters of the idea that policy must be kept separate from administration, for that idea effectively insulates them from the political tumult.[60]

Yet, it is apparent to virtually all public managers that they must interact with this world—at least to some degree. At a minimum, they must maintain routine accountability and respond to occasional press inquiries about their agencies. More important, however, some of the best public sector managers seem to believe that the key to their success lies in embracing rather than avoiding this world.[61] In fact, the Mahoney case teaches us that tragedy can strike managers who do not pay daily attention to the management of their political authorization.

Mahoney is in many respects a virtuous public manager. He believes that his moral and legal duty requires him to resist using the power of eminent domain to facilitate urban redevelopment except in those cases where some significant public value could be produced. The legal criteria that qualify an area for redevelopment offer important clues about how the legislature intended to define public value. But Mahoney also brings views of his own to the definition of public value. He equates it with services to the poor, rather than with the general economic development of the city or the creation of private profits. Since he finds little of this kind of value in the proposed plan for Park Plaza, and since at the outset the governor supported his decision, Mahoney is both duty-bound and politically authorized to reject the Park Plaza proposal.

Unfortunately, having made this decision, Mahoney stops working at sustaining the legitimacy and power of that position. With the decision already founded on the secure rocks of his own moral vision, the law, and the governor's backing, Mahoney rests his case. Meanwhile, the opposition continues pressing its case—its view of public value—in the broader civic arena. Soon, the city council, the mayor of Boston, and the local newspapers join the developers, the builders, and the labor unions in finding the Park Plaza project to be in the interest of Boston. These political forces hope to persuade Mahoney that the private development of the Park Plaza area is sufficiently valuable to justify the use of the power of eminent domain even if the combat zone cannot be redeveloped. If Mahoney does not agree, the political forces will attempt to strip him of his powers (the home rule legislation) or to fire him (the implicit threat from the governor). Mahoney, confident that he has the political backing of the governor, the power of the law, and the force of his own moral vision behind him, does not see fit to mobilize other constituencies to support his view of the project.

Mahoney's failure to develop a constituency for his position on Park Plaza causes a basic shift in the balance of political forces surrounding the Park Plaza decision. That, in turn, puts him in the grip of a cruel dilemma. He must decide whether he is prepared to "learn" from the influence of these political forces or whether he will insist that everyone else agree with him.[62] It is this tension that gives the case its moral drama as well as its technical interest. Mahoney's character and concept of virtue in his office are being tested along with his managerial skills. All this might have been avoided if Mahoney had seen earlier that he needed to do some political work to sustain his effective authority to reject the Park Plaza plan—that his authority was not permanently granted but conditional on the skill with which he used it to advance others' purposes.

Sencer's case, by contrast, reveals the opportunities for leadership that can be exploited by public sector managers. Sencer's position atop CDC alerts him to the threat of the swine flu epidemic. His stature as a scientist, and his relationship with other important scientists, gives him substantial power to shape the views of overseers in HEW, OMB, the executive office of the presidency, the Congress, and the media about the nature of the threat and the actions that would be appropriate to meet it. The capabilities of his organization also ensure that he will play an important role in implementing any national effort to track the threat or to immunize the population. The only question is whether he has the courage and skill to activate this potential for leadership.

That is hardly a trivial question. After all, there is a substantial personal and organizational risk associated with seizing the initiative. If Sencer acts aggressively to mobilize his political superiors, society will attribute any future bad consequences of the swine flu initiative at least partly to Sencer and CDC. Moreover, he cannot be sure that the threat associated with the swine flu will materialize. If it does not, and if bad consequences ensue, Sencer, CDC, and the cause of preventive public health may all be damaged. In short, in exercising leadership Sencer, like Miller in Chapter 3, is "betting the company."

Obviously, a great deal rides on how well managers perform as political managers. In the next chapter, I explore some of the techniques available to guide the calculations and judgments of managers who would like to perform this function well.

CHAPTER 5

ADVOCACY, NEGOTIATION, AND LEADERSHIP: THE TECHNIQUES OF POLITICAL MANAGEMENT

To build political support, establish their legitimacy, and mobilize those beyond the scope of their direct authority, public managers must engage their external political environments.[1] But how?

What may sound like a technical question is an important ethical question as well. How public managers engage their political environments affects the quality of democratic government we citizens enjoy. It influences the confidence we have that the managers are pursuing genuinely public purposes rather than their own selfish interests or their own idiosyncratic views of public value.[2] Techniques that prove effective in allowing managers to dominate or evade democratic politics in the interests of more straightforwardly achieving their goals as managers must be rejected as inconsistent with the best practice of public management. "Best practice" means techniques that are ethical as well as effective.[3]

To explore best practice in political management, consider Mahoney's and Sencer's responses to the situations they confronted. When last seen, Mahoney was pondering his decision on Park Plaza; Sencer was seeking a way to mobilize the nation to counter the threat of swine flu.

Mahoney's Initiatives

In Mahoney's case, the time for effective political management seems past. When we left him, he was standing alone against a project that had acquired substantial political momentum. The limited options available to him measure the price of not having thought about or engaged in effective political management. Yet, in reviewing his performance, a fair observer would have to record positive as well as negative achievements.

Initially, Mahoney succeeded in the central task of political management: he enlisted the governor's support for his decision to reject the Park Plaza plan. Indeed, the governor's support proved so firm that he braved a hail of hard hats to veto the home rule amendment that would have stripped Mahoney of his power. Such backing is rather extraordinary, and Mahoney might have assumed that it would stay solid.

In retrospect, however, the governor's support seems rooted in relatively shallow and shifting sand. It emerged from the ordinary operations of cabinet-level policy-making. A newly appointed political subordinate (Mahoney, in this case) brought a tough issue to the political principal (Governor Sargent). The principal agreed with the decision that the subordinate wanted to make. The subordinate made the decision and took the heat.[4]

The problem was that the issue did not go away. Instead, Mahoney was thrust into continuing negotiations with the BRA and the developers. Those did not go well. Mahoney kept insisting that the developers strengthen the financial plan and make a firmer commitment to the development of the combat zone. The developers refused to make any such concessions. Eight months later, the negotiations yielded the plan that resulted in Governor Sargent's press conference. The "new" plan barely differed from the old, yet somehow this plan was acceptable to Sargent.

To Mahoney, scrambling to find the backing he needed to resist Park Plaza, these events should have raised two questions that would reveal where he had gone wrong in the past and what his (limited) options were for the future. First, why did the negotiations with the developers not go well? Second, why did the governor shift his position?

The difficulty in the negotiations could, conceivably, be traced to the personalities of the protagonists. Mahoney, the BRA director, and the developers, all stubborn and determined men, were quite accustomed to having their way. Such attitudes often frustrate negotiations.[5] The difficulty could also be traced to technical problems in the negotiating process. Mahoney had to negotiate with the developers through the BRA—not directly.[6]

But a more fundamental misconception created the logjam: the parties on both sides assumed they could get what they wanted without negotiating. Mahoney, confident that the governor would continue to support him, thought that if he stood pat, he would be able to stop Park Plaza or dictate terms for his approval. The developers, backed by the

City of Boston—which has a long history of winning struggles with DCA—believed that they would eventually prevail. Thus, neither side had much incentive to negotiate.[7]

Mahoney should have realized that if the developers were reluctant to offer concessions in the past when the governor backed him, they would be even less likely to make concessions after the governor deserted him. To reclaim some bargaining leverage, Mahoney needed to regain the governor's support.

Why exactly did the governor cease to support Mahoney, and in such an abrupt and cavalier way? Three possibilities can be considered. First, the political price of supporting Mahoney's position may simply have become too great. Sargent was willing to back Mahoney for a while, but when the boos became deafening, and no cheers could be heard to offset the boos, the game was no longer worth the candle.

Second, the governor may have become persuaded that Park Plaza was, in fact, a valuable project. He may have continued to have his doubts about the financial viability of the project and its legality. But he may also have decided that, in judging the value of the project to the city, he should respect the views of the city's representatives more than those of a state-level cabinet secretary—even a secretary he appointed.

Third, Sargent may have shifted because the political repercussions of the Park Plaza decision limited his options in dealing with a more important issue in a different domain. While Mahoney struggled with Park Plaza, the governor and his assistant Al Kramer weighed a decision on whether to halt the highway construction then slicing through Boston's neighborhoods. They were inclined to do so but knew that if they did, they would pay a substantial political price—primarily with the construction industry. Unfortunately, that was the same constituency that would be adversely affected by the rejection of Park Plaza. To reject both Park Plaza and road building within the same short space of time would seem like a declaration of war against the construction industry, with dire electoral consequences for the Sargent administration. To decide in favor of Park Plaza and against the highways would soften the blow a bit. Thus, Sargent may have needed Mahoney to say "yes" to Park Plaza to give him the leeway to say "no" to highway construction.[8]

It is significant that neither Sargent nor Kramer explained this to Mahoney. In an effective cabinet team, focused on the overall strategy of an administration and knitted together through an effective strategic planning process, just such conversations would occur.[9] Issues would be seen as important not only in their own right but also in terms of their relationship to one another. The relationships would be calculated not only in technical terms affecting performance and the overall availability of financial and managerial resources, but also in political terms.[10]

But designing and operating such planning systems require a great deal of skill and no small amount of trust among the principals.[11] In this case, the crucial ingredient of trust, built through shared working experience and values, seems lacking. Sargent and Kramer could not be sure that Mahoney would take their problem as his. He would be more apt to view their dilemma as a political problem of no concern to him.[12] Mahoney could even go to the press to complain of political pressure to make a wrong decision on the Park Plaza project. Whatever the reason, the crucial discussion never occurred.

Interestingly, the absence of trust made Mahoney's efforts to develop political support for his decision much harder. He could not get the time or the psychological room with the governor to make his case.

But the lack of trust also hurt the governor. After all, Sargent had the same problem as Mahoney. Sargent needed Mahoney just as Mahoney needed Sargent. Like Mahoney, the governor wanted to put the Park Plaza decision behind him. He hoped the project could proceed on terms agreeable to everyone. It would have been bad for the governor if Mahoney complained publicly that political pressure was being applied on the Park Plaza decision. In short, the governor wanted Mahoney to approve the project with enthusiasm and thereby lend the credibility of his position, his expertise, and his values to the project. Without that, the governor's aims could be frustrated. The governor's need for Mahoney's approval gave Mahoney some continuing leverage with Sargent and some room for negotiation. But Mahoney had to use the leverage delicately lest he be accused of disloyalty or insubordination.

With the governor's backing lost, Mahoney had to reassess his position and calculate how to improve it. In making this calculation, Mahoney realized he had only a week or two to act. The deadlines were tight for three reasons.

First, as noted above, Sargent's announcement that the plan was "finally on the road to reality" unleashed a torrent of press inquiries.[13] Mahoney was called daily to learn whether he had made a decision yet. If he put off the decision too long, those desiring a quick approval (like the developers) would have complained about his delays.

Second, Mahoney had already spent eight months on the problem and made little progress. His reputation for competence was at stake, and any claim that he needed more time to study the plan would have been viewed as incredible.

Third, the deadline for the transportation decision was fast approaching. The governor and his staff, wanting the Park Plaza issue resolved favorably before they decided to halt highway construction, pressed Mahoney for a decision.

The imminent deadline ruled out many options that would otherwise have been available to Mahoney, such as building a constituency for the decision he wanted to make. It was too late for him to reframe the issue from one focused on economic development and home rule to one of fairness and legality, for the newspapers had already come out in favor of the project on terms advantageous to the developers. Because Mahoney had already been considering the issue for many months, it was also too late for him to form a blue-ribbon panel to study the issue.

Perhaps Mahoney should have gone back to the governor to ask for more time or to request that Sargent withdraw his enthusiastic statement about the new plan. This would have given Mahoney more leverage against the developers. There was some chance that Mahoney could persuade the governor to give him a little more time. But it was much less likely that Mahoney could persuade the governor to retract his public statement. Mahoney had limited power despite the fact that both he and the governor knew that he could still hurt the Park Plaza project—and thus the governor, on the transportation decision. Sargent forestalled the need to negotiate with Mahoney by committing himself in advance to support the Park Plaza project.[14]

Essentially, Mahoney had no clout for rejecting the plan other than the formal powers of his office and his conviction that it was both illegal and insufficiently valuable to the public to justify the invocation of eminent domain. He could have turned down the project once again and awaited developments. He could have resigned and complained publicly about the project. He could have approved the project and turned to other matters. Or he could have resigned quietly and let the next DCA secretary approve the project. All were bad choices. They, more than anything, reveal the price of inattentive political management.

Mahoney ended up resigning with a loud blast at the governor. His criticism of the proposed project was strong enough to persuade the developers to withdraw their plan. Little was built on the site for several years. Mahoney's overall strategy for developing and using DCA to promote socially responsible economic development languished without his leadership—all in all, not a very good outcome.

Sencer's Initiatives

At the point we left Sencer, he was in better shape than Mahoney. It was relatively early in the government's decision-making process. His Advisory Council on Immunization Programs had met to discuss the outbreak at Fort Dix, and (with a few dissenting votes) had concluded: that the country faced a "substantial risk" of a swine flu epidemic; and that "heroic action" would be required. The only issue for Sencer was how best to rouse the government to heroic action. The steps he took exemplify classic "political entrepreneurship."[15]

On March 10, 1976, immediately following the council's meeting, Sencer phoned Cooper, his direct superior and the assistant secretary for health. He reported the council's conclusions: (1) that the possibility of a pandemic existed; (2) that while the severity could not be estimated, there were reasons to be concerned; (3) that traditional definitions of high-risk groups were not appropriate because young adults, too, were vulnerable to this disease; (4) that therefore the response had to be a universal rather than targeted immunization program; (5) that the logistics of manufacturing and distributing the vaccine were sufficiently demanding that the government had to act now to have any chance of producing an effective response by the next flu season; and (6) that the possibility that the disease would spread widely, quickly, and invisibly through the population via a process of "jet spread" made it essential that everyone be immunized as rapidly as possible—ideally before the fall.

Cooper heard Sencer out and then explained that he would be out of the country for the next ten days. Cooper considered the matter sufficiently urgent, however, that he asked Sencer to draft a memo and bring it to Washington for discussion. This was the opening for leadership that Sencer needed. He took two days to draft a memo to frame the issue for action. Because it is a key document, and an important part of Sencer's techniques of political management, it is worth describing at some length.[16]

The memorandum, written for Cooper's signature and to be forwarded to David Mathews, secretary of HEW, characterized the issue before the decision-makers as: "How should the Federal Government respond to the influenza problem caused by a new virus?" In helping Mathews, his other staffs, and his superiors at the White House address this issue, Sencer noted, among others, the following "facts":

2. The virus is antigenically related to the influenza virus which has been implicated as the cause of the 1918–1919 pandemic which

killed 450,000 people—more than 400 of every 100,000 Americans . . .
3. The entire U.S. population under 50 is probably susceptible to this strain . . .
7. A vaccine to protect against swine influenza can be developed before the next flu season; however, the production of large quantities would require extraordinary efforts by drug manufacturers.

He also presented the following "assumptions" to guide planning for the government's response:

1. . . .Present evidence and past experience indicate a strong possibility that this country will experience widespread A/swine influenza in 1976–1977. Swine flu represents a major antigenic shift from recent viruses and the population under 50 is almost universally susceptible. These are the ingredients for a pandemic.
2. Routine public health influenza recommendations . . . would not forestall a flu pandemic . . .
3. The situation is one of "go or no go." If extraordinary measures are to be undertaken, there is barely enough time to assure adequate vaccine production and to mobilize the nation's health care delivery system . . . A decision must be made now.
4. A public health undertaking of this magnitude cannot succeed without Federal leadership, sponsorship, and some level of financial support.

Sencer then proposed and analyzed four alternative courses of action:

1. *No Action:* An argument can be made for taking no extraordinary action . . . To date, there has been only one outbreak. The swine flu virus has been around but has not caused a problem among humans since 1930.
2. *Minimum Response:* Under this option there would be . . . primary reliance on delivery systems now in place and on spontaneous, non-governmental action.
3. *Government Program:* This alternative is based on virtually total government responsibility for the nationwide immunization program.
4. *Combined Approach:* . . . The plan would rely on the federal government for its technical leadership and coordination, and its purchasing power; state health agencies for their experience in conducting immunization programs and as logical distribution center

for vaccine; and on the private sector for its medical and other resources which must be mobilized.

After a brief "discussion" reiterating these principal points, Sencer concluded with the recommendation that "the Secretary adopt alternative 4 as the Department's strategy, that the Public Health Service be made responsible for the program, and that he be directed to begin immediate implementation."

To many, this memorandum seemed artfully crafted to achieve Sencer's ambition of engaging top-level decision-makers in a heroic effort to immunize the entire population against the threat of the swine flu epidemic. Without distorting the facts, he made the threat of the epidemic palpable—primarily by frequent references to the 1919 pandemic and the vulnerability of young people. He also made a convincing argument that the choice was "all or nothing." The decision could not be either staged or delayed without sacrificing effectiveness. He implied that any government which failed to act when so alerted would be judged negligent. Then, he made this bitter pill a little easier to swallow by presenting his preferred alternative as one between the (irresponsible) options of "doing nothing" and the (ideologically unacceptable) option of a "governmental response."

Thus, as one participant observed, the memo was crafted as a "gun to the head" of the high-level decision-makers whom Sencer had to persuade to act to achieve his objectives.[17] Faced with the urgency of preparing the country to meet a major threat to its public health, Sencer swept much aside: concerns about money; worry that flu vaccine might have damaging side effects to some citizens; even the personal and institutional reputations of the officials he asked to lead the charge.[18]

Armed with this memo, on March 13 Sencer journeyed to Washington to deliver it to his superiors in HEW. Although Cooper had left the country, he had paved the way for Sencer. He had directed his deputy, James Dickson, to see to it that Sencer be allowed to brief Secretary Mathews on the subject while in Washington, and had also alerted James Cavanaugh, President Ford's health adviser.

Sencer's subsequent march through Washington set off shock waves in other staffs whose advice would naturally be sought by higher level officials.[19] Because the proposed response would require additional federal spending, both the assistant secretary for planning and evaluation in the Department of Health, Education, and Welfare and the comptroller were alerted. Similarly, Paul O'Neill and James Lynn in the Office of Management and Budget were notified. Because the proposed action would require presidential leadership, the White House staff was also briefed.

Although some had doubts about the urgency of the problem and the propriety of the proposed response, their doubts bounced off the solid frame that Sencer had built around the problem and his recommended solution. What made Sencer's take on the issue unassailable was his command of two key political assets: the overriding importance of protecting the public's health—a value that trumped many lesser concerns; and CDC's reputation for neutral competence and expertise. Those together allowed Sencer to cut through the ordinary processes of policy-making in Washington like a hot knife through butter.

Sencer's first visit propelled the issue to the very threshold of the White House, but the president had yet to commit himself. Nevertheless, Sencer, acting through his influence on others, managed to get his foot in the door of the Oval Office. Sencer's briefings within HEW stimulated Mathews to write a brief memo to James Lynn, the director of OMB, reporting, "There is evidence that there will be a major flu epidemic coming this fall," and once again drawing the comparison to the 1919 epidemic.[20] That got the issue through OMB and close to the president. His briefings of Cavanaugh and Cavanaugh's assistant, Victor Zafra, developed his perspective within the Domestic Policy Council—the other key staff channel to the president. Ford first heard of the issue in an afternoon meeting on March 15 devoted exclusively to it. A decision-making meeting among the president's top staff was planned for Monday, March 22.

On Sunday, March 21, Sencer's cause was aided by a story in the *New York Times* suggesting that President Ford was about to make a decision. The article also quoted Sencer, some of his colleagues who oversaw the production and distribution of vaccines, and outside scientists as saying that the United States would have no choice but to mount a large-scale immunization effort. As Harry Meyer, head of the bureau charged with overseeing the production of the needed vaccines (the Bureau of Biologics), said, "It's a choice between gambling with money or gambling with lives."[21]

In this context, it was natural for the president's advisers to see the issue in Sencer's terms. As Paul O'Neill, the deputy director of OMB, explained, "Ultimately, in our judgment—that is to say mine and Jim Lynn's—the President didn't have much choice."[22]

On Monday, March 22, just twelve days after Sencer first alerted Cooper, and nine days after he visited Washington, a meeting was held at the White House to consider what would be done about the threat of swine flu. David Mathews, Theodore Cooper (who had returned from Egypt the day before), and James Dickson attended from Health and Human Services. James Lynn and Paul O'Neill attended from OMB. James Cannon, James Cavanaugh, Spencer Johnson, and Richard Cheney (Ford's chief of staff) came from the White House.

Mathews presented the issue, and the conversation went over much of the same ground that had been previously covered. There was no real substantive opposition to the key points in Sencer's memo. Sencer's only vulnerability showed up on a procedural question. Ford wondered how wide the consultation had been with the scientific community. When he found that it had been narrower than he wished, he asked for a subsequent meeting with outside experts.

That meeting was held two days later. Included in this meeting were such scientific luminaries as Jonas Salk and Albert Sabin, the heroes of the successful fight against polio. The meeting was ostensibly designed to discover differences of opinion in the scientific community and to provide a last check on the analysis of the issue. But White House officials, sure that the president would decide to go ahead, set up press kits announcing the decision before the meeting was held. In the event, they were correct. None of the scientists demurred at the analysis or the recommendations.

Given the scientific consensus, the decision seemed easy. At 4:50 in the afternoon, Ford appeared in the press room with Salk and Sabin by his side and explained that since the "very outstanding technicians" with whom he had just met had advised him that a serious swine flu epidemic was a "very real possibility," he was "asking the Congress to appropriate $135 million prior to the April recess to inoculate every man, woman and child in the United States . . . Finally, I am asking each and every American to make certain he or she receives an inoculation this fall."[23]

Sencer's preferred option had been adopted. There must have been rejoicing in CDC. They had succeeded in mobilizing the executive branch for action, a key first step in mobilizing the country. With the president and the administration committed to a national immunization program, many of the remaining problems—how to get the vaccines tested, manufactured, and distributed—seemed much closer to being solved. The quest for a national immunization program had begun.

Ten months later, in January 1977, there was much less reason for rejoicing. Indeed, the effort had turned into a fiasco. The problems began with the reluctance of insurance companies to cover the vaccine manufacturers against damages that could be attributed to the new, untested vaccine, distributed in a huge national program. Without insurance, the manufacturers proceeded slowly, and the testing and manufacturing schedules slipped badly. Eventually, the matter was resolved when Congress agreed to indemnify the insurance companies and have the federal government assume the financial risk of claims associated with the immunization program. This action set an important precedent in dealing with the risks of immunization and exposed the government to what turned out to be more than $11 million in claims.[24]

The difficulties with production and distribution also played havoc with the program's success in immunizing citizens early. Even though Sencer had declared it urgent that the population be inoculated before the fall, the first inoculations did not occur until October 1. Even though he had said that children should be the highest priority targets for immunization, manufacturers produced only enough vaccine to immunize 1 in 12 children. Ultimately, 40 million were immunized over a period of ten weeks—quite an astonishing accomplishment, but far short of what had been promised or judged to be necessary to provide adequate protection, and far less equitably distributed than had been proposed.[25]

That coverage might still have been welcome had swine flu appeared. But what made the effort particularly tragic was that no additional cases of swine flu in humans arose throughout the summer, fall, or winter. What did occur was deaths associated with the vaccines. Some of these were coincidental; in any program involving 40 million people, some people will die shortly after receiving a vaccine. But gradually it became clear that this vaccine had a particularly damaging side effect—the Guillain-Barre syndrome, which caused paralysis. Ultimately, 54 cases appeared among vaccinees, with 30 occurring within thirty days of their vaccination.[26] And, when the winter flu season did hit, it was Victoria flu that threatened the lives of the elderly and forced others to stay at home. Unfortunately, no vaccine was available because the swine flu effort had preempted all the vaccine-making capacity.

The national immunization program succeeded in protecting many fewer people than it planned to do against a disease that never appeared. It also caused the paralysis and death of some people who took the vaccine and left the population exposed to the ravages of the flu that did appear. It totaled more than $130 million in direct costs, exposed the government to a future stream of damage claims, and set a precedent for the government to be exposed to such claims in the future. Beyond this, of course, the program left the cause of immunization and preventive medicine badly in disarray, the credibility of CDC weakened, and Sencer's own reputation tarnished. It also reinforced the idea that President Ford was a politically motivated bumbler and helped him to lose the election. Some luster may have been lost from the office of the presidency, another poor outcome.

EVALUATION

The denouement of these cases reveals the need and the opportunity for political management but also its hazards, hazards that reach both managers and the wider society.

In Mahoney's case, a potentially important opportunity was lost because of his failure to engage in effective political management. Perhaps a latent constituency existed that would have agreed with his reasons for rejecting the Park Plaza project. Perhaps Mahoney could have used the leverage that would have come from developing this constituency to negotiate a better version of the plan. Perhaps a favorable decision on Park Plaza would have strengthened Mahoney's standing in the Sargent administration and enabled him to pursue his broader overall strategy for DCA. Perhaps all this would have served the public far better than the messy collapse of the Park Plaza project along with Mahoney's plans for DCA. In any case, Mahoney's reluctance to do anything more than cultivate support from the governor left these possibilities undeveloped. It also led to his own downfall. Better and earlier political management might have retrieved this situation.

In Sencer's case, in contrast, an opportunity was exploited through skilled and determined political advocacy. Yet, in retrospect, Sencer might have wished he had been less skillful a political manager, and so might we. Of course, one can argue with this conclusion. One can say that Sencer did the right thing in preparing the country for a dangerous epidemic, and that had the epidemic arrived, he would now be viewed as a hero rather than a goat. But the criticism of Sencer's preferred policy cuts deeper than the superficial (and incorrect) claim that Sencer's actions look wrong only because the epidemic that threatened never appeared. We can criticize Sencer for not properly responding to the uncertainty about the epidemic and not preparing the country to deal with the possibility that the epidemic might not appear.[27]

A proper response to uncertainty often requires two things: first, a continued effort to gather information to reduce the uncertainties; second, a hedged response (that is, a response that may not be the best in dealing with any particular eventuality, but is the best when considered against all the possible eventualities.)[28]

In this concrete case, the government's response to the threat of swine flu could conceivably have been improved in two ways. First, the government could have monitored the international experience over the summer and fall to inform expert judgment about the likelihood of the epidemic.[29] South America's flu season came several months before North America's, and if the swine flu were going to hit North America hard, it would probably have shown up in South America first. If the epidemic did not appear there, some of the government's efforts could have been relaxed to save the risk to vaccinees.

Second, a hedged response was available to the government but was not used: the so-called stockpiling strategy. That strategy called for the government to decide immediately to produce the vaccine, but to wait until later (after more information had been gathered about the likelihood of the epidemic and the side effects of the vaccine) to administer it.

Of course, this hedged approach would have been less effective in protecting the population than the "all out" strategy that was adopted to counter a severe epidemic. But that is always the case with hedged strategies. A hedged strategy is never quite as good at dealing with any particular eventuality once it appears than one designed to deal with that specific eventuality from the outset. A hedged strategy is only better at the outset—before one knows which eventuality will ensue.

Arguably, in the spring of 1977, the stockpiling strategy would have been a better one for the government to adopt since no one could be certain that the epidemic would occur.[30] Because there was a good chance that it would not, the government should arguably have been worrying about the cost and risks of immunizing everyone against a nonexistent epidemic as well as the risk that not everyone would be adequately protected if the epidemic hit. Indeed, this hedged strategy would have looked better and better over the course of the summer and fall as no new outbreaks of swine flu ensued.

It is in this sense that the strategy recommended by Sencer was conceivably wrong and costly. The insurance premium he bought for the country was simply too expensive given the risks.

What is particularly interesting in Sencer's case is that there were important voices that, if taken seriously, would have pushed toward the more prudent response. When it first met, Sencer's Advisory Council on Immunization Programs broached the idea of separating the two decisions and delaying the second, but the council rejected it on the grounds that the epidemic could spread quickly and invisibly and that time would be needed for the immunization to take effect. These assumptions were never fully tested. Most likely everyone thought that heroic measures were needed, and such measures were inconsistent with phased operations. The task was to build urgency and commitment; half-hearted measures would not suffice.[31]

The stockpiling strategy might also have gained force if someone had carefully analyzed the operational feasibility of producing and administering the vaccine.[32] What such an analysis would have revealed is what actually happened: even with optimistic assumptions, only a small fraction of those vulnerable could possibly be immunized before the flu season. If logistics were going to weaken the protection anyway, why not make a virtue of necessity and wait until more data accumulated about the likelihood of the disease? This line of reasoning was, again, cut off, because it seemed inconsistent with the necessary spirit.

Thus, the context of urgency and heroism, partially created by Sencer's interpretation of the problem and his skilled entrepreneurial efforts to advance that conception, had the effect of blotting out information that could have been used to craft a more effective public policy response. That is the price paid for some kinds of political management, and it warns us that not all approaches to the problem of political management are appropriate or useful. For that reason I begin the analysis of political management techniques with a discussion of ethics.

THE ETHICS AND TECHNIQUES
OF POLITICAL MANAGEMENT

In a liberal democracy, leadership of the type being exercised by Mahoney and Sencer is morally suspect. There is no small amount of arrogance in claiming to know the public good. Lurking behind such claims may be nothing more than greed, or ambition, or odd and untested ideas of public value or the public interest.

Moreover, these cases give little cause for reassurance. One manager fails because he does not "do" political management very well, the other because he does it too well. Perhaps it is best to drop the subject altogether.

Yet, on closer examination, these cases together teach an important ethical lesson to public managers. They say that it is fundamentally wrong and dangerous for managers to become so arrogant that they no longer trouble to check their ideas about what is publicly valuable with citizens and those who represent the public. Mahoney's arrogance takes the form of failing to pay continuing attention to his political authorization; Sencer's takes the form of dominating and manipulating the political environment.

I discuss the ethical issues confronting public managers in detail in Chapter 8. For my purposes here it may be enough to observe that, from an ethical perspective, virtue in political management seems to rest crucially on the spirit in which one enters the political lists. One spirit is closed to learning, disrespectful of the views of opponents, manipulative with respect to colleagues, and determined to exploit every loophole to advance one's purposes. This is aggressive advocacy.[33]

At the other extreme is a spirit open to learning. Managers' particular goals and objectives, perhaps even their deepest values, are open to change as a result of the dialogue with opponents. This kind of political management begins with respect for differences. After all, even one's enemies might be defending some important values or have some important information to contribute. In this view, the whole point of deliberation is for managers to expose themselves to learning.[34]

Aggressive advocates may succeed in advancing their purposes, but they run the risk of failing to learn, and of committing the government to a course of action that will prove unwise or shortly be undone.[35] As Karl Deutsch once explained, "In simple language, to have power means not to have to give in, and to force the environment or the other person to do so. Power in this narrow sense is the priority of output over intake, the ability to talk instead of listen. In a sense, it is the ability to afford not to learn."[36] To some extent, this was the fate that befell both Mahoney and Sencer.

Managers who enter political debates with a commitment to learning, however, may well succeed in educating themselves. They may even succeed in articulating a public purpose or value that can command wide, sustained assent, and thereby become effective leaders. But they risk sacrificing their own purposes for the sake of leadership. Of course, many would view this as a virtue in a democracy since the whole point of democratic governance is to realize collective aspirations through governmental operations rather than the vision of any particular individual. One of the most successful techniques of political management is for managers to make themselves agents of others' purposes. But others would say that the point of political management is for managers to find ways to invest their own preconceived purposes with the maximum amount of legitimacy.

Perhaps the synthesis of these competing views is to acknowledge the duty both to represent one's own considered views of what is publicly valuable to do and to learn from others.[37] Managers should also recognize that leadership sometimes takes the form of taking a stand and insisting on the importance of some neglected value or the relevance of some ignored course of action; other times it takes the form of abandoning one's own position in favor of a new synthesis of competing points of view. In political management one cannot entirely rid oneself of the pleasure and the obligation of having and articulating a point of view; nor can one rid oneself of the obligation to learn and to integrate the views of others. It is through such dialogue that the best chance of finding and successfully pursuing public value probably lies; it is this potential that should be cultivated by the techniques of political management.

Below, I review five techniques of political management now being developed in the academic and practitioner literatures on public management. By "technique" I mean a set of ideas that operate at a somewhat higher level of abstraction than advice on what one should say or wear when one is trying to influence others. I mean analytic frameworks that: (1) define the central problem of political management and, implicitly or explicitly, establish a normative orientation to the task; (2) develop a set of diagnostic categories to be used in sizing up the situation and identifying the important pieces of work that must be done; and (3) offer more or less explicit recommendations about how political managers might best proceed to accomplish the goal of building legitimacy and support for their initiatives. The five techniques include: entrepreneurial advocacy; managing policy development; negotiation; public deliberation, social learning, and leadership; and public sector marketing and strategic communication.

Three problems arise in presenting these concepts as answers to the question of how public managers can best engage political environments. First, not all of these concepts were developed as answers to the specific challenge posed by political management. Some—entrepreneurial advocacy, managing policy development, and public deliberation and social learning—*were*. Others, negotiation and public sector marketing, were not. I include them nonetheless because they seem to have important things to say about how public managers could mobilize support for their initiatives. Second, not all of these ideas have been equally well developed for the purpose of guiding public managers in their efforts at political management. This inevitably produces a certain unevenness in their presentation. Third, in summarizing the concepts in a stylized form I give some of the ideas a slightly superficial and elementary treatment.

Despite these difficulties, I consider it important to put the different ideas on the same map so that we in the field as a whole can see them as different, plausibly useful answers to the question of how the function of political management might best be performed. That, in turn, might accelerate the further development of each particular idea and the synthesis of these ideas in a coherent view of this important managerial function.[38]

ENTREPRENEURIAL ADVOCACY

Perhaps the most fully and explicitly developed approach to political management could be called entrepreneurial advocacy.[39] This approach focuses on what a public manager needs to do to maximize the chance that his or her preferred policy will be authoritatively adopted and solidly backed. Mahoney is an entrepreneurial advocate with respect to the rejection of the Park Plaza project. Similarly, Sencer is an entrepreneurial advocate with respect to committing the U.S. government to immunizing the population against swine flu.

The implicit assumption of entrepreneurial advocacy is that political management must assemble a sufficiently powerful coalition to ensure that the managers' preferred policies will be authoritatively endorsed by the government. Given this aim, the crucial *diagnostic* skill is identifying who can, or must, or might play a role in making the decision. The crucial *tactical* skills have to do with finding ways to mobilize support (and neutralize opposition) for the specific choices managers want made.[40]

Diagnosis I: Who Will Be Involved?

Generating the list of players involved in supporting or resisting an initiative is the crucial first diagnostic step in entrepreneurial advocacy. Mahoney must consider whose formal and informal disapprovals are required to block Park Plaza; Sencer must determine whose formal or tacit approvals will launch the national campaign to immunize the population against swine flu. In our complex political system, this first step is a surprisingly difficult task. The group of players is not a fixed or determinate set. Some actors must be involved; others can, if they choose; and still others might be brought into the process. Instead of being able to calculate exactly who *will* be involved, managers can only sketch who *might* be involved.

To be complete in identifying the possible players, managers have to rely on two different methods.[41] The first looks along the formal structure and processes of authoritative decision-making to determine whose signatures on specific documents could formally establish the desired initiative. The second examines the substantive content of the issue (and the way it will be framed) to determine whose interests are engaged and how much particular actors will want to participate. In other words, the first method looks at actors in positions; the second looks at actors with interests.

PLAYERS IN POSITIONS

Sometimes the formal authority to act on a policy question seems to lie no further than the advocate's own front door. As a formal matter, it is Mahoney's signature as the secretary for the Department of Community Affairs that will determine whether the Park Plaza project is approved and whether the flow of powers associated with eminent domain become available to the private developers for use in assembling the land. Similarly, Sencer commands resources and informal influence over a public and private network of vaccine manufacturers, physicians, and public health clinics that can do much of the work of immunizing the U.S. public against the dangers of swine flu.

Often, however, even when officials seem to have the formal authority to take bold initiatives, they recognize that their own formal authority is insufficient. Without additional political work, their decision might well be overruled by one or another of their overseers. Mahoney's decision to reject the Park Plaza project could be overturned by the governor or the state legislature. Sencer's decision to immunize the entire population with an untested vaccine could be reversed or modified by the assistant secretary for health, health policy advisers in OMB or the executive office of the president, the president himself, or the Congress.

This observation underscores the point that although public managers occupy offices with powers attached, the managers do not own them: the powers to act are merely lent to them, and on terms.[42] Their powers can be removed and their actions repudiated if their overseers think they have done something wrong. Moreover, most officials find the formal powers of their office insufficient to achieve the goals for which they will be held accountable.[43] Consequently, most prudent and responsible public officials seek to anchor their decisions in sources of support and legitimacy other than the formal powers of their offices.

Because our constitution divides governmental powers, a public official can seek support and legitimacy by traveling along several different paths.[44] Often, the most obvious route to authorization is simply up the bureaucratic chain of command. Thus, it is natural for Mahoney to think of gaining support from Governor Sargent; and it is natural for Sencer to think of reaching Assistant Secretary Cooper, Secretary Mathews, and President Ford.

Generally speaking, as one moves up the bureaucratic chain of command, getting approvals at each stage of the process, a decision not only acquires *more,* but also a different *kind* of, legitimacy. A bureaucratic initiative starts with the kind of legitimacy that derives from the bureaucrat's technical and legal expertise.[45] Mahoney and his staff decide to resist Park Plaza because the plan seems technically unsound and legally questionable. Sencer and his staff decide to mobilize the country to the threat of swine flu because their scientific expertise alerts them to the risks.

As the decision goes higher in the system, however, greater *political* legitimacy is added. In a democracy, all bureaucratic routes eventually lead to political authorities.[46] The reason, of course, is that democracies join the legitimacy that comes from public support to the legitimacy that comes from compliance with the law and technical expertise. Adding political legitimacy to legal and technical legitimacy is normatively important in reassuring managers and citizens that the managers' judgments about public value are sound. It is also practically important to managers who often need the political platforms and skills of political executives to extend their effective influence over people they need to help them achieve their operational aims.

Thus, Mahoney will probably seek authorization to disapprove the Park Plaza plan from the governor—knowing that if he fails to do so, he might be fired. Sencer will seek authorization from the assistant secretary for health, the secretary of HEW, and ultimately the president, not only because he formally needs their approval to go ahead bureaucratically on the scale and with the urgency he deems necessary, but also because their political standing, access to the media, and political associations will help mobilize the private efforts Sencer needs to make his public leadership successful.

Another path open to public managers seeking support and legitimacy is through legislative bodies.[47] Sometimes this means seeking specific statutes authorizing or directing officials to take actions they want to take. Other times it means gaining the tolerance of legislative overseers for a choice that managers are already authorized to make but which could be overruled by a statute. Still other times it means helping to build political support for a choice that managers want to make to increase the effective scope of their influence.

If Mahoney, for example, is to continue to be successful in resisting the Park Plaza project as currently conceived, he must avoid having the legislature pass the home rule amendment that strips him of the power to review Boston's redevelopment plans. Once was enough, and he can hardly rely on the governor to face another public demonstration and veto it again. Sencer, for his part, might consider going directly to friendly congressional committees for legislation authorizing a national immunization program. Or, if his political superiors in the executive branch seem hesitant, he could implicitly threaten such a move by warning them that Congress might seize the initiative and take unilateral action if the executive branch refuses to act on its own. (Indeed, he did precisely this in his memo.)

A final route, less commonly used but still important, involves the courts.[48] Often the courts intervene in policy decisions unexpectedly: the government is sued by citizens unhappy with the action that has been taken; the public manager seeks to vindicate his action by winning the suit in court, thereby validating the authority he initially claimed in making the decision. Increasingly, however, it seems that officials encourage suits that will force them to take the actions they would like to take. It is as though they and their clients enter into a conspiracy with the courts to claim something more for their clients than the legislature or the political executives were willing to provide.[49] One strategy Mahoney might pursue, for example, is to approve the Park Plaza project but then invite a property owner to sue on the grounds that Mahoney had improperly invoked the powers of eminent domain to do so. Such an act is effective because it helps to give *political* weight to the *legal* requirements of the law that Mahoney administers.

From the perspective of an entrepreneurial advocate, the significance of these different "action channels" is this: because each path engages a somewhat different set of players, with different views about the advocate's preferred policies, each channel offers more or less potential to secure the adoption of the managers' preferred policies.[50] The choice of what channel to use becomes an important tactical decision to be made by the entrepreneurial advocate.

PLAYERS WITH INTERESTS

The second method for identifying relevant players begins with interests rather than formal positions. Of course, there is often a substantial overlap between those who have a formal role in a decision and those who are interested in its outcome. To the extent the government is reasonably well organized, the people with substantive interests in an area will be included in the formal structures and processes for deliberation or will have made themselves part of the informal "issue networks" that oversee governmental policy.[51]

By looking at the issue itself, however, and asking whose interests might be engaged by any potential resolution of the issue, managers might identify some players who are not now formally positioned to act.

These would include players who might care enough about the issue to force themselves into the process, or those who might be persuaded to become active on the issue even though they are not now well positioned to do so.[52]

Of course, most important policy choices produce multiple consequences affecting many potential players. The Park Plaza decision, for example, affects the tax base of the City of Boston, employment in the construction industry, the wealth of banks and entrepreneurs who invest in the project, the future plans of the businesses now occupying the Park Plaza project area, and, if Mahoney has his way, even the availability of hard-core pornography in the city. Obviously, quite different people pay attention to these different aspects of the choice.

Most choices also raise issues of precedent for other decisions or for the process of handling other issues. One of the things that makes success in opposing Park Plaza important to Mahoney is that it would help establish DCA's continuing influence over local redevelopment decisions, including those in Boston—an effect that the BRA has also noted and enlisted the legislature to help resist.

In gauging what players will be involved, then, an advocate must assess how the different substantive and procedural aspects of a choice are linked to important interests and concerns of potential players in the game. That will determine how likely they are to become involved, how aggressively they will play, and in what ways they will seek to influence the process.

Doing such an analysis is both difficult and time consuming. Yet such efforts are not wasted even if the analysis fails to reveal any new players, for the analysis of what stakes individual players have in the ultimate decision helps the manager in deciding which action channel to use; it improves the manager's estimates of how intensively engaged those players who have already been identified will become and what their stand is likely to be. It may also identify some crucial features of the choice that can be emphasized or exploited in persuading or negotiating with other players.

Diagnosis II: Estimating Stands of Players

Once an advocate has identified the players involved in the decision, he or she must guess their likely stand.[53] The most straightforward way of doing this is to find what positions they have taken in the past.[54] History leaves grooves in actors' minds as well as traces of what they value. Both help an advocate guess their likely stand.

If an advocate cannot rely on history, he or she can try to guess how players' interests will be engaged. This depends, in turn, on knowing how the issue will appear to them as well as what they value.

Political actors rarely orient themselves to all the substantive and procedural features of a given choice. There are simply too many. Moreover, most are irrelevant to particular individuals. Consequently, particular players will see the choice before them in only a few dimensions. In this sense, issues present a particular "face" to particular players.[55]

What is true for individuals is also true for the entire group of players and for the way the issue is presented and discussed in public forums. From all the possible things that a decision could be about, only a few will be seen by all or most of the people involved, and only a few will be discussed publicly. These will become the "public face of the issue."

Both the private and public faces of the issue may be shaped by the context in which they arise. Sometimes it is the historical context of the particular issue that is important. Sencer, for example, sees the swine flu issue against the backdrop of the historic flu epidemic in 1918,[56] a context that exaggerates the threat associated with swine flu.

Sometimes the public face of the issue is shaped by what is happening at the same time on other issues. The Park Plaza decision, for instance, becomes entangled with a decision on road building. This context changes the issue from a narrow question, of whether Park Plaza represents an appropriate use of public auspices, to a broader political question, of whether the Sargent administration is pro- or antidevelopment and pro- or anti–construction workers.

These clues help an advocate guess the likely stands of players. Managers could go further of course and produce fine-grained analyses of all potential players: their positions in the organizations they represent, their past history, speeches they have given on the issue at hand or related subjects, their ideological orientations, and so on. But often there is neither time enough nor data accessible enough to support these detailed diagnoses. Managers, then, will be reduced to reviewing the history of an issue or guessing players' interests and how they will see the issue.

Tactics I: Choosing Paths to Decisions

The tactics of an entrepreneurial advocate can be divided into short-run tactics, which take much of the current political setting for granted, and long-run tactics, which allow for changes in the current setting of policy choice.[57]

The existence of alternative routes to authoritative choices gives the advocate one important tactical choice to make. In all likelihood, some routes will be more favorable to the advocate's cause than others. Some will be lined by players favorable to the advocate's view, others by those who are hostile. Some will be well oiled by past interactions; others will be creaky from disuse. Obviously, all else being equal, the advocate should choose those paths to action which are most favorable to his or her cause and most convenient to engage.

Unfortunately, all may not be equal. The different paths to an authoritative decision may vary in terms of their ability to produce powerful, durable mandates. Different processes of choice will have different standing in the eyes of those affected by the choice. They may also look more or less fragile. For example, a piece of legislation that has been thoroughly debated has a much different standing than the decision of an ad hoc committee formed briefly within the executive branch of government to decide a particular matter. It may be worth it to an advocate to take a more difficult path to action if it promises to deliver a more powerful and lasting mandate for that action.[58]

Advocates may also alter existing processes of choice by taking actions that widen or narrow the group of players, or that expand or contract the time for considering the issue.[59] The most common devices used for accomplishing these objectives are managing the level of secrecy or openness with which an issue is considered and creating more or less of a sense of crisis around the issue. In general, the more press coverage given to an issue, the more people will become involved. The greater the sense of crisis created, the less time there will be for deliberation. Thus, secret crises are likely to be the most closely held decisions; widely publicized issues that are not yet at crisis proportions are likely to be the most widely discussed and debated.

What sort of process is advantageous to advocates is, again, a complex issue. They must predict how changes in the decision process will affect who plays the game and how the issue will be debated and resolved. They must trade the potential advantages of closely controlled issues with the disadvantages of narrow or compressed deliberations: the lack of legitimacy and quality, which often makes these decisions vulnerable to reconsideration and half-hearted implementation.

In Mahoney's case a relatively closed process seems appropriate to his purpose since the governor can be reached through such a process and, initially, the governor supports him. Later, as the governor's support wanes, it seems that a wider process would be more valuable. Perhaps he should have established a blue-ribbon commission to review the Park Plaza plan or requested an opinion from the attorney general on the legality of the proposed project. The fact that such options look valuable late in the process may suggest that such activities would have been valuable earlier as well to shore up the governor's initial support.

In Sencer's case it seems clear that he needs a broad, open process from the outset because his aim is not only to secure a particular policy choice but also to establish a broader context in which other choices will be facilitated and a wide social mobilization initiated. For such large enterprises that escape the boundaries of managers' direct authority, only wide and high-level processes will do.

Tactics II: Framing Issues for Discussion

Determining how best to frame issues becomes an important tactical question for advocates because the way an issue is framed might well govern which forum considers the issue and what parties become engaged. Advocates make their job easier if they can frame issues in ways that increase the chance of having them considered in the preferred forum, of mobilizing supporters, and of avoiding arousing or antagonizing opponents.[60]

Unfortunately, however, there are limits to managers' abilities to frame issues for public debate. Substantively, there are limits to the audience's tolerance for having decisions characterized for them in particular terms. People often (but not always) know what are the genuinely important characteristics of a decision and will be unprepared to see the characteristics of the decision substantially altered. If one transcends those limits, the manipulation becomes transparent, and this undermines rather than enhances the advocate's cause. Two recent notorious examples include the Reagan administration's efforts to emphasize the capacity of nuclear deterrence to assure peace by calling a new missile the "peacekeeper,"[61] and to justify the Internal Revenue System (IRS) decision to allow segregated schools to reclaim their tax-exempt status not as a civil rights ruling but as an issue of the authority of the IRS to make the ruling it had made.[62]

Framing is also the area in which the struggles with the press are likely to be the most significant.[63] Advocates of a particular issue seek to shape it for tactical advantage. A journalist, too, looks for a way to shape an issue, for an "angle." But the journalist's angle mixes accuracy with judgment of intrinsic public interest. If advocates can line up their frame with the reporter's angle, they are more likely to succeed.

More often than not, however, the press puts a different face on the issue. Usually, they simplify it.[64] They commonly focus on some dimension that will attract attention because it is emotional, or linked to important values, or connected to something else currently making news.

From the point of view of officials this practice represents a distortion as profound as their own efforts at framing. But the expectation that reporting should be complete and accurate is clearly wrong. People want not only to read things in simple terms but also to act politically on the basis of simple principles.

In resisting the Park Plaza project, Mahoney has trouble finding a way to frame the project as the wrong choice. Although he works to reduce the displacement of poor tenants and answer environmental concerns, these issues are not really powerfully engaged by the proposed project. Few residents are to be displaced, and arguably the environment will be improved. The project does not even involve any government money. Mahoney can only argue that the powers of eminent domain might be wrongly engaged. Hence, the governor demands that the plan be "legal." But that frame only gets Mahoney so far. The fact that it is difficult for Mahoney to find a satisfactory frame could, conceivably, raise questions in Mahoney's mind about whether he is, in fact, protecting any important public values in resisting Park Plaza.

In contrast, one of Sencer's real advantages is that there is a very powerful and effective frame for his issue: the analogy to the flu epidemic of 1918.[65] Never mind that the analogy only partly fits; it does the work of getting people's attention and biasing them toward a particular line of action.

Tactics III: Waiting for a Favorable Moment

The tactics explored so far—choosing the path to authoritative choice and framing the issue—exploit the "play" in a particular setting on behalf of advocates.[66] If advocates can afford to wait for action, however, then additional tactical opportunities become available to them.

One important tactic available to these advocates is simply waiting for the right time to consider an issue. The political authorizing environment constantly changes. A policy issue may be influenced by its own internal development process. It will also be influenced by other issues and events in the environment. Such changes may enhance or lessen the prospects for advocates' causes. Wise advocates wait for opportunities to act.[67]

These observations also help us understand why Sencer has more success than Mahoney at building support for the preferred course of action. In Mahoney's case the time for deciding about Park Plaza is becoming less favorable by the moment. As the decision on road construction approaches, the political environment becomes much less favorable to Mahoney. He was probably in the best position early in the case rather than later, and his error was in failing to recognize that fact and make the best deal possible at that time. In Sencer's case the timing is fortuitous—partly because Cooper is on vacation, and partly because Ford and his political advisers might be looking for an opportunity for Ford to exercise brave, competent leadership and put the lie to his public image as a bumbler. In that world, Sencer's story describing the need for heroic action is very seductive, indeed.

Note that the idea that one should wait for an opportunity to intervene changes one's orientation to management. It acknowledges the lack of control a manager has over particularly political issues. It implies that a fixed agenda might be counterproductive, if expressed in a concrete plan for achieving each particular item on the agenda. Such an effort might cause a manager to spend lots of time working on issues that are not yet ripe for action.[68]

A much different strategy would inspire a manager to hold many issues in mind that would be worth working on, while letting circumstances dictate which ones should be pursued first. Which ones come to the top of the agenda depends on prospects for action—not necessarily on importance. The style is opportunistic and improvisational rather than planned. The crucial managerial skills are diagnosis and monitoring rather than planning and control.

Note that this kind of management works best when one occupies a position in which many issues are likely to be discussed and debated. Then, issues can be spotted and put together,[69] with each decision supporting the next. Thus, being flexible and well positioned is often more important than having detailed plans and ambitions, for one rarely has the wherewithal to pursue all the items on one's agenda.

Tactics IV: Changing the Setting

Of course, the celebration of opportunism may give far too much credit to the flashy "foxes" at the expense of the quieter, more determined "hedgehogs," who have long-range purposes and stubbornly work away at them over the long run.[70] If advocates are prepared to stay in the game over the long run, and to be active as well as opportunistic, they can do many things to change the political environments in which they operate. Things that seem like constraints in the short run can be altered through sustained effort over the long run.

For example, the process can be altered by changing the stands of important players—either by persuading them of the wisdom of the managers' preferred points of view or by enmeshing them in new relationships that help to convert them to the managers' views. On occasion, managers may be able to replace opponents with supporters. Alternatively, advocates can sometimes change the forum within which an issue is being considered, or even construct new mechanisms for considering an issue. The creation of new legislative committees, commissions, or special task forces can be a tool that advocates might grasp to give their issue a more favorable hearing than it would receive in the existing processes.[71]

On the substantive side, if one is prepared to keep at the issue over the long run, one might also be able to change the frame of the issue or the conventional wisdom about the best way to handle a particular situation. A manager can develop and begin using a concept that changes the way an issue is perceived. An excellent example is Stanley Surrey's crusade to view tax exemptions and interest deductions as "tax expenditures" so that they could be readily compared to appropriated money.[72]

Advocates can develop information systems to report on some characteristic of the world that can focus attention on a neglected value. For example, the creation of the Unified Crime Reports tended to focus public attention on street crime rather than other criminal offenses;[73] the sponsoring of a regular survey to determine how many hungry people there are in America inevitably made powerful claims on agriculture and welfare policy.[74]

Advocates can also sponsor program evaluations or basic research studies that change society's perception of how effective particular public policies are. The cumulative research on the success of rehabilitation gradually changed the public's conception of the purposes of imprisonment.[75] The cumulative research on preschool education also changed the public's view of Head Start to the benefit of its advocates.[76]

Finally, over the long run, advocates can build personal relations and credibility so that they can approach policy discussions with more knowledge, greater capacity to construct a sustainable deal with side payments, and greater personal credibility to be lent to the issue. This approach seems to work in the private sector as well as in the public sector. Indeed, according to John Kotter, one of the principal assets that private sector managers bring to their jobs is their cumulative network of contacts, knowledge, and personal credibility.[77] This asset, more than abstract knowledge or skills, seems to make the greatest difference in terms of performance.

Critiques

Although the concept of entrepreneurial advocacy seems a natural and appropriate way to think about political management at the start, the detailed working through of the concept and the recommended tactics tend to raise important ethical qualms. It becomes plausible that with enough insight and determination, aggressive advocates might, in fact, be able to manipulate the government's decisions to suit their aims. And that seems, in the end, wrong for a democratic society. The single-mindedness seems wrong. So does the manipulation. So does the apparent willingness to cut corners of the process in the interests of developing the minimally required coalition. So does the indifference to the long-term sustainability of the decisions made. So also does the indifference to substantive accuracy in the characterization of problems and the analysis of options. It all looks too slick.

Thus, while the techniques of entrepreneurial advocacy offer good advice about how to analyze and diagnose political settings, the tactics recommended lack the spirit one would like to see in policy-making in a democracy. It encourages individual officials to advance their own views without regard for the concerns of others; indeed, it encourages them to do so in a way that defeats the potential influence of those other views and their own opportunities for learning.[78]

MANAGING POLICY DEVELOPMENT

These critiques lead to consideration of an alternative approach to political management: the management of policy development.[79] One crucial feature distinguishes this approach from entrepreneurial advocacy. Managers operating as advocates have a conclusion in mind; they aim to have a particular policy adopted. Officials acting as "policy managers," in contrast, are fundamentally committed to producing a high-quality decision—not any particular decision; they aim to manage a process that invests any decision made with a high degree of legitimacy, power, and accuracy.

Techniques of policy management are used in two somewhat different contexts. In one context, managers, concerned with getting a single important policy decision made well, involve people outside their organizations. They take the lead in organizing a governmentwide deliberation on an important problem among many people who do not work for them, including peers and superiors. Sencer, for example, could see his challenge as one of organizing an effective deliberation across the government (including the Congress, outside experts, and citizens) to produce a widely debated, deeply considered, powerful substantive judgment about the best national response to the threat of swine flu.[80]

In a second context, policy management focuses on designing, developing, and operating an ongoing decision-making process to deal effectively with the full range of decisions to be made within the scope of the manager's responsibility and authority. Thus, for example, President Ford's Domestic Policy Council represents a structure designed to produce an orderly decision-making process to handle the hundreds of important decisions the president must make, not just the decision about swine flu.[81]

Although these contexts for policy management are quite different, both the spirit and many of the techniques are similar: in both contexts, the aim is to run a process that produces high-quality decisions, rather than a specific decision. The building blocks, then, are the particular steps required to produce "well-made" decisions. I consider first high-quality decisions produced in individual cases in which managers work with people outside the scope of their authority; then I turn to designing organizational systems to produce high-quality decisions across the full range of a manager's responsibilities where most participants lie within the reach of the manager's authority.

Diagnosis I: Ingredients of Quality Decisions

Because policy management focuses on producing quality decisions, the first diagnostic step is to identify the ingredients that make for a high-quality decision. Generally speaking, a high-quality decision is one that has a large measure of both *process* and *substantive* virtues.[82] A decision acquires process virtues by emerging from a wide consultation process in which all interested parties have had a chance to be consulted, and all the formal legal rules governing the process of decision-making have been met.[83] A decision acquires substantive legitimacy to the extent that the decision has been able to draw into the policy-making process as many relevant facts as are available, arrayed in an analytic framework that accurately represents the important values at stake in the decision, the principal alternatives open to the decision-makers, and the likely consequences of the alternative choices (reckoned in dimensions of significance to the decision-makers).[84]

Tactics I: Wide Process of Consultation

Given these objectives, to invest a choice with process and substantive legitimacy, a manager must develop a process of wide consultation that reaches out to public officials in various positions, and sometimes even to ordinary citizens. The reason is that consultation draws into the decision-making process the different kinds of legitimacy represented by the different kinds of officials and people consulted.

For example, to lend *political* legitimacy to a choice, one must include officials invested with the particular quality that comes from having stood for election: namely, elected chief executives, elected legislators, and (to a lesser degree) political appointees. Thus, the governor's support for Mahoney at the outset reassures him that his decision to reject Park Plaza is supported politically as well as technically, and that reassurance gives him great confidence in continuing to resist. The erosion of the governor's support later means that he is stuck with resisting a politically popular choice with nothing but a law (that can be changed) and a professional opinion (which has little standing) supporting him. Similarly, Sencer understands that the legitimacy of the decision about swine flu would be immeasurably increased if it was endorsed by the president rather than just the substantive experts of CDC.

Managers can enhance the political legitimacy of a particular decision by inviting ordinary citizens to participate through some kind of hearings process. Mahoney might have strengthened his hand in dealing with Park Plaza if he had held a hearing on the proposed project and invited neighborhood groups to attend.

Similarly, one can invest a process with *legal* standing and power if one consults with chief counsels of departments, or the Department of Justice, or the courts themselves. Mahoney could have asked the governor's counsel, or the state attorney general, for an opinion on the legality of the Park Plaza project.

Managers can lend a decision-making process *substantive* legitimacy by consulting the sorts of people who are thought to embody substantive expertise. They include career officials, outside experts, academics, scientists, and policy analysts.[85] Indeed, it is precisely this kind of legitimacy that both Mahoney and Sencer bring to their decision-making processes because they embody substantive knowledge and expertise. That is the base from which they start. As political managers, they add new forms of legitimacy to the choices they are trying to make.

Tactics II: Getting Closure on Decisions

There is a price to be paid for wide consultation, however: it often produces conflict, disagreement, delay, and compromise, rather than satisfactory resolution. Indeed, often the process reaches a stalemate or threatens to continue indefinitely.[86] Essentially, only two devices exist to help a broadly consultative process come to a conclusion. Either a higher level authority can resolve the ongoing debates or a deadline can be imposed.[87] Often, both are needed to force a decision.

The obvious corollary of this point is that if either of these conditions is absent, then the government may fall into gridlock. If authority is spread so widely across existing institutions that effective cooperation cannot be constructed, or if an existing process of decision-making has been discredited and no replacement yet established, or if there is no crisis forcing a resolution of some issue, it may be hard for anyone to organize a policy process that could reach closure. This situation happens far more often than citizens would wish.[88]

Tactics III: Using Commissions

Managers have sometimes attempted to handle such situations by establishing a special commission. As Nancy Altman Lupu reports, President Reagan used this device to deal with such difficult issues as financing the social security system and deciding how to deploy the MX missile.[89] In both these cases, he charged a commission with a specific problem that had ripened to urgency. The commission typically included officials who were prominent in the debate and held offices whose combined authority was sufficient to resolve the matter authoritatively for the government. In effect, the commission became a back channel of communication, education, and negotiation for officials who had previously been at loggerheads. In other cases, President Reagan used commissions in a more familiar and cynical way: to ward off a difficult issue by studying it until the political pressure for a decision eased.[90]

Tactics IV: Making Policy Analysis Relevant

What makes for a good *substantive* decision is somewhat less clear. In principle, the standards are well known. The analysis should offer a clear definition of the problem, important factual information about its size and character, and accurate reasoning about consequences of choices.[91] These standards counsel extensive use of social science and policy analysis in decision-making. But the fact of the matter is that it has proven somewhat difficult for real decision-making processes to meet these expectations.[92]

Policy analysts sometimes fail to speak to the substantive concerns that policymakers have in particular decisions. The effects that analysts can and do make predictions about are not always the effects that policymakers are most concerned with.[93] Consequently, much policy analysis is viewed as irrelevant. Similarly, policy analysis tends to focus on alternatives that are difficult, sometimes impossible, for a real government to adopt and implement.[94] Although these features have the virtue of stretching the minds and imaginations of the politicians and public officials who implement policies, they contribute to the sense that policy analysis is irrelevant.

Thus, for example, Mahoney's substantive evaluation of the Park Plaza project as a plan that does not contain enough public value to be worth the price of invoking the powers of eminent domain is suspect in the eyes of politicians, and not simply because they are interested in earning votes rather than producing public value. The politicians cannot help noticing that most other people, particularly the people most affected by the project, seem to think that the project is valuable rather than dangerous. Moreover, they quickly realize that even a half-completed project would have some long-run value to Boston in terms of rebuilding its tax base and setting the stage for future development. Somehow, those values do not seem to be reckoned by Mahoney. Mahoney is on strong ground if he can show that the project is illegal. He is on much weaker ground if he claims the project is not substantively valuable, for at that stage he is substituting *his* judgment about what Boston should value, and the kinds of risks it should be willing to run, for the city's own judgment. The methods he relies on to support that claim are not really strong enough to stand against the claims of Boston's own deliberative processes.

Tactics V: Dealing with Uncertainty

The more fundamental difficulty in achieving substantive legitimacy is that there is always a wide gulf between the issues that must be considered in making a decision and the knowledge available to support accurate predictions of relevant consequences. Generally speaking, the science base to support particular decisions is always incomplete. And that leaves decision-makers confronting significant uncertainties—essentially gambles. Despite the power of economics to predict the behavior of economic actors, Mahoney cannot be sure that the developers will go on to develop the combat zone. And despite the power of modern epidemiology, Sencer cannot know for sure whether swine flu will strike. Indeed, he cannot even accurately gauge the odds.[95]

This uncertainty creates a problem for the relationship between managers and social scientists.[96] Managers would rather not gamble with the public's resources. That is why they hire policy analysts in the first place—to tell them with some precision what the consequences of various alternatives would be. Moreover, that is often what social scientists promise to do. Indeed, in their view, policymakers should not make a decision until it can be informed by the hard-won knowledge that science produces. At the start, then, both sides can agree that policy-making should be informed by social science.

Typically, however, social scientists cannot eliminate the uncertainty. There never seems to be enough recorded empirical experience to allow the scientists to predict the relevant consequences of policy choices with any degree of certainty. The result is that managers feel betrayed by the scientists. They feel even more so when circumstances compel them to go ahead and make a decision despite the uncertainty, and then scientists criticize them for acting irresponsibly on less than complete information.

There is an intellectually responsible way of dealing with uncertainty, of course.[97] The techniques call for analysts to estimate the relative likelihood of different consequences and evaluate possible choices against the several different possibilities (weighted by the probability that they will eventuate). That is the logic used to size up Sencer's performance in dealing with the threat of swine flu.

But this logic is a complex and unfamiliar one. Citizens, even policy-makers and social scientists, cannot seem to accept the idea that there could be a good decision that resulted in a bad outcome. Nor can they get used to the idea that the best decision facing an uncertain prospect will never look as good as one designed to deal with the problem as it ultimately occurred. No one (managers, social scientists, citizens) can give up the desire to eliminate uncertainty in the first place. They remain frustrated with the necessity of committing themselves to actions that cannot be optimized with respect to a certain scenario. They do not like not knowing what will happen or knowing that the resolution of the uncertainty can make well-considered choices look foolish. Finding a way to make good decisions that nonetheless produce bad outcomes acceptable in the political world remains a challenge to those who would design policy management processes.[98]

Diagnosis II: Policy Management Systems

So far, I have been considering the design of a process for handling a single policy choice made outside the boundaries of a manager's organization. Such situations crop up commonly in the public sector. Both Mahoney and Sencer face just such problems in the cases discussed here.

But public sector managers encounter policy decisions in a different context as well. As officials presiding over the ongoing operations of organizations with broad responsibilities, they face many policy decisions that must be resolved. Mahoney, for example, receives proposals from Springfield and Worcester as well as from Boston. He must consider questions of appointments to local zoning boards and of how best to allocate his resources between hiring his own staff and relying on outside consultants. He must also try to figure out how his interest in promoting public housing might be advanced by DCA's operations.

To deal with these intra-organizational decisions, managers seek to establish internal systems of decision-making.[99] They do so informally when they indicate to their subordinates what kinds of decisions they would like to review and which they will comfortably delegate; hold staff meetings to learn what issues are being faced by subordinate managers; develop staffs of personal assistants and planners to identify issues that the organization should be facing and to improve the quality of information available to them; and so on. However, many managers try to go beyond these informal approaches and develop systematic approaches to organizational decision-making. Such systems are often described as strategic planning systems, decision support systems, or policy management systems.[100]

Tactics I: Using the Budget Process

In many public organizations managers rely on the budget process as the principal device not only for dealing with the problem of resource allocation but also for providing a framework within which all the important decisions facing an organization may be systematically faced and resolved.[101] This approach reached its zenith in the days when program planning and budgeting, zero-based budgeting, and management by objectives were enshrined as key management systems within the agencies of the federal government.[102]

Gradually it became apparent, however, that these systems could not cope with the variety of policy decisions that public managers faced. Their fixed calendars made it difficult for them to take up issues that emerged out of context.[103] Because these systems forced managers to systematically review all aspects of their agencies' operations, managers could not focus attention on the much smaller number of areas in which critical investments had to be undertaken to position the organizations more effectively for the future.[104] Finally, there were many issues that did not involve financial resources but were nonetheless strategically important. The EPA and the National Highway Traffic Safety Administration, for example, both discovered that they needed special systems to monitor their regulatory decisions, in which they spent not money but the authority of the state.[105] Public sector managers needed strategic planning systems that were to some degree separated from the systematic demands of financial planning, management, and control.

Tactics II: Centralized Planning, Ad Hocracy, and Multiple Advocacy

Roger Porter delineates three different ways of organizing policy management systems.[106] One approach he describes as "centralized management."[107] In such systems the chief political executive is viewed not only as the client of the system but as the dominant decision-maker.[108] He or she is served by a large staff that digs out issues, assigns subordinate agencies to develop the relevant information, oversees the quality of that work, makes recommendations to the chief executive about what decision should be made, and monitors the implementation of those decisions. The systems are centralized in that they are designed to maximize the influence and control of the chief political executive.

A second approach he characterizes as "ad hocracy."[109] In this approach issues are taken up on a piecemeal basis as they arise. Special task forces, composed of those most able to deal with the issue, are created to manage each distinct issue. Often, no formal mechanisms exist to assure the quality of the information developed or to oversee the process of implementation.

A third approach he describes as "multiple advocacy."[110] In this approach the principal staff work is done by line managers whose responsibilities are affected by the particular decision under consideration. The central staff is kept small and plays the role of "honest broker," rather than quality controller or recommender, to make sure that all views have been heard and that an issue is ready for a decision.[111]

Although Porter is careful to describe the strengths and weaknesses of each of these approaches, he seems partial to multiple advocacy. There is enough "system" in the approach to ensure that important decisions will be identified and properly staffed, that chief political executives will be able to make the decisions if they so desire, and that the decisions will be well debated and reliably implemented. At the same time, the openness of the system increases the likelihood that interested and participating agencies will contribute what information they have and be more willing to implement the decisions that emerge than they typically are under the rigid, somewhat insulting controls associated with centralized management.

One question that Porter does not explicitly address is whether a particular system for decision-making is consistent across all decisions or not. For example, are there some issues that a basically centralized decision process could handle on an ad hoc or multiple advocacy basis? If so, who would make such a decision?

One way to treat this situation is to view policy management systems as a production process designed to produce well-made decisions. From this perspective, managers can ask whether they consider the policy management system as a kind of "production line," in which all decisions are made in about the same way, or whether it is more like a "job shop," in which each decision is handled through a unique process customized particularly for that decision.

The issue is significant, for it influences how much work must go into the design of a process for each decision and who will do it. If, on the one hand, managers think of the process as a production line, then the system can be designed at the beginning of a manager's tenure and used routinely thereafter. Indeed, it may be important to have consistent procedures to help teach participants in the process how decisions will be handled and to train them in the suitable orientations and techniques.

If, on the other hand, they think of the process as a job shop, then there is a continuing need for design. Indeed, managers would have to imagine having the honest broker go through the exercise of designing a process like that sketched above for each decision that the organization faces.

Tactics III: A "System of Systems"

In subsequent work, Richard Darman has analyzed policy management systems in terms of an abstract set of functions that such systems must be able to perform—not only with respect to each issue but also for the whole set of issues the organization faces.[112] His list of functions includes the following:

1. Issue identification/nomination
2. Issue weighting for importance and urgency
3. Political analysis of issues
4. Substantive analysis of issues
5. Process controls to guarantee "due process" to stakeholders
6. Relating issues to one another and to overall strategy
7. Issue tracking
8. Monitoring and evaluation of implementation

Like Porter, Darman, too, comes to reject highly centralized systems that depend on large, central staffs to make the decisions in favor of more decentralized, bottom-up systems. Indeed, like Porter, he insists on distinguishing the "quality control" function of a central staff from its "process control" function. Moreover, he emphasizes the preeminence of the process control function that guarantees "due process" to all those in the organization who have a stake in the issue. His reasons for preferring these open systems, like Porter's, have to do with the advantages that such decentralized systems have in attracting the cooperation of subordinate managers whose information and control over implementation make them valuable participants in any policy-making process.

He does make one possible exception to this rule, however. He recognizes that when an organization is considering a basic shift in its overall strategy, a system that relies heavily on the organization's current principal managers may fail to identify or appropriately resolve the central strategic issues.[113] In the short run at least, many of the current managers are likely to be opposed to a basic change in strategy.[114] Thus, the basic strategic decisions may have to be identified, resolved, and acted upon by a different group.[115]

One of Darman's other key insights is to see that an important function of policy management systems is not just to ensure that each decision is made well (including wide participation, good policy analysis, and political and bureaucratic analyses of feasibility), but also to recognize relations among different decisions so that the effect of one decision on another can be observed and taken into account.[116] He also notes that issues could be related to one another through such familiar linkages as the need to make budgetary trade-offs or to ensure effective operational coordination, and through less frequently considered linkages such as the impact of particular decisions on various constituencies and their tolerance for other decisions being considered, or the symbolic impact of a decision in enhancing or reducing the credibility of management's commitment to an overall strategy. One can easily imagine that if Governor Sargent had designed, developed, and operated such a system of policy-making, Mahoney might have better understood the relationship of Park Plaza to the pending highway decision and have been prepared to yield more gracefully to the governor's broader purposes.

Criticisms

These ideas about how best to manage the process of policy development are not without their critics. To many, the prescriptions seem too formal and mechanical. They are skeptical that structures and processes alone can resolve the deep conflicts that commonly underlie policy debates in a democracy.[117] They ask how a process alone could cause people who disagreed at the outset to reach an agreement. In seeking an explanation, they tend to look past and through the mechanical process to see how the basic material of *interests* was shaped within that process to produce an agreement. Such critics tend to see policy choices as a deal struck among the players and the policy process as creating a climate within which a particular deal was made. For these analysts, then, the fundamental paradigm for political management is multilateral negotiation.

NEGOTIATION

Negotiation becomes valuable when a manager wants something but needs someone else to help get it.[118] This is, in many ways, the paradigmatic problem of political management. Public managers want a policy adopted; but, given the system of divided powers, they cannot accomplish this goal unless they can persuade others to go along. At the outset, then, there seems to be much that negotiation analysis can teach political managers.

Despite the potential importance, negotiation analysis was long ignored as a potentially useful guide to political managers for essentially three reasons. First, the analysts who studied negotiations typically assumed, explicitly or implicitly, that individuals negotiated only for their material self-interest.[119] They referred to the paradigm of negotiation over the price of a house or a car.

Self-interest is hardly absent from politics; indeed it may undergird much that occurs there.[120] But many players active in politics claim to be, and in fact are, motivated by more altruistic goals such as the pursuit of public value—or at least their particular idea of public value. Some are interested in nothing more than a fair process of decision.[121] Moreover, most political managers want to believe that it is possible to change or refocus people's interests from their immediate self-interest to concerns with the public good or procedural fairness.[122] They even think that such appeals in the past have succeeded in producing political agreements.[123] But the traditional negotiation paradigm seemed to allow little room for such hopes. As long as these concerns were ignored, political managers had little interest in the negotiation framework. It did not seem to focus on their problem, nor recognize their tactics.

Second, negotiation analysts were far more interested in predicting and evaluating the outcomes of negotiations than in suggesting concrete tactics for negotiators. Of course, they had to make assumptions about the tactics of negotiators in order to make their predictions about how "negotiation games" would turn out. But the tactics they assumed abstracted from the concrete circumstances facing those who actually carried out negotiations. Since most political managers wanted advice on tactics, the focus of much traditional game theory on outcomes seemed beside the point.[124]

Third, the original analysts focused on relatively simple situations, in which two parties negotiated over one issue, where each party's stakes were easy to identify.[125] That seemed a long way from the complex situations that most political managers face. The paradigmatic situations involve multiple actors, each with complex interests, facing multiple issues where the outcomes of each choice are hard to evaluate.

Recently, however, negotiation analysts have turned their attention to far more realistic situations and focused on giving advice to negotiators.[126] As they have done so, their capacity to engage and help political managers has increased substantially. The key advances have come in three areas.

First, the new paradigms not only admit but encourage negotiators to recognize the variety of interests and goals that people could have.[127] This change is crucial to making negotiation analysis applicable to political management because much that is negotiated in this domain concerns the public interest, proper procedures for decision-making, and personal reputation and prestige rather than private material interests.[128] Thus, for example, the new framework for negotiation would recognize Mahoney's interests in conserving the power of eminent domain for situations where some real public value was being created, and his interest in establishing DCA as a power to contend with in local redevelopment. It would also recognize Sencer's interests in taking heroic measures to protect the public and thereby advance the cause of public health prevention.

Second, the new negotiation analysts emphasize that some of the most important moves in determining the outcome of a negotiation happen "away from the table."[129] *Framing* the negotiation (determining the context for the negotiation, the issues to be negotiated, and the parties to negotiate) is often much more important in determining the outcome than what happens "at the table." The traditional analysis assumed that the basic framework of the game was set, and thus abstracted from many important tactics that could be used by political managers. In contrast, contemporary negotiation analysts see moves away from the table—such as the development of managers' alternatives to negotiation,[130] or the addition of parties and issues to the negotiation—as devices that can be used to give advantages to the bargainers.[131]

The new negotiation analysts would recognize and approve of the Boston developers' moves to persuade the Massachusetts legislature to pass the home rule amendment that erases Mahoney's authority and, with that, his bargaining power. They might also appreciate Sencer's efforts to publicize the threat of swine flu and liken it to the 1918 epidemic, which, by increasing the chance that Congress would act independently, forced President Ford to confront the issue. Such moves away from the table significantly widen the tactics available to negotiators and make the advice offered by negotiation analysts much more relevant to political managers.

Third, the contemporary views of negotiation analysis add new insights into how agreements can be produced. Many emerge directly from expanding the sorts of interests that negotiators could have. If negotiators care about public value, processes of decision-making, and reputations, then these interests could become material for producing agreements where none seemed possible. Even more significant, the analysts note that differences in negotiators' views of the world can sometimes be used to make deals that would not be possible if they shared the same view.[132] Jack Sprat and his wife, for example, found it possible to dovetail their differences in a very satisfactory food-sharing agreement.

Thus, the new negotiation analysts offer a revised and potentially useful way of approaching the problem of political management. To capture the flavor of their approach, let us look at how they recommend analyzing negotiating situations and what sorts of tactics they propose to political managers.

Diagnosis I: Issues

Negotiators begin their diagnosis the way entrepreneurial advocates start their calculations: with the identification of an issue and interests that could form the basis for a negotiation. By definition, such an issue is one where two or more agents can make themselves better off in their own terms by reaching an agreement than they could without the agreement.[133]

Take the issue created between Miles Mahoney and the Boston Redevelopment Authority by the BRA's need for Mahoney to approve its proposed plan. While Mahoney is reluctant to grant approval for the current plan, he would presumably not be adverse to approving a plan that included a commitment to develop the combat zone. That might not be impossible from the perspective of the developers.

An issue for negotiation exists, then, when there is some value to be created by reaching a joint agreement. If this were not true, if no interdependence existed among the players, or if each could do better alone, there would be no basis for negotiation.

Diagnosis II: Interests

The analysis then proceeds by identifying the *interests* the players have in a given issue.[134] In looking at the BRA's interests, Mahoney could calculate that the agency would favor increasing the tax base of the city by encouraging development, that it has bureaucratic and organizational interests in encouraging as much development as possible, that the particular plan is one that would help the City of Boston, that even some small commitment to the development of the combat zone is better than nothing, and that, in any case, the project is cheap in any currency that matters to the BRA.

In looking at his own interests, Mahoney might conclude that he is interested in establishing the precedent that DCA will be an influential player in local redevelopment projects and in using what leverage he has to increase the developers' commitment to developing the combat zone. Mahoney might also want to promote his reputation for competence and integrity in the Sargent administration. It is in terms of these interests that the value of any particular resolution of the Park Plaza controversy will be evaluated, and it is in these terms that the resolutions can be reconfigured to provide more or less of a sweetener to one party or the other.

Diagnosis III: The Best Alternative to a Negotiated Agreement

In the third step, negotiators assess each party's "best alternative to a negotiated agreement," or BATNA.[135] The BATNA establishes the minimum amount that each party must get out of the negotiation to be willing to participate in the negotiated agreement. If the agreement does not do at least as well for each of the interested parties as they can do without negotiating, they will walk away from the table.

As noted above, at the outset of their negotiations Mahoney has relatively little reason to negotiate because he thinks his best alternative to a negotiated agreement with the BRA is simply to reject the Park Plaza project. He thinks the law, his own expertise, the political backing of the governor, and his own moral vision will allow him to claim the value of stopping the project. Similarly, the developers have little reason to negotiate with Mahoney because they think the political support of the mayor and the labor unions will be enough to "roll" Mahoney. Later in the negotiations, once the developers have succeeded in enlisting the governor's support, they have even less reason to negotiate, because they can be even more sure that they will get what they want without having to negotiate. Either the governor or the legislature will compel Mahoney to give in.

Tactics I: "Hard" versus "Soft" Bargaining

Given that there is an issue to be negotiated, and that the parties to the negotiation have interests that could be advanced by reaching agreement, a political manager then must think about tactics for the negotiation. At this point, one comes to a remarkable schism in the world.[136] On one side are those who recommend hard-nosed bargaining tactics such as concealing one's interests, making irrevocable commitments to positions that claim most of the potential advantages of the agreement for one party and leave just enough on the table to induce the other to go along, and doing everything one can to weaken the other person's BATNA.[137] On the other side are those who recommend much softer and more open tactics such as candidly indicating one's interests, proposing several different ways of resolving the issue, trying to find some shared notion of justice or fairness in the negotiation that could provide the basis for a principled settlement, and so on.[138] The contrast in recommended bargaining tactics is so stark that one suspects that both approaches cannot be recommended—that one must opt for one or the other.

David Lax and James Sebenius argue, however, that these different prescriptions arise from a fundamental dilemma.[139] They observe that all negotiations are always and inevitably both about *creating* value through joint action and *claiming* value for each party, since all proposals and all agreements will apportion the value created by joint action as well as create the conditions for producing it. When focusing on the value-creating aspects of negotiation, one naturally sees cooperative joint efforts that make everyone better off. When focusing on the value-claiming aspects of negotiation, one naturally thinks in terms of much more aggressive tactics to ensure that one will get at least one's fair share, and perhaps more. Lax and Sebenius find no solution to this dilemma. The only thing to be done is for each party in the negotiation to keep both aspects of the problem in mind in responding to the tactics and attitudes of the other players.[140]

Note that the negotiation over the future of the Park Plaza project ensued in a hard-nosed, value-claiming mode. By consulting the governor at the outset, and gaining his support for rejecting the Park Plaza plan, Mahoney enormously strengthened his bargaining position vis-à-vis the City of Boston. From that position, Mahoney thought it would be possible to prevent the city from going ahead on any terms unacceptable to him. And, since he preferred no progress on Park Plaza to a proposal that did not include a strong commitment on the combat zone, he refused to compromise.

For their part, the developers, in league with the City of Boston, immediately began doing the political work necessary to undercut Mahoney's position. They lobbied the legislature to pass the home rule amendment. Since they thought (correctly) that it would ultimately pass, they too had little reason to compromise. As a result, the discussions commissioned by the governor made little progress. Indeed, these tactics illustrate two other key ideas about negotiating that have moved to the center of the new literature.

Tactics II: Adding Issues and Players

First, political managers may be able to increase the value created, or claim more of it, or reach an agreement with greater ease, if they change the game by adding new issues or new players.[141] This insight resembles the technique of advocacy associated with changing the frame of the decision or widening the scope of conflict. By changing the issue from a technical consideration of whether the proposed Park Plaza project did or did not meet the statutory criteria for approval to an issue of home rule, and by bringing in the legislature to the debate, the City of Boston dramatically increased its ability to negotiate for the policy decision its representatives preferred.

Tactics III: Influencing Alternatives to Negotiation

Second, political managers can position themselves to claim more of the potential value if they improve their own BATNA and weaken their opponent's.[142] Mahoney scores an early tactical advantage in negotiating for an improved version of the Park Plaza plan when he unexpectedly rejects the proposal with the backing of the governor. At this stage, his BATNA is simply to reject the project and establish the precedent that he is a power to be reckoned with.

But he soon suffers a significant loss when representatives of the city manage to persuade nearly everyone else that Mahoney's decision is arbitrary and counter to the legitimate interests of those most affected by the project. At that stage, the developers' BATNA is to wait for Mahoney to approve the plan or be fired, and Mahoney seems powerless to escape this position.

Criticisms

The negotiation paradigm, while providing many useful insights and helpful guidance, provokes criticism. Critics commonly charge that it, like the advocacy approach, takes too individualistic and cynical a view about the process of reaching collective decisions. Such criticisms have been muted to some degree by the recognition that idealistic aims, such as serving the public's interest or participating effectively in a fair and competent decision-making process, could be interests that negotiators could seek to advance in their negotiating activity.

But what still rankles is the individual basis of the analysis. It is as though each person decides alone what is in his or her or even society's interest without reference to what others think. That perspective may be appropriate when looking at each individual as the unit of analysis and, in effect, counting individual votes. What this perspective leaves out is the possibility that social collisions among people trying to reach collective judgments might actually shape individuals' views of what is important and worth doing. They do not just bring social rather than individual interests to the forefront, or simply make them more important in the ultimate choices; these collisions might actually change what people think is important for themselves and for the society.[143] In short, critics claim that people might be made to think and act like *citizens* rather than self-interested clients of policy decisions, or people with odd and idiosyncratic notions of public value.[144] Those interested in exploiting this set of ideas tend to look to the ideas of "public deliberation," or "social learning," or "leadership" for guidance in political management.

PUBLIC DELIBERATION, SOCIAL LEARNING, AND LEADERSHIP

So far, the techniques of political management have been narrowly focused. They have made influencing formal policy decisions the main objective of political management. Consequently, they have focused attention on the relatively small number of people in positions of formal authority. The techniques have offered advice on how to facilitate decision-making processes in some particular way—to make it more likely that managers' preferred positions will be adopted, or that high-quality decisions will be produced, or that negotiated settlements will result.

In contrast, a fourth approach to political management seeks a wider compass: one that reaches well beyond those now in positions of authority.[145] Moreover, instead of assuming that individuals' interests and views about public value are fixed, it assumes that they can be changed through social interaction. Finally, it allows the public as a whole to act on problems directly, without the mediation of government, and political managers to be as concerned with accomplishing this end as with organizing the decision-making processes of government.

Indeed, this fourth approach considers government's role as authoritative policymaker a potential problem rather than a solution to many public problems. In this view government becomes a way for citizens to avoid making the changes in their perspectives and actions that are required to solve important collective problems.[146] Instead of encouraging conflicting groups to reach their own accommodations, government policy has fostered reliance on the government to arbitrate disputes. Instead of encouraging thousands of individuals to work on collective problems, government has taken all the responsibility for solving the problems—even when it has no powerful solutions.[147]

This approach offers the alternative, then, of using government authority not to make public policy decisions but instead to create environments in which the citizens who face collective problems can decide together what they would like to do.[148] In this world, government leadership changes from providing authoritative solutions to collective problems to nominating issues for public attention and creating the environment within which citizens can act on their own.[149] Although this approach has a unified theme, it can be most usefully discussed in two parts: one focused on using public deliberation to improve public policy-making, the other focused on helping citizens contribute to the solution of public problems by facilitating their adaptation to "problematic realities" through a particular kind of leadership.[150]

Diagnosis I: Public Deliberation

The concept of "public deliberation" holds that citizens can and should be asked to confront policy questions affecting them directly, and that they should do so in a forum in which opposing interests can also be heard.[151] Such forums encourage people to face policy problems not as individuals or clients with particular interests and odd ideas of the public interest, but instead as citizens who can incorporate the views of other citizens in their own "civic discovery" of what constitutes public value.[152]

In this conception the ordered policy deliberations of the government often get in the way of effective policy-making because they allow citizens to petition the government to adopt their own views of public policy wholesale. That, in turn, allows individual citizens to avoid confronting one another and, through that experience, learning how the problem appears to other contending parties. In short, citizens are insulated from the need to learn about the interests and perceptions of other citizens.

This process inevitably results in a decision that satisfies no one except the government officials who made the decision. They are the only ones who were forced to integrate and synthesize the conflicting claims. They were the only ones who had to take the views of the contending parties seriously and, therefore, to learn the full set of values at stake in the decision.

If government officials had gotten out of the way, the argument goes, and let the opposing forces confront one another directly, perhaps each side might have learned to identify a little more closely with the concerns of the others and to understand the ultimate decision more sympathetically than they otherwise would. They might even have been able to invent a solution to the problem superior to any the government officials could design.

This is an attractive idea, but it smacks of utopianism. After all, it seems as likely that contending parties would come to blows, become locked in a stalemate, or prevail by bullying the others, as that they could produce a creative resolution of their conflict. Indeed, it is precisely to avoid such outcomes that the authority to decide public policy was given to the government in the first place. If people could reach agreements without governmental authority, there would be no need for government. And, for public managers charged with the responsibility for deciding on public policy, it often feels irresponsible to give up their control to an unpredictable process. Both Mahoney and Sencer would feel derelict in their duty if they did not accept the responsibility for deciding, respectively, to resist Park Plaza and accelerate the nation's response to swine flu. That is what they are paid to do.

Yet those advancing public deliberation have a point. It may be that for many of the most intractable and difficult problems facing the government, there is no alternative but to turn the issue over to the contending parties for a resolution. Interestingly, William Ruckelshaus reached precisely this conclusion in dealing with an intractable environmental dispute during his second stint as administrator of the Environmental Protection Agency.[153]

Faced with a cruel choice of shutting down an Asarco smelting plant in Tacoma, Washington, that was emitting hazardous wastes in the air or leaving it in operation to provide jobs for a large number of local citizens, Ruckelshaus decided that he, alone, as a public official, could not make the decision on any technical or legal grounds. Instead, he created a process by which the citizens themselves could debate the issue and reach an agreement.

Ultimately, the citizens decided to leave the plant in operation and accept the environmental risk. Although some in the community were disappointed and continued to fear the health threat represented by the Asarco emissions, they understood more fully than they otherwise would why they were exposing themselves to this health risk: namely, to protect the jobs of others in the town.

According to David Kirp, these techniques have also proved useful in managing the hot controversies that have erupted in several communities facing the question of whether children infected with the AIDS virus would be allowed to attend school.[154]

One can also imagine how this concept of "public deliberation" might have been used by Mahoney and Sencer to deal more effectively with the problems they faced. Instead of spending eight months on fruitless negotiations with the BRA over the future of Park Plaza, Mahoney could have organized public hearings on the plan. Had he done so, he might have discovered earlier how much local support existed for the project and how few wanted to turn it down. He might also have been able to mobilize some public concern for dealing more effectively with the combat zone through this project, and that concern, in turn, might have swayed the developers. As is always the case, opening a process to wide discussion often has quite unpredictable results, but it seems clear in this case that such a move might have improved Mahoney's political intelligence and perhaps broadened his options.

Similarly, instead of pressuring the government to make a full-scale commitment to immunizing the nation against the threat of swine flu based on his own technical judgment, Sencer might have organized an ongoing process of deliberation that would include epidemiologists, the vaccine manufacturers, public health physicians, private physicians, and ordinary citizens. Their task would have been to monitor the country's efforts to deal with swine flu and to raise warnings and considerations that were not particularly salient in the minds of the heroes attempting to save the country from the threat.

Had he done this, Sencer might have been forced to acknowledge much earlier than he did the truth that not everyone could be vaccinated. Consequently, he might have taken a closer look at the virtues of the hedged solution as well as the problems. Similarly, if the issue had been left open, the lack of evidence that the swine flu was spreading might have been kept more prominently in view. That, too, might have counseled the wisdom of a more hedged response. For their part, the citizens and other officials might have learned that it was wise public policy to be prepared to meet the epidemic head on even if it did not materialize. In short, the reality that society and government had to face might have stayed in focus.

Diagnosis II: Social Learning and Leadership

The ideas associated with social learning are similar in spirit to the ideas associated with public deliberation.[155] They both focus a political manager's attention on a wide group of people outside the boundaries of the formal structures of government who are interested in, affected by, and capable of responding to the problems that the government is trying to solve. They both recognize the potential informational value of encouraging deliberation among those affected by governmental action. And they both view the tendency of citizens to give problems to the government to solve as problematic because it shuts off individual learning and adaptation.

Still, the approaches differ slightly. For one thing, ideas associated with social learning and leadership are as concerned with mobilizing citizens to act on their own as with organizing them to give advice or reach collective agreements. In short, they aim to mobilize citizens for action—to move right into the implementation of both collective and individual solutions.[156]

Furthermore, social learning and leadership focus more attention on how actions by individuals exercising leadership can invent solutions and mobilize action. This aspect may be particularly important when the "solution" to a public policy problem requires many individuals to invent their own adaptations to the problematic realities they face—including a recognition that they can no longer be insulated from the problems by powerful others.

Indeed, the most important insights associated with the concept of social learning and leadership stem from two important observations about public policy-making in democratic systems. First, many public policy problems cannot necessarily be solved by senior public officials working out a technically competent and politically acceptable conclusion.[157] Many problems can be solved only by ordinary citizens learning to adjust or devising their own solutions. Second, this exceedingly unpleasant reality is often resisted by citizens who would like the government to solve problems for them.[158]

Thus, viewed from the perspective of social learning, political management must find ways for the government to refrain from taking action and must shift the burden of taking action onto others. Since both sorts of actions by government are often experienced by citizens as great losses, the issue often becomes one of encouraging society to face up to a problematic reality.[159]

Tactics: Managing the Pace of Learning

One key technique associated with managing social adaptation is managing the pace of learning.[160] On the one hand, if the government forces citizens to face the problem too rapidly, and with too little assistance, then the citizens will become angry and the government discredited. They will turn to any official who promises some solution rather than none. On the other hand, if the government proceeds too slowly, then the society will not ready itself to deal adequately with the problem it faces. In both cases, moreover, public officials can never quite be sure that they have accurately identified the problem they are trying to solve.

A health scare that occurred in Woburn, Massachusetts, illustrates these abstract ideas.[161] As part of its routine statistical reporting, the Massachusetts Department of Public Health (DPH) produced data indicating that Woburn, a small town north of Boston, had unusually high rates of liver cancer and leukemia among children. Somewhat coincidentally, DPH also reported that some of the state's most dangerous toxic waste dumps were located in Woburn.

The two reports, coming close together, alarmed the town. Woburn's citizens reasonably worried that their health had been jeopardized by the toxic waste sites. They wanted something done about the situation. In response, DPH conducted a sophisticated set of studies to determine whether the town's elevated rates of cancer were truly significant and whether they could be traced in any way to contaminated water and toxic waste dumps. The answers, based on the best scientific evidence produced, were negative: the elevated cancer rate fell within the normal range of variation, and no link could be found between the cancers and the toxic waste sites. Therefore, DPH deemed government action unnecessary.

When this conclusion was announced, the town rejected it out of hand. Indeed, citizens' demands for governmental action to clean up the sites and to provide treatment for the cancer patients increased in stridency. Although the government held to its conclusions and the uproar eventually subsided, a legacy of suspicion and bitterness remained.

Those who look at political problems from the perspective of social learning would see in this case many predictable problems. They would begin their analysis with the observation that the citizens of Woburn faced a problematic reality: namely, that they seemed to be exposed to an elevated risk of cancer. They responded to the problem as people typically do: first with denial, then with a demand that someone do something to reduce the threat or alleviate the condition.

An effective governmental response would have to begin by acknowledging the citizens' predicament, their loss of security. If the government does not acknowledge that loss, its response will be discredited. Yet the government's response must also be designed to help the community learn that the problem is not as severe as it first appears, and that the government's response to that problem will be limited. In a situation in which the community is already frightened and is looking to the government for help, the government's position will come as yet another piece of bad news. The conclusion that the community is not particularly at risk should be good news, but in this context it will be viewed an excuse for the government to escape responsibility. The conclusion that the government will do little is always bad news, since it would be more valuable to citizens if government would clean up the dumps and treat those with cancer.

The government, then, must help the citizens of Woburn learn that the reality as best it can be ascertained is that they are not particularly vulnerable and hence the government will do little to help them. Clearly, simply announcing the scientific conclusions is an ineffective political management strategy. That forces people to learn much too fast from media they do not trust.

A better strategy would design a process to pace their learning. Such a process would begin by acknowledging the citizens' position and presenting information known about the rates of cancer and the assumed links to the toxic dump sites. Particular channels of communication that had credibility would have to be engaged for giving the scientific information. Some graphic illustrations of the scientist's confidence in their findings would have to be developed, along with demonstrations that other citizens in Woburn who were particularly concerned about the problem found their conclusions convincing.

Instead of simply assuming that the citizens of Woburn could absorb the government's information through a technical publication presented at a news conference, an advocate of this learning and leadership approach would design a more sustained and sophisticated process of teaching citizens what the government thought it knew about the problem. If the public officials had thought in terms of managing the pace of social learning, they might have emerged from the Woburn controversy with the same substantive result, but with the reputation of government and the Public Health Department enhanced rather than eroded.

PUBLIC SECTOR MARKETING AND STRATEGIC COMMUNICATION

The concept of social learning and the Woburn case brings us to the last frame within which a public sector manager might view the problem of political management. This frame has been labeled "public sector marketing" or "strategic communication."[162] What is strategic in the communication is not that it is designed to be manipulative, but instead that it is designed to advance particular policies or organizational strategies by making them comprehensible and by enlisting the support and cooperation of those who must work together to produce the intended result.

At the outset, one cannot but feel a deep suspicion about the role that marketing and persuasion should play in public sector management. To talk of such things recalls deep anxieties about the power of government propaganda.[163] The terms seem to place in the hands of government officials the tools to defeat proper accountability and conceal their failures, or to control the private lives of individual citizens. From this perspective, government officials should not be in the business of trying to persuade anyone of anything. They should simply report what they have done, and what is known about problems that individuals face, and let the citizens and their representatives draw their own conclusions. Anything else shows disrespect for representative government and the capabilities of citizens, and risks an all-too powerful government.

It is hard not to sympathize with those who express these concerns. But it also seems clear that they misunderstand the basic concepts of marketing; they fail to acknowledge the importance of strategic communication in helping government become responsive to citizens' aspirations and succeed in achieving those complex goals.

Diagnosis I: Marketing as Increased Accountability to Customers

Many in the public sector think that private sector marketing makes customers want to buy a bad product by making false claims about its virtues or by linking the product to things that customers like but are largely irrelevant to the product. For example, toothpaste is sold by persuading people that it will prevent cavities (which is not necessarily true) and that it will make them happy and sexy (which is, in the minds of many, both false and irrelevant to the real nature of the product).

This common perspective ignores, however, the key insight in modern marketing: that producers should start by finding out what attributes of products might be of interest to consumers.[164] A successful company is not one that begins with an unattractive product and then uses marketing techniques to sell it. A successful company uses marketing techniques such as focus groups, surveys, and so on to discover what particular features consumers desire in a product. That way, the company can design a product that fits consumers' desires. In this sense, marketing becomes a way of tapping the current of consumer desires and giving it force in the process of product design and manufacturing.

Taking this concept into the public sector, one might say that the task of public sector marketers is to find out what features of governmental performance are judged to be relevant and important by those who pay for the organization's product: namely, the citizens and their political representatives. As observed in Chapter 2, what such groups "consume" is some aggregate properties of the organization's operations. Thus, in marketing their organizations to the elected overseers, public managers would first have to find out what those overseers wanted and expected of the organization and then have to try to produce it. That would enhance rather than reduce accountability.

Similarly, in recent years, we have seen major investments made in the government's efforts to survey its "clients" to determine their satisfaction with the government's operations. Recreation departments, schools, even police departments are beginning to conduct surveys and focus groups to learn directly what citizens think about the services they receive.[165] This, too, increases rather than decreases the accountability of public sector managers to the public, but this time to clients rather than to citizens and their representatives.

Diagnosis II: Marketing as Social Mobilization

The argument that public sector managers should not give close attention to the issue of how their communication with citizens, overseers, and clients is designed fails to take account of the importance of such communication in helping government organizations achieve their collectively established objectives.[166] The case of Ira Jackson, who became commissioner of the Massachusetts Department of Revenue, provides a good illustration of this point.[167]

Jackson considered his public responsibility collecting taxes fairly and efficiently. His ability to accomplish that mission was based on two critical factors: first, the perception the citizens of Massachusetts had of the determination, competence, and fairness his organization showed in imposing tax liabilities on citizens; and second, the ease with which reasonably well motivated taxpayers could discover and record their tax liabilities. Both represented problems of public sector marketing even though what was being marketed was an *obligation* rather than a product or service.

With respect to the first objective, he had to find a way to project an image of a tough, vigorous, but fair tax collector to create the climate in which citizens would feel motivated and obliged to pay their taxes. With respect to the second, he had to find a way to make it easy for citizens to pay their taxes.

He accomplished the first through a series of highly visible actions designed to persuade the citizens of Massachusetts that they faced an imaginative and aggressive tax collector whom even the rich and powerful had to pay. In front of television cameras, he seized yachts owned by people who had outstanding tax liabilities.[168] He also tried to collect taxes from the members of visiting professional athletic teams who performed some of their work in Massachusetts.[169] Perhaps most important, he experimented with a widely publicized amnesty period in which he promised not to prosecute those who had not filed tax returns in the past if they would come forward and file within the amnesty period.[170] Such actions soon created a public perception that the Department of Revenue was an organization to be taken seriously.

With respect to the second objective, he redesigned the forms so that they were easier to read and fill out, mailed the returns out earlier, and staffed taxpayer information offices with more responsive and knowledgeable officials.[171] He also promised to send refunds to those who filed early, within three weeks of receiving the return.

The combination of these actions, all conceived as enhancing the effectiveness of the communication among the agency, its overseers, and its clients, helped Jackson achieve his socially mandated goal: to collect taxes less expensively and more fairly than the commissioners who had come before. The reason that strategic communication was so important in this case is precisely that so much of the task of collecting taxes lay beyond the control of Jackson's own organization. It lay, instead, in the motivations and capabilities of the commonwealth's citizens. And the only way they could be reached was through the images of the organization that appeared in the mass media and through the character of the correspondence and other individual transactions with the organization. Obviously, these techniques would be equally important to Sencer's efforts to mobilize citizens to immunize themselves against swine flu.

Criticisms

No doubt, there remains an important danger associated with encouraging public officials to become more effective communicators. There is always the risk that they will be able to deceive their overseers and patronize citizens. But there are also some advantages in having public sector managers become marketers and communicators. The new role might well make them more rather than less responsive to the expectations and demands of their overseers, just as marketing has made private companies more responsive to their customers. It might also provide them with the means of mobilizing the operational assistance they so often need to accomplish their goals. A method better than discouraging public sector managers from developing and using these skills, then, might be increasing the capacity of overseers to ensure that the information being communicated is candid, accurate, and consistent with the overall mission of the organization rather than deceptive, false, and manipulative.

HELPING TO DEFINE
AND PRODUCE PUBLIC VALUE

To review, political management is a key function that public sector managers must perform to be effective in their jobs on behalf of the broader society. But it is also a difficult and ethically sensitive part of their job. What makes political management necessary is that public managers share responsibility with other officials, and with citizens, for deciding what would be valuable to produce with public resources and for actually producing what they agreed would be valuable to produce. They must interact with people over whom they have no direct authority to determine the ends and organize the means of their enterprises.

Yet, in engaging in political management, they must walk a fine line between, on the one hand, exercising too little influence over the judgments of overseers and the actions of coproducers to be effective in achieving attractive public purposes and, on the other, exercising so much authority that they risk the quality of democratic governance and the freedom of the citizens.

Techniques exist to help managers walk this fine line. But they are far from foolproof as practical guides and hardly immune to powerful normative critiques. No doubt, in the future, the techniques of advocacy, policy management, negotiation, public deliberation, social learning, and public sector marketing will grow through continued refinement and development.

What is important for the moment is that we have them in our sights as possible answers to the question of what public managers can do to legitimate their enterprises and to mobilize those beyond the boundaries of their authority to help them achieve their mandated objectives. These are some of the most difficult and challenging of the public manager's tasks. Indeed, they may be the tasks that are unique to public sector management.

PART III

DELIVERING PUBLIC VALUE

CHAPTER 6

REENGINEERING PUBLIC SECTOR PRODUCTION: THE FUNCTION OF OPERATIONAL MANAGEMENT

In seeking public value, we come finally to what many believe is the essence of management: the self-conscious, skilled deployment of legal, financial, material, and human assets to produce concrete results. It is one thing for managers to have visions, and still another for them to mobilize a flow of resources to their enterprises. But the heart of management lies in *delivering* the envisioned value. That is what management (as opposed to leadership or entrepreneurship) is all about.[1] To see the challenges of operational management clearly and concretely, consider the daunting circumstances that Harry Spence and Lee Brown confronted when they took over (respectively) the Boston Housing Authority and the Houston Police Department.

HARRY SPENCE AND THE BOSTON HOUSING AUTHORITY

In July 1979 Massachusetts Superior Court Judge Paul Garrity, frustrated beyond endurance by the inability of the Boston Housing Authority to meet the obligations it had assumed under a negotiated settlement to a class action suit brought by its tenants, took an unprecedented step: he ordered the Boston Housing Authority (BHA) into receivership.[2] In justifying the unusual step, the judge declared that the BHA board's "alleged gross mismanagement, nonfeasance, incompetence, and irresponsibility have been shown to exist beyond any question."[3] In effect, Garrity declared the BHA bankrupt.[4]

Predictably, the BHA board challenged this decision. But its challenge only delayed the inevitable result. Six months later, following the Massachusetts Supreme Court's decision to uphold his ruling, Garrity suspended the BHA board and appointed Harry Spence as the court's "receiver." Spence's task, according to the judge, was to "take any and all actions necessary, desirable, and appropriate" to bring the BHA's housing units into compliance with the state sanitary code and other applicable federal, state, and local housing regulations.[5]

The Task

Spence's task was formidable. The authority owned and operated 68 developments consisting of 17,000 housing units and 60,000 people—almost 10 percent of the city's population. Much of this formerly valuable housing stock lay in shocking disrepair. A *Boston Magazine* reporter sketched a riveting portrait of one project's once proud "village green": "Separating two rows of three-story brick buildings, the 'green' is a wholly inhospitable, desiccated plain of concrete, dust, and broken glass . . . No banner has flown from the rusted flagpole in at least a decade. The two visitors pass by the remnants of a playground swing; with the seats all gone and one of the legs buckled, the whole structure looks like some wounded, staggering animal."[6]

Given the dilapidated state of the BHA's projects, it was hardly surprising that many vacancies existed. In 1980 the average vacancy rate for the family housing projects reached 28 percent. In the most troubled projects—Mission Hill and Fidelis Way—the vacancy rate exceeded 40 percent. And in Columbia Point—a sprawling development of over 1,500 units in 39 buildings—the vacancy rate had climbed to 70 percent.

More and more of those left stranded in the decaying projects were poor. In 1953 the BHA reported that only 4 percent of its families were "on relief." By 1975 the number of families with no wage earners had risen to nearly 80 percent. In 1980 tenant incomes ranged from about $3,700 to $6,400 per year—the lowest in any public housing in the country.

Increasingly, single-parent families—most headed by women—dominated among BHA tenants. In 1969 single-parent households occupied less than half the units in the family projects. By 1978 the fraction had increased to more than four-fifths. One important result was weakened adult supervision of minors. In Mission Hill, for example, more than 60 percent of the population consisted of minors. Spence described the consequences: "If you have an entryway with nine families—all female-headed—you have a large problem with male teenagers. They're . . . brutal. That's why they fight all the wars in the world. They pick these hall-ways out because there's no one there who can scare them out."[7]

Financial Resources

The BHA needed substantial financial resources to simultaneously maintain the deteriorating buildings and care for the increasingly desperate people. Unfortunately, few were available.

The U.S. Department of Housing and Urban Development (HUD) provided about $20 million annually to subsidize the BHA's operations. This amount was dictated by a formula estimating how much it should cost a well-managed housing authority to operate projects of the style, vintage, and construction of those managed by the BHA. State government contributed another $7 million, and the BHA collected an additional $7 million from its tenants in rental income.

Unfortunately, annual operating costs were such that at the time Spence took office, the BHA faced a $5 million deficit. This deficit had forced the BHA to delay much-needed repairs and to trim other services to tenants. As a result, the buildings deteriorated, vacancies increased, and rental income fell—the familiar downward spiral that leads private real estate ventures to bankruptcy.

Unexpectedly, some funds were available to break this vicious cycle. In 1969 HUD had initiated a "modernization" program to provide funds to qualified public housing projects for specific renovation projects. Each year the BHA had applied for these funds. Each year it received some. Because the BHA was so badly managed, however, it had failed to spend the money. The result was that it had accumulated a $30 million pot of unspent money.

Conceivably, rental income could also be increased. Current tenants owed $1.4 million in uncollected rents. Improved collections could produce a short-run windfall and, if sustained, guarantee continuing higher revenues into the future. Additional rental income could also be realized by increasing the number of higher-income, working people living in the projects.

This potential revenue source was limited by two important rules, however. The first required the BHA to rent only to those people whose incomes were less than 80 percent of the area's median income. The second prohibited the BHA from charging tenants more than 25 percent of their annual income in rents.

These rules embodied a particular view of what sort of public value the agency was to produce: they ensured that the BHA's publicly subsidized housing was delivered to Boston's poorest citizens and, further, that the rents the BHA charged would not be unduly burdensome. To citizens and overseers who thought the agency contributed the most value by being a good and generous landlord to Boston's poorest residents, these rules were fundamental to ensuring that it achieved its purpose. To citizens and overseers who sought to ensure the BHA's continued financial viability, however, and who were willing to sacrifice some of the benefits to the poorest of the poor for achieving this somewhat different purpose, the rules were an unfortunate obstacle. Indeed, they were forcing the BHA down a path toward ruin.

The Organization: Its Managers, Structure, and Systems

To act on the problems, Spence needed a well-structured, highly motivated, operationally focused enterprise. Unfortunately, the BHA was anything but. The long period of litigation leading to Spence's appointment had produced deep divisions at the top and widespread demoralization at the bottom of the organization.

THE MANAGEMENT TEAM

For two years prior to Spence's appointment, the BHA's operations had been overseen by Robert Whittlesey, a "special master" appointed by the court to monitor the agency's compliance with a consent decree negotiated between the tenants and the BHA administration. To help him with his work, a special staff had been created: the Division of Planning, Development, and Modernization.

Partly as a consequence, the old management structure of the organization had atrophied. The positions of administrator and deputy administrator had been vacant since October 1977. Kevin Feeley, the assistant administrator for administration had served (reluctantly) as acting administrator.

Relations between the two staffs were far from cordial. The newcomers in staff positions tended to view the old-timers in line positions as corrupt and incompetent—unable to make plans, to account for their actions, or to produce results. For their part, the old-timers viewed the newcomers as neophytes who, while refusing to take responsibility for managing the organization, had plenty of criticisms for those who did. They wrote plans and filed reports, but they never interviewed a client or fixed broken plumbing.

ORGANIZATIONAL STRUCTURE

Beneath the top levels, the problems were graver still. About 700 people worked for the BHA. They were distributed across three major divisions and twelve sections. (Figure 6.1 presents an organizational chart.) About 200 worked in administrative positions in the new Division of Planning, Development, and Modernization or the old Division of Administration. They made plans or kept accounts. The remaining 500 worked for the Division of Operations. They admitted tenants, collected rents, and fixed buildings.

The Division of Operations divided its work by function and program. One unit was responsible for maintenance; another for security; a third for occupancy (including tenant selection); and a fourth for tenant services. In addition, the division employed 30 people as project managers. Their task was "to ensure the efficient operation and management" of one or more particular housing projects.

Once, the project managers had been all-powerful. They had determined who would be allowed to live in the projects and the priority given to requests for repairs. Gradually, however, their functions had been stripped away and placed in specialized, central offices. The aim had been to achieve economies of scale and to ensure greater consistency in the treatment of residents in the different projects. In 1972 maintenance efforts had been centralized. Later, the project managers lost direct control over rent collection, tenant selection, and transfers. As the functions were centralized, the power of the project managers to shape life in the individual projects drained away. With the loss of power went any sense of responsibility. By the time Spence took office, their job had shrunk to dunning delinquent rent payers.

POLICIES AND PROCEDURES

Despite the centralization of maintenance, tenant selection, and security functions, performance remained poor, at least partly because of poor design of the policies and procedures that guided work in these domains.

Maintenance, in particular, had long been a quagmire. The BHA employed about 300 skilled craftspeople and laborers to maintain buildings and grounds. Much of their work was routine. In addition, maintenance crews dealt with 100,000 repair orders each year. Responses to these were slow: it took crews more than ten days to respond to emergencies; more than three weeks to deal with nonemergencies.

Work rules established and enforced by a powerful union—the Building and Construction Trades Council— handicapped efforts to increase productivity. These rules made rigid distinctions among different kinds

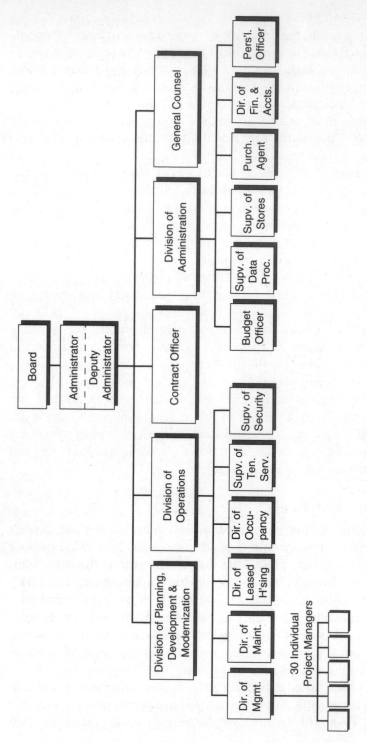

Figure 6.1 Organization of the Boston Housing Authority, circa 1980 (Source: U.S. Department of Housing and Urban Development, Boston Area Office, *Management Review of the Boston Housing Authority*, June 1976)

of work and the workers allowed to do it. A frustrated BHA official described the consequences: "If you had a leak under the sink, a laborer had to go and break open the wall. A plumber would have to get in there and fix the pipe. A carpenter had to come back up and frame the hole back in. The plasterer would have to plaster. And the painter would have to paint."[8] No wonder their response was slow.

Patronage and civil service protection also made it difficult to use discipline to maintain standards. As Robert Whittlesey recalled: "If you were a maintenance man and you were challenged, your reply might very well have been, 'You can't do anything to me, because I'm a friend of X.' As I've heard it described, there were geological layers of patronage that went back years and years."[9] Furthermore, although BHA workers did not have to qualify for the jobs through civil service exams, they were automatically protected by the state's civil service laws once they had worked for the BHA for five years.

Finally, to add insult to injury, the BHA lacked the power to negotiate wages. They were set by the commissioner of labor and industries. He had for years pegged those rates at 80 percent of the prevailing wages for unionized construction workers. These workers, of course, received high wages to compensate for the lack of year-round work, paid sick leave, and paid holidays—all benefits that *did* accrue to BHA employees.

Although maintenance was probably the BHA's worst operational component, serious problems also existed in tenant selection and security. The key problems in tenant selection involved both policies and operational procedures for screening tenant applications. Existing policies, designed to ensure that the housing would be open to all, stated that applicants could be declared ineligible only if they had a "chronically poor record of meeting their financial obligations"; a history of disturbing people or destroying property; or a record of eviction from BHA property for unpaid rents. Because only two people staffed this function, records were poor. Moreover, even if the information could be obtained, the legal staff of the BHA was notoriously reluctant to contest a legal challenge from a prospective tenant. For the most part, tenants were admitted as a matter of right.

The weak screening procedures contributed to serious security problems, but BHA security was threatened by other weaknesses as well. It was as difficult to oust tenants who engaged in vandalism, theft, and drug dealing as to prevent them from being admitted in the first place. To be fair to the BHA legal staff, policies designed to protect the rights of tenants against arbitrary evictions by the BHA had made successful eviction proceedings quite difficult. But they had essentially given up trying. As a result, criminals operated in the projects with little fear of retribution. Eventually, the projects became so dangerous that the police stopped answering calls for assistance or came only in force.

The operational problems in maintenance, tenant selection, and security were potentially solvable with proper control mechanisms and information systems to ensure that existing policies were being followed. But the BHA had almost no such systems.

The agency prepared a central budget without reference to actual cost data. It made no effort to track expenses against budget allocations. The only part of the financial system that seemed to work was the identification of tenants who failed to pay their rent (who then became the focus of the project managers' collection efforts). Indeed, this was the only financial information collected and reported at the level of individual projects. All other information about costs, activities, and performance were aggregated for the organization as a whole, or for particular functions such as maintenance or security.

None of the employees faced effective performance standards. Project managers were accountable for achieving quantitative goals in areas such as rent collection, vacancy turnovers, appearances at the projects, and visits to tenant apartments. But no information about their performance was recorded or audited. Nor were any of these data used to adjust their pay or influence prospects for promotion. Similarly, the authority could have monitored the productivity of skilled craftspeople through data contained in the authority's computerized work-order system, but these data were considered incomplete and unreliable.

To Spence, it was clear that there was a great deal of managerial work to be done in improving the performance of the BHA. The important question was where to start.

LEE BROWN AND THE HOUSTON POLICE DEPARTMENT

Lee Brown became chief of the Houston Police Department (HPD) in April 1982—the department's seventh chief in eight years.[10] The frequent turnover reflected rapid changes in the city itself and a continuing debate about the kind of policing the sprawling, ambitious, and increasingly diverse city needed.

Background

In less than two decades Houston had changed from a small, complacent southwestern city to a large, growing metropolis. Its growth had attracted the ambitious from many domains: executives to guide the multinational oil companies based in Houston; space scientists to staff burgeoning NASA facilities; urban developers (and the lawyers and insurance agents who attended them) to create office complexes, malls, and residential communities; and African Americans, Hispanics, and others who sought the American dream.

The changes produced enormous conflict along with wealth. The wealth encouraged a kind of license. Inevitably, the demands on the Houston Police Department increased. Riots and civil disturbances erupted in the late sixties. In the mid-seventies Houston was dubbed the nation's murder capital.

The police department initially responded by holding the line. The principal tactic was described by Tim James, a police officer who joined the force in 1968 and rose to become its general counsel: "In 1970 there were two Tactical Units—one for the north side, one for the south. Each had sixty officers . . . Our mission was . . . to stop crime . . . In units of 4–5 men, we would go into the bad-ass clubs and check the patrons for papers, guns, drugs and so on with very little regard for the subtleties, the niceties, the constitutional nuances. If there was a liquor license, that was probable cause enough for us . . . We made hundreds of felony arrests."[11]

To support these operations, the HPD aligned itself with the old power structure rather than the new. As the editor of the *Houston Post* explained: "In 1968, Houston was run by the 'good ol' boys.' It was not just police, but fire, sanitation, and public works. As a result, there was a lot of conflict between the police department and the minorities."[12]

In short, in the late sixties and early seventies, the HPD believed that its support and legitimacy depended on maintaining the existing social order. The most vivid display of its commitment to this goal was its response to a relatively small civil disturbance in 1968. Officer James recalls the events: "We had all seen pictures of the looting on television. We were all mobilized . . . I remember standing out in the parking lot among the cruisers. Herman Short [then the police chief] came out, and climbed up on top of one of the cruisers with a bull horn. He said, 'There will be no looting in Houston. Looters will be shot on sight. Get on your loudspeakers and tell them to stay inside their homes and they'll be safe.' It sent chills up and down my spine. We left the parking lot in a convoy of cruisers, driving slowly, lights flashing."[13]

Over the decade of the seventies, the Houston Police Department acquired an unenviable national reputation as a "cowboy" department. Pappy Bond, chief of the department in this period, allowed the officers to wear what they wanted and arm themselves as they wished. Cowboy hats and pearl-handled automatics appeared at the department's roll calls. When the department needed to hire more officers, it mounted a national advertising campaign inviting officers from all over the country to come to Houston, "where the action is."

The result was an unprecedented level of violence by the HPD against Houston's citizens. Mary Sinderson, an assistant U. S. attorney for the Southern District of Texas, remembers the time: "In the first part of 1977, the Houston Police Department was killing people left and right. It was a blood bath. Something like 13 people in a three month period [were killed]. In the middle of that, the Joe Campos Torres case came along."[14] Harry Caldwell, soon to be appointed chief of the police department, described the Campos Torres case: "Five HPD officers took Joe Campos Torres drunk from a bar, whipped his ass, and threw him in Buffalo Bayou."[15] According to subsequent court testimony, one of the officers involved had said, "I always wanted to see a wetback swim."[16] Caldwell, reflecting bitterly on the event, said, "He didn't swim. He sank."[17]

The case plunged the Houston Police Department into its first serious reconsideration of the overall strategy for policing Houston. Pappy Bond resigned and was replaced by Harry Caldwell. Caldwell had previously headed the department's Community Relations Bureau and had done much of the key staff work for the previous chiefs. Caldwell defined his goal as "establishing accountability" within the department.

In setting this goal Caldwell attempted to synthesize the apparently conflicting demands of the old and new Houston. He took from the old a continued focus on hard-nosed law enforcement as the essential mission of the organization. He took from the new the aim of professionalizing and disciplining the department. To achieve these purposes, he began publishing administrative rules regulating dress, weapons, and the use of deadly force. He also made spot checks to see that his officers were on assignment and properly uniformed and equipped. Those found wanting were publicly disciplined.

These changes upset Houston's rank and file. Already traumatized by the Campos Torres incident, they formed a union. The union produced a report documenting the low morale of the police and proposing changes in personnel policies to protect officers from arbitrary discipline and public scapegoating.

Caldwell's response was characteristically authoritarian. Bob Thomas, a patrol officer who became head of the union, recalled Caldwell's speech to the 300 Houston police officers who attended a meeting that Caldwell called to allow the officers to air their grievances: "He said,

'I'm a goddamned dictator, and if you don't like it, you can hit the fucking door' . . . He didn't even read our report. He just took it, tore it in half, and threw it in the wastebasket."[18]

Nor was Caldwell any easier on his own command staff. A veteran member of the higher ranks of the department recalls: "Harry created the Inspections Command. He reached down into the ranks until he found two sergeants he thought could do the job, and passed by a whole lot of Captains and Lieutenants along the way . . . The staff went to war with him. They fought him. Everything he did they made him turn around and eat. They just wore him down."[19]

Caldwell was eventually replaced by B. K. Johnson—a much more popular man in the department. Former chief Pappy Bond commented favorably on the appointment: "What Houston needs is a chief like Johnson who will concentrate on protecting the city from criminals. He is a low key, professional policeman with tremendous compassion for everyone."[20]

Minority groups in Houston were less keen, and Johnson's first actions gave them little reassurance. He tested an open microphone at a public meeting by reciting portions of "Little Black Sambo." Sweeps of the downtown areas with foot patrols filled Houston's jails with people whom Johnson described as "vagrants and winos." In response to urgent requests from the Hispanic community to solve a rash of homicides in their neighborhoods, Johnson promised to send fleets of patrol cars. "Don't be upset when you see them," he said. "We're not trying to harass you. We really don't have time for that."[21] Soon thereafter an organizer of Houston's large gay community was shot and killed by a Houston police officer.

By the fall of 1981, Houston's minority communities were up in arms. Even the newer establishment of Houston was embarrassed. Kathy Whitmire, running for mayor on a platform of political and administrative reform, supported by a "rainbow alliance" of minority populations and newly arrived professionals, won election. Following a national search to find someone to lead the Houston Police Department, she appointed Lee Brown.

The Task and the Resources

At the time Brown took command, crime in Houston had reached record levels. Over the decade 1970–1980, the reported crime rate had increased from 0.065 major crimes per person per year to 0.090. The number of homicides had nearly doubled. Rapes had more than tripled. Robbery was up 70 percent for the decade.

The Houston Police Department met the increased crime with a budget of $142 million and a force of 3,200 officers. By national standards, the force was too small. Houston employed 1.9 sworn police officers per 1,000 citizens—just over half the national average of 3.5 officers per 1,000 citizens. It fielded 6 officers per square mile compared with the 15 officers per square mile fielded by the Los Angeles Police Department.

Moreover, the attacks on the HPD had taken their toll on the morale of the department. From 1970 to 1978, only about 3 percent of the officers left the department each year. From 1978 to 1981, this rate doubled to 6 percent per year. Exit surveys of departing officers found that 60 percent felt they had been underutilized by the force. More than half the officers rated management of the department as "fair" or "bad." Many expressed concern about the poor quality of vehicles and equipment.

The Organization: Its Structure, Systems, and Performance

The department was organized along functional lines. Beneath the chief there were three principal commands: the Field Operations Command, the Investigations Command, and the Support Command. (Figure 6.2 presents an organizational chart.)

The Field Operations Command took primary responsibility for deploying 1,600 patrol officers across the city. With that force, it staffed 160 patrol vehicles twenty-four hours a day, seven days a week. Three geographically defined Patrol Bureaus and six geographically defined Patrol Divisions supervised the patrol force. Two of the three Patrol Bureaus also supervised one or more specialized units of the department: the South Patrol Bureau supervised the Helicopter Division; the Metro Patrol Bureau, the Accident Division and the Special Operations Division.

The Investigations Command deployed the department's detectives to conduct criminal investigations. That command also had three bureaus: Criminal Investigations, which investigated cases of homicide, robbery, burglary, assault, and theft—each with its own division; Special Investigations, which investigated narcotics, vice, and juvenile offenses—each with its own division; and Staff Services, which was responsible for criminal records, the development of management information

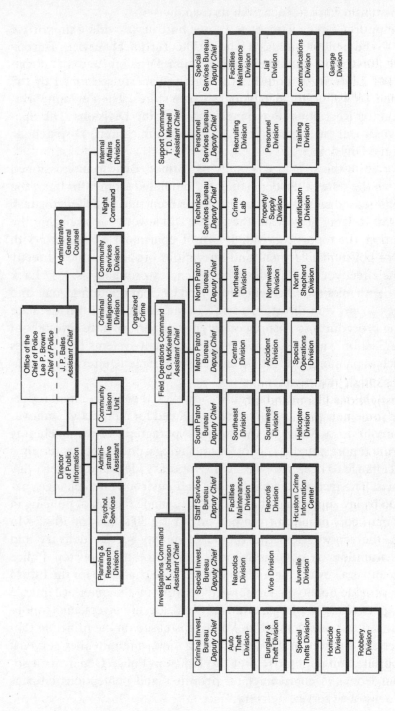

Figure 6.2 Houston Police Department Organizational Chart, May 1982 (Source: Liz Brown, "Assessment of the Department: Problems and Issues," September 1982, p. 25)

systems for the department as a whole, and facilities maintenance for the department as a whole—each with its own division.

The Support Command managed three bureaus providing supportive services to the organization as a whole. The Technical Services Bureau included the Crime Lab, the Identification Division, and the Property/Supply Division, responsible for stolen property reclaimed by the department as well as the department's own stores. The Personnel Bureau included Recruiting, Personnel, and Training Divisions. The Special Services Bureau included the Jail, Communications, Dispatchers, and Garage Divisions.

To learn how this structure actually performed, Brown commissioned a report on the state of the department. Completed six months later, the report painted a dismal picture of the department and a challenging task for Brown. Relying heavily on the classic framework for analyzing the organization, the report concluded: "The Department is . . . faced with a series of police management and operations problems which directly impact its effectiveness."[22] It described such key problems as: (1) "Lack of an in-depth mission statement supported by clear operating goals and objectives to provide direction to the organization"; (2) "Inadequate operating procedures to ensure consistency of performance throughout the organization"; and (3) "Lack of management systems that address areas such as planning, budgeting, career development, internal communications and deployment."[23]

Beyond this traditional perspective, however, the management report sounded some new themes. It stressed the need for a proactive, innovative approach to policing. In the opening paragraph of its concluding section, the report stated: "The job of managing a police agency requires constant change to keep pace with contemporary ideas and modern-day techniques. The increased complexities and environmental changes experienced by law enforcement agencies have made the job of policing in the 80's markedly different from policing in the 50's, 60's, or 70's."[24] In addition, the report stressed a theme of quality service delivery and focused attention on community impressions of the Houston Police Department as a key managerial objective: "The challenge for the future is . . . to provide quality police service delivery in a manner acceptable to the expectations of a large, ethnically and socially diverse metropolitan area . . . Law enforcement in America is based on the principle that the police are a part of and not apart from the community they serve. It is appropriate and imperative that the Houston Police Department solicit input from the community on priorities and perceptions citizens have about police service delivery."[25]

Finally, the report pointed to key assets the police department might use to develop its future capabilities and to some important programmatic innovations that had occurred. "Community Support" headed the list: "The community wants to be involved in assisting the police. Several important citizen support activities currently exist, including the neighborhood-oriented 'Houstonians on Watch' program, and the annual Hundred Club Awards for individual officer heroism."[26] The list also included the Crime Stoppers Program (designed to attract information from the community on an anonymous basis about the commission of crimes) and the Spanish Language Program, designed to teach officers how to speak Spanish and to promote better relations with Houston's large Hispanic community.[27]

Brown's freedom of action in exploiting these assets seemed sharply limited, not only by the legacy of the past but also by deep personal suspicions of him. Houston's strong civil service system had deposited two former chiefs in powerful positions in Brown's organization: J. P. Bales, who remained as Brown's deputy, and B. K. Johnson, who remained as the assistant chief commanding Investigations. When Brown took command, the chief's car had already been assigned to Bales, and all the furniture from his office had been removed. Brown was left with a yellow Plymouth and a pile of boxes to launch his administration.

THE FUNCTION OF
OPERATIONAL MANAGEMENT

These two cases offer vivid illustrations of the operational challenges facing public sector managers. To a degree they also challenge conventional images of public administration.

Surprisingly, if performance falters disastrously enough, even public enterprises can go bankrupt.[28] The bankruptcy is explicit in the case of the BHA: a court has declared the organization unable to meet its mandated responsibilities and placed it in receivership. Bankruptcy is only implicit in the HPD case: the HPD has lost its credibility with the local community, and the incoming mayor has gone outside the department for effective leadership.

Neither political aspirations nor operational tasks remain constant; they both change. With change comes the need to adapt and innovate. The BHA and the HPD reach the public sector equivalent of bankruptcy in part because of their difficulty meeting the challenge of change.

Looking up to politics, both Spence and Brown find complex, shifting expectations. Initially, the BHA had been charged with the task of providing transitional housing to upwardly mobile poor. Then, it had been encouraged to focus more of its resources on the desperately poor. Now, it is also expected to preserve the quality of the housing it owns and become financially self-sufficient—goals that are, to some degree, in conflict. Similarly, in the past the HPD was expected to produce law and order. Now, it is being encouraged to do so with less use of force and more respect for the rights of a diverse citizenry.

Looking out to the task, Spence and Brown also find new, diverse challenges. The BHA finds the task of housing desperately poor, single-parent households different (and more challenging) from housing upwardly mobile families. The HPD is learning that coping with urban violence, exacerbated by increasing ethnic and class tensions, is different from maintaining order in a more homogeneous and stable society. Both organizations have noted and responded to the new political expectations and substantive tasks but not with enough creativity and energy. Bankruptcy has resulted—just as it would if private sector organizations failed to adapt to their markets.

The cases support my observation in Chapter 2 that government is not exclusively (perhaps not even primarily) a "service" sector.[29] Both the BHA and the HPD oblige their clients as well as serve them. Both agencies use public authority as well as public money to accomplish their aims.

The BHA is most obviously a service agency: it delivers publicly subsidized housing to poor people. Yet, on close inspection, we see that it obliges as well as serves its clients. It obliges them to pay rents, dispose of their trash properly, and not deal drugs. The BHA can demand no more from tenants than the rules for admitting and evicting tenants allow. And these rules are drawn tightly because citizens, their representatives, and the courts want the agency to treat clients fairly and to deliver public housing to those who truly need it. Still, within these limits, the BHA has the formal authority to require clients to behave in particular ways on pain of eviction if they fail to comply.[30]

The HPD, by contrast, is most obviously an obliging agency: it exists to oblige citizens to obey laws.[31] Yet, on close inspection, the HPD is also a service agency. It provides first aid and tourist information as well as reassurance to citizens that no burglars lurk in their houses. It also aids crime victims and witnesses who want to help the police solve crimes and see justice done.

As noted in Chapter 2, an important consequence of being a public agency using both public funds to provide services and public authority to impose obligations is that the agency must perform for two quite different audiences. At the *business* end of its operations, the agency must try to satisfy the clients who use its services or are the focus of an obligation: the BHA must get extra heat to Mrs. Jones, who just came home with her new baby; the HPD must persuade Mr. Smith, who is suspected of an armed robbery, to come along quietly. At the *reporting* end, it must satisfy its overseers that the job is being done well. The BHA must satisfy Judge Garrity that it is not only providing minimally satisfactory services to its clients but also admitting people fairly. The HPD must satisfy the new mayor that it can invent a style of policing that reduces criminal victimization and uses the force and authority entrusted to it economically and fairly.

Interestingly, in these two cases overseer dissatisfaction more than client dissatisfaction produces the bankruptcies. True, the BHA's rotten service to clients caused the court to push the organization into receivership. But what the court is doing in backing (some of) the claims of tenants is converting the individual interests of the BHA's clients into claims that society as a whole will take as its own to satisfy. In effect, the court converts the private interests of clients into public commitments that the BHA must meet, and the private value of satisfying such interests into public value.

It is true as well that the interests of Houston's minorities in being policed fairly (along with the desires of other citizens for improved crime control) caused the HPD to lose its credibility. But what happens, once again, is that the election of Mayor Whitmire converts what were once the private interests of individuals, and the parochial interests of particular groups, to the status of *public* interests. It is through social choice mechanisms such as court decisions, elections, and legislation that once private interests are redefined as public interests, and the value associated with satisfying private interests transformed into public value that public managers are pledged to produce.

A close look at these cases indicates that one of the most important challenges facing public sector managers is how best to enlist the cooperation of their clients in producing the results for which the managers are held accountable. In seeking to maintain high-quality public housing for poor people, for example, Spence focuses on how tenants can be mobilized to help him keep the buildings and grounds in good repair. In trying to produce public order and allay fears, Brown usefully focuses on how Houston's citizens could be enlisted in this cause. Client cooperation is important because citizens and clients do not stand outside the production process; they participate in it.

These cases also make it clear that many public organizations fall well short of traditional ideals of public administration. Both organizations seem out of control. They lack basic administrative mechanisms to ensure tight accountability. In all likelihood, Spence and Brown could substantially improve production by doing the traditional things: establishing sensible policies, hiring tough supervisors, and monitoring levels of performance.

Yet the problems facing Spence and Brown require more than these basic steps. Both Spence and Brown need to rethink the basic mission and product of their organizations. They need to reengineer their operations. Most important, they must find the room to innovate.[32] In this work, they have to invent a strategic rather than a technical view of operational management.[33]

A Strategic View of Operational Management

By "strategic view of operational management," I mean one built on many of the observations made so far in this book. It includes the idea that managers are accountable for their use of authority as well as money. Moreover, because the funds they expend are raised through coercive power, the managers must be consistently responsible for fairness in the way the government operates, even when they are delivering services. It also means that public value is created in the satisfactions of overseers met at the reporting end of their organizations as well as in the satisfaction of clients met at the business end of their organizations. It encompasses the idea that because public managers confront changing political expectations and substantive tasks, they must be responsible for creating adaptable and flexible organizations as well as controllable and efficient ones. Finally, strategic management focuses attention on the possibility that operational capacity often lies outside an organization's boundaries.

Note that the interest in strategic management does not eliminate the value of the conventional view of public sector production. Many times a conventional perspective on public management is entirely appropriate—for example, in running the U. S. Mint.[34] The conventional view can be seen as a special case of a more general view of public sector value creation—one that is appropriate to situations in which little political conflict or change occurs, minimal operational innovation is needed, and most of the required operational capacity lies within the boundaries of the organization. A strategic view, in contrast, is needed when change and conflict exist and, with them, the need for innovation.

Note also that these observations on the nature of public management dramatically increase the importance of political management as a managerial function, even when one is focused on the operational challenges of achieving substantive results. Because political changes are what occasion the need (and create the opportunity) for operational changes, effective political management is key to learning what managers should be trying to produce. Because powerful political backing is essential to mobilizing coproduction, political management is often key to effective operational management. Thus, one cannot talk about effective operational management without also talking about effective political management. The strategic triangle introduced earlier conveys that basic message, and the chapters on political management reinforce the point.

Still, a strategic view of management eventually does require a hard-nosed, operational focus. Something has to be produced as well as envisioned. A "story" offered to the authorizing environment must be kept alive through real performance captured in measurement systems. To meet these responsibilities, strategic managers must focus their attention downward and inward, toward their organization's production processes as well as up and out, toward politics. As in the exploration of political management, the important question is what normative purposes and analytic techniques should guide their efforts to improve operations.

Reengineering Public Sector Production

In my view, operational managers should seek, find, and exploit opportunities to create public value. Their task is not to increase the size of their organizations, institutionalize current policies, insulate their organizations from the demands of politics, or perfect the administrative systems that guide their organizations. Their task is to make their organizations more valuable, in the short and long run.[35]

In principle, greater value can be produced by: (1) increasing the quantity or quality of public activities per resource expended; (2) reducing the costs (in terms of money and authority) used to achieve current levels of production; (3) making public organizations better able to identify and respond to citizens' aspirations; (4) enhancing the fairness with which public sector organizations operate; and (5) increasing their continuing capacity to respond and innovate. To locate these opportunities to create additional value, public managers, like private managers, must reengineer their organizations.[36] They may do so by analyzing five key issues.

First, they must establish what concrete products, services, or obligations are to be produced for particular clients and determine how performance in delivering the products, services, and obligations will be reported to the organization's overseers. These are the tasks associated with what the private sector would call marketing and product engineering. The "products" must be consistent with the vision contained in the organization's overall strategy and appeal to both overseers and clients. Often, increased value can be gained by building new qualities into old activities, or developing new product lines to reflect new aspirations, or giving effective responses to new problems.

Second, managers must design the particular operations through which the products, services, and obligations will be produced. This is the task of production engineering. Often, to improve operational performance, process innovations will be required.

Third, to keep the organization performing well, managers must use and adjust their organization's administrative systems: their structures, policy-making processes, personnel systems, and control mechanisms. Operational managers may have to make changes in these systems to increase productivity, improve the quality of reporting to overseers, accommodate important product or process innovations, or produce more flexible organizations. Thus, managers must often make administrative innovations as well as product or process innovations.

Fourth, in making process and administrative innovations, operational managers have to keep in mind the effects of these innovations on their capacity to engage those outside the organization in the achievement of the organization's objectives. An administrative change that produces a more economical use of the organization's own resources but sacrifices the ease with which the organization can engage the efforts of clients may lead to less efficiency and effectiveness than one focused on the total resources committed to a task. Inevitably, this focus will involve public managers in the kinds of political management that helps them mobilize "coproducers."

This sounds like a very complex calculation. And so it is. But managers must remember that wisdom in operational management begins with recognizing that many of these issues have been previously resolved. Typically, organizations have established purposes, particular products and activities judged to be consistent with those purposes, well-practiced programs and routines for achieving them, and administrative systems well designed to focus the attention and the resources of the organization on its key tasks. That is what has allowed the organization to survive so far.[37]

Operational managers do not typically face the problem of designing the organization's products, production processes, or administrative systems from scratch, then. Instead, their job is to consider how current operations might be altered at the margin through product, program, or administrative innovations to enhance their value. On occasion, managers may even have to make strategic innovations that reposition their organizations in their political and task environments.[38]

The question of how much and what kind of innovation is required defines the fifth issue for operational managers: they must consider how much work they need to do with their political authorizing environments to create the room they need to innovate at the rate they think appropriate. Innovations require capital and entail risks—to clients, to citizens, and to managers. To raise the capital and reduce the risks, operational managers will have to engage their political environments—this time for authorization rather than assistance in production.[39] How much innovation they can support depends on how much political credibility they enjoy.

To illustrate these calculations, consider the problems facing the BHA and the HPD through the eyes of a strategically oriented operational manager.

DEFINING ORGANIZATIONAL MISSION AND PRODUCT

In Chapter 3, I stressed the importance of defining the mission and goals of an organization in a simple, overarching concept. Such goals help managers remain focused and purposeful. They may also help in building strong organizational cultures.[40] Still, most organizations need more than one simple phrase to guide their operations. Most organizations operate, explicitly or implicitly, with a *hierarchy* of goals and objectives.[41] At the top of the pyramid are the organizations' broad, relatively durable goals; at the bottom are more particular, changeable operational objectives.

The logic connecting the goals at the top with the more particular objectives at the bottom can be variously understood. To some, the goals at the top describe the ends of the organization; the objectives at the bottom the means to achieving them.[42] To others, the high-level goals focus on the long term; those at the bottom on the short term.[43] Perhaps the easiest and most general way to describe the logic of a hierarchy of goals and objectives is to say that both high-level goals and low-level objectives seek to point the organization in particular directions. The only difference is that they do so at *different levels of abstraction*. Thus, the lower level objectives simply describe what is meant by the higher level goals or what particular things the organization will do in pursuit of, or as an expression of, the higher level goals.[44]

The pyramid of goals and objectives comes into existence at least partly because, in setting goals, managers seek to communicate with different parts of their authorizing environments, and they have learned that different parts of that environment converse in different languages. Politicians and the media prefer the poetry of simple, value-laden sound bites. For them, managers need rhetoric that inspires and gives meaning. The "green eye shades" in budget agencies and congressional appropriations committees, however, want much more concrete and quantifiable accounts. For them, the prose of numbers, statistics, and accomplishments speaks far more eloquently than empty rhetorical goals.

But pyramids also exist because managers find them useful in leading and directing their enterprises. Without the higher level abstractions, their organizations would lack inspiration and become confused about their ultimate purpose. Without the lower level abstractions, midlevel managers and employees would lack operational guidance and accountability. Goal hierarchies thus contribute to both external accountability and internal direction and control.[45]

Predictably, at the time Spence and Brown take office, the highest level missions of the BHA and the HPD are reasonably well established. Spence starts with the assumption that the BHA's goal is to provide decent, publicly owned and subsidized housing to those who, by virtue of their poverty, deserve it. Brown starts with the understanding that the HPD's goal is to protect life and property from criminal attack through professional enforcement of the criminal law.

What makes questions about mission and product worth further consideration, however, is that Spence and Brown take office at a time of intense dissatisfaction with their organizations' performance. The quality of the housing delivered to BHA tenants has been deemed inadequate by a state court. The political and legal community of Houston has become dissatisfied with the price paid for the limited security the HPD has provided. These perceptions of organizational failure could, on close inspection, reveal nothing more than a failure to execute established procedures to achieve traditional purposes. But they might also be an indication that the overall mission, goals, and operational objectives of each organization have been wrongly conceived and that a new hierarchy of goals and objectives must be developed. It is this second possibility that creates the opportunity for strategic leadership.

Defining the Mission and Product of the BHA

For Spence, a central issue must be what citizens want from public housing and how they perceive and reckon the value of what the BHA currently produces.[46] He knows what the public can see of his organization's performance: dilapidated, boarded-up buildings inhabited by residents who seem indifferent to and destructive of their surroundings. In all likelihood, that image conflicts sharply with what citizens would like the BHA to produce. They probably want the agency to provide clean, well-maintained buildings inhabited by conscientious homeowners. Because the buildings are so badly decayed, most citizens will conclude that the BHA is failing. The buildings they bought and paid for are being destroyed. To some degree, that is what the court sees, too. It decries the quality of the housing being provided to the BHA's tenants, and it judges (for the rest of the society as well as the tenants) that the tenants have rights to something far better.

Given this situation, Spence could focus the BHA's resources on making the buildings (and the human communities they house) look more attractive to citizens. He could consolidate the number of housing units (thereby allowing him to concentrate limited modernization resources on these units and reducing the costs associated with preventing the vandalization of other vacant units); and he could change the composition of residents (to favor people who can afford higher rents, need less care, and are less likely to vandalize the buildings). Such changes would also increase the value of the housing to clients, since living conditions would substantially improve. Moreover, such changes in BHA operations could be justified. They are broadly consistent with the abstract goal of "providing safe, decent, subsidized housing to those who cannot afford it."

Yet Spence must acknowledge that, at a more concrete level, these changes would importantly alter the basic product and service that the BHA now provides. The overall *quantity* of public housing would diminish as housing units were mothballed (that is, completely boarded up, sealed tight, and with utilities shut off). And, although the *quality* of the remaining stock would probably increase (thereby giving current residents a larger net benefit than they now enjoy), the beneficiaries of this improved quality would be different. The BHA's clients or beneficiaries would shift from the poorest populations in the city toward the working poor. That, in turn, would change the distribution of the benefits of the BHA and the overall public value of the enterprise. In effect, the organization would change its basic product from providing emergency housing to the most desperate citizens of Boston to providing slightly higher quality housing to a population that is better off in social and economic terms.

Alternatively, Spence might try to focus public attention on the value of providing large quantities of emergency housing to Boston's poorest citizens. He could observe that what citizens take for terrible housing is actually relatively good housing compared to what the residents would have if public housing were not available. Thus, the BHA is creating value for its clients. Moreover, he could remind citizens that their aims for the agency include a sharp focus on the most disadvantaged, and therefore most needy, citizens. This focus fits the particular conception of justice embodied in public housing to begin with.

The difficulty, of course, is that this story runs up against powerful middle-class values. The middle class wants the buildings to be protected, not allowed to deteriorate. Moreover, although it wants benefits to go to the poor, it also wants the poor to adopt middle-class values with respect to homeowning. And finally, if clients are to be served by the government, they must be served in a way that is consistent with a middle-class notion of decent service. The government should not be a slumlord. Indeed, that is what the court decision established. As a result, Spence is charged with producing clean, attractive communities in which some of Boston's poorest can make investments to pull themselves out of poverty, all at a low cost in terms of money and authority. How best to accomplish this goal turns out to be a decision about the valuable and sustainable proper ends of public housing as well as about means.

Defining the Mission and Product of the HPD

For Brown, the issues are even more complex. As in the case of public housing, there is a widely shared idea of what a police force should do and how it should operate. This particular idea has been refined over time, as policing has developed as a profession and police organizations have interacted with their overseers in the nation's cities.[47]

In that conception, the goals of policing are clear: to reduce crime and enforce the law. To achieve these goals, police departments conventionally deploy a motorized patrol force to drive through the city looking for crime and responding quickly to calls for assistance. They also field trained investigators capable of solving crimes and presenting evidence effectively in court. Both patrol officers and detectives should be trained to judge when arrests are warranted and to make arrests with the minimal use of force. To a degree, the Houston Police Department approximates this model.

Unfortunately, an accumulating body of evidence casts doubt on the value of this basic strategy of policing. Experimental studies have shown that patrolling cars have less impact on levels of crime than originally hoped and do little to reassure citizens.[48] Other studies have indicated that rapid response to calls for service also fails to reduce crime.[49] And, most disappointing of all, it seems that detective bureaus can solve crimes only when victims and witnesses tell them who did it.[50] Without such information, they are all but helpless.

These studies have shaken public and professional confidence in the current strategy of policing. And no one has yet developed a strategy that can be shown conclusively to be superior. Nonetheless, the search for an improved strategy is now being guided by four key observations.[51]

First, it seems abundantly clear that successful crime control depends on close—even intimate—relations with the community being policed. Without information from the community, both patrol forces and detective bureaus are powerless. Moreover, unless citizens make efforts to defend themselves, police efforts are largely in vain. Thus, the first line of defense is always the community itself.[52]

Second, fear is an important problem in its own right.[53] It makes life miserable for those who fear and prompts citizens to take actions that make their neighborhoods even more dangerous. When citizens stop going out, buy guns, hide behind closed shutters, or fail to confront offenders, a neighborhood can no longer defend itself. Significantly, the police can reduce fear, but not necessarily through the same means they now use to confront violent crime.[54] Because fear is most commonly triggered by evidence of disorder in a community, such as graffiti, noisy kids, or public drunkenness, to reduce fear, police must shift some of their attention toward dealing with these "quality of life offenses."[55] Police officers can also reduce fear by getting out of their cars and establishing more regular, personal encounters with citizens.[56]

Third, citizens want to use the police for many things other than crime control.[57] They do not restrict their calls to occasions of robbery, assault, or burglary; they call when accidents happen, when domestic quarrels get too loud, or simply when they feel afraid. Such calls have traditionally been viewed as nuisances to be screened out as soon as possible. Now, however, those calls are being reevaluated. Some might present an opportunity for crime prevention; others for dealing with frightening kinds of disorder. Or, they might simply be an opportunity for the police to provide "quality service to customers," which may be important in itself. Such quality service might also create the public support that the police need to help them identify robbers, quell an urban disorder, or justify a police shooting.[58]

Fourth, what the police see as incidents are often the indicators of continuing, underlying problems.[59] Indeed, analyses of calls for service show that a large portion of the calls comes from a small number of locations—now designated as "hot spots."[60] Perhaps instead of continuing to respond to the individual calls for service, the police could analyze the situation and find a better and more permanent response.[61]

Taken together, these four observations point toward major changes in the way the police do their work. In this new vision, the police would still be focused on reducing crime. They would still field a patrol force and respond to calls for service. They would still have a detective unit investigating crimes. But they would take responsibility for a wider set of problems than they now do and deal with them through a more varied response than just arrests.

Specifically, the police would have to enlarge their mission beyond crime control to include crime prevention, fear reduction, and crisis response as well.[62] Officers would have to spend more time out of their patrol cars in direct contact with citizens. And they would respond to incidents with some curiosity about whether the incident reflected a continuing problem and what could be done to resolve it.[63] For example, a successful police response to a wave of residential burglaries in Santa Ana, California, included not only traditional efforts to catch the burglars, but also a successful effort to use civil regulatory authority to restore to its original purposes a local motel that had become a drug-trafficking center.[64]

In addition, the police would have to develop new mechanisms for community groups to bring problems to their attention. As things now stand, the police hear about two different kinds of problems from two different sources. On the one hand, they learn about the problems of individual citizens through the individual calls for service. On the other, they hear about citywide problems from the newspapers and the elected representatives of the people. What they do not hear about are neighborhood problems that exist between individual and citywide levels.

Police department organization simply does not facilitate this kind of communication. The geographic organization of the patrol division ensures citizens of a precinct a captain to whom a local community group could address their concerns. But, typically, the precinct captain thinks his or her job is to maintain the focus of the local unit on citywide priorities and to insist on conformity with uniform standards of performance. Furthermore, because precinct commanders command only the patrol force, they do not necessarily have access to resources from the detective bureau or the narcotics unit. Consequently, both their inclination and capacity to deal with community problems are limited.

Two important consequences result from this inability to identify and respond to community-nominated problems. First, the police are deprived of useful information about what local communities value and want from them. Without that information, they are free to define their own priorities, but those may or may not match the priorities of the communities. Second, the police lose the opportunity to develop a trusting working relationship with a potentially important partner in reducing crime. Citizens, particularly those who have a big enough stake to have developed a community-oriented outlook, are potentially an extremely valuable ally for the police. It is they who will take voluntary actions to help control the streets. If the police can serve only individuals, and not community groups, they will lose an opportunity to strengthen a neighborhood's first line of defense.

Obviously, the pursuit of these new ideas about the best strategy for policing would require important changes in the specific, concrete behavior of the Houston Police Department. The new product or new set of product lines would emphasize efforts to control fear and disorder as well as serious criminal victimization. It would emphasize the servicing side of policing as well as its obliging side. It would require the police to respond to community-nominated problems as well as to individual incidents or citywide priorities.

Thus, both Spence and Brown face important choices about how to define the mission, product, and activities of their organizations. They could rely on past definitions. But precisely because their organizations are failing, they have the occasion to reexamine their purposes in light of their operations. To determine whether it is possible to achieve something more with their organizations, they must explore how their organizations are now operating and how those operations might be altered.

REDESIGNING PRODUCTION PROCESSES

In principle, managers can distinguish an organization's product from the process of producing it. As a practical matter, however, product and production process are very closely intertwined—particularly for public sector enterprises. Three different reasons for this closeness come to mind.

The first is obvious: one cannot design a production process without knowing what product is desired. To produce a housing project that accommodates poor people, preserves the value of the buildings, and does so at low maintenance costs, the agency must design the process of tenant selection, building design, and maintenance specifically to produce that result. To field a patrol force to respond promptly to calls for service, the police department must divide the city into sectors, schedule its officers, purchase vehicles, and equip the cars with radios. The desired product dictates the required production process.[65]

The second is somewhat less obvious: in service and enforcement operations, the distinction between product and process blurs because clients experience the latter as well as the former. If the public housing authority is slow in delivering requested maintenance services, that is part of the experience of living in a public housing project. If the police use sirens to get to a location quickly, that will be part of the experience of having a police car respond. In effect, the organization's interactions with its clients are not restricted to, or channeled through, the medium of a physical product; they include the way in which the product, service, and obligations are produced and delivered. The contact with the client is ongoing and multidimensional, and each aspect affects the client's perception of the service.[66]

Third, specific attributes of the production process are often important to the overseers of the enterprise. In the BHA case, for example, many overseers want to keep the specialized staffs needed to achieve the objectives of the modernization program as small as possible, to wring the most value out of the program.[67] They want small staffs (even though in practice this weakens the organization's performance) because they think that low administrative costs signal efficiency. Similarly, in Houston, overseers demand a centralized homicide bureau, believing that such a unit increases the capacity of the police to solve homicides, despite the lack of evidence supporting this claim. Others pay close attention to the allocation of police across the city—not only out of concern for efficiency but also out of concern for fairness and equity. Because overseers have views about *how* things should be produced as well as *what* should be produced, the process a government agency uses is often part of the product.

Despite the difficulty of distinguishing the operating programs and technologies of the organization from the product being produced, it is useful to do so because it focuses operational managers' attention on three concrete questions: how an enterprise is actually operating to produce a result; what attributes or features of that process turn out to be important in determining the clients' and overseers' satisfaction with the enterprise; and what key assets are being deployed.

The Production of Public Housing

In the BHA case, the largest portion of the production process lies in the buildings themselves: the buildings store past expenditures and then release value to those who live in them. The capital stock of the BHA is its productive heart: when it changes, the product changes.

Of course, the buildings do not stay as they were originally constructed. They are vulnerable to decay, to neglect, and to vandalism. This means that maintenance and rehabilitation are important parts of the production process as well. Indeed, shortfalls in this domain have been the principal cause of the agency's downfall.

Another key component of the BHA's production process, however, is its procedures for selecting and removing tenants. Tenants affect the quality and value of the BHA's production process in at least three important ways.

From the perspective of citizens subsidizing the public housing, it matters who lives in the project and how they were admitted. As noted above, the public value of housing services delivered to the poorest and most deserving tenants is different from the public value of housing services delivered to relatively well-off tenants who happen to be friends of politicians or housing managers. Because citizens and taxpayers are interested in the justice and fairness with which public benefits are distributed as well as the total quantity and quality of the services, both the targeting of the services and the procedures that admit people to the projects are central to the BHA's value-creating activities. Ideally, the agency will deliver subsidized housing to the deserving poor (as defined in their enabling statutes) and will treat individual applicants with fairness and accuracy.

From the perspective of the tenants, fellow tenants will have a decisive impact on the quality of life. If tenants commit crimes against one another, then life will be miserable even if the housing structures remain attractive. If they are decent and helpful, even poor housing may come to be attractive. Similarly, if tenants care for the housing, and make the small investments required to keep it in good repair, the housing will last longer than if they vandalized it or used it carelessly.

Over the longer run the characteristics of the tenants and their behavior may affect their future life prospects and those of their children. Most people are not simply good or bad regardless of their environment. Their conduct is shaped by the examples and expectations of people around them. Mechanisms that change individuals or the human environment of the projects might be as important as the mechanisms that select tenants initially. The Office of Client Counseling—a small organizational unit within the BHA—reflects a prior, somewhat equivocal commitment to this idea. So does the assumption that social services ought to be provided to residents from a base in the project. Perhaps the most radical idea, however, is that the most important way to transform desperate individuals into a functioning, competent community is by encouraging the process of self-governance. In this sense, tenant services and tenant governance can be seen as part of the production process of a housing project.

Thus, the BHA's production process consists of housing services—produced by a combination of capital structures and ongoing rehabilitation and maintenance—delivered to a particular group of clients according to procedures for determining eligibility, screening applicants, and evicting problem tenants. The tenants figure prominently in the production process through behavior that protects or erodes the physical structures themselves. The product is evaluated by clients or beneficiaries who live in the projects, and by a group of overseers who want to see the capital investment maintained and the public subsidy justified by ensuring that the benefits of the project go to deserving and needy people.

The Production of Community Order

Unlike public housing, the capital equipment of a police department plays a relatively limited role in its production process. True, the organization uses cars, station houses, radios, guns, and computers. But the greater part of the organization's production process emerges from the particular way that individual officers do their work. Indeed, typically more than 80 percent of a police department budget goes to paying its personnel.[68] An important implication, then, is that a police department's operational "technology" lies in the orientations and capabilities of the officers and the policies and procedures that guide their work.

In this respect, police departments resemble service enterprises in the private sector. We should not be too surprised, for police departments provide many important services. Yet, initially, the police look less like service providers than obligation imposers. Indeed, one could define their fundamental business as the "retail delivery of obligations." In imposing obligations, the police make use of public authority as well as money. As the Philadelphia Police Study Task Force explained: "The police are entrusted with important public resources. The most obvious is money: $230 million a year flows through the Philadelphia Police Department. Far more important, the public grants the police . . . the use of force and authority. These are deployed when a citizen is arrested or handcuffed, when an officer fires his weapon at a citizen, and when an officer claims exclusive use of the streets with his siren."[69]

The use of state authority and force is a resource that receives particularly close scrutiny by overseers. They want to be sure public authority and force are used properly (only in situations where it is warranted), economically (with the smallest amount required to achieve the objective), and fairly (equally on all those who face legal vulnerabilities). Those interests exist because citizens and their representatives value justice and fairness as well as efficiency and effectiveness.[70]

But using force justly may also increase its efficacy. Force that is legitimated and used sparingly may be able to command more obedience from those subjected to it than force used abusively or negligently. Those subjected to legitimated force have no basis for appeal. The crowd, standing on the sidelines (both literally and figuratively), will be inclined to support the police rather than the suspect. In such situations, suspects may come along more willingly. In this sense, the police must learn to "husband" their authority as well as to deploy it. Selective use of force reveals their expertise and lends quality to their operations.

The pressure on the police to use their force properly leads them to emphasize operational consistency: to treat like cases alike. This aim, in turn, leads them to consider their productive activities more a production line than a job shop. By definition, a production line produces the same product over and over again. Adam Smith's pin factory is the prototype. A job shop, by contrast, produces a different product each time it goes to work. An architectural firm producing customized designs for buildings is a quintessential job shop.

Although at the extremes, production lines and job shops form a sharp contrast, these ideal types actually lie on a continuous dimension. Close to Adam Smith's pin factory but moving toward a job shop would be an automotive factory that produces customized models. Close to the architectural firm but moving toward a production line would be a machine tool company that earns 50 percent of its revenues by producing one basic kind of machine. Essentially, what this continuum traces is how much new engineering and design goes into the organization's production processes for each discrete unit of production. If most of the design is done in advance and embedded in machinery, policies, job descriptions, and training, then one is operating a production line. If, however, much of the design has to be done at the moment each product is being fashioned, then one is operating a job shop.

To a great extent, the interest in ensuring a consistent response has caused police executives to view police departments as production lines rather than job shops. Police departments manifest this attitude when they try to specify, in advance, all of the particular situations that officers might encounter, and to write down the rules for how they should behave in those situations. That is the sense in which the policy and procedures manual of a police department defines its operating technologies. The drive to codify the department's operational procedures could be justified as a method for achieving organizational effectiveness by ensuring that every police officer used what the organization had learned was the best and most appropriate technique for dealing with a particular problem. But this drive toward standardization probably becomes equally useful as a device to increase the consistency (therefore the fairness) of the police department's response. Codification reduces the scope for individual officer discretion and therefore reduces the chance that officers will misbehave.[71]

Unfortunately, the world dishes up extraordinarily varied circumstances to police officers.[72] Often, adaptation and invention are necessary (or at least valuable) in dealing with the particular situations encountered. Absent the concerns for consistent treatment and effective control over distrusted agents, an effective organizational response would be to "commission" the officer to make the appropriate adaptations—in short, to organize the police as a job shop rather than a production line.[73] In such an enterprise, the presumption would shift from the expectation that all problems are well known and similar to an acknowledgment that each problem might be slightly different and require an adaptive or innovative response. The process of diagnosing the problem and inventing the new response would be left up to the "craftsperson" who faced the problem.[74] He or she could call on the past experience of the organization, accumulated in its policies and procedures, as a resource to suggest how the problem might be solved. But the officer would also rely on what he or she learned about the nature of the particular problem encountered, and on past experience in facing other problems, to work out the solution.

Note that in job shops, and particularly those with large numbers of immediate jobs to produce, the people of the organization provide the key resource. For that reason, the organizational systems that recruit, develop, and deploy personnel are the keys to high performance. In a police department, that system consists of a great deal of technical apparatus that defines the operational routines of the organization: for example, schedules, deployment systems, and dispatching systems. But the system also consists of the training the officers receive and the formal and informal systems that guide what they do on the street. In an important sense, the production process of the organization is the combination of its technology and its culture.

At the time Lee Brown took office, the technology and culture of the Houston Police Department had a distinctive shape. The technical system was embedded in the scheduling system, the communication system, and the huge manual that defined what officers could and could not do. The cultural system was embedded in a set of shared understandings about the purposes of the organization, the marks of virtue and competence among officers, and the paths to success in the organization.

At a cultural level, the organization understood and articulated its job in terms of controlling predatory street crime. Its virtues lay in a combination of technical proficiency and aggressiveness.[75] It responded to calls, determined whether a criminal violation had occurred, and made arrests where appropriate. It viewed its individual and collective success in terms of making arrests.

Beneath the explicit culture of the organization lay a more hidden, subterranean culture. At this level, the organization understood its mission in terms of protecting the good people of Houston from the bad. It understood that it had to do a dirty job, and that none of the citizens really wanted to know exactly how that job got done. It had to present an attractive face of disciplined professionalism to salve the public conscience, while behaving much differently on the street.[76]

To some extent that subterranean culture resulted from the mismatch between the way that the organization tried to represent its operations and the actual conditions it confronted on the street. The effort to superimpose the administrative systems associated with a production-line agency on an organization whose task environment was essentially that of a job shop created a great deal of stress throughout the organization. Supervisors sometimes winked at rule violations if they were invisible to the broader public. When, however, the violations became public, the police managers would crack down to save their own reputations.

In such a world, the officers felt quite vulnerable—not only to those whom they encountered on the street but also to their own superiors. They became cynical and created a whole different set of understandings about what they were supposed to do and why they should do it. The formal apparatus of control became increasingly irrelevant.

The police culture in Houston and elsewhere also emphasized police independence from politics and from the community. As agents of the law, officers viewed themselves as separate and apart from the community. Their self-image projected them above the community as imposers of the law rather than placing them in the community, where they could work with citizens to create a normative order.

To a degree this cultural commitment to independence matched the formal ideals of policing. The police had won a forty-year struggle to free themselves from the taint of political corruption precisely by separating themselves from politics and finding their legitimacy in the neutral application of the law and their technical expertise.[77] Moreover, there were many occasions when society did depend on the police to stand apart and impose the law—for example, when the police were asked to help integrate public schools or to protect pro-life demonstrations. That was what police professionalism was all about.

But the desire to be independent, autonomous, and powerful had its roots in the darker side of the police culture as well. The police felt socially isolated from the rest of the society—cut off by their complex schedules and their unique experiences.[78] They saw more pain and evil than most others in society, and that, in their eyes, set them apart. They also felt extremely vulnerable not only to attacks by offenders but also to being scapegoated by citizens and their own managers.[79] To protect themselves, they had to stick together. All this helped to build a wall between the police and the community.

In viewing themselves as separate and apart from the community, however, they ignored the extent to which policing was ultimately dependent on close connections with the community. Police success depended on the community alerting them to crimes that occurred and helping them identify the offender. It also depended on citizens taking steps on their own to reduce their vulnerability to crime. Above all, it depended on citizens reacting to the presence of the police with feelings of security and self-confidence. Without that, the police could not achieve the objective of reducing fears and building strong, competent communities.[80]

Thus, the production process for the police department consisted of a complex technology embedded in a culture that motivated and directed the behavior of officers on the street. The perceived value of the department was rooted in its ability to adapt to the varied circumstances it encountered and to account for its operations. It was held accountable for the economical uses of funds as well as the fair and economical use of state authority. In addition, like the housing authority, the police department was fundamentally dependent on its clients in producing its desired results.

USING ADMINISTRATIVE SYSTEMS TO INFLUENCE OPERATIONS

To ensure that important objectives are achieved and valued services delivered, managers use administrative systems to animate and guide organizational activity. Key administrative systems are those that: (1) establish domains of authority, responsibility, and accountability for those employed by the organization (organizational structure); (2) set up the deliberative processes the organization will use to make and review key policy decisions (strategic planning systems); (3) define the principal policies, programs, and procedures of the organization (organizational technology); (4) recruit, select, train, evaluate, reward, and promote employees (personnel systems); and (5) develop and report information about the organization's use of resources, levels of activity, and achievements (management information and control systems). A strategic perspective on how to use these systems to enhance the value of an organization's productive efforts must look at the administrative systems together and evaluate their contribution to the organization's overall strategy.[81]

Administrative Systems in the BHA

At the time the BHA slid into court receivership, it was structured along the lines commonly viewed as the best for the efficient performance of its tasks. Initially, BHA operations were guided principally by project managers who served as general managers of particular projects. They handled many functions including maintenance, tenant selection and eviction, rent collection, and overall costs. Often, they lived in the projects they managed. Their activities were only loosely supervised by higher level managers, and little information was collected about their performance.

Eventually, this way of running the BHA was criticized for being insufficiently structured. BHA overseers and central managers judged that efficiencies could be gained by centralizing common functions across projects. Every housing project did not need its own plumber, furnace repairer, or tenant screener; these jobs could be performed by centralized personnel deployed where needed. In addition, centralizing these functions would enhance consistency. One project would not receive advantages over another because it had a manager who was particularly determined about maintenance, for example. Finally, centralized functions seemed likely to increase accountability since each functional manager would become responsible for ensuring the quality and consistency of his or her particular function.

These considerations led BHA management to transfer functions from the individual project managers to specialized, central offices. The centralized units were not expected to understand any particular project but specialized in knowing how to perform a particular function across all the projects, at least in theory. In practice, however, the systems did not perform as intended. As the power of the project managers was reduced, the organization lost its sense of responsibility for the overall quality of life in a given project. Instead of seeing the individual projects as communities, staff focused on the bundle of functions to be performed. Implicitly, midlevel managers and employees felt more responsible for satisfying central managers than for responding to clients who lived in the projects.

Even worse, none of the other systems that might have allowed the centralized offices to work well came into existence. There were no policies for tenant selection and no useful information about maintenance performance. Personnel policies, negotiated with the unions, made it difficult to motivate existing employees and change existing personnel. Thus, the BHA's administrative systems allowed employees to feed off revenues without contributing much to the achievement of its mission. In fact, almost nothing in the BHA's administrative systems focused the staff on the *accomplishment* of its mission.

The centralized, functional structure of the BHA also frustrated tenants in their attempts to get what they wanted from the agency, either as individuals or as communities. If individual tenants needed to have something repaired, or to complain about the conduct of neighbors, they had to file reports with an anonymous central office and wait for some action to be taken. They could not easily organize as tenant groups to take effective action in the projects, for, again, they would have no one to talk to at the project level. They had to reach the center of the organization to get a response, although they could not be sure the center would provide one.

Because all important functions were centralized, the only way BHA tenants could effectively demand a response from the organization was to organize a citywide tenant group. That was hard work and took a long time to achieve. When the tenants finally established themselves, however, the city found itself the target of a powerful lawsuit. That form of petition, in turn, did not encourage the development of solutions to particular problems in particular locations. It also made the relationships adversarial. As a result, a group of people essential to achieving the BHA's goals were frustrated and at odds with the agency. A potentially valuable partnership was ruined.

Administrative Systems in the HPD

At first glance, the Houston Police Department looked far more sophisticated than the BHA. It had a formal, complete, and hierarchical structure. Detailed policies and procedures covered all aspects of HPD operations. Important information was collected and reported about the performance of the organization at the aggregate and individual level. In these respects, the organization met standards of formalization.[82] But the strategic question is not whether formal systems exist, but whether they help the organization do its work. Judged from this second perspective, the HPD's systems look far weaker.

Perhaps the greatest problem lay in the illusion of control created by the comprehensive formal systems. From the outside, everything seemed under control. Written policies and procedures specified what actions were to be taken. Narrow spans of control guaranteed close supervision. Harsh discipline was meted out when officers erred.

In reality, however, officers worked with relatively little supervision. The informal culture encouraged them to break rules to get the job done. When caught, they were alternately protected and scapegoated by their superiors. Such conditions generated an enormous amount of stress and cynicism in the organization. It also made creativity in doing the work a form of deviance. Thus, the key productive asset of the organization—the commitment, talent, and orientation of the officers themselves—was being wasted.

Moreover, like the Boston Housing Authority, the police department was handicapped in achieving its goals by the centralized, functional structure it had adopted. Initially, like the BHA, urban police departments were geographically decentralized. Precinct commanders operated like local chiefs of police. But this decentralized structure allowed powerful local politicians to use the police for their own purposes.[83] Hiring and promotion decisions were corrupted to support local political machines. Enforcement practices, too, became ways to reward the party faithful and punish its enemies.

To guard against inappropriate political influence, police departments throughout the country were reorganized into centralized, functional units. As in the BHA, the local precinct commanders gradually had functions stripped away and placed into the centralized units. The justification for the police force's centralization was identical to that for the centralization of the BHA: the centralized units would develop greater skills in performing particular functions and could be deployed more efficiently across the entire police force. Reformers also claimed that the centralized units would ensure consistent, citywide performance.

The reorganizations accomplished what they were designed to do. They weakened the power of local politicians. Skill levels did improve. Police operations became more consistent. But, as with the centralization of the BHA, there was a price to be paid for these advantages: the working partnership between the police and the community began to break down. True, by investing in elaborate dispatching systems, the police wired themselves to the needs of individual citizens. But the focus on responding to individual calls for service subtly undermined the importance of communicating with larger community groups and learning the problems they faced. As long as the police provided services to *individuals,* they tended to think of security in individual rather than group terms. With no community groups as partners, the police could not find any effective leverage over the larger problems of the local community. With no one to talk to in the police department, little incentive existed for community groups to band together.

Unlike the BHA, the HPD had some powerful information systems to measure its overall performance, but these measures also locked the agency into a particular view of its mission. The key performance measure was the level of reported crime. These data, tallied in a particular way defined by the FBI's system of Unified Crime Reports, were collected consistently across the nation's cities and within Houston over time.[84] Thus, analysts could compare Houston's performance with other cities, and with itself, at different times. Because citizens and overseers monitored the comparisons, these measures attracted a great deal of managerial attention.

To the extent that these measures gave the organization an operational focus, they served a purpose. To the extent they focused the organization on a key component of their mission, they were also desirable. Despite these advantages, the reported crime statistics had three weaknesses.[85] First, they captured only the crimes reported to the police—not all the crimes experienced by citizens. Because the "dark figure" of unreported crime remained unknown, a great deal of uncertainty inevitably remained about how bad the crime problem was, whether it was getting better or worse, and where it was located.[86] Second, because many factors other than police performance affect crime rates, it was hard to hold the police strictly accountable for any changes in the level of crime. The changes could have been caused by shifts in the social structure or the economy, or by the inability of the criminal justice system to respond appropriately to arrested offenders. Third, the statistics tended to emphasize only one part of the police mission—the part that concerned reducing homicides, rapes, robberies, assaults, and burglaries. The role that the police might play in promoting community order and security through other activities was implicitly deemphasized by measurements that accounted only for their crime-fighting role.

In addition to these data, the police collected and reported output measures that described their own operations. But those data, too, had limitations. The police reported how many arrests they made and what fraction of the crimes reported to them had been "cleared" by arrest. These numbers were useful in recording levels of organizational activity, but without knowing what happened later to the cases in the court system, a crucial piece of information about the quality of police operations was missing. They also collected information about "response times," but no one really knew whether response times were a valued attribute of service, nor whether response time correlated with the chance of making an arrest and clearing a case.

The HPD's personnel systems were similarly well developed and formalized, and quite well adapted to the goal of hard-nosed law enforcement, but only imperfectly related to other visions of the organization's mission. The systems for recruiting and selecting officers, for example, emphasized the capacity to use force in a disciplined way. Men applied for the police far more often than women. Height requirements existed to ensure that officers could be physically imposing. Any record of prior misconduct was disqualifying. Similarly, recruit training emphasized physical training and skills over knowledge of the law and development of judgment and human relations skills. Indeed, the compelling experiences of recruit training focused on learning how to wrestle resisting suspects to the ground, drive a car in hot pursuit, and fire a gun in self-defense.

Once on the force, officers had two principal routes of advancement. The quickest way up was promotion from patrol officer to detective. Officers qualified themselves for such promotions by showing initiative in making "collars." Once officers became detectives, their pay increased, and their working conditions improved dramatically. They had more freedom to plan their work and set their own schedules. Even more important, they could put aside the uniform (colloquially called the "bag") that exposed them to any and all demands from citizens.

The other route to advancement was up through the supervisory ranks. This path involved civil service exams, which tested substantive knowledge of the job rather than managerial or leadership skills. Promotion to a supervisory position in a patrol bureau meant better pay and slightly better working conditions. Officers could get off the street. But they exchanged the arbitrary demands from citizens for the arbitrary demands from their superiors.

These personnel policies undermined the caliber of the organization's patrol operations. The best officers left patrol for the detective bureau. Those who became managers in patrol were distinguished more by their ability to pass exams than their ability to perform on the street as police officers or in the office as effective managers. Because the detectives were considered the heroes of the organization, the culture of the department remained focused on crime fighting and crime solving rather than on any other value-creating aspects of their operations.

In sum, although the administrative systems of the HPD gave it the appearance of a well-controlled task-focused organization, it was actually quite volatile an only imperfectly focused on its most important work. Centralized structures had weakened ties to local communities so that useful partnerships had not developed. Statistics kept the attention of the police on goals that described only a part of the public value police departments could create and on operational programs whose effectiveness was suspect. The personnel system tended to recruit people for a narrow vision of the task and to drain the patrol force, the organization's key operational unit, of its best people and its organizational status. Unlike the BHA, the Houston Police Department's administrative systems focused the attention and energy of the organization on a mission; unfortunately, it was not entirely clear that the mission being pursued so zealously was the right one.

INNOVATING AND CAPITALIZING

Any analysis focused on an organization's product, production processes, and administrative systems in light of its overall strategy will generally identify important gaps in what the organization produces and incongruities in the way it is organized. For example, analysis of the BHA reveals the gap between the need for effective maintenance and the strong procedures and administrative systems that such operations would require. It also shows the gap between, on the one hand, the need to organize the tenants to produce a high-quality community life and, on the other, the weakness of the organization's structure in facilitating the development of strong local communities. Analysis of the HPD hints at the incongruity between the organization's control systems and the conditions under which most officers work. It also uncovers the lack of any program for reducing fear or for mobilizing citizens to undertake their own self-defense.

Identifying such gaps and incongruities is important, for they identify the need for managerially led innovation. Each gap or incongruity becomes a plausible focus of thought, planning, and investment—in effect, an occasion for innovating. In meeting the successive challenges posed by the gaps and incongruities, managers set their organizations on a course toward improved performance.

How much innovation work must be done depends on how well adapted the organization is to its political and task environments. If managers take over bankrupt organizations, they will find much to be done. If they take over organizations that have operated successfully in a stable environment, they will generally find less to do.

Managers need to know roughly how many and what kinds of innovations are required because innovations use certain kinds of organizational assets intensively. In many public sector organizations, employees are unaccustomed to innovation, and authorization for innovative initiatives is closely held by top-level managers and their staffs. In such organizations, sustaining a rapid pace of innovation strains both the organization's top managers and the capacity of the organization's strategic planning system to nominate, analyze, design, approve, and track innovations.

Innovations also tend to use up the tolerance of managers' employees. Chester Barnard observed that, to be successful, managers have to operate within their employees' "zone of indifference." They cannot ask their employees to do something beyond the scope of their implicit contract with the organization.[87] If managers make demands beyond that zone, employees resist, and managers fail. One of the hardest things that public managers ask their organizations to do, of course, is to change, for many public sector employees have grown accustomed to their current modes of operation. Indeed, they have come to see stability as a virtue— a characteristic of a well-run, well-planned organization. Consequently, when things become unsettled by too much change, many employees begin to fear for their organization's future, and they become resistant to further change. Their discomfort constrains how much change can occur within any period of time.[88]

Innovations also create political risks.[89] Initially, the media are attracted to innovations simply because they are news. Indeed, public executives are sometimes tempted to launch innovations for no reason other than gaining visibility. The problem, however, is that if the projects fail, the media often seek a scapegoat.[90] So do political overseers who opposed the innovation. Both the media and political overseers will attack the managers for being irresponsible. They shouldn't have *experimented* with the public's money. If they couldn't be sure that their idea was going to work, they shouldn't have tried it. Against such a background, public managers can withstand some failed experiments, but they cannot endure a long succession of them.

In sizing up the innovations that need to be undertaken, managers should distinguish several different types. Some could be characterized as *policy* or *program* innovations. These innovations define new ways of using an organization's resources to accomplish its overall mission. Thus Spence might change the BHA's policies governing tenant selection, or develop youth recreational programs in the housing projects. Brown might develop a program to deal with fear.

Other kinds of innovations could be characterized as *administrative* innovations. These innovations involve new methods for organizing, accounting for, or controlling the organization's operations. For example, Spence might develop an information system to measure the performance of his maintenance unit. Brown might decide to decentralize the patrol function so that stronger relations could be developed with local communities.

Still other kinds of innovations could be characterized as *strategic* innovations. These innovations seek to redefine the basic purposes or core technologies of an organization. Spence might judge that, if the BHA is to succeed, it will have to take in more upwardly mobile families and reduce its focus on the most poor; he would recognize this shift as a change in the BHA's mission: from providing emergency housing to the most desperate to providing transitional housing for the upwardly mobile. Brown might see a need for the HPD to shift its focus from hard-nosed crime control to efforts to reduce fears and improve the quality of service to Houston's diverse neighborhoods.

There are important relationships among these different kinds of innovations. A strategic innovation usually requires a great many programmatic and administrative innovations if it is to succeed. Indeed, only when managers envision a strategic innovation in concrete detail can they accurately see what kinds of programmatic and administrative innovations must be undertaken. The latter innovations close the gap between what the organization now is and what it can become.

As a corollary, programmatic and administrative innovations represent the concrete path toward a strategic change. Managers cannot move their organizations instantaneously to their newly envisioned strategy. They can move them only by undertaking specific, concrete measures. Those are usually the smaller innovations characterized as administrative or programmatic.

Note that these smaller innovations may be adopted because they lead to a new strategy or simply because they seem to solve a current operational problem. Sometimes, the innovations adopted because they seem to solve a current operational problem suddenly open a new vista that allows the manager to see a whole new strategy.[91]

The smaller innovations may also be more or less catalytic by stimulating the changes required to make the transition to a new strategy. All innovations seem to have second- and third-round effects on the organizations in which they are introduced. Sometimes these effects accelerate the organization's course toward a new strategy. Other times they hold the organization back.[92] Being able to distinguish between powerfully catalytic and relatively inert innovations is very important for those managers who want to make big changes quickly.

One particularly important kind of strategic innovation is designed not only to move the organization to new purposes and methods but also to increase the organization's future capacity to learn and innovate.[93] To some degree, any large change in an organization produces these effects. Once an organization has had to make the many changes required by a shift to a new strategy, it has learned how to sustain a high rate of innovation; those "muscles" have been extensively exercised. But it may also be that some particular kinds of organizational structures keep the organization open to learning.[94] Principally, these structures seem to be those that expose the organization to many external stimuli, permit lots of decentralized decision-making, and allow employees to team up in many different units to get the work of the organization done.[95] Organizations guided by values and performance measures, rather than regulations and rules, seem most capable of maintaining this openness.[96]

At any rate, an operating strategy for an organization often requires some degree of innovation. The innovations may be administrative, programmatic, or strategic. The more ambitious the plans, or the more desperate the circumstances of the organization, the more the need for innovation. Viewed from this perspective, the BHA and the HPD, at first glance, look quite different.

Innovation in the BHA

The problems facing the BHA look as though they might be solved with a few, simple administrative innovations. Essentially, the organization seems demoralized and badly run. Thus, Spence has to find a way to improve basic operations: to release the flow of modernization funds to upgrade the buildings, improve the quality and timeliness of maintenance, tighten policies on tenant selection and eviction, and enhance rent collections.

Behind these operational problems, however, lies a disguised strategic problem. Spence has to find a way to rebuild the commitment of citizens and their representatives to public housing by making it appear that the housing projects are attractive communities in which public value is being preserved rather than squandered. That requires him to think in terms of mothballing some of the worst projects and changing the strategy from providing housing to the most desperate citizens of Boston to serving those who are slightly better off. Such changes would require larger adaptations in the policies and procedures of the BHA and a different way of relating to the authorizing environment than now exists.

Innovation in the HPD

The Houston Police Department could also be described as having an operational problem—particularly with respect to the way it uses force and authority. That could, perhaps, be solved by improved training programs or by new administrative systems designed to identify officers commonly accused of excessive force.

But in Houston the strategic problem is more evident. The essential question facing Brown is whether he will continue to police Houston as it has been policed in the past, or whether he will break from tradition and pursue a new untested strategy—one that makes the problems of fear and disorder as important as effective crime control, that seeks to develop more effective relationships with the communities of Houston, and that changes the administrative style of the organization to allow greater use of the patrol officers' own initiatives and capabilities.

Such changes would require a far more fundamental adjustment of the organization's culture and orientation. They may be pursued by specific, concrete changes in the organization's administrative systems. They will be expressed in countless details of the organization's operations. But the changes will be so numerous that they represent an overhaul of strategy rather than simply shifts in administrative systems or in operations.[97]

Once managers have gauged how much innovation is required to pursue a higher value strategy, they can calculate more closely how much capitalization is required to achieve their goals. The more ambitious the goals, the more capitalization they need.

In the public sector, capitalization comes in different forms. Obviously, new funding is one source, as are new grants of authority. Perhaps the least obvious form of capitalization is the most important, however: the political tolerance of errors. These forms of political capital come from the authorizing environment through the exercise of political management.

The other source of capital is internal. New resources and new capabilities for action can often be found in the "slack" that exists in the organization.[98] More resources can be generated if managers can find the means to reprogram current resources, usually by liquidating old commitments and transferring the resources freed up to new initiatives. Unfortunately, such efforts are generally met by intense internal resistance. People who have made commitments to the development of particular programs or administrative arrangements, and whose careers seem to depend on the continuation of those programs, do not like to give up their claims on the organization's budget. Nor do they want to shift their efforts to new functions.

Outside political pressure can overcome such internal resistance. Experience teaches that most subordinate managers in organizations will not release their claim on an organization's resources until it is absolutely and incontrovertibly necessary. They will not refocus their energy or effort until the demands for change are inevitable. For this reason, they will generally respond to initial demands for change made by their superior managers with skepticism and covert resistance. They will look right *through* their superiors to determine the strength and durability of the claims to change that the managers represent. Only over time will actions by superiors and support by others in the political world reveal the strength of those claims.

One of the important and interesting features of these cases is that the incoming managers—Spence and Brown—have, at the outset, a great deal of flexibility. That flexibility comes from the very weakness of their organizations, the explicit or implicit declarations of bankruptcy. As in other bankruptcies, the new managers are relatively free to restructure operations. Some of the old managers have departed. With their departure, the expectations of subordinates have become unsettled, leaving employees more willing to respond to managerial initiatives.

These observations probably apply to Spence more than Brown. After all, in Spence's case the organization has been officially declared incompetent and has operated without any top management for several years. In Brown's case the organization has made a few mistakes but still enjoys widespread support. Moreover, none of the top-level managers have left; indeed, four former chiefs remain lodged in key positions just under Chief Brown.

When we look at the opportunities for mobilizing outside support in the future, however, the situation seems reversed. Spence will face the difficult task of generating enthusiasm for a new mission for public housing. He might be able to produce a sense of relief that conditions within the BHA are starting to improve. But it is hard to imagine how any broad new constituency will flock to the enterprise. Brown, by contrast, has a vision of policing that might turn out to be attractive to a great many citizens of Houston. Its appeal may allow him to succeed even in a world in which his organization has not yet decided that radical change is necessary.

FROM DIAGNOSIS TO INTERVENTION

This assessment of the operational problems and opportunities of the two organizations is meant to sensitize operational managers to the opportunities to create value through transformations of their organizations' productive activities. Although the assessment does not give an answer to what a specific manager must do to realize a specific opportunity, it does provide clues about what might be valuable. To learn what managers must do to realize operational value, we must turn to the question of how best to implement a strategic vision. That is the subject of Chapter 7.

IMPLEMENTING STRATEGY: THE TECHNIQUES OF OPERATIONAL MANAGEMENT

To implement a shift in organizational strategy, managers must take a series of particular, concrete actions.[1] They cannot simply command an organization to pursue new goals, or invent new operational programs to achieve them.[2] They cannot even transform an organization's administrative systems with a stroke of the pen. Instead, they must prod their organizations toward new purposes through specific, concrete actions: some that communicate new purposes, some that build outside support, some that reengineer operations, and some that restructure responsibility and accountability among their subordinates.

Often, managers believe that strategic actions are those they plan: the ones that emerge from processes such as management retreats, formal budgeting systems, or major reorganizations.[3] Observation tells a different story, however.[4] Many strategic issues are plucked opportunistically from the tide of issues that breaks over their heads as media and political overseers suddenly take an interest in their operations, or that sluices through their in-boxes.[5] Thus, good strategic managers learn not only how to plan actions but, as important, how to exploit unanticipated opportunities as they arise.

In Chapter 3, I indicated that an important device for remaining purposeful in a chaotic world was to envision a broad strategic direction rather than develop a detailed strategic plan. The direction had to be specific enough to identify the key political and organizational work that had to be done to allow the organization to achieve the envisioned value. But I identified those tasks as general problems to be attacked through both improvised and planned action. When things go well, and managers are wise, nimble, and lucky, each intervention they make, whether planned or opportunistic, helps shape the context for the next intervention and thereby amplifies its effects. On rare occasions the sequence of managerial interventions accumulates to produce that most unusual of organizational phenomena: a real change in organizational strategy. To see what this looks like in practice, consider the actions Spence and Brown took to realize their strategic visions.

SPENCE: REHABILITATING PUBLIC HOUSING IN BOSTON

Judge Garrity ordered the BHA into receivership in October 1979.[6] Shortly thereafter, he selected Spence as the court-appointed receiver. Because appeals by the BHA were not exhausted until February 1980, Spence had a full three months to prepare his takeover of the BHA.

Paving the Way

Spence used this time to complete two key tasks. First, he shored up his mandate by negotiating the terms of his accountability with Garrity. Second, he recruited a core management staff.

Spence jointly drafted his formal "order of appointment" with Garrity. In the final version of this mandate, the judge ordered Spence to "provide relief to the Plaintiff Class of Tenants." To do so, he was afforded "full power to direct, control, manage, administer, and operate the property, funds and staff of the BHA."[7]

To ensure he remained accountable, Spence agreed to submit semi-annual progress reports to the judge and to participate in annual hearings to determine whether the receivership should be continued. Spence also agreed to establish a Housing Advisory Committee made up of academics, tenants, and members of the Boston business community, to provide for him and the judge the benefit of their independent views of the BHA's progress.

Finally, Spence and the judge agreed that Spence would be the public spokesman for the BHA and the court's efforts to improve conditions therein. Through these devices, Spence was put on the spot to deliver important results—a position he welcomed.

To help meet his newly defined obligations, Spence recruited a small management team from among his professional associates. He hired Carol Gutt to be his secretary, Kay Gibbs to be his executive assistant,

Howard Cohen to be his chief counsel, Rod Solomon to be in charge of special projects, and David Gilmore to be his deputy for operations. He had previously worked with Gutt, Cohen, and Gilmore. In recruiting this staff, Spence said: "The first issue was loyalty, I admit . . . I had a lot of concern, obviously, for competence. But I wanted to be certain that they were people I could absolutely trust."[8]

Finally, on the eve of his formal appointment, Spence telephoned several other key individuals whose support he would need: Byron Matthews, the secretary of the Massachusetts Executive Office of Communities and Development, which provided the state funding for the BHA; Marvin Siflinger, the director of HUD's New England Area Office, which provided the federal funding to the BHA; and the heads of the two local unions representing the majority of BHA workers—the Teamsters (representing the BHA white collar workers including the field managers of the organization), and the Building and Construction Trades Council (representing the skilled craftspeople in the BHA's maintenance operations). He informed each that he was about to be appointed the BHA receiver and looked forward to working productively with them.

Challenging the Staff

At 10:00 the next morning, Spence walked into his first senior staff meeting as the receiver of the BHA. He asked the senior staff to prepare reports describing the work of their offices and giving their assessments of their key staff members.

Following the meeting, Spence reached deeply into BHA operations. He dug into the piles of paper that had accumulated over the long months of waiting. Issues long neglected began to be addressed. A steady flow of memos streamed out from the receiver's office.

Spence also became a visible presence in the field. At least twice a week he arrived at a housing project for an unannounced tour. He convened a regular, semimonthly senior staff conference during which BHA managers were asked to report on their activities, issues, and accomplishments.

All this added up to an aggressive engagement with both the work and the people of the BHA. The engagement, in turn, alerted Spence to "just about every issue . . . in the authority." It also allowed him to assess the competence, energy, and orientation of the BHA staff. Most important, the encounters enabled Spence to establish and enforce standards of performance. He explained: "By day two I was doing things like taking letters back and saying, 'This has a typo in it.' That kind of thing was fundamental because the agency was so sloppy. [There were] just no standards whatsoever . . . In some sense, this was ludicrous little stuff. [But] in another sense it says, 'This represents the quality of the work we do, and this is crap.'"[9]

To reinforce his commitment to exacting standards and personal accountability, Spence also took more consequential steps: he drafted official letters of reprimand and commendation and inserted them in official personnel folders. Two managers, long regarded by the rest of the organization as "classic survivor types," left the agency after they had been subjected to disciplinary actions. Their departures began a wider exodus. Within six months, all the top staff of the authority had departed.

Reorganizing

The resignations gave Spence an opportunity to reorganize the BHA to accomplish two goals: to focus the organization's attention on its key tasks; and to exploit the talents of his key subordinates. In one strategic move, Spence lifted the Construction Management Bureau out of the Division of Planning and Redevelopment and made it into a separate division reporting directly to him. The change reflected his judgment that producing visible improvement in the physical condition of the BHA's deteriorating projects was the single most urgent task facing him. The changes also allowed Spence to recruit a first-class manager— Robert Tierney—to lead it. As Spence explained, "I never could have gotten a person of that caliber for a job with lesser status or lesser pay."[10]

In a second key move, Spence removed the Department of Occupancy from the Operations Division and appointed David Gilmore to be his special deputy for operations. In this case, Spence sought less to emphasize the importance of tenant selection than to establish Gilmore's firm control over two other functions Spence had singled out for long-term emphasis: security and maintenance. In Spence's mind, these issues were ultimately the most important ones facing the organization. But they would also take longer to solve than either the construction or tenant selection issues. Spence wanted his principal assistant to begin work immediately on these large, long-term problems. And he wanted that work done without distractions.

Building Support and Attracting Resources

These organizational changes freed Spence to focus his own attention on mobilizing external political support for the BHA. The wide publicity given to the appalling conditions in the projects had produced an attentive political audience. If Spence could show that he could improve the agency's performance, many would step forward to help.

Spence met this test in part simply by being energetic, determined, and optimistic. In addition, Robert Tierney's early successes in initiating modernization projects (discussed below) produced concrete evidence that something was happening at the BHA. Together, they inspired confidence in the future of the agency.

To sustain the political support, Spence paid close attention to the demands of Massachusetts legislators. He named John Washek, originally hired as a planner in 1978, as his special assistant and made him responsible for political liaison. In the past the BHA had built legislative support through patronage. In the new regime Spence and Washek hoped to substitute "excellent information services" for the older approach. The basic idea was to keep legislators informed on matters that interested them rather than accommodate their demands. Washek's "excellent information services" resulted in generous appropriations: $20 million for the rehabilitation of the D Street Project in 1980, and over $8 million for modernization in 1981 (the first such award since 1977).

In another sign of trust, the legislature gave the BHA wider discretion in construction contracting. The agency had long sought an exemption from the "filed sub-bid requirement"—an onerous procurement regulation that required public agencies to divide large construction jobs into smaller subprojects so that small subcontractors could successfully compete for public construction work.[11] Although originally designed to widen competition and enhance fairness, the rule had the additional, unwanted effect of frustrating the efforts of general contractors to assemble teams capable of taking on an entire job. General contractors had to use subcontractors who had already filed bids. The net effect was to slow the pace and increase the cost of construction.

Under Spence and Washek, the legislature finally agreed to exempt large BHA construction projects from this burdensome requirement. Washek recalled: "That was a major political victory . . . It was a very important piece of legislation. The sub-bidders (who are very well organized and connected) and labor fought us tooth and nail . . . I think in a case like that our legislative relations came out quite well."[12]

Spence was equally effective in lobbying at the federal level. Within six months of his appointment, Spence announced a special award of $13.5 million in modernization funds to "stabilize" the authority's six most distressed developments. In addition, HUD permitted the BHA to combine previously unspent development funds with infusions of new money to create a pot of $26 million, which could be used to support a massive rehabilitation of Fidelis Way, another of the BHA's deteriorating projects.

Following the election of Ronald Reagan in 1981, however, Spence found the federal government less forthcoming. Indeed, the Reagan administration sought to reduce HUD's operating subsidies to local authorities by 15 percent in fiscal year 1981 and 30 percent in fiscal year 1982. Deciding that "there was no effective national lobbying," Spence created the Council of Large Public Housing Authorities (CLPHA). In March 1982 Spence testified as CLPHA's spokesman before the Subcommittee on Housing of the Senate Committee on Banking, Housing, and Urban Affairs. Terming HUD's proposed cap on operating subsidies "totally disastrous for public housing," Spence concluded that, if HUD had its way, "Within a few years there will no longer be any public housing in this country that can provide shelter for low-income people."[13]

Spence's lobbying efforts paid off. In both fiscal year 1981 and fiscal year 1982, Congress approved supplemental funds to maintain federal support at the accustomed levels. Later, when HUD cut the housing subsidies administratively, CLPHA successfully sued and helped pass legislation that forced HUD to spend the appropriated funds.

Spence attributed the success of the lobbying effort to CLPHA, which, with the aid of private foundations, had expanded into a full-time research and lobbying organization. Others credited Spence himself. Said former court-appointed master Robert Whittlesley, admiringly: "[Spence] has been such a brilliant national leader in this thing . . . He's getting a lot of money which is helping him . . . [but] the guy in Chicago is getting more, too, because of Harry Spence."[14]

Operations I: Rebuilding the Housing Stock

The new funds and more flexible contracting authority gave Robert Tierney the wherewithal to begin rebuilding the BHA's deteriorated housing. The question was where to start. Spence and Tierney decided to deploy the resources to support two strategic goals.

First, they sought to stabilize the authority's largest, most vacant, and most rapidly deteriorating projects. Stabilization involved three steps: families living in the worst buildings were moved into better buildings; the vacant buildings were mothballed; and the newly filled buildings were improved with new plumbing and heating.

From one perspective, the stabilization program improved life for clients and BHA management. The residents benefited from living in projects with lower vacancy rates and better plumbing and heating. The BHA gained by simplifying its maintenance tasks.

From another perspective, however, the stabilization program hurt potential clients of the BHA. Mothballing took many apartments out of service. Arguably, this was not a great loss, since many of them would have been vacant in any case. Still, because stabilization reduced the number of public housing units in the city, some potential clients of the BHA went unserved.

Second, Spence and Tierney focused on reconstruction: major rehabilitation of particular projects. Three projects received special attention. One was the D Street Project—a predominantly white project, and a pet of Senate President William Bulger. Indeed, shortly after Spence's appointment, the Massachusetts legislature had appropriated funds to rehabilitate D Street with little encouragement from Spence. To maintain racial balance, the legislature also appropriated similar funds to rehabilitate the Franklin Field Project—a predominantly black project in Dorchester. In addition, as described above, Spence negotiated with the federal government to create a $25 million pot to work on Fidelis Way, a racially mixed project.

In selecting these particular projects for reconstruction, Spence signaled the key public values he judged important to achieve through the BHA's operations. The deal with Bulger indicated that, while Spence was not adverse to having the authority's assets be used to benefit politically influential white populations, he was also determined that the agency deliver housing services to poor minorities. The focus on Fidelis Way showed the importance that Spence placed on community organization—particularly in racially mixed communities. As he explained: "I wanted to demonstrate around the city that where a resident group came together as competently as [the one in Fidelis way] had, and developed plans like that, and worked well with the staff of the BHA, that was the place we'd put money."[15]

Operations II: Enhancing Security

The construction work that stabilized and reconstructed some of the BHA's worst projects gave clear evidence that the agency was making progress. But Spence knew those physical gains could be sustained only if security in the projects could be enhanced. In a speech in April 1981 (later published on the *Boston Globe*'s op-ed page), Spence pointed to the "collapse of order and community among the residents of our projects" as a major problem to be solved. In his view much of the problem came from the withdrawal of "responsive ordering institutions" such as the police and the housing authority itself. As evidence, Spence pointed to the reluctance of the police to enter troubled projects and the unwillingness of the authority to enforce leases.[16]

To solve these problems, Spence proposed that the Boston Police Department, joined by a complement of BHA security guards, establish "team policing" units to patrol the BHA's worst projects. In a successful lobbying effort, Spence and the Tenants Policy Council (the plaintiffs in the suit against the BHA) pried $2 million from Boston's Community Development Block Grant for this purpose over the objections of a vindictive Mayor Kevin White. In May 1981 fifty Boston police officers and twenty-three civilian investigators began patrolling the BHA's thirteen most crime-plagued projects.

Spence also decided to strengthen the BHA's capacity to evict troublesome tenants. This involved, on the one hand, focusing the resources of his legal staff on the problem, and, on the other, seeking new and broader powers. His chief counsel, Howard Cohen, drew these assignments.

Cohen succeeded in focusing legal resources on tenant evictions by making an informal deal with the Boston Housing Court. Previously, the BHA's legal staff had spent most of its time defending BHA staff against complaints filed by tenants about violations of the housing code. Although most of the complaints were minor, they were nonetheless treated as criminal offenses. Cohen persuaded the Boston Housing Court that such cases should be treated as civil rather than criminal violations. Because the civil proceedings were far less onerous, staff resources became available to pursue tenant eviction cases.

To make these newly available resources more productive, Cohen also sought to shorten the time it took to evict troublesome tenants. He reasoned that a major obstacle to successful evictions was the reluctance of other tenants to testify against them when the complaining tenants would have to live next door to their troublesome neighbors during the long months it took to complete the eviction process. If the time could be shortened, more tenants would testify, and the cases could be handled more quickly.

In May 1980, Judge Garrity granted Cohen's request for an expedited eviction procedure in cases where a tenant had committed, or threatened to commit, a serious crime. Under the emergency procedure, the BHA could bypass a previously mandated administrative grievance panel and bring the case directly to court. Further, such cases would be brought to Garrity himself.

Wasting no time, the Boston Housing Authority invoked the procedure against George and Irene Reeder, residents for thirty years at the Charlestown Project; their son was accused of stabbing another resident when she refused to hide him from the police after he had engaged in a lethal racial assault. The Reeders were tried by jury before Garrity and ordered evicted in August 1980. They quickly appealed the case. The Massachusetts Supreme Court reversed the jury's findings, holding that the emergency eviction procedure had been improperly adopted. The court went on to say that although such a procedure was not constitutionally impermissible, it would require enabling legislation. Accordingly, Spence filed a bill to permit the BHA to bypass a grievance hearing and go directly to court in cases involving serious crime. The bill became law in November 1981.

Looking back, the dispute over the emergency procedures may have been a mistake. Spence and the BHA lost credibility with one of their principal allies—the Boston legal community. Even worse, the emergency provisions had little practical effect. Nevertheless, Spence had served notice that he would go after troublesome tenants, and he had courted conservative support by showing that he was prepared to be tough on crime. The real progress in evicting troublesome tenants came in the more common but less spectacular nuisance cases. In those, the previously toothless legal staff succeeded in evicting fifty tenants.

In another effort to promote security, Spence instructed Washek to "dig deep" into tenant selection procedures and recommend solutions. What Washek found was an operation that, like the legal staff, was spending most of its time on the wrong problem.

Under the BHA's old policies, any application for BHA residency triggered a complete investigation of the applicant's eligibility and suitability, which was then updated annually. That process would have made sense if immediate prospects for occupancy existed. But the waiting list held eight thousand names! The average time spent waiting for residence was several years. Many applicants moved (or even died) before being admitted.

Washek's proposed reengineering of this process effectively reversed the system. Under the new regime, applicants would face only a cursory eligibility test. Once passed, their case would receive no further attention until their name approached the top of the waiting list. At that stage, they would undergo a much more intensive investigation than the BHA had previously done. Staff assigned to this final stage increased from two to six. The method of investigation changed from telephoning references to conducting home visits.

In principle, the criteria for selection remained constant through the changes. These included statutorily defined income criteria to ensure that the poorest citizens were being served and standards of conduct for the tenants to protect the value of the projects for current and future tenants. Applicants could be declared ineligible if they had "a chronically poor record of meeting their financial obligations"; a history of disturbing people or destroying property; or prior evictions and unpaid rents in other BHA units.

Nonetheless, the revised procedures seemed to produce important changes in the resident population. For one thing, the BHA began rejecting applicants. In May 1983 it turned down roughly thirty applicants. In addition, the screeners and field managers began paying attention to how applicants would fit in particular projects. As Spence explained: "If you have an entryway in which you have, say, three families a floor for three stories—that's nine families—and they're all female-headed households, you have a terrible problem with the large number of male teenagers. They pick those hallways out because there's nobody . . . who can scare them out. I haven't come to terms with how we deal with that one . . . But I do think . . . when you do tenant assignment . . . it is reasonable to say, 'Good God in heaven, we either need a very powerful woman or we need a man in this hallway to control the kids.'"[17]

Finally, a new feature introduced by the BHA to speed the process of filling vacant apartments turned out to have subtle screening effects. Under Spence, the BHA had established a homesteading program in which new tenants did the work of preparing a vacant unit for occupation using BHA-provided materials. Leslie Newman, the lawyer for the tenant class, explained how this program effectively screened tenants:

[The BHA has] a real problem getting refrigerators to a vacant unit . . . So they say to a family that's number one on the waiting list, "We have a unit for you. If you can . . . work and . . . provide your own refrigerator, we can move you in immediately." And the family—a mother of three children—says, "I don't see how I can do that, I can't afford a refrigerator." And the BHA says, "Well, then, as soon as we can get a refrigerator, we'll admit you. You're not losing your place on the waiting list." But they'll go to number two and ask, "Can you move in and fix this place up?" And if the second household on the waiting list has a male head of the household, and they are both working, and they can afford a refrigerator, the BHA will move them in first.[18]

This subtle process was entirely consistent with Spence's goals for altering the mix of tenants. Since 1974 HUD regulations had permitted (even urged) public housing authorities to establish criteria that would achieve "the basic objective . . . of housing tenant families with a broad range of income, representative of the range of low income families in the [Public Housing Authority's] area of operation."[19] The only criterion was that tenants had to have incomes lower than 80 percent of the median family income. Some housing authorities, most notably New York City's, had long pursued income mixing as part of their tenant selection policy. As a result, only 25 percent of New York City's tenants were on welfare, and 50 percent of its operating revenues came from rental income. These numbers contrasted with the statistics for Boston, where 75 percent of the residents were on welfare, and 25 percent of the BHA's revenues came from rental income. In fact, Boston's tenants had the lowest per capita income of any housing authority residents in the country.

Such comparisons focused Spence's and his staff's attention on the advantages of income mixing as a tenant selection policy: "What we thought had to happen was some kind of mix—not so much of income as of working and non-working families." Spence explained the reasons: "There is a very big difference between a community made up of non-working people and . . . [one] . . . that has lots of working people in it . . . We started trying to get a tenant organization going at Franklin Field. Fifteen percent of the population of Franklin Field works. We had some meetings. Who turned out? Two thirds of them were working people! From that tiny proportion of the population! They were the only people who believed it was worth coming to a meeting . . . we've [concluded that] we've got to increase the number of working people in our developments."[20]

Spence contended that the kind of income mixing he envisioned did not subvert public housing's mandate to aid the poor. "If you're a working poor family—that's gross income between $5,000 and $12,000 before taxes—you are equally desperate for housing in Boston today as if you were on welfare."[21] But Kay Gibbs insisted that the policy would encourage arbitrariness and discrimination: "Let's suppose you have somebody who's been on a waiting list for five years, but they're on welfare, and you'd much rather admit somebody who applied yesterday who has a job. It's not fair to do that."[22]

This abstract discussion about income mixing policies became concrete in the spring of 1983. Fidelis Way contracted with a private concern to manage the project. In drafting the contract to direct their activities, the tenants, the BHA, and the firm agreed that, except for existing families at the development who would be guaranteed rehousing once reconstruction was completed, "Households will be selected in such a fashion as to achieve and maintain ... moderate income occupancy in 25% of all units." The contract defined moderate income as "family income between 75% and 100% of the applicable income limit for admissions."[23]

Operations III: Community Organization

In addition to these security efforts, Spence initiated tenant-organizing programs within each housing project. Although these programs included literacy, alcoholism treatment, and job-training components, their main thrust was away from the social work and toward activities that tenants could do for themselves. In his fifth semiannual report to Judge Garrity in August 1982, Spence offered this rationale for the change in direction: "The Receivership's interest in helping to build resident capacity reflects an acknowledgement that management improvements and capital investment alone may not ensure the long-term reconstruction of BHA's housing developments; that secure viable communities can be developed only in partnership with strong, capable resident bodies."[24]

Typical of the new effort was the Supportive Services Program launched by Spence in 1982 and funded by a $1 million grant from the state. Under this program, the BHA signed contracts with tenant task forces in three developments—Mission Hill, Mission Hill Extension, and D Street—to hire staff to assist them in providing educational, employment, counseling, and community-organizing services.

Spence initiated a similar program called Community Capacity Building in other projects. Using private funds, six BHA projects received money to hire community organizers who aided tenants in setting up committees to deal with issues such as maintenance, teenagers, gardening, and recreation programs. The net effect of these efforts was described by Leslie Newman: "The number of tenants who can now participate in open, forward looking local membership organizations is much greater than before receivership."[25]

Eventually, these project-level organizing efforts brought Spence into conflict with the citywide tenant organization—the Tenants Policy Council. Although often a partner to Spence's efforts to improve conditions in the BHA, the Tenants Policy Council gradually began to see Spence and his local organizing efforts as a threat. Spence and the council solicited the same foundations for money. The organizations Spence nurtured in his projects began to think and act independently of the council. Policy was being made at the local, rather than city (council), level.

Spence had announced his intention to challenge the council. He later recalled: "I began pushing very early on at the [council] saying, 'Hey, look, number one, you've got no local base; number two, our theme is decentralization. From my view, in order to solve the problems of our developments, we've got to have local tenant organizations that are strong.' Well, as soon as you start talking about strong local organizations, that was terribly threatening."[26]

The festering debate erupted in May 1982. In a letter approving the council's budget for 1983 of $85,700, Spence wrote: "In approving the ... budget for fiscal 1983, however, I wish to emphasize that the BHA continues to be concerned about ... staff productivity at the [council] ... [Its] staff activities too often are uncoordinated or of brief duration. Rather than supporting and encouraging strong LTPCs [Local Tenants Policy Councils], the Director (Myra McAdoo) often seems more intent on dominating the affairs of weak LTPCs."[27]

Spence eventually undermined the council. On May 17 its board voted to ask McAdoo, who had been the organization's executive director since 1975, for her resignation. The change in directors did not, however, satisfy most of the organization's critics. Consequently, in February, Garrity ordered the council defunded, effective April 18, 1983. He instructed the receiver, the plaintiff class, and the Housing Advisory Committee to "implement a plan to solicit proposals for funding both to replace the [council] and to start up tenant organizations in local developments where there are none currently."[28]

To further strengthen the BHA's efforts to build strong communities, Spence wanted to reverse the BHA's tendency to centralize functions and, instead, decentralize responsibility to local project managers. In his second report to Garrity, Spence wrote: "Since the needs of public housing are not uniform, but instead vary substantially from project to project and community to community, prompt and informed decision-making requires decentralization of decision authority."[29] Later in that same report Spence introduced the Operations Division by declaring: "Philosophically and practically, our day-to-day functions are performed with the principle in mind that the field management structure is the first and major line of service to tenants, and the other functions of the Division are to facilitate and support the field operation."[30]

Spence targeted five areas for decentralization: maintenance, security, occupancy, income and expenditures, and capital improvements.

Over the first three years of receivership, devolution of control across these areas was quite uneven. Decentralization of tenant selection, for example, had not passed beyond the proposal stage. Indeed, as noted above, some aspects of that function had been centralized to make fundamental changes in operations.

In other areas, though, change had occurred. For instance, by 1982, all field managers had assumed budgetary responsibility for their projects. Instead of receiving money and personnel according to the dictates of the central office, managers determined their own priorities. They did not have total control over their budgets. They could not, for example, shuffle money between line items or make their own decisions about purchasing material or contracting for services. But they had nonetheless become a "responsibility center."[31] Similarly, under the receivership, instead of having off-duty police patrolling family developments and privately contracted security guards stationed at elderly projects, the BHA assigned its own investigators to work full-time at the projects. Nonetheless, as a formal matter, these officers remained under the supervision of the director of security.

The chief reason for the relatively slow and uneven pace of decentralization was, according to Spence, that "we had a very mixed group of field managers . . . [A] majority were terrible [managers] . . . and you can't have decentralization with an incompetent set of people."[32] Early efforts at including field managers in decision-making were, Spence acknowledged, "largely symbolic"; but as significant departures from past experience, they served to test and challenge the managers. For example, field managers joined in headquarters meetings to design the stabilization program. "They had never [before] been involved in that kind of planning process," said Spence. He chose the next cautious step—having the field managers draw up their own budgets—because "control of resources was an immediately valuable thing for a manager to have. In addition, you could track what people were doing with their new authority."[33]

Spence also explained that the decentralization efforts went slowly because it took him a while to "figure out that the staffing pattern in operations was wrong for decentralization."[34] Initially, the BHA had a very steep organizational structure with four layers of supervision above the level of the individual project manager: Spence at the top; then David Gilmore, head of operations; then the director of field management; then six district directors to oversee the individual project managers. The district directors—initially established under the consent decree—were, according to Spence, "originally conceived as super-managers who were going to manage around those incompetent union members (i.e., the Project Managers themselves), because the District Directors would be non-union."[35] However, as the quality of project managers gradually improved, the district directors had less and less to do. As a result, they became intrusive and undermined the emerging autonomy of the project managers.

Eventually, after lengthy consultations with the field staff, Spence and Gilmore agreed on a solution. In February 1983 they eliminated the position of director of field management and replaced the six district directors with four area directors who would report directly to Gilmore. Under this new scheme, each area director was responsible for overseeing the project managers at about seven or eight developments. "It means," explained Spence, "that everybody's busy . . . There's much less defensiveness about letting decision authority go, because no one's afraid they're going to lose their role."[36]

Operations IV: Routine Maintenance

In the key area of routine maintenance, Spence made major changes by establishing a system that assigned skilled laborers to individual projects. More far-reaching changes resulted from the merging of the once divided functions of maintenance and field management. Under the reorganization introduced by Spence, maintenance superintendents, who deployed and supervised project-based maintenance employees, now reported directly to the project manager. The project manager had the ultimate say about which maintenance projects would be done. The old Department of Maintenance, which had once directly controlled all maintenance work for the agency, was reduced in size and retitled Central Maintenance. Its task was to perform major repair work beyond the capacity of the project-based work crews, for example, roofing, boiler work, and preparing vacancies for occupancy.

Even under the receivership, the decentralization of routine maintenance was not complete, however. Many project managers did not have adequate skilled laborers on hand and had to rely on "swing" craftspeople who rotated among projects on schedules drawn up by the maintenance superintendents. It was not unusual for those schedules to be disrupted by emergencies, so that project managers often found themselves unable to respond to local, routine repair requests.

Overall, the changes in the organization of routine maintenance received mixed reviews. In the words of one field manager: "Routine maintenance is improving all the time. I think that, as opposed to 3 or 4 years ago, on a scale of 1 to 10 we're now about 6 or 7, where we were a 2. We can handle day-to-day maintenance repairs within a week."[37] But, in an otherwise quite laudatory February 1983 memorandum to Garrity, lawyer Newman reserved some sharp criticism for the operations side of the agency: "The tenants of the Boston Housing Authority primarily seek ... a living environment with decent, safe and sanitary housing. The establishment of the basic practices necessary to accomplish this goal has proven to be the most intractable element of the receivership, as it was for the pre-receivership Authority. Lack of direction and purpose, lack of systems designed to do the work and lack of data needed to evaluate the work persist in the maintenance and field management areas. These persistent deficiencies undermine the ultimate success of the receivership."[38]

Not surprisingly, the BHA did not entirely agree with Newman's criticisms. David Gilmore in particular felt that maintenance had improved. To explain why the tenants were not all satisfied, he offered a time-honored explanation—inadequate resources. But in his comments, he also indicated a different set of priorities in responding to the demands for maintenance, one that reflected an orientation to citizens rather than clients: "I will send a glazier to replace a broken window in a flash. I won't necessarily send a plasterer to scrape a little peeling paint or to repair a hairline crack in the wall. Let me tell you why. The broken window says something to a lot of people. If you've got a development full of broken windows, you're sending a message. If you have a development full of hairline cracks in the wall, there's no message being sent to anybody but the resident."[39]

Gilmore's solution to the nagging maintenance problem was "to come to closure with the resident population."[40] Closure meant acknowledging that some requests for minor, cosmetic repairs would simply not be honored by the BHA. It also meant helping the tenants find other ways of making the repairs, such as providing the tenants with the materials. Gilmore noted that the BHA had already given away "hundreds of thousands of gallons of paint" to tenants.[41]

The State of the Authority: Spring 1983

By spring 1983 much of Spence's hard work, and that of his staff, was clearly beginning to pay off. In financial terms, the operating deficit of several million dollars had been eliminated. The BHA was even beginning to accumulate a modest reserve.

In operational terms, the rot had stopped. The modernization projects in the BHA's worst projects established a new image for the agency among citizens and overseers and created far better living conditions for the tenants. These changes were both cause and consequence of a new spirit among the residents that led to the appearance of more effective resident organizations. Maintenance remained a source of frustration, but with the improved resident organizations emerging and the quickening pace of decentralization, there was every reason to imagine that even this most intractable problem would be solved.

As one indication of success, Spence emphasized the significant reductions in vacancies in the projects—from 2,800 to 2,300. Spence believed that by the end of 1984 the agency would have 100 percent occupancy rates in all units except the ones going through reconstruction. He judged this significant because it indicated that the projects had been restored to valuable uses and because it suggested that progress could be sustained. That much was true.

But it was also true that the reduced vacancies had been achieved at least partly through the reduction of the total number of living units available through the BHA. This reduction had occurred partly in the early stages of "stabilization" and partly in the later stages of "reconstruction," during which the density of units was reduced as they were fitted to the needs of the larger families that tended to occupy the projects. Overall, the resident population in the BHA had been increased during the period of the receivership, but by less than vacancies had been reduced.

Perhaps the most important accomplishment of the receivership was an intangible one—the restoration of public confidence in the enterprise of public housing. Describing his tactics in the early days of the receivership, Spence once remarked: "You can establish yourself first as a person with credibility, and later you can pass that on. The restoration of an agency comes first through highly personalizing it."[42] Spence had little trouble establishing his own credibility. What is remarkable is that he succeeded in transferring that credibility to the organization he left behind.

BROWN: EXPLORING
THE FRONTIERS OF POLICING

Lee Brown assumed command of an organization bitterly opposed to his appointment.[43] Within twenty-four hours of his appointment, all but one of his twelve-person command staff had publicly announced their opposition. Not to be outdone, the local union dispatched a delegation to Atlanta to investigate Brown's tenure there and, on the basis of this trip, proclaimed Brown unqualified for the job. Despite the opposition, Houston's City Council voted eleven to three to confirm him.

New Themes: Setting the Course on the Future

Brown initially acted to avoid sharp confrontation. Immediately following his confirmation, he called a closed-door meeting with his command staff. He emerged later to meet the press and declare that he intended "to work with all people who want to make the Police Department the showcase of the nation."[44] He said of his command staff, "I'm sure we'll work together fine in achieving our mutual objectives."[45] Of police brutality, he said: "Misuse of police authority is not . . . [to] be tolerated. Police should not break the law to enforce the law."[46] And, as to the importance of being black, he explained: "It's important for the entire citizenship of the city, including its minority citizens, to come to respect and support [their] police. The successful achievement of the police mission is contingent upon having all segments of the community support it."[47]

These themes, articulated early, signaled the ideas that Brown would use to guide the development of the HPD. On one hand, he reassured the department by focusing on its future rather than its sorry past and by emphasizing strengths rather than weaknesses. On the other, he made it clear that the department would have to change if it were to fulfill his ambitions. Above all, he insisted that the HPD had to become more valuable to the city by binding itself more closely to the problems of Houston's diverse communities.

To shape the department's future, however, this general vision had to become much more concrete. Thus, Brown commissioned Sergeant Richard Sander of the department's Planning and Research Division to write an assessment of the department. Brown instructed Sander to: (1) record the state of policing in Houston as he found it; (2) inventory the department's basic strengths and weaknesses; (3) define the fundamental goals of the organization; and (4) trace the implications of those goals for the operational and administrative innovations that needed to be introduced.

Consulting with Houston's Communities

Having initiated work inside the organization, Brown then turned his attention outward. Over the summer he consulted members of the Houston business community and residents of the city's diverse neighborhoods. He asked each group what attributes of performance they wanted to see in the HPD's operations—the qualities that would make the department valuable to Houston and a showcase for the nation.

Meanwhile, the old guard of the department was breathing easier. To them Brown seemed more interested in external politicking than internal management. That suited them fine, since they remained ensconced in powerful positions. As noted above, two former chiefs of the department, B. K. Johnson and John Bales, remained as assistant chiefs. Johnson headed the Investigations Command. Bales was temporarily without portfolio, since Brown's appointment had ended his tenure as acting chief. The other major positions in the department—those responsible for field operations and administration—were filled by John McKeehan and Thomas Mitchell, both HPD veterans.

The assessment report might have posed a threat to the insiders. But its designated author was a relatively low-ranking officer whose future might depend more on the old guard than on Lee Brown. It was unlikely that he would develop any radical ideas. Instead, the report seemed to be shaping up as a mere plea for more resources. As for Lee Brown, they were confident he would remain a figurehead whose leadership they would have to endure for no more than a year or two.

Operationalizing the New Themes: The Assessment Report

Late in the summer the organization's pulse rate quickened when Brown's dissatisfaction with the progress of the report became apparent. Brown had regularly informed Sander of what he had learned in his community consultations and had asked Sander to incorporate these perspectives in the report. Under pressure from his former bosses, Sander continued to file drafts that reflected the department's views of itself rather than what the community thought of the HPD.

Eventually, Brown hired a consultant, Robert Wasserman, to help Sander complete the report. According to Sander, mild curiosity about the report soon turned to "hallway anxiety." Commanders stopped him in the halls hoping for a preview. "Are they going to show the real problems in the units I commanded? Am I going to be mentioned in the report?" they asked. Sander reassured them, but the department waited for the other shoe to drop.

It dropped late in September when Brown convened his command staff in a day-long retreat in the borrowed boardroom of a local corporation. The setting symbolized the support Brown had cultivated over the summer among the local business community; *he* was now the establishment, and the old guard the invited guests. The intimidating board-room environment also presaged new standards for managerial per-formance—standards that many of the old guard were not sure they could meet.

At 8:00 A.M., the four assistant chiefs and eight deputy chiefs entered the room to find a horseshoe table set with name cards, a packet of information including an agenda and a copy of the report, and two flip charts to indicate that the participants were expected to contribute to the meeting. "It was," Sander recalled, "a highly structured corralling of the team."[48] It was also the first time any of them had seen the report. Brown took them through it, page by page.

The report's basic structure showed how Brown and Wasserman wanted the organization to think about itself. Part I, entitled "The Overview," discussed Houston's development, the tasks that that devel-opment imposed on the organization, and the opportunities it created. Part II, entitled "The Houston Police Department," was an exhaustive, detailed description of the organization and operations of the depart-ment as they then existed. Part III, entitled "Organizational Observa-tions," identified the basic challenges facing the department. The novel feature of this structure was that it represented the HPD as an organiza-tion with demands to meet and tasks to perform that were set by the changing environment of the city itself. The value of the department would be determined by what the city wanted and needed, not what the police department wanted to provide.

The point was made forcefully and directly in Part III of the report. After cataloging "a large number of excellent programs and attributes which have served as models for the nation and about which the depart-ment can be proud," the authors turned to what they saw as the crux of the problem confronting the HPD: "As the city has spread out, rapidly grown, and attracted a new workforce, the police department has at-tempted to keep up with . . . a continually expanding . . . demand . . . Lacking a carefully developed management system, the department has been reactive . . . The challenge for the future is to move from reactive to proactive; to develop a . . . capability which will permit effective use of limited resources to provide quality police service delivery in a man-ner acceptable to the expectations of a large, ethnically and socially diverse metropolitan area."[49]

To justify the idea that the police department had to provide quality services in a "manner acceptable to expectations," the authors asserted: "Law enforcement in America is based on the principle that the police are a part of and not apart from the community they serve. It is appropriate and imperative that the Houston Police Department solicit input from the community on priorities and perceptions citizens have about police service."[50]

Having established this point, they went on to use the information that Brown had obtained in his meetings with local community leaders to identify three key areas the community thought needed improvements: service quality, fear of the police, and police management. With respect to service quality, they wrote:

> The major concerns expressed by citizens . . . [about the] . . . quality of service were the lack of visibility of police in their neighborhoods, the attitudes of officers toward citizens, and the excessive amount of time it takes for police to respond to a call . . . Many citizens . . . express the desire for the return of the "cop on the beat" . . . Minority members of the community would like to see more minority officers responding to their calls. Hispanics request additional bilingual officers who they feel would be more sensitive to language problems and specific community problems such as "glue sniffing" among the young . . . Citizens . . . feel that police should be "a friend," someone you can depend on—not invisible faces who only show up after a crime.[51]

With respect to fear of the police, they reported:

> There remains a fear of police in Houston, particularly in some parts of the Black and Hispanic communities. Citizens complain about officers' use of "ethnic" language to insult people and the use of excessive force following arrests . . . Citizens, again, believe the solution to this perceived fear of police is . . . tied to the critical need for positive interaction between the community and the police.[52]

And with respect to the management of the police, they wrote: "Citizens feel that HPD's managers, generally, are crisis oriented . . . They also feel that HPD's management concepts and philosophies are 'unsophisticated, self-serving and unsympathetic.' Top management, some say, is hindered by some members [who] are unable or unwilling to seek or accept advice from outside HPD."[53]

Hammering on these points, Brown told his command staff that instead of operating separately from (and to some degree above) the community they policed, the Houston Police Department would commit to operating in partnership with the community. Their task was to build an organization in which the "spirit of service" replaced the "spirit of adventure." Further, he insisted that it was up to HPD managers to produce the necessary changes, and it was urgent for them to get on with the job.

The assessment report concluded by identifying two key steps to "lay the foundation for improvement in operational effectiveness and resolution of the pending issues": "Develop an interim organizational structure correcting the functional disparities in the current structure"; and "Develop a plan of action laying out a program of improvement to correct the deficiencies noted in this report."[54]

Brown spent nine hours with his command staff in the boardroom discussing the report. "At the retreat I told the Assistant and Deputy Chiefs I wanted a model police department. Not just a model—but the number one police department in the nation. I explained what that meant—what our value system was going to be, what the ultimate outcomes were that we would expect. Our reason for existing is to serve the people, I said."[55] Rick Sander recalled the impact: "It was right out of Peter Drucker. Brown wiped out the argument . . . that he was an outsider and couldn't understand the problems of Houston. One thing was clear to all in the room. Lee Brown was in command and knew it . . . The retreat . . . was the epitome of good management. 'Here are our problems,' he said. 'Give me the solutions.'"[56]

Establishing Accountability

In subsequent months Brown and Wasserman exploited the initiative they had seized through the report and the retreat. They began pushing the responsibility for making change deep into the organization by restructuring the organization and demanding that HPD managers begin to manage.

REORGANIZING

The knottiest and most urgent task was to decide what to do with Brown's four highest ranking subordinates: Assistant Chief Thomas Mitchell, head of the Administration and Support Services Command; Assistant Chief John McKeehan, head of the huge Field Operations Command; Assistant Chief B. K. Johnson, a former chief of the department and now head of the politically powerful Investigations Command; and John Bales, also a former chief of the department, now without portfolio. These men held civil service ranks and could not be demoted or removed without cause. Moreover, all but Bales (who had sacrificed his standing with the others by currying favor with the newly elected mayor in hopes of being appointed chief) met each week for what they called "tea time" to complain about how the department was going to the dogs, and sometimes to plot against Brown.

In principle, Brown had many options for dealing with this mutinous group. He could have pressured them to resign. He could have asked the Texas Civil Service Commission to grant him additional powers. He could have circumvented their authority by setting up a separate reporting channel through staff officers to line commanders at lower levels. In the end, Brown did none of these. Instead, he decided to make the organizational structure work with the people he had.

His most urgent problem was that he had more assistant chiefs than positions to place them in. Brown solved it by persuading the City Council to provide an additional assistant chief position. He then split the Administration and Support Services Command into two separate commands. He left Johnson in charge of the Investigations Command and Mitchell as head of the (now shrunken) Administration Command. In an important shuffle, the head of Field Operations, McKeehan, was transferred to the new, slimmed down Support Services Command. Bales, the only member of the command staff who had not publicly opposed Brown's nomination, was put in charge of the huge Field Operations Command.

The most important feature of this reorganization was the appointment of Bales to Field Operations. To some degree, it helped to ensure Bales's future loyalty. In addition to feeling disappointed at his failure to be appointed chief, Bales knew that his efforts to claim the job had alienated him from his peers, and possibly from Brown. By placing him in a powerful position, Brown rehabilitated him in the eyes of the organization. Moreover, Brown and Bales agreed that the success of the Houston Police Department depended on improvements in patrol force operations. This shared conviction cemented their emerging working partnership. Finally, Bales was considered a strong and important figure by the department's rank and file, particularly in comparison with the relatively accommodating McKeehan. Thus, by replacing McKeehan with a newly energized, broadly experienced Bales, Brown signaled that patrol operations were to be the highest priority in the department. Brown recalls his reasons for this appointment succinctly: "Bales and I didn't have a difference. We basically agreed on the importance of patrol. And I didn't need a Chief of Staff."[57]

MAKING MANAGERS MANAGE

Having committed himself to working through these managers, Brown next had to stimulate them to become active and accountable. To this end he decentralized the budgeting process and made the department's top and midlevel managers accountable for the development and execution of the department's annual budget. In many respects this was not a difficult assignment, for nearly 90 percent of the organization's budget was spent on personnel. But the HPD's managers had never before had this responsibility. Instead, one man, George Hogan, a civilian administrative assistant with forty years of experience, had always prepared the department's budget. Brown asked Bob Wasserman, who had been appointed as director of planning and research, to oversee the new process. He also hired an accountant from Peat, Marwick, and Mitchell (who happened to be a black woman) as the HPD's budget director to instruct the department's managers in the rudiments of budgeting.

Under these conditions Hogan soon retired, and the assistant chiefs were left exposed. They met Lee Brown alone. One staff assistant described the first meetings:

> The Assistant Chiefs were all in a conference room with Brown; just the Chiefs—no army of police officers or [accountants] with armloads of numbers and charts. Every now and then an Assistant Chief would duck out into a hallway . . . [They were] whitefaced . . . [T]hey didn't know jackshit about their budgets. Brown made the command budget based on that meeting. Bales [lost] half his mechanics because he didn't know what he was getting into.[58]

Wasserman also recalled the meetings, but he emphasized a different effect on the department's managers:

> It's true the Assistant Chiefs didn't know anything about their budgets. And Lee Brown asked tough questions . . . [As] important, however, was that once a budget request was agreed upon, whenever Lee met with City Hall, he brought the entire Command Staff and their staffs. I remember once the city budget director came to have the annual private budget negotiation meeting with the chief and was confronted by 40 commanders in a conference room . . . Lee played hardball in these situations—both with his staff and with City Hall.[59]

Developing the Action Plan

Alongside the effort to construct the department's annual budget, Brown directed a separate planning process—the effort to write the "action plan" that would define exactly how the department would exploit the opportunities and remedy the deficiencies that had been described in the assessment report. Brown released the action plan in the spring of 1983. Three aspects of the form and function of this report are important quite apart from its substantive content.

First, although the report was prepared internally by the department and focused primarily on how the department proposed to operate, the report was addressed externally to the community as well as internally to the police department. The Introduction explained: "This document sets forth the Houston Police Department's Plan of Action for . . . improv[ing] . . . management, service delivery, and effectiveness . . . This Plan of Action . . . is a public statement by the Department on its goals and objectives for improvement."[60] Lest anyone miss the importance of this fact, the report continued: "By issuing such a statement, the Department hopes to signify to the community that it wants the public to be deeply involved in all aspects of police program development, general improvement and direction."[61] Thus, the HPD was making itself accountable to the citizens of Houston.

Second, the plan sought to legitimate the proposed reform program through several interlocking logics: that the specific reforms represented the best response to the particular problems facing Houston; that the proposed solutions emerged from an expert, professional internal analysis; that the solutions drew on the best experience from the field of policing as a whole; and that the proposed solutions would build on the acknowledged traditions and strengths of the department. The plan, and the demands it made on the department, were thus firmly anchored in practical wisdom and necessity.

Third, the plan of action was written at several different levels of abstraction, self-consciously linked to one another. It began with a broad overview of the problems of the Houston community. It then presented the "key values and beliefs underlying the police commitment to improvement." Finally, it described in more concrete particularity what would be done to improve the performance of the Houston Police Department.

In effect, Brown offered the plan as a hierarchy of goals and objectives dictated by the requirements of the HPD's political and task environments. The broadest and most abstract goals were those that defined the values of the organization. The more specific programs and objectives laid out particular, concrete responsibilities that managers within the organization would be expected to meet. The plan was publicized to help make the organization accountable for executing it. Brown and Wasserman thought that anchoring the plan in community expectations would help give it a life of its own—that it would become an inexorable force making powerful claims on the day-to-day behavior of the organization and personnel. That was important, for the plan called for significant changes.

ESTABLISHING ORGANIZATIONAL VALUES

Surprisingly, the general values the plan articulated were its most radical points. In comparison, the specific operational initiatives were relatively tame. The report identified ten fundamental values to guide current operations and future development of the HPD:

Value #1: The police cannot carry out their responsibilities alone . . . they must be willing to involve the community in all aspects of policing which directly impact the quality of community life.

Value #2: The police department . . . [should] . . . react to criminal behavior in a way that emphasizes prevention and is marked by vigorous law enforcement.

Value #3: The police department adheres to the fundamental principle that it must deliver its services in a manner that preserves and advances democratic values.

Value #4: The department is committed to delivering services in a manner which will best reinforce the strength of the city's neighborhoods.

Value #5: The department is committed to allowing public input in the development of its policies.

Value #6: The department will collaboratively work with neighborhoods to understand the true nature of the neighborhood's crime problems and develop meaningful cooperation strategies which will best deal with these problems.

Value #7: The department is committed to managing its resources in the most effective manner possible.

Value #8: The department will actively seek the input and involvement of all employees in matters which impact job performance, and manage the organization in a manner which will embrace employee job satisfaction and effectiveness.

Value #9:   The department is committed to maintaining the highest levels of integrity and professionalism.

Value #10:   The department believes that the police function most effectively when the organization and its operations are marked by stability, continuity, and consistency.[62]

Both the order and the content of these values were significant: taken together, they defined new functions the police should perform and proposed a new relationship to local communities.

For example, the commitment to react to criminal behavior by emphasizing prevention opened up a significant front in the war against crime and gave increased priority to a set of activities within the department. The commitment to advance democratic values and to maintain "the highest levels of integrity and professionalism" meant that the police would finally acknowledge their responsibility to protect constitutional rights. The commitment to "involve the community in all aspects of policing which directly impact the quality of community life" and to "deliver police services in a manner which will best reinforce the strength of the city's neighborhoods" implied a decision to embrace public cooperation rather than professional autonomy.

These values did not sit well with the existing department members. They believed in apprehending offenders far more than preventing crime. Their history placed them among the police departments that had been most disdainful of constitutional protections. And they were far more interested in maintaining their professional autonomy than in consulting with citizens. But the values probably did speak to the new Houston community—both those progressive, middle-class citizens who had recently arrived on the scene, and the minorities who were at last finding a chief who would be responsive to their concerns.

The tension between the values that could command support from the Houston community and those supported by the department is precisely what gave the statement of values its potential force in reshaping the police department.[63] If the values could be held in place as obligations that the department could learn to honor, then the culture of the organization would be transformed. If they crumbled owing to lack of external and internal support, or if they were ignored as irrelevant pieties by those with operational tasks, then they would become nothing more than a public relations device.[64] Thus, much depended on the particular, concrete improvements in the performance of the department's commands, improvements the report promised to deliver.

Significantly, the report began with recommendations for changes in Field Operations. That opening reflected Brown's conviction that reforms in patrol operations were necessary and would be sufficient to improve the overall quality of policing. It was also consistent with his decision to rely a great deal on John Bales, who headed this command. With respect to patrol operations, the report committed the organization to "move toward achieving" five key operational characteristics.

Maximum visibility from patrol resources.

Rapid response to citizen calls for emergency assistance.

Effective crime interception activities undertaken by police and community to developing crime patterns.

Stability of assignment for police officers working neighborhood beats, permitting the development of a close police–neighborhood resident relationship.

Neighborhood involvement in setting the priorities that determine how police officers will spend the time they are on neighborhood patrol.[65]

To some degree, one could read this list as nothing more than a restatement of the status quo. The first three points reflected the traditional emphasis on patrol and rapid response to calls for service. But read closely, the list revealed some subversive, new elements. Crime interception was to be accomplished by the police *and the community*. Officers were to be assigned to stable, neighborhood beats, not only to increase visibility but also to *permit the development of close relationships*. Citizens would be involved in setting priorities for the time that the police were on neighborhood patrol. In such language were sown the seeds of a different style of policing that emphasized contact with citizens, dialogue about neighborhood problems, and crime prevention over arrests.[66]

Brown's intention to foster the new style becomes even more clear if one inspects the list of more particular activities that the Field Operations Command was to perform to approach these operational characteristics. The command pledged to: redesign patrol beats to correspond to neighborhood boundaries; determine the number of officers required for response to emergency calls for service; develop a system to manage the time of officers when not responding to emergency calls for service; develop an analytic capability to support proactive problem-solving efforts to prevent crime; and resolve problems nominated by local communities for police department attention. These specific objectives identified the organizational innovations that would allow the Field Operations Command to take an active approach to community-nominated problems.[67]

Although the heart of the action plan lay in the statement of values and the specific plans for the Field Operations Division, several other features deserve mention. Brown advanced his campaign to decentralize responsibility and hold his managers accountable by obliging individual functional commands to develop detailed policies and procedures and to do so in consultation with community groups. This requirement opened up the department both to operational innovation and to an unprecedented level of public scrutiny. Brown also established an Inspection Division in the chief's office to conduct annual performance audits for each major operational unit in the HPD. Until that time, no mechanism had existed for reviewing the performance of departmental units; only crises triggered high-level review.

Similarly, Brown's determination to "make the patrol officer the backbone of the department" was reflected in proposals to train patrol officers to conduct preliminary investigations at crime scenes, and to eliminate the special rank of detective by giving all detectives the rank of patrol sergeants. In addition, Brown proposed new efforts to audit the department's claimed "clearances" (the number of reported crimes solved by investigations) and new methods for controlling criminal investigations. These changes had the effect of reducing some of the independence and stature of the department's detectives relative to its patrol officers.

Key Innovations

Taken together, Brown's initiatives produced a great deal of ferment in the department. A few managers, betting on Brown's success, undertook innovations that moved the department toward Brown's vision of policing. Three innovations became particularly important, operationally and symbolically.

THE WESTSIDE COMMAND STATION

One key innovation predated Brown's arrival but suited his purposes admirably. In 1979 Houston's voters had authorized the city to borrow $35 million to renovate and build police substations. The department planned several small facilities, each housing a modest motorized patrol force. Detectives would remain stationed at headquarters.

Lieutenant Jerry DeFoor, head of the long-range planning unit thought that this plan enshrined a mode of policing that had been discredited. In 1979 he proposed an alternative: a "multipurpose command center" to serve the burgeoning western section of the city. He recommended decentralizing *all* police functions, including detective work, to the new command station.

His idea was to design and use the substation to facilitate the integration of the police into neighborhood life. The station would reject the image of the police as "an occupying army"; it would promote close contact. To create that intimacy, every function of the department— whatever an officer or citizen might need on a day-to-day basis—would be represented at the station, including detention facilities, courtrooms, motorpool, radio repair, administrative offices, male and female patrol facilities, detective offices, and facilities for community activities.

Although the ideas of decentralization and integration were first occasioned by demands to change the physical architecture of the HPD, the department soon made the leap to change the organizational architecture as well. B. K. Johnson, then chief of the department, authorized DeFoor to convene a Decentralization Study Group, composed of thirteen functional task forces representing each departmental interest likely to be affected by decentralization. By July 1981 the group had completed its report. It offered a plan for the full decentralization of the Houston Police Department. But, with the mayoral election looming and Chief Johnson's own future uncertain, DeFoor's plan languished.

Lee Brown breathed new life into the plan. The decentralized Westside Command Station, now designed and budgeted at $17 million, symbolized his vision of neighborhood-based policing. In the spring of 1983 Brown and the mayor both asked the City Council to support the plan. The council stonewalled. Many councillors—some of whom were the first to represent newly redistricted areas of the city—wanted a command station of their own. Ultimately, the council agreed, but only by authorizing three more command stations. On October 1, 1984, the mayor and the chief of police broke ground for the new Westside Command Station—a concrete symbol of Brown's neighborhood-oriented policing.

THE DART PROGRAM

DeFoor also sponsored the second of Brown's major policy innovations pointing toward the HPD's future. His Decentralization Study Group had recommended that Houston deploy its forces in Directed Area Responsibility Teams (DART). The essential elements of DART included:

1. Assignment of responsibility for all of a geographic area's crime and disorder problems to an integrated group of patrol officers and detectives reporting to a single patrol commander.
2. Maintaining "beat integrity" through policies that prohibited the dispatching of DART officers outside their area except in the most urgent circumstances.
3. Greater use of one-officer patrol cars to promote visibility and keep response times low.
4. The operational integration of patrol officers and detectives in DART teams, assuring more effective cooperation in the gathering of information and job enrichment for patrol officers.
5. The use of "beat profiles" to encourage officers to learn about the neighborhoods they patrolled.
6. "Crime analysis" to identify crime patterns in their areas of responsibility.
7. Formal consultations with civic leaders, ministers, and private citizens to develop lists of community problems to which the police could respond.
8. The development of "tactical action plans" to produce solutions for the crime patterns and problems that had come to the DART team's attention through its information-gathering efforts.
9. The use of these tactical action plans to guide the activities of officers when not responding to calls for service.

Bob Wasserman recalled that DART furthered the three basic elements of Brown's reforms: correct past bad practices, build local confidence in policing, and move Houston into the national scene of progressive policing:

The importance of DART rests on the fact that Houston policing ... [had been] ... characterized by "frontierism"—police officers wildly racing around a large area in "packs." No localized accountability. No interface between detectives and police officers. No community interface. DART focused on correcting these in a rather simple way. It could keep officers in beats, decentralize a group of detectives, provide some kind of supervisory accountability to neighborhood groups. They had not yet figured out several important things—leadership, shift supervision, neighborhood sergeant assignments, and so on. So, Lee decided to let them try it in one area and see what happened. He wanted to encourage change, so he let them go at it even though it had flaws.[68]

Brown assigned responsibility for a DART pilot project to John Bales, gave him 110 officers in the Field Operations Command, and scheduled operations to begin in one district in the fall of 1983.

THE HOUSTON FEAR REDUCTION EXPERIMENT

With the action plan complete and DART in preparation, the Houston Police Department sought and won a National Institute of Justice grant to test several strategies to reduce fear of crime in Houston neighborhoods. It had been Wasserman's view that Brown and the department would soon need more than planning and proclamations for the future. They would need a "win"—something that demonstrated Brown's capacity to lead and the department's capacity to mount successful reform programs. A favorable national spotlight could improve the department's own self-image and give Houstonians something to boast about, perhaps strengthening Lee Brown's hand. Wasserman recalls: "When the fear reduction program was announced . . . we went after it . . . We fought to get it to Houston. We saw it as a chance to give our people hands-on experience with something having . . . national importance. And we committed ourselves to developing the ideas to be used from the bottom up . . . So we formed a police officer task force . . . They came up with the ideas and made it work."[69]

The task force working with Brown and Wasserman would test six fear-reducing strategies in four Houston neighborhoods. One, known as Community Organizing Response Teams, deployed police officers to "help organize the community around specific crime-related, as well as quality of life issues such as disorder, vandalism, and so on." A second, Neighborhood Information Networks, committed the HPD to publishing a newsletter providing accurate information about the risks of crime. A third, Storefront Police Stations, supplemented the command stations with smaller, more informal offices staffed by police officers. A fourth, Victim Follow Up, required police officers to call citizens who had recently been victims of crime to offer their sympathy and support. A fifth, Police Service Response, committed officers to soliciting citizens' views of the quality of service they provided by mailing postcard surveys to citizens who had called for service. A sixth, Directed Citizen Contact, provided the police with a survey instrument and methodology to inventory the concerns of local citizens. These particular programs reflected the important themes that Brown had been stressing for the department's operations.

Engaging the Mainstream of the Department

With the important administrative changes called for in the action plan under way, and with all the talk and planning for the Westside Command Station, DART, and fear reduction, the look and feel of policing in Houston began to change. Some still worried, however, that these interventions were superficial and vulnerable. DART and the fear reduction experiments had both been evaluated favorably, but Brown had been unable to expand either program. In most of Houston's substations and police cruisers, the traditional culture of policing prevailed. The question remained: how could the department move from a series of individual, innovative programs to a whole new philosophy of policing?

In response, Brown continued two important initiatives. First, he sought to anchor his vision of neighborhood policing in the political environment of Houston to ensure continuing support and demands for the kind of policing he was trying to produce. Second, he used his formal and informal powers to create an organizational context in which those who shared his vision could succeed both personally and operationally.

Throughout 1984 and 1985 Brown pursued the first objective by cultivating support for Houston policing among the city's civic, financial, and political establishments. Brown had discovered that except in times of crisis, the Houston Police Department had been closed to civic leaders. He changed that, forming committees and waging a strong campaign on behalf of his plans. "We use the business community a lot for support," Brown explained. Building their commitment to Houston policing helped to create a "favorable impression" for Brown and his budgets with the mayor and the City Council. "All those people who do something for us buy into us," Brown said. "They now have a stake in what we are all about."[70]

He pursued the second objective by assigning new young leaders to lead the reform charge. Lieutenant Thomas Koby exemplified the next generation of aggressive midlevel managers on whom the chief relied to build the future of policing in Houston. Koby had taken every promotional exam as soon as he was eligible and had risen rapidly through the ranks. Brown appointed him a captain and assigned him to Houston's toughest police district, the North Shepherd substation.

Koby arrived at North Shepherd in 1983, shortly after the fear reduction experiment began there. He recalled it as "one screwed up division." North Shepherd's supervisors and officers were resisting the department's new work rules and accountability measures. The division's captain and lieutenant had been on leave for a month. The substation seemed on the verge of revolt.

Koby attributed the substation's problems to the prior regime's practice of cutting itself off from the concerns of the rank and file and leaving significant personnel problems to fester. At first, Koby did not know where to begin. Then, the solution came to him. "I did what Lee Brown did," Koby said. He looked for capable officers with positive attitudes—those who "didn't like the mess out there, officers who had some enthusiasm, commitment and sense of pride that was waiting to be tapped, channelled, and inspired."[71]

Koby soon developed his own version of neighborhood policing. He expanded his one storefront police station to four, and his officers started doing beat profiles and crime analysis. From Koby's perspective, the storefront police stations worked like a charm. He liked the idea that "you put a good thing in the middle of bad things to turn the bad things around."[72]

Koby also incorporated community relations into the activities of his regular patrol operations. The department's practice of dispatching designated community service officers from headquarters to deal with local community groups struck Koby as wrong. Those officers had no ties to the substation or to the neighborhoods. How could a pair of them deal effectively with all North Shepherd's schools? How could they manage the division's local Houstonians on Watch program? Koby's heretical alternative was simple: "My people should be doing that." He proposed to Brown that his substation take on this previously centralized function. Brown quickly agreed.[73]

Tom Koby and others like him spotted the opportunities and challenges in Brown's vision of policing. They staked their careers on moving in the innovative directions suggested by Brown. But the issue still remained whether the reforms would outlast Brown's tenure. Until that was clear, the future of policing would be uncertain.

With three years of administrative ferment and operational innovation behind him, with the external political support and demands on the organization strengthened, and with a rising cadre of internal managers in place, Brown needed some mechanism to reduce his own importance in the organization. He wanted some device to identify the new strategy of policing as the ambition and accomplishment of the organization itself.

He found it by convening a set of meetings involving a large number of Houston police officers from all ranks to discuss the future of the department. In the first such meeting, participants agreed that the future of policing in Houston lay in the values articulated by Brown and in the general concept of neighborhood policing. In subsequent meetings, they worked through a set of operational issues that still bedeviled the department. In effect, the organization as a whole went through another round of "action planning." This time, however, the plan that emerged was the department's—not Brown's or Wasserman's.

The State of Policing in Houston, 1988

In 1989 Lee Brown was appointed police commissioner of New York City. A young woman manager, firmly committed to the concepts of neighborhood policing, replaced him. In her first act, Elizabeth Watson declared that the Houston Police Department would continue on the path marked out by Brown. After all, continuity in direction was one of the values to which the department was committed.

REENGINEERING ORGANIZATIONS: WHAT STRATEGIC MANAGERS THINK AND DO

These cases, combined with others, and set in the context of literatures on public and private management, offer clues about what public sector managers could do to improve the performance of public sector organizations.[74]

Embracing External, Political Accountability

Perhaps the most important lesson comes from observing how much attention Spence and Brown focus on *political* management, specifically, in building political support by embracing accountability and in negotiating the terms of their accountability to overseers. Spence works closely with Judge Garrity to delineate the scope of his powers and responsibilities, and they agree on a process of regular reporting. As though that weren't enough, Spence establishes an advisory board to which he is also accountable. Similarly, Brown articulates his overall goals at his initial press conference. Next, he consults widely with Houston's diverse constituencies. Finally, because the declarations he makes in these processes are too informal and unspecific, he goes on to publish both the *Assessment of the Department* and the *Plan of Action*. These documents lock Brown into achieving specific objectives.

Such actions run counter to what public managers often do.[75] Instead of exposing their organizations to the pressures of external accountability, managers often seek to insulate them.[76] They worry that embracing accountability will take too much time and expose their organizations to too many conflicting demands.[77] As bad, they worry that too much attention to external politicking will be interpreted by those within the organization as a sign of their own personal ambition, or their disinterest in meeting the substantive responsibilities of running the organization, or their weakness and inability to protect the organization from improper external influences.[78]

Against these common practices, the examples of Spence and Brown stand out. They embrace rather than shun accountability, and they stimulate rather than dampen public expectations. Moreover, this tactic seems to work; the performance of the organizations they lead improves. Why? Two reasons stand out.

First, because the newly established terms of accountability reflect the aspirations of political overseers, by embracing political accountability, Spence and Brown are able to command enhanced political support. From the overseers' perspective, the organizations Spence and Brown lead are finally becoming responsive and doing what they are supposed to do. They are becoming valuable. Thus, previous stinginess becomes generosity, and prior skepticism turns to trust. The attitude of overseers, in turn, increases Spence's and Brown's power because it gives them more resources to be deployed and more discretionary power over how to use them. Hence the paradox: by giving power away to overseers, Spence and Brown increase their power and their ability to achieve their ends.

Second, by committing their organizations to quite specific objectives, and anchoring those objectives in specific agreements with powerful overseers, Spence and Brown increase their ability to challenge their own organizations. Once their purposes are linked to the expectations and demands of powerful overseers standing behind them, their strategic visions cease being the idiosyncratic views of transient figureheads; they become, instead, a "reality" to which the organizations have to respond.[79]

Of course, close inspection reveals that neither Spence nor Brown exposes his organization haphazardly to political overseers. Instead, they seek out those overseers who are likely to demand what Spence and Brown think is most valuable to deliver. Indeed, they deliberately disrupt the political coalitions supporting the old strategies of their organizations and forge new political coalitions that demand from them an organization whose substantive purposes are more to their liking.[80] Once armed with a powerful external constituency demanding the changes they want to make, the task of changing their organizations becomes much easier.[81]

Indeed, at that stage, the process of organizational change assumes a rather familiar form. Like Ruckelshaus and Miller, Spence and Brown assume the leadership of organizations that have become the focus of intense criticism by emerging political forces. The criticism has discredited the current organizational strategies and forced the agencies into public sector bankruptcy. As in private sector bankruptcies, new managers are appointed who have no loyalties to the past. Thus, they are free to liquidate some of the organization's previous commitments and shift operations toward new purposes and goals. The overseers, accustomed to unresponsiveness and lackluster performance, are sufficiently impressed by the new initiatives to provide additional "capital." The employees, sufficiently frightened by their prospects in the absence of change, respond to minimal managerial prodding. The net result is that most unlikely of miracles: an important change in organizational strategy.

This common scenario for an organizational turnaround may not be too difficult to execute if the situation is right.[82] Thus, students of management might imagine that the device of embracing rather than shunning accountability works primarily in situations where an organization's political environment has changed, and a new manager (whose goals are closely aligned with the new mandate) has been recruited to implement a strategic change.

Yet the device of embracing external accountability applies far more generally. Indeed, embracing accountability is *always* important in the public sector. There may be some situations where it *appears* that managers can avoid taking this step: for example, in situations stable enough for past traditions to carry into the future, or when organizations have developed such formidable reputations that they can resist effective oversight.[83] Although managers can get away with rejecting accountability in these cases, in doing so, they risk subsequent disaster.[84] The reason is that they risk losing touch with the important values that political overseers want expressed through their organizations' operations.[85] They get too far away from one important kind of "customer." That, over the long run, courts disaster.

Similarly, by resisting accountability, managers lose some of their ability to challenge the organizations they lead.[86] Without being exposed to external demands, they become vulnerable to their own subordinates' desires to be protected from demands for change. In the interest of protecting morale, a manager will come to think that his or her responsibilities as executive are to insulate the organization from these demands rather than give the demands increased force within the organization.[87] In effect, such a manager becomes an agent of the organization's employees vis-à-vis its overseers rather than an agent of the overseers vis-à-vis its employees. The net effect is to reduce the organization's responsiveness and value to citizens and to its overseers.

Whether embracing accountability is generally valuable can await further testing. For now, we can say that if managers seek strategic changes in organizations, embracing accountability seems to be an important tool.[88] Without such an embrace, managers confront their organizations alone. With it, managers can focus the massed force of public expectations for change on their organizations—a far more advantageous position.

Organizational Structure and Staffing

Less surprising than the embrace of accountability is the use that Spence and Brown make of recruiting their key subordinates and designing organizational structures to focus attention on the organization's key tasks. All managers know they are fundamentally dependent on their key subordinates. Thus, they naturally recruit those personally loyal to them and reshape their organizations to make the most of these employees' talents.[89]

BRINGING IN ONE'S OWN TEAM

To a degree, both Spence and Brown follow this pattern. Spence appoints Robert Tierney to head the elevated Construction Management Bureau and David Gilmore to be the special deputy for operations. Brown recruits Bob Wasserman to help develop the two reports that become his strategic plan. They differ from each other, however, in that Brown decides to rely far more heavily on the organization's existing line managers than Spence. Brown recruits fewer outsiders, and those he does recruit are given staff rather than line positions. For operations, Brown puts all his chips on the organization's old managers. And he does so despite the fact that many of them have openly declared their opposition.

The differences could be explained as the result of different institutional constraints. Spence has a freer hand in developing and filling high-level positions than Brown. But the difference also reflects a real difference in managerial style. Brown *always* decides to work with those in a setting designed to emphasize that standards of managerial performance are to be raised. Such efforts make the point that performance matters, that differences in performance will be noted, and that everyone will have to work a little harder to satisfy the new regime.

But these interventions have another important effect as well: they tend to focus the attention of the organization on the new managers. The small disciplinary acts taken by Spence and Brown take on unusual significance. The organization searches these actions closely to learn how high the standards of performance will be, and in what direction the organization is headed. At this stage the managers have an attentive audience for their explanations of what they want and how their standards differ from those previously used.

Of course, given the context of these takeovers, neither Spence nor Brown has to do much to get employees' attention or to set high standards. Because the organizations are already failing, and because the managers are new, people expect standards to be raised. Since everyone expects this result, even small acts will have dramatic effects.

The point is, however, that Spence and Brown self-consciously use the limelight naturally afforded them to challenge rather than reassure their organizations. Neither Spence nor Brown complains about his organization publicly. Indeed, both publicly express support. Instead, through example, through symbolism, and through individual conversations with managers, they establish the idea that standards are going up throughout their organizations.

In the second phase, the higher standards of performance become less symbolic and general, and more concrete and specific.[94] Spence and Brown find ways to distribute challenging operational assignments across their organizations. Employees learn in detail what is expected of them. People who do not want to live up to the new standards (or fear that they cannot) decide to leave. Others begin working and, as they succeed, become committed to their new roles. The attention of the organizations shifts from worries and speculations about new bosses to the specific tasks that the new bosses have handed out.

Spence and Brown use budgeting and planning processes to accomplish these aims. Such processes have long been viewed as important to the success of public sector organizations, and so they seem to be.[95] But Spence and Brown use the budget process for purposes different from the common ones. In their use of the budgeting and financial systems, instead of emphasizing centralized staff planning for resource allocation, they use the budget process to put pressure on line managers to begin accepting responsibility for the operations of their units.

Thus, they both *decentralize* their budgeting processes; they shift the responsibility for developing budgets from central staff offices to operating line managers. In making this shift, they give up some degree of technical competence in preparing the budget and a certain amount of credibility with overseers who have grown accustomed to dealing with the organization's traditional budget office.[96] In return, they get the opportunity to distribute managerial responsibility more widely throughout their organizations. This arrangement takes some of the burden of managing off their shoulders and places it squarely on their subordinates. When Brown brings his managers to the meetings with the city's budget director, for example, he is doing more than "mau-mauing" City Hall; he is inviting both City Hall and his managers to see the subordinate managers as he wants to see them—as principals in the effort to make the Houston Police Department the best in the nation.

Spence and Brown also rely on planning processes that are separate from the budgeting process. Brown, in particular, relies on a strategic planning process to produce the assessment report and the action plan. This particular strategic planning process differs from the usual budgeting process in that it focuses the organization's attention on only a few areas judged to be key for improved future performance. In general, the weakness of budgeting as a tool for strategic management is that it ordinarily tries to be comprehensive and to justify all the organization's activities.[97] Since a manager often uses budgeting for these purposes, every piece of the organization demands to be recognized. Inevitably, then, the budget gives a more accurate picture of the organization's past than its future. Strategic planning, by contrast, is deliberately selective.[98] It does not try to give an account of everything that happens in the organization. It focuses only on the key problems and opportunities facing the organization, and the adaptations the organization must make to deal with the problems and exploit the opportunities.

Brown self-consciously uses strategic planning efforts to focus his organization's attention on the key tasks. Spence does so to a lesser degree. Perhaps this difference occurs because Spence's operational tasks and goals are so clearly spelled out in the terms of the receivership that no additional strategic planning is required: the complaint and the settlement decree define the general and specific tasks that must be completed. They function as the strategic plan. Brown, however, must develop his own. The difference could also result from Spence's bringing in most of his own staff. The strategic planning may have been done as Spence was negotiating their assignments with them. Brown has to develop his assignments publicly.

the community than would have been tolerated in days preceding Brown's tenure. In both cases, the additional authority turns into improved performance: Spence's housing projects become more attractive and safer, Brown's city less fearful and more secure.

Three factors help these managers succeed in gaining additional resources: the preexisting political context, personal attributes they bring to the job, and specific actions they take. In the preexisting political context their organizations were in desperate straits; a strong public interest (backed by specific, energized constituencies) remains interested in improving their performance. Thus, the prima facie case for additional, new resources has already been made.

Among important personal attributes, Spence and Brown bring creditability, competence, energy, and commitment to attractive values. To some degree, these characteristics could be transferred to their organizations. That, in turn, makes them more attractive targets for investment.

The important actions they take resemble those techniques described in Chapter 5. Spence and Brown both spend a great deal of time cultivating relationships with those in their authorizing environments. They attend meetings with business groups, speak on radio shows, and issue a stream of press releases that keep them in the news. Like Kaufmann's federal executives, Spence and Brown spend more than a third of their time managing externally rather than internally.[100]

It also probably matters that they both have something like a strategic plan establishing terms of accountability, and that they report regularly on their accomplishments. Their embrace of accountability attracts confidence from overseers. That confidence, in turn, releases money and authority for operations.

Undertaking Major, Publicized Initiatives

Because these conditions come together, and are skillfully exploited, Spence and Brown benefit from an increased flow of resources. That, alone, might improve performance. But they go beyond these gains and attempt to change the ways that their organizations do their work; that is, they innovate, or stimulate their organizations to become generally more innovative.[101]

Some of the important innovations occur in a few major, widely publicized initiatives.[102] Spence consolidates the organization's worst projects, rehabilitates three key projects, and reestablishes powers over tenants who destroy the quality of life for others in the project. These actions fundamentally change the production processes of the BHA.

already in the organization, with only the slimmest of staff recruited from the outside.

What is important is that both approaches seem to work. This observation flies in the face of the common managerial advice that managers should "always have around them people whom they can trust." These cases show that managers can succeed even if their top subordinates are neither personally loyal nor substantively committed to the managers' visions. Brown seems to cope with the opposition of his staff by giving them important organizational assignments whose results can be easily assessed. That, at least, is what he does with John Bales and his colleagues. In such arrangements, performance on key organizational tasks, rather than personal loyalty, becomes the tie that binds managers to key subordinates. Over time, these working relationships may ripen into personal loyalty and commitment to the mission. But this does not have to be true at the outset. Brown achieves significant organizational changes by working through people who have declared their opposition.

Of course, working with opponents makes the job tougher. It is far more comfortable psychologically, and far more efficient operationally, for managers to surround themselves with people they can trust to do the right thing without having to be closely supervised. But Brown's example suggests that it is possible to manage even when one cannot recruit one's own team. Indeed, by doing so, a manager may be able to gain the benefits both of staying in touch with the knowledge and traditions of the organization as he or she found it and of avoiding charges of cronyism.

Whether managers can succeed in organizations without having key subordinates who feel personal loyalty or a strong sense of shared purpose may be largely determined by personality. Those who are personally secure may fare better without close allies than those who are more anxious. But managers' capacities to survive without close allies inside their organizations may also be affected by the support they get outside their organizations. The more outside support they get, the less inside support they may need—either psychologically or operationally.

In deciding how large a group of people to import to the organization, the differences between the quality of the people in the organization and those known to the incoming manager may also matter a great deal. Most incoming managers have a network of associates.[90] That pool of talent may be deeper and wider than that available in the existing organization. Or it may, as in the case of Spence, cover some specialties that the organization has not yet developed. In such cases it may be entirely appropriate to bring in more outsiders as a way of inexpensively upgrading the managerial talent or specialized skills of the existing organization.

FITTING STRUCTURE TO PEOPLE AND KEY TASKS

Decisions about whom to hire are closely linked to decisions about organizational structure. For example, Spence reorganizes to create a job for Richard Tierney and David Gilmore. Brown reorganizes to accommodate his four assistant chiefs.

Both managers also use these occasions to define the strategically important jobs that need to get done. Spence signals his determination to "rehabilitate" and "build" by elevating the Construction Management Bureau in the organization's hierarchy. Similarly, Brown emphasizes the importance of the patrol function in his new vision of the police department by appointing Bales head of that division. In short, organizational structure is made to serve strategic purposes by allowing the manager to focus managerial talent on the tasks that he or she thinks are important for the short- and medium-run development of the organization.[91]

Note that in using organizational structure for these purposes, the managers do not think they are establishing an organization structure that will operate in a steady state forever; they are developing a structure that allows them to focus their managers' attention on the key jobs that must be done now to reposition their organizations for the future. Against this imperative, the niceties of organizational theory, and the desire to have a consistent organizational logic, carry little weight. Thus, both Spence and Brown end up with organizational structures that mix functional, programmatic, and geographic logics.[92]

Establishing Internal Accountability

Early in their tenures, Spence and Brown challenge their organizations by elevating *internal* standards of accountability as well as by embracing external accountability. Indeed, the latter logically implies and requires the former. Only by embracing external accountability can they convincingly raise internal standards.[93] Because the embrace of external accountability takes time to develop, however, both Spence and Brown find other means to communicate their sense of urgency internally. Interestingly, their efforts operate in two phases.

In the first phase, Spence and Brown intentionally shock their organizations by establishing new, exacting standards of performance. Spence returns sloppy letters for retyping and files letters of commendation and criticism in official personnel files. Brown holds his management retreat

Yet these differences may also reflect a real difference in managerial style and technique. In general, Spence's style seems a little more closed than Brown's. That difference may well have implications for the long-run durability of their strategies. Because Brown's style is more open, and his strategy more public and explicit, he is more vulnerable to changes in political fashion. If the world remains persuaded of the desirability of Brown's reforms, his openness will strengthen the reforms. If the world changes, however, then openness will hasten his strategy's demise.[99] Because Spence has been less open and explicit about his overall plans, he is less able to mobilize external support for his objectives but may be better able to weather a change.

Gaining Additional Resources

Spence's and Brown's successes depend not only on doing more with available resources but also on gaining new resources. Spence secures additional funds from both the Massachusetts legislature and the federal government. He also succeeds in avoiding the disastrous cuts in the HUD operating subsidy that otherwise would have occurred. Brown manages to increase his budget even in hard fiscal times in Houston and to attract money from the federal government for undertaking nationally significant experiments.

Gaining the additional resources gives Spence and Brown the wherewithal to improve the quantity and quality of services as perceived by clients and overseers. It also allows them to undertake particular new innovations and build up specific, new capabilities they consider particularly important to the future of their organizations. Finally, their success is viewed as a symbol of their power and influence in local and national communities, and therefore as a signal of their durability. To the extent that they succeed in bringing in additional resources, then, their influence over the organization's development extends beyond the mere purchasing power of the additional funds.

Just as important, both these managers seek and receive wider authority as well as more money. Spence clearly needs additional authority: he fights for and gains greater control over tenants who have the power to destroy the BHA's housing stock and make the projects uninhabitable. Brown's need is more subtle. Brown's attempt to reach out to local communities could be attacked as an effort to "politicize" the police and expose them to corrupting influences. Because his values reflect a heightened concern for legalism and the protection of constitutional rights, however, the police are given broader latitude to engage

(They also express and enact a shift in strategic focus from providing emergency housing to the most desperate to providing sustainable housing to the working poor.) For his part, Brown builds local, multifunctional police stations, introduces the DART program on an experimental basis, and initiates nationally significant fear reduction programs.

In the context of these managers' overall efforts, these specific innovations seem to do double or triple duty in influencing the development of the BHA and the HPD. On one hand, each of the innovations is important in its own right: higher quality services get delivered to specific clients as a result of implementing the innovations. On the other hand, the innovations produce important indirect effects on the organization as a whole. For one thing, the initiatives symbolize key values that Spence and Brown advance within their organizations. Spence uses construction to symbolize the BHA's commitment to quality, to renewal, to investment, and to preservation, thereby transforming the shame, hopelessness, and despair that afflict both tenants and employees. Brown uses his programs to advance a "spirit of service" in the organization and to establish the value of the organization's patrol and service functions as well as its investigative and crime control functions. In short, the initiatives become concrete symbols of the broad directions in which the managers are trying to lead their organizations.

The initiatives also provide opportunities for Spence and Brown to test the quality and commitment of their senior and midlevel managers, and then to expose those managers to a set of experiences that may change the way they think about themselves and their organization. Those who manage the key innovations experience the organization as one that challenges them to undertake new tasks and that has different purposes than those previously served. As they succeed, they not only acquire new skills but also become converts to the new purposes and methods. Spence and Brown thus develop effective partners in managing the changes they wish to make inside the organization as well as outside.

Finally, the innovations demonstrate that the purposes Spence and Brown articulate and the methods they propose can, in fact, succeed. They give concrete proof that steps previously considered unrealistic can be taken and that devices considered useless can be valuable. No amount of discussion or planning could have this impact. Nor could it be produced by seeing people in other organizations and other cities. What matters is that people in the BHA and the HPD make the innovations work. Thus, many of the usual arguments used to defeat public sector innovations cannot apply.

The symbolism of the initiatives, their impact on the managers and employees involved, and their demonstration that Spence's and Brown's ideas are both feasible and valuable all give the key initiatives importance beyond their immediate effect. They help create a climate within the organization that is more favorable to the changes that Spence and Brown seek and, indeed, more open to change generally.[103] What pertains inside the organization pertains outside as well. The initiatives prove that the strategic vision is being realized, that the strategic plan is being executed. That success, in turn, provides still more resources, authority, and latitude to Spence and Brown. As a result, the organizations become even more responsive, as employees see the managers as forces to be reckoned with and hear an increasing number of voices in their own organization arguing that the directions being pursued are interesting and attractive.

Reengineering Basic Operational Programs

Much of what has so far been discussed could reasonably be considered superficial. It seems neither novel nor particularly important that new managers would give brave speeches about new missions, reorganize their organizations' top levels, shake up their staffs, institute new budgeting and planning procedures, and secure additional resources to undertake new initiatives that embody new purposes. We have seen many managers do precisely these things and then move on to bigger and better jobs, leaving little more than their shadow behind.[104]

Yet I think there is more to these actions than temporary results. Such actions prepare organizations to make more significant changes in particular directions.[105] They create new possibilities for organizations. Whether this new potential can be successfully exploited, however, depends on the continuing efforts of the managers to encourage changes. What sets Spence and Brown apart is precisely that they go further than generating this surface turmoil: they use the turmoil to reengineer some of the basic operational procedures of their organizations. They go after their organizations' "core technologies."[106]

In Spence's case, this assault takes the form of recognizing the central importance of the tenants themselves in producing high-value public housing and then adjusting the BHA's activities to exploit that fact. In trying to improve tenant contributions to the BHA's production of quality housing, Spence is, to a degree, caught in a dilemma. On one hand, he values the part of his mandate that directs him to focus the BHA's efforts on providing emergency housing to those most in need,

and to do so in a fair and nondiscriminatory manner. On the other hand, he knows there are many eligible tenants who use the housing in ways that reduce the value of the housing for everyone else in both the short and long run. Thus, he has to find some way to keep the housing services focused on the poor and needy, while ensuring that the particular poor and needy who become tenants will be good tenants.

Existing policies deal with this problem by establishing qualifying and disqualifying tenant characteristics. Thus, eligible clients have to be poor. But poor tenants can be refused if they have a history (in BHA projects or elsewhere) of destroying property or creating disturbances. The difficulty is that the BHA does not apply these criteria in approving applicants or move effectively to evict tenants who violate the rules. Spence and Washek must make important changes in the basic operating procedures guiding the key functions of tenant selection and eviction.

With respect to tenant selection, Washek institutes four significant changes. First, he changes the application system to one in which detailed eligibility investigations are done only at the end of the application process when actual occupancy looms. This allows for more thorough and more current investigations. Second, with the additional time provided by this new procedure, the intake staff can do much more intensive follow-up interviews with former neighbors and friends of the applicants. This increases the chance of basing tenancy decisions on accurate, current, and complete information about the applicants. Third, while in the past the ultimate decision to admit the applicant was made by a centralized unit, Spence and Washek give the ultimate decision to the local manager accountable for the overall quality of the BHA services in his or her area. This changes the relationship between the tenant and the BHA. The tenant no longer answers to an abstract entity with little knowledge about him or her and with only bureaucratic procedures to satisfy. The tenant now answers to someone who visits on a regular basis and is far more knowledgeable about and interested in his or her impact on the quality of community life in the project. Fourth, in the past, vacancies were filled only when the apartment had been certified as ready for occupancy, with all repairs done and all equipment in place. Under the new "homesteading program," a tenant willing to reside in an apartment not quite ready may do so under the condition that he or she make it ready. This gives resourceful tenants a slight edge over those more dependent on the BHA to provide the necessary services and equipment.

These changes produce a marked shift in the characteristics of those admitted to the BHA. Incomes rise a little; the fraction employed (at low wages) rises more; the ratio of adults to children improves. These changes in the characteristics of those served by the BHA may lessen the value associated with providing housing to the most needy in the society. But they also increase the quality of housing to those only slightly less desperate tenants who now occupy the projects. These changes also help maintain the credibility of public housing in the eyes of many citizens and overseers, who want the BHA to deliver reasonably high-quality public housing to poor people able to preserve the housing for the future. The increased credibility may, over the long run, increase the overall supply of public housing to the poor, since it keeps the idea of public housing alive.

Whether Spence's new strategy increases public value or not, by transforming a basic set of operational procedures governing tenant selection, Spence makes an important systemic change in the product that the BHA delivers to clients and citizens. The basic operational technology of the organization changes, as does the product of the BHA's efforts.

In Brown's case, the important change in the HPD's core technology comes from shifting the organization away from its obsessive focus on crime control and its near exclusive reliance on arrests as its most effective response to crime to a strategy that: makes crime prevention as important as reactive arrests; focuses on reducing fears as well as controlling crime; and reorganizes patrol operations to ensure that officers maintain close contact with citizens and communities so that they can better identify and respond to community problems.[107]

The new concept, DART, eventually becomes an official policy of neighborhood-oriented policing.[108] Implementing neighborhood policing citywide requires many operational and administrative innovations including: (1) the redesign of neighborhood beats and sectors to reflect the boundaries of existing neighborhoods; (2) the introduction of a "call management system" to reduce the number of priority-one calls, and thereby allow more calls to be answered by local beat officers, and allow patrol officers more time to work on community-nominated problems;[109] (3) the development of new evaluation procedures to encourage officers to engage in crime prevention, problem solving, and fear-reducing activities, as opposed to random patrol in the periods in which they are not responding to high-priority calls; and (4) the training and authorizing of patrol officers to undertake preliminary criminal investigations.

Introducing these innovations requires a great deal of organizational effort to test the techniques and see if they work, to rewrite existing policies and procedures, and to train officers and supervisors in the new

techniques. But changing these basic procedures produces significant organization-wide changes in the nature of the service being supplied by the HPD and thus in the value it creates for the citizens of Houston.

Organizing for Coproduction and Responsiveness

In choosing their strategies and reengineering their operations, both Spence and Brown recognize their organizations' clients not only as recipients of services but also as an important part of the production processes.[110] Spence understands that the BHA cannot succeed in supplying high-quality public housing to those in need unless the clients who are attracted to the service use it in ways that make the housing valuable to other clients and to citizens who contribute money to the enterprise. Brown understands that the HPD cannot succeed in apprehending offenders or producing community security unless citizens alert officers to crimes and take some responsibility for self-defense. In this sense, citizens, clients, and governmental organizations coproduce the value attributed to public sector organizations.

If public organizations are to depend on citizens and clients to help them achieve their results, then managers must devise means for increasing these contributions from outside. Interestingly, both Spence and Brown hit on the same device: decentralizing their operations to make citizens and clients feel that they have effective influence over the organization's operations and purposes. Spence and Brown implicitly assume that if citizens and clients "own" the organization, they will be more inclined to support the organization both as authorizers and as coproducers. In short, decentralization helps to build a working partnership.[111]

True or not, the aim of building effective working partnerships with citizens and clients was difficult to achieve under the old BHA and HPD. Like most public sector agencies, the BHA and the HPD were centralized, functional organizations.[112] By "centralized," I mean an organization in which all but the most routine operational decisions must be made at the top of the organization. By "functional," I mean an organization in which the top levels are differentiated by function rather than program or geography.

The public sector's commitment to centralized, functional organizations is not an accident. It reflects the legacy of the progressive era's mistrust of politics and its confidence in principles of scientific management. In political terms, centralized, functional organizations were judged to be superior to decentralized, geographic organizations because they broke the corrupt relationships that could grow up between locally powerful politicians and locally organized service delivery organizations.[113] They also promised the uniform application of administrative rules. In operational terms, centralized, functional organizations were judged superior because they encouraged the development of specialized expertise and allowed for the exploitation of significant economies of scale and the avoidance of wasteful redundancy.[114]

But just as confidence in scientific management has begun to yield to the principles of "getting close to the customer" and "a bias toward action" in the private sector, so Spence and Brown seem to be trying to break down their centralized structures to get their organizations closer to citizens and clients and more open to street-level initiative.[115] Spence seeks to return powers over tenant selection, eviction, repairs, security, and social services to project managers, and to flatten the BHA by eliminating levels of supervision and allowing middle managers the freedom and responsibility to act without checking with a superior. Brown redefines his geographic boundaries to ensure that they correspond to natural political communities, physically disperses his troops to new ministations that house the many diverse functional specialties that constitute a police department, and authorizes patrol officers to conduct criminal investigations.

Such efforts will make it easier for organized groups in the public housing projects of Boston and the neighborhoods of Houston to form working partnerships with the BHA and the HPD, respectively. These groups will find someone in the organization's structure who can respond to whatever concerns they have. BHA tenants can find a project manager; the citizens of Houston can find a division commander. Each is able to act as a minicommissioner with control over many of the organization's diverse functions.

These cases teach us that it is no easy task to shift from centralized, functional organizations to decentralized, geographic organizations. It seems to involve two key steps.

Initially, decentralizing managers must engage in the bruising effort to break up the centralized, functional units and redistribute their functions (or their people) to the geographically decentralized units. The gentlest way to do this is simply to relocate the personnel physically, leaving their organizational reporting relationships intact. Thus, Spence assigns centralized maintenance workers to work "out of" particular projects, and Brown assigns investigators to the new Westside Command Station.

Somewhat more bruising is to break the monopoly that the specialized units have on particular kinds of work and redistribute that work to

others. Brown does this by authorizing patrol officers to conduct preliminary investigations. Spence, hemmed in by union rules, cannot do this without renegotiating labor contracts, but he eventually does get some concessions on maintenance work.

The most brutal way to make the change is to place the functional specialists under the command of the newly defined geographic managers. Such action usually provokes protest and much public criticism of the manager, who is alleged to be undermining the competence and morale of the specialist units that were once the elite of the organization. To prevent such complaints and preserve the specialized competence that the functional units represented, many managers decide not to transfer all the specialists to the geographic units. They retain a small, specialized unit to undertake the few operations most dependent on the specialists, oversee the quality of the performance of those personnel in the new commands, and provide training for the specialists now deployed to other commands. Thus, Spence retains a centralized repair unit to work on emergency or specially complicated repairs. Brown never disbands his homicide detectives. The trick, of course, is to keep the specialized skills alive in the new multifunctional commands without letting the centralized units reform at the center of the organization.

Once managers have broken up the centralized, functional units, they must undertake the second step, preparing the decentralized, geographic managers to think and act as general managers encompassing all the functions of the organization rather than as the specialist managers they were in the past. Ordinarily this switch presents quite a shock. In functional organizations, managers become managers by knowing their functional specialty better than others. Their job is to ensure that their subordinates do the job as well as they could by correcting technical errors when they see them. In the new organizations, the midlevel managers preside over several functions—only some of which they understand well. Thus, they have to redefine their idea of what it means to be a manager. Their job is to help the functional specialists work together as a team, not to perfect any particular function. Moreover, to the extent that these managers are expected to develop effective working partnerships with local groups, they also need training in the techniques of political management, for it is those skills that will be tested in this assignment. In short, midlevel managers change from being substantive specialists supervising the work of other substantive specialists in an insulated bureaucratic environment to managers orchestrating the efforts of different substantive specialists in an interactive dialogue with local community groups.

Geographic decentralization also depends on developing control mechanisms for holding the decentralized, geographically based units accountable for performance. At a minimum this involves making adjustments in the organization's financial management and performance measurement systems to ensure that the organization's traditional measures of effectiveness and accomplishment can be disaggregated to correspond to the newly created organizational units.[116] More ambitious mechanisms for ensuring accountability would include new systems designed to reinforce the importance of responsiveness, such as client surveys. Or they might include explicit efforts to develop after-the-fact, aggregate reviews of the performance of the local units. Thus, for example, Brown establishes an inspection team in his office to begin reviewing, on an aggregate basis, the overall effectiveness of various commands. It is through devices such as these that managers like Spence and Brown seek to create operationally decentralized but centrally accountable client-responsive organizations.

One last feature of shifting to geographically decentralized organizations is worth noting. Insofar as geographic decentralization succeeds in tying organizations more closely to their clients, the organizations will remain continually responsive to community concerns. That will force the organization to maintain a continuing capacity for adjustment, adaptation, innovation, and renewal associated with changes in local demands. Just as the market stimulates adaptations and innovations in private sector organizations, close connections with clients to determine what they value may stimulate change in public sector organizations.[117]

ACTING IN A STREAM

To the extent that one can generalize from these cases, six important conclusions emerge about the role of individual managers in bringing strategic change to organizations.

First, the successful implementation of an organizational strategy involves elements of both leadership and management.[118] These managers do not limit themselves to working inside the organizations or to perfecting existing administrative systems. They work *outside* their organizations, partly to build support, but also to expose their organizations to criticisms, demands, and expectations not currently palpable. They assume the responsibility for articulating purposes and negotiating terms of accountability with their authorizing environment. They focus attention on areas where innovations and improvements are required as well as on their organizations' accomplishments. In short, they challenge as well as protect their organizations.

Second, these managers seem closely attuned to the amount of pressure they put on their organizations.[119] Challenges are followed by reassurance; criticisms, by praise; exacting demands, by new resources. Early opposition and defections are taken as a matter of course, but the managers know they will have to create some partners inside their organizations if they are to achieve their goals.[120]

Third, the managers influence operational performance only partly through the manipulation of administrative systems. When they use administrative systems to guide their organizations, their calculations are not guided by abstract notions of what constitutes completeness, perfection, or modernity in the systems; they are guided instead by commonsense calculations of what will help them focus organizational effort on the work that they think needs to get done.[121] They do not spend a great deal of time drawing new organization charts or introducing new systems for performance evaluation. Instead, they stay focused on the substantive problems their organizations face. To prod their organizations toward higher value strategies, they rely on selective exposure to external pressures and demands, symbolic actions designed to communicate their vision of the values that should guide their organization's development, and detailed attention to a few key innovations.

It is not that they do not use administrative systems at all. Indeed, both Spence and Brown make important changes in structure, in planning processes, in personnel systems, and in performance measurement. Nor can we say that changes in administrative systems do not themselves produce important changes in the ways the organizations operate. Indeed, the big changes in administrative systems—such as the shift from functionally centralized to geographically decentralized structures, or from internal organizational measurements of performance to external measures—not only sustain certain patterns of development but also trigger another round of changes.

The argument is simply that the big changes in administrative systems seem to follow rather than lead the process of persuading the organizations' employees to think and operate in a new way. Administrative shifts reinforce rather than carry the message of change. They facilitate rather than dictate the organizations' efforts to change. And they are calculated with an eye to improved operational performance.

Fourth, the managers seem to operate not according to a detailed plan but improvisationally.[122] They have a general sense of what they are trying to do. They have even identified detailed areas in which improvements are essential and to which they are committed. But they do not act on these plans systematically; they innovate only as opportunities present themselves. It is as though they keep in mind (and before the organization) a set of problems to be solved, and then wait for propitious moments to act on them.

Fifth, the managers accept contributions from others. It is not important to them that they initiate every solution. They appropriate many initiatives taken before they arrived on the scene. When someone solves a problem that was on their agenda, that is great news and celebrated as such. When someone brings forward both a new problem and a new solution, that, too, is treated as good news.

Sixth, the managers know that the pace and sequence of their actions matter. If they go too quickly, their organizations will rebel. If they go too slowly, they may lose the momentum they need to execute a large organizational change.[123] Similarly, they know that their organizations' responses to particular actions they take depend a great deal on what else has recently been undertaken. Speeches followed by actions patently inconsistent with the speech dilute the message of both. In contrast, speeches followed promptly by supportive actions amplify the message of both.

In sum, managers who implement basic changes in strategy act through a series of concrete actions, some planned and some improvised. The actions unleash somewhat unpredictable influences throughout the organizations they lead, and managers must make many adjustments to keep their efforts to change on course. Only some of the interventions they make involve changes in the organizations' administrative systems. More involve keeping the broad and specific purposes of their organizations in constant view, developing structures and planning systems that distribute important tasks across the organizations, and concentrating on product and process innovations that move the organizations toward higher value strategies. Often, they influence their organizations most powerfully by selectively exposing them to external challenges that had previously been resisted. Just as private sector executives have learned that it is important to the success of their organizations that they get close to their customers, so public sector managers are learning that being close to citizens and their representatives is key to making their organizations perform better. Without close contact and active support from their political environments, managers can neither know what is worth producing nor achieve it.

CONCLUSION:
ACTING FOR A DIVIDED,
UNCERTAIN SOCIETY

Consider the managers whose problems we have faced, and whose calculations we have shared, in the pages of this book: the reflective librarian of Chapter 1; the hard-driving sanitation commissioner of Chapter 2; the bold leaders of the Environmental Protection Agency and the Department of Youth Services of Chapter 3; the enterprising heads of the Department of Community Affairs and the Center for Disease Control in Chapters 4 and 5; and the determined operational strategists of the Boston Housing Authority and the Houston Police Department in Chapters 6 and 7. As presented, these managers exhibit a certain kind of consciousness: they are imaginative, purposeful, enterprising, and calculating. They focus on increasing the value of the organizations they lead to the broader society. In search of value, their minds range freely across the concrete circumstances of today seeking opportunities for tomorrow. Based on the potential they see, they calculate what to do: how to define their purposes, engage their political overseers and coproducers, and guide their organizations' operations. Then, most remarkably of all, they go ahead and do what their calculations suggest they should.

This sort of enterprise may be rare. Moreover, society may not much value such qualities among public executives. Indeed, some citizens may fear that if public executives commonly possessed such qualities, initiative in defining public purposes would shift to appointed rather than elected officials, with deleterious consequences for the quality of democracy. Yet, my purpose in this book is precisely to encourage

Inconsistent Images of Virtue

That we citizens hold these two images of virtue is somewhat surprising, for, superficially at least, they seem inconsistent. Starkly put: in the first view, public officials are *discouraged* from having (let alone acting on) their own views of what is right; in the second, officials are morally *obligated* to have (and act on) their moral views.

Clearly, we are ambivalent: on the one hand, we fear the idea that public officials might have their own views of public value and pursue them at the expense of society's true interests and values. When we think this way, we implicitly put a great deal of trust in the capacity of our political institutions and processes to define and establish society's true interests and values, and we are quite concerned about the power of bureaucratic agencies to upset these deliberations.

On the other hand, we also fear a world in which our public officials have no moral responsibility. If they are not morally accountable for their actions, then one of the bulwarks against corruption or injustice in the political system might weaken.[7] When we think this way, we remind ourselves that political institutions are often vulnerable to the corruption of short-term particular interests and may have to be resisted by conscientious officials who take the wide and long view of the public interest.

Reconciling Inconsistent Views

To some degree, of course, the views that I have presented as stark opposites can be reconciled. One could argue, for example, that managers' obligations to act on their own moral views depend on the importance and universality of the values they are defending. If the conflict between political overseers and managers concerns mere policy differences, then bureaucratic officials are obligated to keep their mouths shut. After all, gaining the right to have one's policy preferences count in the formation and execution of public policy is precisely what democratic elections are about, and that right should not be undermined by bureaucratic resistance.[8]

But if the conflict concerns either fundamental injustice or corruption, then subordinate officials are obligated to shout their indignation from the rooftops, for no election gives public officials a right to do injustice or to steal. Often, this distinction between policy differences, on one hand, and fundamental injustice or corruption, on the other, is quite clear, and these simple rules will clearly indicate when managers should yield gracefully and when they should actively resist specific political pressures from overseers.

At times, however, the distinction blurs as human passions come into play. It is all too easy for public officials who disagree with one another to attribute their differences not to disagreements about policy but to either injustice or corruption among their opponents. For example, it is evident that Jerry Miller views deinstitutionalization as something more than just a desirable policy or a better means for controlling juvenile crime; he considers it fundamentally wrong and unjust to keep children locked up. From such a premise, it takes only a small step to conclude that his opponents are not simply people who disagree with him but are, instead, citizens who support injustice and whose moral claims on him can therefore be discounted.

The Miles Mahoney case suggests that it is even easier to find corruption among those with whom one has policy differences. Mahoney and his staff come to suspect the developers, Mayor White, and BRA officials of being corrupt—not because of direct evidence but simply because they have important policy differences. Mahoney and his staff's suspicions widen naturally to include the governor's aide, Al Kramer, because he appears to be in league with the others. Only Governor Sargent is spared their suspicion, but perhaps only because he is their boss and is thereby protected by their hope that their leader is a good one. As time goes on, they even come to suspect that badly motivated aides manipulate Sargent or that misguided political ambitions rule him.

A different way to reconcile the apparently conflicting views of virtue is to say that public officials have the duty to act as advocates for their views *before* policy decisions are made. Once a decision is made, however, their obligation shifts to ensuring faithful implementation of the newly adopted policies.[9] Thus, for example, once it becomes clear to Mahoney that Sargent wants him to approve the Park Plaza project, he must do what he can to implement that decision, regardless of his own views. It would be particularly wrong for him to resist overtly the governor's desires to approve the project.

This approach fails to account for the ongoing nature of decisions. In both the theory and practice of democracy, policy decisions remain open to review. This is not quite to say that nothing ever gets decided. There are moments when collective, authoritative judgments are made and codified in laws, executive orders, or policy agreements. In those moments, some public values are judged more important than others, and resources and organizational performance shift in response. Moreover, given the difficulty of bringing the complex political systems to these imagination, purposefulness, enterprise, and calculation among public executives. Inevitably, then, I must confront the ethical and psychological challenges of exercising this kind of leadership. If the managerial orientation and techniques proposed herein threaten democracy, they should be rejected. If they cannot be embraced by the many ordinary people who will be asked to do these jobs, then they will be irrelevant.

ETHICAL CHALLENGES
OF PUBLIC LEADERSHIP

When we citizens imagine the virtues of public executives, two quite different images come to mind.[1] One is the image of public servant. In this conception, managers act as faithful agents of their political masters. Their sole moral duty is to lend their substantive and administrative expertise to the achievement of whatever purposes have been sanctioned by laws, elections, or courts.[2] The more neutral and responsive they become, the better public servants they make.

Note that in this conception the managers' own views of valuable public purposes are treated as irrelevant at best, and suspect at worst. Indeed, the managers are specifically obligated to suppress their own ideas of what would be in the public interest in favor of the (normatively superior) judgments of their political overseers.

A second, contrasting view casts the public executive as an independent moral actor. The Nuremberg trials following World War II most powerfully expressed this view.[3] There, Nazi officials were executed for war crimes despite protestations that they had simply followed orders. The court judged that public officials could never entirely forsake their personal moral responsibility: even though they were bound by authority to their political masters, they remained independent, accountable, moral actors.

Note that this conception requires public officials to express their own views of what is right and good. Indeed, it obligates managers to use their moral views to resist commands by superiors that are illegal or immoral.[4] Nor should they remain silent in such cases. Instead, their duty is to protest—loudly enough that others who care about the values that are being sacrificed may rally to their cause.[5] The public executive as moral leader shows a "profile of courage" in the face of either injustice or venality, even when these are allied with intimidating political power.[6]

cism—not all of it coherent or consistent. The managers' duty, then, is to use that commentary to revise their efforts to define and produce value as the technical and administrative possibilities present themselves.

Thus, the librarian of Chapter 1 might learn whether her local community wants her to provide services to latchkey children by making a proposal to do so and awaiting a policy decision. Alternatively, she could simply initiate the program, report on its performance, and wait for the response. The sanitation commissioner of Chapter 2 might initiate an experiment with privatization, use the resources saved to seek more effective rat control programs in the city's ghettos, report on these initiatives, and wait to see what response comes from the mayor, the city council, or the newspapers. Ruckelshaus, the EPA administrator of Chapter 3, launches an aggressive enforcement program against the most obvious polluters and judges the value of this initiative not only by assessing its value against the effect that these efforts have on stimulating "polluters" to begin the process of cleaning up, but also by sensing the political reaction to his efforts.

"After-the-Fact" Accountability

Note that in this image of public sector management the nature of the dialogue that managers have with their overseers—the ways in which they are held accountable—diverges from the process envisioned by the classic paradigm. In the classic paradigm, authorization is supposed to occur "before the fact." If managers have new ideas, they are supposed to present them for approval before they initiate action. In the ideas suggested here, before-the-fact consultation remains an attractive and desirable option. In that mode, managers listen, consult, and respond to the varied concerns of their many overseers. They may even offer a vision to balance the competing interests at stake in their domains of responsibility. But the ideas presented here also give public managers greater leeway to consult with their authorizing environment after the fact, through evaluations of what they have accomplished.[21]

Of course, after-the-fact evaluations have always been a part of the dialogue with overseers in the conventional paradigm.[22] But once one sees managers as explorers searching for public value through effective action, then the relative importance of the after-the-fact discussion of results increases. Indeed, it may be easier for managers to learn what is both possible and desirable by producing it first and seeing how people points of decision, once a decision has been made, a strong desire not to reopen the decision acts to hold decisions fairly constant.

Yet, even with these qualifications, it remains true that all decisions will come up for reconsideration sooner or later. Indeed, experience in implementing policies will often give new reasons for review. And, once there is a reason for review, the moral duty of the public executive will shift again to giving voice to the objections.[10]

Such a process could have occurred in the case of Sencer and swine flu. If Sencer had either more accurately visualized the process of implementation or actually responded to the problems that arose during implementation, he might have shifted from a strong advocacy position (motivated by a fervent desire to prepare the country for the worst consequences of the epidemic) to a more hedged position (one that would have been worse if the epidemic had occurred but would have been much better in the increasingly likely case that the country was spared).

Obviously, if decisions are so frequently reconsidered that little time passes between a decision and its reconsideration, then public officials may nearly always have the duty to voice their views, and their duty to remain silent and cooperative in implementation will disappear.

These approaches to reconciling conflicting ideas of virtue may work enough of the time to save the apparently inconsistent images of virtue among public officials. Viewed from the perspective of conscientious managers who would like to manage both effectively and democratically, however, these images remain quite unsatisfactory. On the crucial questions of how public managers should engage their overseers in valuable discussions about what is worth doing and what important innovations should be undertaken, the images (even with reconciliations) provide only a few alternatives: silent, dutiful obedience; aggressive advocacy followed by quiet obedience or resignation depending on the outcome of the decision; or noisy martyrdom. None of these particularly appeals to individuals who would like to make sustained, individual contributions to the public good.

Doubtful Assumptions and Unwarranted Cynicism

Even worse, the images of virtue seem to be based on some dubious assumptions about how democratic governance really works. They seem contrived more to reassure citizens and overseers that public managers are effectively under control than to recognize the moral dilemmas of public managers and to give them useful guidance. Two false assumptions undergird and distort this discussion.

The first is the comfortable assumption that the actions of public managers are now guided by clear, coherent, and stable mandates, forged in the sustained heat of ongoing political debate.[11] Of course, some such mandates do exist. And where they are present, there can be no doubt that the manager has the moral duty to implement them.

In the far more typical case, however, managers are guided by mandates in which political conflicts have been papered over rather than resolved.[12] Even if resolved, the resolution is often temporary, and conflict will reopen at the first sign of difficulty in implementing the new policies.

Where conflict continues unresolved, it is by no means clear to whom government managers are accountable or for what particular purposes. Often, they have to decide for themselves how the competing forces in their political environments should be balanced. And they tend to do so in the ongoing course of implementation by adapting to criticisms rather than by reopening the policy debate to secure a clearer and more coherent mandate. Thus, decisions made by managers in implementation are often as important as policy choice in determining what the policy will be.[13]

The second false assumption is that those who choose to work for the government are content with putting their own moral views about the public interest and public value in abeyance. In reality, many people work for the government precisely because they want to enact some particular view they have of the public interest.[14] Indeed, that is one of the small compensations the government provides in what is otherwise an uncompetitive effort to recruit some of society's most talented individuals.[15] Moreover, we citizens often join the managers in judging it a virtue for public managers to have causes. We like officials who have purposes they are willing to pursue at a financial sacrifice. Yet if we organize our governmental institutions to attract and compensate people who have specific causes they would like to pursue, we ask a great deal from such people in requiring them to abandon their cause when politics or policy fashion changes and to establish a different public purpose as paramount.[16]

Because the traditional images of virtue among public sector managers are founded on sand, they not only fail to provide useful guidance but also foster cynicism and hypocrisy among practicing managers. Often, public managers will *claim* to represent the virtues they are supposed to possess. They may even think they are loyal to them. In reality, however, they will search covertly for ways to express their real values.[17] Instead of trying to accommodate conflicting claims in new syntheses, they will decide instead to anchor their preferred vision of their purposes with that portion of their (divided) authorizing environment that agrees with them. Thus, the secret image of virtue among government managers becomes one of skilled advocates building powerful dikes protecting themselves, their organizations, and their causes from the political tides that sweep over the more gullible, dutiful bureaucrats.[18]

Judging by their secret image of virtue, many public managers find Mahoney wanting—not because he did not adjust his vision of what would be valuable to do in the face of overwhelming political opposition to his views, but because he failed to find some constituency that would share his view. Conversely, many public managers find Miller more compelling not just because he takes an agreeable policy stance, but because he finds enough support and authorization in his political environment to carry out his ambitious and risky project. In short, managers are judged by how skillfully they recruit a political constituency to support their preferred policy position, rather than by how creative they are in integrating or adapting to conflicting political forces.

Public Managers as Explorers

There is a different way of thinking about the proper role of public sector executives—one tied much more closely to the reality of modern governance but geared to preserving, even enhancing, the ideals of democratic accountability. In this image, public executives are neither clerks nor martyrs. Instead, they are *explorers* commissioned by society to search for public value.[19] In undertaking the search, managers are expected to use their initiative and imagination. But they are also expected to be responsive to more or less constant political guidance and feedback. Their most important ethical responsibility is to undertake the search for public value conscientiously.[20]

"Conscientiously" in this context means something quite simple: they have to be willing to openly state their views about what is valuable, and to subject those views both to political commentary and to operational tests of effectiveness. They should not hide their views or frustrate efforts to test the value of their operational or administrative theories. They must report honestly on what their organizations are seeking, doing, and accomplishing. Based on those reports, overseers of the organizations can offer a continuing commentary of praise and criti-

respond rather than by trying to get them to say what they want in the first place.[23]

Strategy as Enhanced Accountability

In this new paradigm public managers are duty bound to have and present ideas of public value. They even have the right and the responsibility to nominate new ideas for consideration as circumstances change. And these ideas will be their own in the sense that the managers will fashion them, articulate them, and be viewed as responsible for having suggested them.

But if the ideas are to succeed, they will have to incorporate much from the surrounding environment. They will have to fit with the political aspirations of overseers. They will have to engage the employees who will be asked to help achieve the new goals. And they will have to meet the test of plausibly representing a set of purposes that citizens and taxpayers would choose to support if they had deliberated carefully on the question.

Note that these are the same tests that must be met by the development of a sound corporate strategy in the public sector.[24] Indeed, these are all the reasons why Ruckelshaus's vision for the EPA turns out to be both practically useful and morally compelling. Although Ruckelshaus himself articulates the proposed mission for the EPA, and the idea therefore becomes associated with him individually, the idea he presents is designed to express what society as a whole thinks is the best thing to do in the circumstances that he confronts. It is in this sense that having a coherent strategic vision responds to a *moral* as well as a *practical* requirement.

Substantive and Operational Risks

Of course, as noted in Chapter 3, there may be many possible strategic visions—many different paths to creating public value. In choosing among them, managers will inevitably face difficult moral choices.[25] Often the difficult moral question will be how much substantive risk managers should impose on society in pursuing their adopted strategies. In committing to a particular strategic vision, public managers often have to bet on how political values will change or hope that some new programmatic capabilities can be developed in their organizations, rather than know these things for sure. In guessing, they expose society and their organizations to risk.

The greater the substantive and operational risks foisted on the society, the greater managers' personal responsibility. This is one of the important ways in which Miller and Sencer, on the one hand, differ from Ruckelshaus, Spence, and Brown, on the other. Arguably, Miller and Sencer take far greater risks on behalf of society than any of the others. They "bet their companies" on responding to new problems with new methods.

Ruckelshaus, by contrast, takes a smaller substantive and operational risk. True, he commits the society to cleaning up the environment when he cannot be sure that the environment has become endangered or that his methods will be the best for the job. But the risks simply seem smaller and easier to discount than for Miller and Sencer.

Spence and Brown lie somewhere in the middle. Their visions risk some dimensions of public value. Spence gives up some quantity of emergency housing for Boston's most desperate citizens; Brown risks some degradation in police response times. But they perceive potential gains to be harvested by making the changes they do and assume that once society sees these other gains, it will judge that the value of their enterprises has increased.

Risking Democratic Accountability

At times the difficult moral question to be decided in committing to a particular strategy will focus not on substance and operations but on politics and accountability. The issue will be how aggressively, and on behalf of what values, public managers should engage and respond to their political environments.

As Chapter 5 indicated, managers can choose to be more or less aggressive and manipulative in advocating their views. Precisely because political conflict exists, managers can choose their allies and play one side against the other. Because they control information and have important relations with constituency and client groups, they can help to amplify or repress particular voices and interests in the political environment. Because their operations will strengthen or weaken particular constituencies, managers can lend aid and comfort to particular outside groups, or deny it. And, in implementing policies, they can choose to exaggerate, accommodate, or resist the claims made by different outside groups.

In making such choices, managers expose themselves to moral risks, for each of the political forces surrounding them can reasonably make a claim to be heard and accommodated. Therefore, a manager willfully supporting or ignoring one claim at the expense of another is making an

important decision not only about what is publicly valuable but about to whom they are democratically accountable.

Thus, Miller makes an important moral decision in aligning himself with advocates for children and cutting off relationships with those in the legislature and the judiciary who want to retain some of the capacity that the old reform schools represent. Ruckelshaus makes an important and different moral decision in deciding to keep lines of communication (and influence) open not only to President Nixon but also to Senator Muskie, the environmental groups, and the farmers interested in continuing to use pesticides.

In general, in a democracy, it is probably a greater virtue to keep lines of communication and accountability open to many people with interests and views in what should be done. That remains true until such openness allows too many "special interests" to creep in and makes it impossible for managers to respond to new political or technical possibilities.

Obligations to One's Subordinates

Other times the tough moral question facing managers will be how deeply to challenge their own organizations. The moral dilemma arises here because, over time, most public sector organizations (and the particular purposes they embody and the particular skills they depend on) have become at least a home, sometimes even a temple, to those who work there. If managers commit to a strategy that makes a wrenching change in their organizations' purposes and, with that, their architectural arrangements and most important tasks, many employees will be discomforted. They will lose their utility and value. Even worse, they will lose their faith. They will feel betrayed by their managers and leaders, whom they had trusted to protect them. They will press that view on the managers whose decisions forced the unwelcome changes on them. For their part, the managers will feel their employees' pain and wonder if they did the right thing. That is an important moral question as well as an operational one.

For example, it is morally important that Miller, Spence, and Brown all challenge their organizations to do something quite different from what they have done in the past. No doubt, those working in the juvenile institutions feel that Miller has sold them down the river rather than helped them succeed. No doubt, the former senior managers of the BHA feel humiliated by Spence's appointment. No doubt, the Houston Police Department's top command and many of its rank and file feel indignant about the new ethic that Brown seeks to instill in the HPD.

Because such people have served well in the past, they may have the right to expect decent treatment and support from their incoming managers. It is not their fault that the world has changed. They may be entitled either to the opportunity to make the case for their way of doing things or to enough time and retraining to see if they can make the necessary changes.

The Limitations of Traditional Answers

One of the things that make the moral questions raised by the adoption of a particular organizational strategy so interesting and compelling is that the commonly given answers to the troubling moral questions are almost certainly wrong. For example, a common answer to the question of how much risk a manager should impose on society is "none"; public managers shouldn't gamble with the public's money! But that cannot be the right answer, for managers always impose risks on society. The cases in this book suggest that standing pat in changing circumstances is often far more hazardous to managers, to organizations, and to the public than groping in a direction that seems suited to the new politically expressed values or the new technical or administrative possibilities.

But there ought to be some relationship between the degree of risk imposed and the amount and neutrality of the consultation managers rely on for authorization. Arguably, Spence and Brown insulate themselves from harsh criticism as they experiment with their organizations by working hard at remaining properly accountable while making the changes. Even so, as the case of Jerry Miller suggests, sometimes managers may need to take the lead in showing society a new kind of value, one previously unconceived or not taken seriously.

Similarly, with respect to the issue of what political claims managers should accommodate, it is almost certainly incorrect to say either that they should respond to all claims or that they should answer only claims made by elected chief executives. The first is wrong because there are many political claims that should be rejected since they reflect too particular an interest or too idiosyncratic a conception of public value. The second is wrong because the claims of other elected overseers in legislatures, and the claims of past political agreements expressed in laws, also demand allegiance from public managers. Thus, managers often have no choice but to exercise their own discriminating judgment about which claims from their political authorizing environments should be accommodated and to what degree.

Finally, with respect to the important question of how much managers owe their employees and the past traditions of the organization, it is

certainly wrong to say that their duty is to protect their employees or guarantee the continuity of their organizations. Often organizations need to be challenged to rethink their purposes or methods. Other times ways must be found to reduce their claims on the public purse, not because their cause is not important but simply because other enterprises now seem more important. In such circumstances, public managers may have an affirmative duty to expose rather than insulate their organizations to these harsh realities.

Yet it is also clear that they owe their employees, and their organizations' tradition, some respect. These should not be written off casually, for there are both moral claims and practical wisdom in what employees and organizations have done in the past.

The Duties of Public Executives as Explorers

Perhaps the best that can be said, then, about the moral obligations of public executives is that they owe a conscientious, publicly accountable, effort to search for public value. In that search they are duty bound to have and articulate a vision. But that vision has to accommodate the aspirations of those in their authorizing environments, as well as what they know or think is important based on their professional or administrative expertise, or what techniques of policy analysis and program evaluation can tell them. They are also responsible for accurate reporting on what they are doing and what is being produced. The articulation of their purposes and the reporting of activities and accomplishments become the crucial signposts that allow them to be held accountable to—and, through their accountability, learn from—their overseers.

Sometimes, the feedback and pressures they receive from the political forces in their authorizing environment will carry them forward in their search and away from past practices. In those circumstances they must bear the moral burden of deciding how deeply they should challenge their organizations and the employees who have come to attach meaning to the organization as it operated in the past.

PSYCHOLOGICAL CHALLENGES OF PUBLIC LEADERSHIP

Living up to the moral challenges of leading public sector organizations helps to clarify why being a public sector executive is psychologically as well as ethically challenging. Because public executives work for all of us, because we all have different ideas about what would be valuable for them to do, and because we all feel entitled to express those views, an enormous amount of pressure accumulates within their offices. Precisely because they channel public aspirations, they become lightning rods for social conflict.[26] Hardly ever can they act to universal applause. At best, their actions are greeted by a grudging tolerance. Their critics' voices always seem louder and more public than their supporters'. Indeed, because character assassination has become such an important tool of policy advocacy, they often become the focus of unfair or damaging attacks on their personal values and conduct as well as on their professional performance.[27]

The False Search for Refuge

Under such intense pressure, public managers naturally seek psychological refuge. They typically find it in one or both of two common forms: deep convictions about the rightness of their cause; and consistent encouragement from a small circle of close associates who either share their public purposes or care for them personally.[28] Sometimes that small group of supporters is drawn from those in the political environment who share their views. Other times it comes from within the organizations they lead—the people with whom they have long worked.[29]

But if the managers are to live up to their stern moral obligations to seek visions of public value that are politically inclusive and (sometimes) challenging to the organizations they lead, then they must distance themselves from these common sources of comfort. They must be skeptical of their convictions about their purposes because they have to hold open the possibility that their view of public value is wrong, or idiosyncratic, or not suitable to the times. They must hold at arm's length the comfort of close allies because they are duty bound to hear and respond to the views of others who disagree with their supporters. They must resist the comfort of their subordinates because they may have to challenge them to perform in new ways.

"Walking the Razor's Edge"

The job of the public manager is psychologically demanding, then, because public sector executives must strike a complex balance between two commonly opposed psychological orientations. First, they must have strong enough convictions about what is worth doing that they are willing to work hard for them and to stake their reputations on the values that they pursue. Yet their convictions cannot be so strong that they are impervious to doubt and the opportunity for continued learning.[30] Their views, the ones for which they labor so mightily and with which they are closely identified, must be held *contingently*. Second, they must be willing to act with determination and commitment while retaining a taste and a capacity for thought and reflection.[31]

Moreover, these difficult balances between conviction and doubt, action and reflection, must be struck not once but every day, in the way that managers approach their jobs—sometimes insisting on their views and taking actions that commit their organizations to a particular course of action; other times leaving themselves open to the views of others and changing the direction of their organizations.

My colleague Ronald Heifetz characterizes such challenges as learning to "walk on the razor's edge."[32] He points out that a high degree of balance and poise is necessary to avoid two different kinds of failure common to leaders of groups and organizations.

One kind comes from lacking the courage to challenge current understandings and arrangements in the political and organizational realm. This kind of failure sacrifices the responsibility that leaders have to identify and pursue opportunities to produce value.[33] This failure allows the current balance of political forces, organizational tradition, and past practices to determine what is worth doing. While allowing this may be appropriate on many occasions, it is wrong to assume in advance that this is always true. Indeed, given the enormous pressures to preserve the status quo, one might even treat one's first considered judgment that such a course is appropriate as suspect.

A second kind of failure comes from challenging current arrangements so deeply, and at such an accelerated pace, that managers are metaphorically "assassinated" either by their political overseers, or their subordinates, or both, because these groups cannot stand, or do not agree with, the direction in which their leaders are trying to take them.[34] This kind of failure sacrifices managers' continued capacities to be useful.

The Crucial Role of Partners

In Heifetz's view, the only way to walk the razor's edge confidently is to reach for the balancing poles that come from both feedback and reflection. Managers must step forward again and again. But to keep their balance, they have to absorb the reactions from those affected by their actions, including clients, overseers, and staff. Managers cannot hear only from those who are applauding, because supporters might be leading managers down a path that gets narrower and narrower and finally disappears. Such was the path for David Sencer and perhaps Miles Mahoney.

Managers must have partners to help keep them upright.[35] Without partners, it is impossible for managers to succeed, or to be sure that they are on the right course, or to have the psychological confidence and energy required to carry on. But our cases also suggest that managers must draw their partners from the ranks of their opponents and rivals as well as from their supporters, for the opponents are almost certainly telling managers or leaders something important. They are opposed, and powerfully opposed, because some important value is being sacrificed. It is not just that they are corrupt or evil. Public managers in a democracy must acknowledge and respond to their concerns. Thus, as part of learning how to doubt, managers must learn how to take their opponent's views seriously.

The Vocation of the Public Executive

In discussing the "vocation of the politician," Max Weber once wrote about the need for "passion" as one of the most important qualifying psychological characteristics of politicians.[36] He was careful to say that he was not talking about a kind of passion he called "sterile excitation" and attributed to "a certain kind of Russian intellectual."[37] He instead referred to passion in the sense of "matter-of-factness"—"the ability to let realities work upon [the politician] with inner concentration and calmness."[38]

What makes this observation so interesting is that Weber combines two qualities ordinarily thought to be opposed: the psychological strength and energy that come from being committed to a cause; and a capacity for diagnosis, reflection, and objectivity that is associated with disinterestedness. Weber's key insight is that it takes psychological energy to do the hard work of facing up to the reality of conflict and uncertainty and, furthermore, to chart actions realistically adapted to the situation at hand, however favorable or unfavorable that situation might be to one's initial goals.

That cool, inner concentration, in the end, can and should guide the calculations of those who would lead public organizations. It describes the "managerial temperament" that is appropriate for those who would lead organizations that work for a divided and uncertain society. And it is that kind of temperament which this book seeks to encourage among public sector executives in the interests of achieving more effective, more accountable, more responsive, and more democratic management of our public institutions. The ideas and techniques offered here can be no substitute for good character and experience. But, with luck, they might help to extend the limits of one's character and experience.

NOTES

INTRODUCTION

1. I am indebted to my colleague Michael Barzelay for properly characterizing this work in these terms. For a vigorous defense of practical reasoning, see Donald A. Schon, *The Reflective Practitioner: How Professionals Think in Action* (New York: Basic Books, 1983).

2. For a book that does an outstanding job of explaining why public sector organizations behave as they do, see James Q. Wilson, *Bureaucracy: What Government Agencies Do and Why They Do It* (New York: Basic Books, 1989).

3. For a book that admirably fills this particular niche, see Herbert Kaufman, *The Administrative Behavior of Federal Bureau Chiefs* (Washington, D.C.: Brookings Institution, 1981).

4. Richard E. Neustadt described the effect of the constitution on American presidents: "And the need to bargain is the product of a constitutional system that shares formal powers among separate institutions." See Neustadt, *Presidential Power and the Modern Presidents: The Politics of Leadership from Roosevelt to Reagan* (New York: Free Press, 1990), pp. 191–192. Laurence E. Lynn, Jr., observes that what is true for presidents is equally true for lower level public executives. See Lynn, *Managing the Public's Business: The Job of the Government Executive* (New York: Basic Books, 1981), pp. 3–17. Graham T. Allison points to this effect as one of the most important things that distinguish public from private sector management. See Allison, "Public and Private Management: Are They Fundamentally Alike in All Unimportant Respects?" in Jay M. Shafritz and Albert C. Hyde, eds., *Classics of Public Administration,* 2d ed. (Chicago: Dorsey Press, 1987), p. 519. I refer to Shafritz and Hyde's excellent anthology throughout this chapter.

5. Laurence E. Lynn, Jr., and David DeF. Whitman treat the president as a manager in *The President as Policymaker: Jimmy Carter and Welfare Reform* (Philadelphia: Temple University Press, 1981), p. 35. Martha Weinberg gives an account of governors in these terms in *Managing the State* (Cambridge, Mass.: MIT Press, 1977). And Doug Yates views Mayors at least partly as managers in *The Ungovernable City: The Politics of Urban Problems and Policy Making* (Cambridge, Mass.: MIT Press, 1977), p. 28.

6. Herbert Kaufman makes these officials the focus of his attention in *The Administrative Behavior of Federal Bureau Chiefs*. So do Jameson Doig and Erwin C. Hargrove in *Leadership and Innovation: A Biographical Perspective on Entrepreneurs in Government* (Baltimore: Johns Hopkins University Press, 1987).

7. Jerry Mechling, "Analysis and Implementation: Sanitation Policies in New York City," *Public Policy,* vol. 27, no. 2 (Spring 1978): 263–284. These positions may be similar in function to new product managers or "integrators" that are commonly used in the private sector to give point to an organization's new initiatives. See Paul R. Lawrence and Jay W. Lorsch, "New Management Job: The Integrator," *Harvard Business Review,* November–December 1967, 142–151.

8. For a discussion of how these officials exercise influence on appointed political executives, see Hugh Heclo, *A Government of Strangers: Executive Politics in Washington* (Washington, D.C.: Brookings Institution, 1977).

9. Joel D. Aberbach, *Keeping a Watchful Eye: The Politics of Congressional Oversight* (Washington, D.C.: Brookings Institution, 1990), pp. 217–219. See also Morris S. Ogul, *Congress Oversees the Bureaucracy: Studies in Legislative Supervision* (Pittsburgh: University of Pittsburgh Press, 1976), p. 11.

10. The case of the Boston Housing Authority, presented in Chapters 6 and 7 of this book, represents an example of judicial management of a public organization. For a more general discussion of this phenomenon, see Robert C. Wood, *Remedial Law: When Courts Become Administrators* (Amherst: University of Massachusetts Press, 1990).

11. For a vivid portrayal of an interest group leader who has left a powerful trace on public enterprises, see Charles McCarry, *Citizen Nader* (New York: Saturday Review Press, 1972).

12. E. S. Savas is encouraging this trend. See Savas, *Privatizing the Public Sector* (Chatham, N.J.: Chatham House, 1982). John D. Donahue points out some of the limitations and requirements. See Donahue, *The Privatization Decision: Public Ends, Private Means* (New York: Basic Books, 1989).

13. For a critique of the "actor-centered" view of public management, see Laurence E. Lynn, Jr., "Public Management Research: The Triumph of Art over Science," *Journal of Public Policy and Management,* vol. 13, no.

2 (Spring 1994): 231–259. It is also significant, I think, that David Osborne and Ted Gaebler focus most of their attention on systems changes and say relatively little about changing managerial doctrines. See Osborne and Gaebler, *Reinventing Government: How the Entrepreneurial Spirit Is Transforming the Public Sector from Schoolhouse to Statehouse, City Hall to the Pentagon* (Reading, Mass.: Addison-Wesley, 1992).

14. For a discussion of total quality management in the public sector, see Steven Cohen and Ronald Bran, *Total Quality Management in Government: A Practical Guide for the Real World* (San Francisco: Jossey-Bass, 1993).

15. I am indebted to Marc Zegans for introducing me to the view that particular ideas about how public managers should do their work, held by the managers themselves or their overseers, could be considered an important institution. See Zegans, "Innovation in the Well-Functioning Public Agency," *Public Productivity and Management Review,* vol. 16, no. 2 (Winter 1992): 141–156. Hugh Heclo makes a somewhat similar point: "Civil servants have appeared on the government scene in a way that seems somewhat detached from the accepted structure of American political institutions . . . Perhaps the most important effect of their detachment from constitutional history has been within the minds of bureaucrats themselves. There is less basis for American senior bureaucrats to feel sure of their place in government as civil servants . . . Their profession as civil servants has never been a part of the constitutional culture." See Heclo, "The State and America's Higher Civil Service" (Department of Government, Harvard University, photocopy, 1982), p. 5.

16. I confess that I am a little encouraged by the experience I have had in presenting these ideas to public sector executives from around the world. The students at the Kennedy School include public officials from more than forty different countries. I have also presented these ideas in executive programs in Australia, Canada, England, Poland, Spain, and Ukraine. In all cases, the executives are able to make the translations to their particular cultures and particular institutions. Still, this is hardly a proof of the generality of my approach.

17. For an excellent overview of the context of American government, see James Q. Wilson, *American Government: Institutions and Policies* (Lexington, Mass.: D. C. Heath, 1981). For an excellent discussion of the policy-making process, see Charles E. Lindblom, *The Policy-Making Process* (Englewood Cliffs, N.J.: Prentice-Hall, 1980). For a sharp discussion of the contemporary setting in which public managers operate, see John E. Chubb and Paul E. Peterson, eds., *Can the Government Govern?* (Washington, D.C.: Brookings Institution, 1989).

18. For an insightful analysis of the United States Congress, see David Mayhew, *Congress: The Electoral Connection* (New Haven, Conn.: Yale University Press, 1974); and Richard Fenno, *Congressmen in Committees* (Boston: Little, Brown, 1973). On the nature and behavior of legislative

oversight of executive branch agencies, see Aberbach, *Keeping a Watchful Eye*. On the interactions of public executives with the Congress, see Philip B. Heymann, *The Politics of Public Management* (New Haven, Conn.: Yale University Press, 1987).

19. See, for example, Harry M. Clor, ed., *The Mass Media and American Democracy* (New York: Rand, McNally, 1974); Martin Linsky, *Impact: How the Press Affects Federal Policymaking* (New York: Norton, 1986); Stephen Hess, *The Government/Press Connection: Press Officers and Their Offices* (Washington, D.C.: Brookings Institution, 1984); and Leon V. Sigal, *Reporters and Officials* (Lexington, Mass.: D. C. Heath, 1973).

20. The classic in this field, of course, is Neustadt, *Presidential Power and the Modern Presidents*. For a discussion of governors, see Robert Behn, *Governors on Governing* (Washington, D.C.: National Governors' Association, 1991).

21. See, for example, Walter Nicholson, *Microeconomic Theory: Basic Principles and Extensions,* 2d ed. (Hinsdale, Ill.: Dryden Press, 1978), pp. 607–678. For a summary, see Edith Stokey and Richard Zeckhauser, *A Primer for Policy Analysis* (New York: Norton, 1978), pp. 292–319. See also Richard Zeckhauser and Derek Leebaert, eds., *What Role for Government: Lessons from Policy Research* (Durham, N.C.: Duke University Press, 1983).

22. Dwight Waldo observes: "It can be argued with some persuasiveness that the proper role of a bureaucracy is to act as a stabilizing force in the midst of vertiginous change, and that this is what it is doing when it seems to be unresponsive and stupid. In this view it has a balance wheel or gyroscopic function." It is significant, however, that Waldo goes on to reject this view in favor of increased responsiveness or leadership from public managers. Waldo, "Public Administration in a Time of Revolution," *Public Administration Review,* 28 (July–August 1968), reprinted in Shafritz and Hyde, *Classics,* p. 367. Rufus Miles worked out a particular set of ideas about the extent to which career civil servants should adapt to the demands of incoming political executives in "Administrative Adaptability to Political Change," *Public Administration Review,* September 1965, 221–225. For a set of cases describing the responses of career civil servants to rather dramatic political change, see "Surviving at the EPA: David Tundermann," KSG Case #C16-84-588.0; "Surviving at the EPA: Mike Walsh," KSG Case #C16-84-589.0; "Surviving at the EPA: Mike Cook," KSG Case #C16-84-590.0; "Surviving at the EPA: Bill Hedeman," KSG Case #C16-84-591.0; "Surviving at the EPA: Gary Dietrich," KSG Case #C16-84-592.0; "Note on the EPA under Administrator Anne Gorsuch," KSG Case #N16-84-587.0 (all Cambridge, Mass.: Kennedy School of Government Case Program, 1984).

23. John W. Pratt and Richard Zeckhauser, *Principals and Agents: The Structure of Business* (Boston: Harvard Business School Press, 1985). For a critique of these ideas in the public sector, see Mark H. Moore and Mar-

garet J. Gates, *Inspectors-General: Junkyard Dogs or Man's Best Friend?* (New York: Russell Sage, 1986).

24. Howard Raiffa, *The Art and Science of Negotiation* (Cambridge, Mass.: Harvard University Press, 1982).

25. For a general introduction to organizations, see Gareth Morgan, *Images of Organizations* (Thousand Oaks, Calif.: Sage Publications, 1986). For a discussion of why public sector organizations behave as they do, see Wilson, *Bureaucracy.*

26. The classic in the field is James G. March and Herbert Simon, *Organizations* (New York: Wiley and Sons, 1986). See also Herbert Kaufman, *Red Tape: Its Origins, Uses, and Abuses* (Washington, D.C.: Brookings Institution, 1977). For a contemporary treatment of obstacles to innovation and ways to get around them, see Rosabeth Moss Kanter, *When Giants Learn to Dance: Mastering the Challenge of Strategy, Management, and Careers in the 1990's* (New York: Simon and Schuster, 1989).

27. For a comprehensive account of the traditional view of public administration, see Shafritz and Hyde, *Classics.* In addition, classic texts include Leonard D. White, *Introduction to the Study of Public Administration* (New York: Macmillan, 1926); E. Pendleton Herring, *Public Administration and the Public Interest* (New York: McGraw-Hill, 1936); Dwight Waldo, *The Study of Public Administration* (New York: Random House, 1955); Frederick C. Mosher, *Democracy and the Public Service* (New York: Oxford University Press, 1968). For more contemporary approaches, see James W. Fesler and Donald F. Kettl, *The Politics of the Administrative Process* (Chatham, N.J.: Chatham House, 1991). For a critique, see Michael Barzelay with Babak J. Armajani, *Breaking through Bureaucracy: A New Vision for Managing in Government* (Berkeley: University of California Press, 1992).

28. Mosher, *Democracy and the Public Service*; and Judith E. Gruber, *Controlling Bureaucracies: Dilemmas in Democratic Government* (Berkeley: University of California Press, 1987).

29. See the "POSDCORB" acronym developed by Luther Gulick in "Notes on the Theory of Organization," in Shafritz and Hyde, *Classics,* pp. 79–89.

30. Kaufman, *Administrative Behavior of Bureau Chiefs;* Herbert Kaufman, *The Forest Ranger* (Baltimore: Johns Hopkins University Press, 1960); Jeffrey Manditch Prottas, *People Processing* (Lexington, Mass.: D. C. Heath, 1979); Martha Derthick, *Agency under Stress: The Social Security Administration in American Government* (Washington, D.C.: Brookings Institution, 1990). For an effort to link managerial action to the performance of public sector organizations, see John J. DiIulio, Jr., *Governing Prisons: A Comparative Study of Correctional Management* (New York: Free Press, 1987).

31. Richard B. Stewart, "The Reformation of American Administrative Law," in *Harvard Law Review,* vol. 88, no. 8 (June 1975): 1667–1813. Jerry L.

Mashaw, *Due Process in the Administrative State* (New Haven, Conn.: Yale University Press, 1985).

32. Jerry L. Mashaw, *Bureaucratic Justice: Managing Social Security Disability Claims* (New Haven, Conn.: Yale University Press, 1983).
33. The private sector management literature includes classics such as Chester Barnard, *The Functions of the Executive* (Cambridge, Mass.: Harvard University Press, 1938); Peter F. Drucker, *Management: Tasks, Responsibilities, Practices* (New York: Harper and Row, 1973); Thomas J. Peters and Robert H. Waterman, *In Search of Excellence: Lessons from America's Best-Run Companies* (New York: Warner, 1982); and Michael E. Porter, *Competitive Strategy: Techniques for Analyzing Industries and Competitors* (New York: Free Press, 1980).
34. Porter, *Competitive Strategy.*
35. Kanter, *When Giants Learn to Dance;* and Donald K. Clifford and Richard E. Cavanagh, *The Winning Performance: How America's High-Growth, Midsize Companies Succeed* (New York: Bantam, 1985).
36. John Kotter, *A Force for Change: How Leadership Differs from Management* (New York: Free Press; London: Collier Macmillan, 1990).
37. There is an emerging literature on public management and public entrepreneurship that takes up these same issues and forms an important new tradition in which I am writing. Key works in this domain include: Lynn, *Managing the Public's Business*; Gordon Chase and Elizabeth C. Reveal, *How to Manage in the Public Sector* (Reading, Mass.: Addison-Wesley, 1983); Doig and Hargrove, *Leadership and Innovation: A Biographical Perspective*; Laurence E. Lynn, Jr., *Managing Public Policy* (Boston: Little, Brown, 1987); Heymann, *The Politics of Public Management*; Steven Kelman, *Procurement and Public Management: The Fear of Discretion and the Quality of Government Performance* (Washington, D.C.: AEI Press, 1990); Erwin C. Hargrove and John C. Glidewell, eds., *Impossible Jobs in Public Management* (Lawrence: University of Kansas Press, 1991); Robert D. Behn, *Leadership Counts: Lessons for Public Managers from the Massachusetts Welfare, Training, and Employment Program* (Cambridge, Mass.: Harvard University Press, 1991); Martin A. Levin and Mary Bryna Sanger, *Making Government Work: How Entrepreneurial Executives Turn Bright Ideas into Real Results* (San Francisco: Jossey-Bass, 1994); and Richard N. Haass, *The Power to Persuade: How to Be Effective in Government, the Public Sector, or Any Unruly Organization* (Boston: Houghton Mifflin, 1994).
38. For a partial listing of these cases, see Case Program of the Kennedy School of Government, *The Kennedy School Case Catalog,* 3d ed. (Cambridge, Mass.: Kennedy School of Government Case Program, 1992).
39. Nelson Polsby, personal communication.
40. These practitioners included such people as Nancy Altman-Lupu, Robert Blackwell, Manuel Carballo, Hale Champion, Gordon Chase, Richard

Darman, Michael Dukakis, Richard Haass, Martin Linsky, and James Verdier.

41. On the limitations of these hopes, see Mark H. Moore, "Policy Analysis vs. Social Science: Some Fundamental Differences," in Daniel V. Callahan and Bruce Jenning, eds., *Ethics: The Social Sciences and Policy Analysis* (New York: Plenum Publishing, 1983).

42. Graham T. Allison and Mark H. Moore, "Special Issues on Implementation Analysis," in *Public Policy,* vol. 26, no. 2 (Spring 1978); and Daniel A. Mazmanian and Paul A. Sabatier, *Implementation and Public Policy* (Glenview, Ill.: Scott, Foresman, 1983).

43. Mark Moore, "Gordon Chase and Public Sector Innovation" (Kennedy School of Government, photocopy, 1987).

44. John E. Chubb and Paul E. Peterson, eds., *Can the Government Govern?* (Washington, D.C.: Brookings Institution, 1989).

45. For discussions about the importance of flexible, innovative, value-seeking organizations in the private sector, see Peters and Waterman, *In Search of Excellence;* Kanter, *When Giants Learn to Dance;* and Donald K. Clifford and Richard E. Cavanagh, *The Winning Performance: How America's High-Growth Midsize Companies Succeed* (New York: Bantam, 1985).

46. Chris Argyris has forever disabused us of the idea that "espoused theories" are the same as theories "in use." See Argyris and Schon, *Organizational Learning.*

47. William A. Niskanen, Jr., thinks this is the principal motivation of public sector executives. See Niskanen, *Bureaucracy and Representative Government* (Chicago: Aldine-Atherton, 1971). James Q. Wilson has expressed his doubts about this as a positive description in *Bureaucracy,* pp. 118–120. I am arguing here that it is wrong as a normative criterion, a much easier argument to make.

48. Survival and growth are important normative tests of managerial accomplishments in the private sector, for they indicate that the organization has continued to meet market challenges. Indeed, building organizations that could survive and flourish was the managerial accomplishment celebrated by Peters and Waterman in *In Search of Excellence.*

49. Robert Caro, *The Power Broker: Robert Moses and the Fall of New York* (New York: Knopf, 1974). See also the stories of J. Edgar Hoover and Robert Moses in James W. Doig and Erwin C. Hargrove, eds., *Leadership and Innovation: Entrepreneurs in Government* (Baltimore: Johns Hopkins University Press, 1990).

50. See, for example, Phil Heymann's account of the Federal Trade Commission in *The Politics of Public Management,* pp. 15–17.

51. See the discussion of this point in Chapter 5 (on the ethics of entrepreneurial advocacy) and in Chapter 8.

52. Peters and Waterman focused not simply on survival and growth but also on sustained *profitability*. That is the concept for which we need an anal-

ogy in the public sector. See Peters and Waterman, *In Search of Excellence,* pp. 22–23.

1. MANAGERIAL IMAGINATION

1. The case I describe here is a hypothetical one stimulated by a discussion in my hometown of Belmont, Mass. What librarians should do about latchkey children seems to be a hot issue. A computer search yielded twelve recent citations of the problem. The most comprehensive discussion is by Frances Smardo Dowd, *Latchkey Children in the Library and the Community* (Phoenix: Onyx Press, 1991). On the difficulty of managing use of library spaces by children and adults, see Paul G. Allvin, "Library Goes by the Book: Restrictions on Children Faulted by Andover Parents," *Boston Globe,* July 22, 1990, p. 27.

2. Aaron B. Wildavsky observes this kind of behavior in the federal budgeting process. See Wildavsky, *The Politics of the Budgetary Process,* 4th ed. (Boston: Little, Brown, 1984), pp. 108–123.

3. This thought is an example of what David Osborne and Ted Gaebler consider "enterprising government." See Osborne and Gaebler, *Reinventing Government: How the Entrepreneurial Spirit Is Transforming the Public Sector from Schoolhouse to Statehouse, City Hall to the Pentagon* (Reading, Mass.: Addison-Wesley, 1992), pp. 195–218.

4. For a discussion of the difficulties one faces in determining what price should be charged for governmental services, see Joseph T. Kelly, *Costing Government Services: A Guide for Decision Making* (Washington, D.C.: Government Finance Research Center, 1984).

5. A similar problem arose in a much different and somewhat unexpected context: financing the Gulf War. In that case, America's allies had agreed to pay the United States some of the costs associated with prosecuting the war. The question was to whom that money should be paid. One possibility was directly to the U.S. Department of Defense (DOD). A second was to the Congress of the United States, which would then appropriate the money to DOD. The first option seemed by far the simpler one, but DOD's overseers in Congress balked. They did so for two reasons. First, it would remove Congress from being able to effectively control monies going to the Pentagon. Second, it would suggest that the DOD had become a mercenary force for the world and was entitled to charge "clients" for military operations taken on their behalf. If the money was paid to the U.S. Congress, instead, and then appropriated to the DOD, the DOD would be kept more firmly under democratic control, and there would be a stronger presumption that the expenditures reflected appropriate U.S. national purposes rather than DOD institutional purposes. I thank Sean O'Keefe for the story.

6. Note that "going back to the Town Meeting for guidance" resolves several important problems for the librarian. First, it relieves her of the responsi-

bility (and the privilege!) of having to decide whether or not it is publicly valuable for her to use library resources to meet the needs of latchkey children. Second, depending on *how* she goes back and what transpires in the deliberations, the Town Meeting would or would not transform the collective interests of individual latchkey parents into a public interest in meeting their individual needs. She could enter this debate as an advocate for the parents, by minimizing the cost and inconvenience associated with accommodating the latchkey children, or as an opponent, by maximizing the difficulty, expense, and inconvenience to others of meeting the demands. In deciding whether and how to enter into this discussion, she might be influenced by her own views about what was desirable, by her sense of her organization's most basic mission, or even by her sense of how "rational" the deliberation in the Town Meeting might be. If, for example, she thought that some politicians might use the issue to attack single-parent families for their neglect in raising children and the burdens they placed on others, she might decide that the question of whether it was publicly valuable for the library to respond to latchkey children could not be effectively engaged, and therefore that openness was not in the best interests of the society. Or, she might decide that this was an important issue to discuss, and then think about how the issue might best be framed. In any case, she faces a decision not only about whether to go back to the Town Meeting but also about what approach to take. These issues are discussed extensively in Chapters 4, 5, and 8.

7. The United States has always prided itself on (and been admired by others for) a civic culture that seems to nourish voluntary associations of various kinds. In the mid-nineteenth century Alexis de Tocqueville noted how common and important this feature of American democracy was in *Democracy in America,* ed. Francis Bowen (New York: Vintage Books, 1945), pp. 198–206. More recently, Robert Putnam has observed the importance of voluntary associations in determining the quality of local government in Italy. See Putnam, *Making Democracy Work: Civic Traditions in Modern Italy* (Princeton, N.J.: Princeton University Press, 1993). For an interesting case drawn from contemporary American experience, see "Finding Black Parents: One Church, One Child," KSG Case #C16-88-856.0 (Cambridge, Mass.: Kennedy School of Government, Case Program, 1988).

8. For a general discussion of the possible roles and missions of the public library, see David Gerard, ed., *Libraries in Society: A Reader* (New York: K. G. Sauer, 1978). For an argument that they ought to actively search for ways to be helpful to citizens, see Bernard Vavrek, "Public Librarianship: Waiting for Something to Happen," *Wilson Library Bulletin,* vol. 67, no. 8 (April 1993): 70.

9. The claim that public managers are responsible for finding the most valuable use of the resources entrusted to them may sound unexceptionable. In fact, it is a controversial statement in that it encourages managers to

scan their environment for useful things to do. This, as will be described below, is consistent with what we expect *private* sector managers to do, but not *public* sector executives. Public sector executives are supposed to have been constrained as to their proper purposes and to search only for more effective means to achieve their mandated purposes. Thus, it is more common for public managers to say that they are responsible for "achieving their mandated purposes as efficiently and effectively as possible" than that they are responsible for "finding high value uses of the resources entrusted to them." Working through the implications of this apparently simple but actually quite profound change in conceiving of the role of public managers—to change them from functionaries who have little role in the search for public value to one in which they are explorers with important roles to play—is the whole point of this book.

10. Key sources of this conception include Woodrow Wilson's classic article "The Study of Administration," *Political Science Quarterly*, 2 (June 1887): 197-222; Frank J. Goodnow, *Politics and Administration: A Study of Government* (New York: Russell and Russell, 1900); Leonard D. White, *Introduction to the Study of Public Administration* (New York: Macmillan, 1926); E. Pendleton Herring, *Public Administration and the Public Interest* (New York: McGraw-Hill, 1936); Luther Gulick, "Notes on the Theory of Organization," in Luther Gulick and Lyndall Urwick, eds., *Papers on the Science of Administration* (New York: Institute of Public Administration, 1937); and Louis Brownlow, Charles E. Merriam, and Luther Gulick, *Administrative Management in the Government of the United States* (Washington, D.C.: United States Government Printing Office, 1937). Significant excerpts from these classic sources have been collected and usefully interpreted in a single volume by Jay M. Shafritz and Albert C. Hyde, *Classics of Public Administration*, 2d ed. (Chicago: Dorsey Press, 1987).

Specific examples of the language these authors used to help frame the tasks of public sector executives in these ways include the following. Woodrow Wilson wrote: "It is the object of administrative study to discover, first, what government can properly and successfully do, and, secondly, how it can do these proper things with the utmost possible efficiency and at the least possible cost either of money or energy" (quoted in Shafritz and Hyde, *Classics,* p. 10). He went on to introduce the classic distinction between "policy," which was concerned with what government should do, and "administration," which was concerned with the efficient doing of the government's business: "Administration lies outside the proper sphere of *politics.* Administrative questions are not political questions. Although politics sets the tasks for administration, it should not be suffered to manipulate its offices" (Shafritz and Hyde, *Classics,* p. 18). He also described what constituted "good" behavior for public administrators: "Steady, hearty allegiance to the policy of the government they serve" (Shafritz and Hyde, *Classics,* p. 22). Goodnow echoed Wilson's distinction between politics and administration: "Politics has to do with policies or expressions of the state will. Administration has to do with the execution of these policies" (quoted in Shafritz and Hyde, *Classics*, p. 26). White, writing many years later, explained in more detail what the function of administration was: "Public administration is the management of men and materials in the accomplishment of the purposes of the state . . . It leaves open the question to what extent the administration itself participates in formulating the purposes of the state . . . The objective of public administration is the most efficient utilization of the resources at the disposal of officials and employees . . . In every direction, good administration seeks the elimination of waste, the conservation of material and energy, and the most rapid and complete achievement of public purposes consistent with economy and the welfare of workers" (quoted in Shafritz and Hyde, *Classics*, pp. 56–57).

It is important to consider, however, that the tradition based on the separation of politics from administration, and the assumption that the purpose of administration was to achieve mandated purposes as efficiently and effectively as possible, always had a subordinate theme indicating that things were not quite so simple. Thus, for example, White recognized that "the problems which crowd upon legislative bodies today are often entangled with, or become exclusively technical questions which the layman can handle only by utilizing the services of the expert. The control of local government, the regulation of utilities, the enforcement of the prohibition amendment, the appropriation for a navy, the organization of a health department, the maintenance of a national service of agricultural research, are all matters which can be put upon the statute book only with the assistance of men who know the operating details in each case . . . These men are not merely useful to legislators . . . ; they are simply indispensable. They are the government" (Shafritz and Hyde, *Classics*, p. 59). This point is also made emphatically by Emmette S. Redford in *Democracy in the Administrative State* (New York: Oxford University Press, 1969), pp. 31–36. Herring went even further, recognizing the key importance of the initiative of public managers in defining as well as executing purposes, and found the reasons not only in the expertise of the managers but also in the imperfections of politics. He wrote: "Upon the shoulders of the bureaucrat has been placed in large part the burden of reconciling group differences and making effective and workable the economic and social compromises arrived at through the legislative process. Thus Congress passes a statute setting forth a general principle. The details must be filled in by supplemental regulation. The bureaucrat is left to decide as to the conditions that necessitate the law's application. He is in a better position than the legislators to perform these duties. His daily occupation brings him into direct contact with the situation the law is intended to meet" (quoted in Shafritz and Hyde, *Classics*, p. 74).

So, the question of whether public administrators should be skilled technicians who could devise efficient means to achieve legislative intent, experts who could help legislators deliberate, officials who could defend the public interest against short-sighted or badly motivated politics, or something other than all these has remained unsettled in the field of public administration and in the broader public. As Frederick C. Mosher stated in 1968, "The developments in recent decades in the 'real world' of government have brought to the policy-administration dichotomy strains which have grown almost beyond the point of toleration. In fact, on the theoretical plane, the finding of a viable substitute may well be the number one problem of public administration today. But this concept, like most others, dies hard. There are built in obstacles of motivation in favor of perpetuating it. By and large, legislators prefer not to derogate their importance by advertising that it is smaller than it appears to be, and when they do it is usually to denounce administrative (or judicial) 'usurpation' of legislative power. Likewise, administrators . . . prefer not to advertise, or even to recognize, that they are significantly influencing policy for fear of provoking such charges." See Mosher, *Democracy and the Public Service* (New York: Oxford University Press, 1968), p. 6. Thus, even though academics and practitioners have long known there were flaws in the traditional doctrine of public administration, they have been hard-pressed to replace the conventional theory in the academy, among practitioners, or in the general population. For an account of why this theory has hung on so long, see Alasdair Roberts, "Demonstrating Neutrality: The Rockefeller Philanthropies and the Evolution of Public Administration, 1927–1936," *Public Administration Review,* vol. 54, no. 23, pp. 221–228.

11. Judith E. Gruber, *Controlling Bureaucracies: Dilemmas in Democratic Governance* (Berkeley: University of California Press, 1987).

12. Woodrow Wilson, "The Study of Administration."

13. This, at least, is what legislative processes are supposed to accomplish. See Dennis Thompson, *Political Ethics and Public Office* (Cambridge, Mass.: Harvard University Press, 1987), pp. 96–122.

14. See Herbert Jacob's discussion of the form that laws take in *Law and Politics in the United States* (Boston: Little, Brown, 1986), pp. 241–243.

15. For a discussion of how Congress exercises its oversight functions and holds agency managers accountable, see Joel D. Aberbach, *Keeping a Watchful Eye: The Politics of Congressional Oversight* (Washington, D.C.: Brookings Institution, 1990), pp. 195–198. On the question of whether Congressional oversight is bound by the terms of legislation, see Harvey C. Mansfield, Sr., "Accountability and Congressional Oversight," in Bruce L. R. Smith and James D. Carroll, eds., *Improving the Accountability and Performance of Government* (Washington, D.C.: Brookings Institution, 1982). For a discussion of how inspectors general help to hold government managers accountable to legislative requirements, see Mark H. Moore and Margaret J. Gates, *Inspectors-General: Junkyard Dogs or Man's Best Friend?* (New York: Russell Sage, 1986).

16. See n. 9 above.
17. Edward C. Banfield made the distinction between the "substantive" and "administrative" expertise of managers in "The Training of the Executive," *Public Policy,* vol. 10 (1960): 20–21. Michael Barzelay notes that the "bureaucratic reform model" created different organizational positions for these two different kinds of expertise: the substantive experts were put in charge of line operations, while the administrative experts were placed in staff elements concerned with administration and management. Barzelay with Babak Armajani, *Breaking through Bureaucracy: A New Vision for Managing in Government* (Berkeley: University of California Press, 1992), p. 5.

   The importance of substantive knowledge for government managers is implicit in the fact that civil service systems routinely establish knowledge and experience in the profession as an important qualifying characteristic. How important substantive or specialist knowledge as compared with administrative or generalist knowledge, however, has long been a contentious issue in public administration. For a long period, an effort was made in the United States to emulate the example of England and other continental governments and establish an administrative class whose expertise lay in its knowledge of the general principles of administration rather than of any particular field. For a skeptical view of whether this approach is feasible or desirable in the United States, see Rufus D. Miles, "Rethinking Some Premises of the Senior Executive Service" in Bruce L. R. Smith and James D. Carroll, eds., *Improving Accountability and Performance of Government* (Washington, D.C.: Brookings Institution, 1982), pp. 41–45.
18. What constitutes "administrative" competence is set out in White, *Introduction to the Study of Public Administration,* and Luther Gulick, *Papers on the Science of Administration* (New York: Institute of Public Administration, 1937).
19. Over the last decade or so, I have often concluded executive development programs at the Kennedy School by writing a list of words on the blackboard that describe people who take responsibility for large enterprises. The list includes the following words: leader, entrepreneur, executive, manager, commissioner, administrator, and bureaucrat. I then draw a line beneath the words "leader" and "entrepreneur," and above the words "commissioner," "administrator," and "bureaucrat," and ask the participants if they sense any difference between the words that are above the line and those below the line. They usually can sense a difference and tend to locate the difference in how much freedom and initiative the different words suggest, with leaders and entrepreneurs assuming that they are authorized to act and the others having to wait for others to authorize them to act. They also sense a great deal of risk in being a leader and an entrepreneur and more safety in being any of the others. They associate the risk with having to be creative and in assuming the responsibility for

charting an uncertain course. It is important that the words below the line—"commissioner," "administrator," and "bureaucrat"—are also largely considered public sector words by the participants.

20. For this view of bureaucracy, see Edward C. Banfield, *Political Influence* (New York: Free Press of Glencoe, 1961); and William A. Niskanen, *Bureaucracy and Representative Government* (Chicago: Aldine-Atherton, 1971), p. 40.

21. The winds of change are being fanned by two important books: Osborne and Gaebler, *Reinventing Government,* and Barzelay, *Breaking through Bureaucracy.*

22. For a comprehensive treatment of the distinction between these two offices and how the incumbents of each engage one another in the direction of public efforts, see Hugh Heclo, *A Government of Strangers: Executive Politics in Washington* (Washington, D.C.: Brookings Institution, 1977).

23. Niskanen, *Bureaucracy and Representative Government,* p. 39. Terry Moe agrees with Niskanen: "Once an agency is created, the political world becomes a different place. Agency bureaucrats are now political actors in their own right. They have career and institutional interests that may not be entirely congruent with their formal missions, and they have powerful resources—expertise and delegated authority—that might be employed toward these selfish ends. They are new players whose interests and resources alter the political game." Moe, "The Politics of Bureaucratic Structure," in John Chubb and Paul Peterson, eds., *Can the Government Govern?* (Washington, D.C.: Brookings Institution, 1989), p. 282.

24. David R. Mayhew, *The Electoral Connection* (New Haven, Conn.: Yale University Press, 1974).

25. Niskanen, *Bureaucracy and Representative Government,* pp. 138–154. Terry M. Moe, "Political Institutions: The Neglected Side of the Story," *Journal of Law, Economics, and Organization,* vol. 6 (1990): 213–254.

26. See discussion below in Chapter 2.

27. Graham T. Allison, "Public and Private Management: Are They Fundamentally Alike in All Unimportant Respects?" in Shafritz and Hyde, *Classics,* pp. 510–529.

28. This is the view advanced by Herring in *Public Administration and the Public Interest.*

29. Herman S. Leonard, "Theory S and Theory T" (Kennedy School of Government, photocopy, 1984). Robert D. Behn has advanced a similar view. See Behn, *Leadership Counts: Lessons for Public Managers from the Massachusetts Welfare, Training, and Employment Program* (Cambridge, Mass.: Harvard University Press, 1991), pp. 203–209.

30. This is increasingly the world which private sector managers operate. See Thomas J. Peters, *Thriving on Chaos: Handbook for a Management Revolution* (New York: Knopf, 1987).

31. The distinction between self-serving and misguided is potentially impor-

tant. See Mark H. Moore and Malcolm K. Sparrow, *Ethics in Government: The Moral Challenge of Public Leadership* (Englewood Cliffs, N.J.: Prentice-Hall, 1990). Also see discussion in Chapter 8.

32. See n. 9 above.
33. See Robert A. Caro, *The Power Broker: Robert Moses and the Fall of New York* (New York: Knopf, 1974). See also Jameson W. Doig and Erwin C. Hargrove, *Leadership and Innovation: A Biographical Perspective on Entrepreneurs in Government* (Baltimore: Johns Hopkins University Press, 1987).
34. Michael Maccoby, *The Gamesman: The New Corporate Leaders* (New York: Simon and Schuster, 1976). Laurence E. Lynn, Jr., has usefully picked up and applied this image to the public sector. See Lynn, "Government Executives as Gamesmen: A Metaphor for Analyzing Managerial Behavior," *Journal of Policy Analysis and Management,* vol. 1, no. 4 (Summer 1982): 482–495.
35. For evidence that effective management matters in the public sector, see John J. DiIulio, Jr., *Governing Prisons: A Comparative Study of Correctional Management* (New York: Free Press, 1987); and Osborne and Gaebler, *Reinventing Government.*
36. For a basic reference on program evaluation, see Carol H. Weiss, *Evaluation Research: Methods of Assessing Program Effectiveness* (Englewood Cliffs, N.J.: Prentice-Hall, 1972). For a useful guide about how to do program evaluations in concrete contexts, see Jerome T. Murphy, *Getting the Facts: A Fieldwork Guide for Evaluators and Policy Analysts* (Santa Monica, Calif.: Goodyear Publishing, 1980). On the problems of getting organizations to use program evaluations routinely to improve their performance, see Aaron Wildavksy, "The Self-Evaluating Organization," *Public Administration Review,* 32 (September–October 1972): 509–520.
37. Edith Stokey and Richard Zeckhauser, *A Primer for Policy Analysis* (New York: Norton, 1978), pp. 134–158.
38. Osborne and Gaebler, *Reinventing Government,* pp. 166–194.
39. On the importance of managers having overall goals and objectives, see Philip Selznick, *Leadership in Administration: A Sociological Interpretation,* rev. ed. (Berkeley: University of California Press, 1984); and Peter Drucker, *Management: Tasks, Responsibilities, Practices* (New York: Harper and Row, 1973). On the concept of corporate strategy in the private sector, see Kenneth Andrews, *The Concept of Corporate Strategy,* rev. ed. (Homewood, Ill.: R. D. Irwin, 1980); and Michael E. Porter, *Competitive Advantage: Creating and Sustaining Superior Performance* (New York: Free Press, 1985).
40. Philip B. Heymann, *The Politics of Public Management* (New Haven, Conn.: Yale University Press, 1987), pp. 12–15; David A. Lax and James K. Sebenius, *The Manager as Negotiator: Bargaining for Cooperation and Competitive Gain* (New York: Free Press, 1986), pp. 264–267.

41. For additional insight on the notion of "indirect management," see Lax and Sebenius, *Manager as Negotiator,* pp. 315–330.

42. Heymann, *The Politics of Public Management.* Also, Richard N. Haass, *The Power to Persuade: How to Be Effective in Government, the Public Sector, or Any Unruly Organization* (Boston: Houghton Mifflin, 1994).

43. Laurence E. Lynn, Jr., and John M. Seidl, "Bottom-Line Management for Public Agencies," *Harvard Business Review,* vol. 55, no. 1 (January–February 1977): 144–153; Roger Porter, *Presidential Decisionmaking: The Economic Policy Board* (Cambridge: Cambridge University Press, 1980).

44. Lax and Sebenius, *Manager as Negotiator.*

45. Robert B. Reich, *Public Management in a Democratic Society* (Englewood Cliffs, N.J.: Prentice-Hall, 1990); Ronald A. Heifetz, *Leadership without Easy Answers* (Cambridge, Mass.: Harvard University Press, 1994).

46. Philip Kotler and Eduardo L. Roberto, *Social Marketing: Strategies for Changing Public Behavior* (New York: Free Press, 1989).

47. For theoretical discussion of the moral obligations facing public officials, see Arthur Isak Applbaum, "Democratic Legitimacy and Official Discretion," *Philosophy and Public Affairs,* vol. 21, no. 3 (Summer 1982): 240–274; and John P. Burke, *Bureaucratic Responsibility* (Baltimore: Johns Hopkins University Press, 1986). For a more applied discussion, see Moore and Sparrow, *Ethics in Government.*

48. I am indebted to my colleagues Robert Leone, Michael O'Hare, Steven Kelman, and Michael Barzelay through our collaboration in several courses for teaching me to think this way about public sector operations.

49. For a discussion of how to create innovative organizations in the private sector, see Rosabeth Moss Kanter, *The Change Masters: Innovation and Entrepreneurship in the American Corporation* (New York: Simon and Schuster, 1983); and Peter M. Senge, *The Fifth Discipline: The Art and Practice of the Learning Organization* (New York: Doubleday, 1990). For a discussion of how the lessons carry over into the public sector, see Alan Altshuler and Marc Zegans, "Innovation and Creativity: Comparisons between Public Management and Private Enterprise," *Cities,* February 1990, pp. 16–24; and Mark H. Moore, *Accounting for Change: Reconciling the Demands for Accountability and Innovation in the Public Sector* (Washington, D.C.: Council for Excellence in Government, 1993).

50. On ethical obligations and commitments, see n. 31. On appropriate psychological stances, see Max Weber, "Politics as a Vocation," in H. Gerth and C. W. Mills, trans., *From Max Weber* (New York: Oxford University Press, 1958); and Heifetz, *Leadership without Easy Answers.*

2. DEFINING PUBLIC VALUE

1. This case, like the case of the librarian, is a hypothetical one based on a common story. It comes generally from the experience of public managers

but is not the precise history of any particular manager. I use it to illustrate the kinds of problems that managers do face and the ways in which they might think.

2. Richard A. Brealey and Stewart C. Myers, *Principles of Corporate Finance,* 4th ed. (New York: McGraw-Hill, 1991), p. 22.

3. It may not be strictly true that *managers* in the private sector are responsible for *conceiving* products or services. More often, it seems that they are responsible for producing products that have been conceived by others—the chief executive officers of the firm and the marketing people. Yet, if we think of the chief executive officers and marketing people as "managers" as well, then it is true that the managers of a firm are responsible for conceiving as well as producing products. Moreover, it is increasingly true that private sector firms are structuring themselves to encourage entrepreneurship among midlevel managers. See, for example, Rosabeth Moss Kanter, *The Change Masters: Innovation and Entrepreneurship in the American Corporation* (New York: Simon and Schuster, 1983), pp. 129–179. This also seems to be occurring in the public sector. See United States Department of Agriculture, Forest Service, "The Evolution of Middle Management in the Forest Service," *New Thinking for Managing in Government* (Washington, D.C.: USDA, Forest Service, n.d.).

   The fact that we often want to separate the conception of a product (which could be understood as the imagination of something that would be valuable to produce) from the production of that product (which is more often understood as a technical problem), and to associate the conception of products with "leadership" and "entrepreneurship," reflects the discussion in n. 9 in Chapter 1. Apparently, we associate leadership and entrepreneurship with the use of imagination to find things that are valuable and management and administration with devising the technical means for achieving what our imaginations suggested would be valuable. For further evidence on the vitality of this distinction, see John Kotter, *A Force for Change: How Leadership Differs from Management* (New York: Free Press; London: Collier Macmillan, 1990), pp. 1–18. For an interesting interpretation of how the distinction between leadership and management is being used in both the theory and practice of management, see James Krantz and Thomas N. Gilmore, "The Splitting of Leadership and Management as a Social Defense," *Human Relations,* vol. 43, no. 2 (February 1990): 183–204.

4. These are the criteria Thomas J. Peters and Robert H. Waterman use to identify the firms that embody "excellence"; and it is the creation of organizations that are capable of maintaining profitability over the long run that they take to be the key managerial challenge in the private sector. See Peters and Waterman, *In Search of Excellence: Lessons from America's Best-Run Companies* (New York: Warner, 1982), pp. 121–125.

5. Of course, it is not strictly true that the profitability of a firm in either the short or long run gives certain evidence of the firm's ability to create value.

Insofar as the firm uses unowned and unpriced resources valuable to others in its productive activities, such as air or water, or unidentified risks to workers, its financial success may give a distorted view of its overall activity. Still, as a first approximation, the financial success of a firm does create a presumption that some value has been created for consumers and, therefore, for society at large.

6. James W. Fesler and Donald F. Kettl also treat authority as a key resource for public managers in *The Politics of the Administrative Process* (Chatham, N.J.: Chatham House, 1991), p. 9. Terry M. Moe considers the state's control over the use of public authority one of the things that attracts individuals to use the government for their own interests or to impose their idiosyncratic views of the public interest on public policy. See Moe, "Political Institutions: The Neglected Side of the Story," *Journal of Law, Economics, and Organizations,* vol. 6 (1990): 221.

7. For a discussion of how "obligations" to pay taxes might be mobilized, see Mark H. Moore, "On the Office of Taxpayer and the Social Process of Taxpaying," in Philip Sawicki, ed., *Income Tax Compliance* (Reston, Va.: American Bar Association, 1983), pp. 275–291.

8. Interestingly, the economics profession no longer seems to feel as though it has to defend markets philosophically as an appropriate way to allocate goods in the society. Reading through several microeconomics texts in search of a ringing philosophical endorsement of market mechanisms, I came up empty. To find the philosophical justification, one must go back to earlier writers who thought they were producing a normative political theory as well as a technical discussion of how economies functioned. See John Stuart Mill, *Utilitarianism and Other Writings,* ed. Mary Womack (Utica, N.Y.: Meridian, 1974), pp. 21–30. For more contemporary defenses of the social value of markets in allocating scarce resources, one has to go to books interpreting economics for others. See Steven E. Rhoads, *The Economist's View of the World: Government, Markets, and Public Policy* (Cambridge: Cambridge University Press, 1985), pp. 62–64.

9. The point of view I am alluding to here is one associated with "welfare economics." For a very good summary of these ideas and how they relate to social decision processes, see Edith Stokey and Richard Zeckhauser, *A Primer for Policy Analysis* (New York: Norton, 1978), pp. 257–290. The fundamental idea in welfare economics is that the overall value of a society's activities can be captured by the satisfaction that individuals derive from the activities of that society. In principle, of course, that satisfaction could include the satisfaction that comes from living in a society organized to produce what each individual views as justice and fairness as well as from the efficient production of consumer goods. In practice, however, welfare economics generally focuses on the satisfaction that is produced by achieving the efficient production of goods and services that individuals can consume. It devotes less attention to the satisfac-

tions that might come from living in a just society and still less to the satisfactions that might come from participating in political processes that allowed individuals to deliberate with others and then express through the institutions of government a shared idea of a just or virtuous society or what such a society might choose to do in a particular domain of policy. What is particularly alien to welfare economics is any "collectivist" notion that satisfaction could be found anywhere outside an individual's experience. Individuals—their tastes, preferences, and satisfactions—are always the units of analysis; families, groups, or polities never are. In this respect welfare economics departs from Aristotle's understanding of human nature and society and follows John Stuart Mill's. For a discussion of why individuals should not be viewed as existing in isolation from these other mediating structures and how the preferences of individuals expressed within the context of these intermediate structures are the ones the public sector should respond to, see Michael Sandel, "The Political Theory of the Procedural Republic," in Robert Reich, ed., *The Power of Public Ideas* (Cambridge, Mass.: Ballinger, 1988), pp. 109–122.

10. Rhoads, *The Economist's View of the World,* pp. 62–63.

11. In proposing the existence of a coherent "we," I am departing from a prevailing commitment to "liberal" political and economic philosophies that emphasize the importance of individuals, and the difficulty or impossibility of assembling individuals into coherent wholes that can have preferences, formed within the group through a political process, to develop a meaningful collective aspiration. I am entering the realm of "communitarian" philosophies that take a more optimistic view of the possibility (and desirability) of forging individuals into citizens of communities that can have collective aspirations. For some representative examples of works in communitarian philosophies, see Michael Sandel, *Liberalism and Its Critics* (New York: New York University Press, 1984); Amy Gutman, "Communitarian Critiques of Liberalism," *Philosophy and Public Affairs,* vol. 14, no. 3 (Summer 1985): 308–322; George Will, *Statecraft as Soulcraft: What Government Does* (New York: Simon and Schuster, 1983); and Robert Reich, *The Power of Public Ideas* (Cambridge, Mass.: Ballinger, 1988). For a specific argument consistent with the position I am adopting here, see Sandel, "The Political Theory of the Procedural Republic," pp. 109–121. Such philosophies do not seem all that far from the position that John Rawls also takes in formulating his conception of justice. He asserts: "If men's inclination to self-interest makes their vigilance against one another necessary, their public sense of justice makes their secure association together possible. Among individuals with disparate aims and purposes a shared conception of justice establishes the bonds of civic friendship; the general desire for justice limits the pursuit of other ends"; see Rawls, *A Theory of Justice* (Cambridge, Mass.: Harvard University Press, 1971), p. 5. For an argument that American government can actually

approximate some of the ideals of a communitarian political philosophy, see Steven Kelman, *Making Public Policy: A Hopeful View of American Government* (New York: Basic Books, 1987).

Note that I am adopting a communitarian view of government partly because I prefer it as a philosophical stance. More important, however, public managers must adopt a communitarian stance simply because they cannot make philosophical sense of their lives unless they do. This is the only stance that makes sense when we ask them to deploy public resources for the general benefit of society and instruct them (quite imperfectly) about where public value lies through imperfect political processes.

12. What that marketplace looks like, and what it is trying to purchase, is, as a positive matter, the focus of political science. As a normative matter, it is something that all citizens, elected representatives, and public managers have to be concerned about. For one "hopeful" view of how this market now functions, see Kelman, *Making Public Policy*. For an argument that even that most vilified of institutions, the United States Congress, also aims to produce the public good, see Arthur Maass, *Congress and the Common Good* (New York: Basic Books, 1983), pp. 4–12. And for a view that this is the process that guides the politics of regulation, see James Q. Wilson, "The Politics of Regulation," in James Q. Wilson, ed., *The Politics of Regulation* (New York: Basic Books, 1980), pp. 357–364.

13. William F. Willoughby emphasized the importance of providing accurate information about how plans have been carried out by public administrators in 1918: "The popular will cannot be intelligently formulated nor expressed unless the public has adequate means for knowing currently how governmental affairs have been conducted in the past, what are present conditions, and what program for work in the future is under consideration." Willoughby, *The Movement for Budgetary Reform in the States* (New York: D. Appleton, for the Institute for Government Research, 1918); Jay M. Shafritz and Albert C. Hyde, eds., *Classics in Public Administration*, 2d ed. (Chicago: Dorsey Press, 1987), reprint Willoughby's text. This view is also central to the idea of a proper relationship between "citizen principals" and their agents—legislators and bureaucrats. See John W. Pratt and Richard Zeckhauser, *Principals and Agents: The Structure of Business* (Boston: Harvard Business School Press, 1985), pp. 1–24.

14. Kenneth A. Shepsle, "Positive Theories of Congressional Institutions," occasional paper 92-18, Center for American Political Studies, Harvard University, 1992. For theoretical criticism of political processes, see William Niskanen, *Bureaucracy and Representative Government* (Chicago: Aldine-Atherton, 1971), pp. 138–154. For empirical criticism, see Robert Dahl, *Who Governs: Democracy and Power in an American City* (New Haven, Conn.: Yale University Press, 1961).

15. John Chubb and Paul Peterson make this point succinctly: "The problem of governance in the United States is mainly one of creating institutions or

governing arrangements that can pursue policies of sufficient coherence, consistency, foresight and stability that the national welfare is not sacrificed for narrow or temporary gains." See Chubb and Peterson, eds., *Can the Government Govern?* (Washington, D.C.: Brookings Institution, 1989), p. 4. I would agree with this statement even more strongly if I were sure that, first, they included in their idea of "institutions and governing arrangements" an ethic that guides the work of public sector managers and, second, they accepted the idea that the definition of the "national welfare" was importantly influenced by politics and might well change over time as collective aspirations and objective circumstances changed.

16. See Chapter 1, n. 9.

17. For a defense of this position, see Kelman, *Making Public Policy.*

18. Woodrow Wilson, for example, thought that the crucial question politics had to resolve in committing the government to action was to "discover, first, what government can properly and successfully do." Wilson, "The Study of Administration," *Political Science Quarterly,* 2 (June 1887), reprinted in Shafritz and Hyde, *Classics,* p. 10. Modern economists also prefer that the processes that engage governmental action meet these conditions. See, for example, Stokey and Zeckhauser, *Primer,* pp. 283–285, 292–293, 310–319.

19. Richard Zeckhauser and Derek Leebaert observe: "Our governmental structure requires only that beliefs and values be expressed through the electoral process, whether those beliefs are well- or ill-informed, whether those values are self-serving or public spirited. In practice, our nation has taken minimal steps—most significantly through the support of public education—to encourage a more informed outcome of the political process. Still, the United States has soundly rejected the notion of placing educational requirements on franchise, and has refused to deviate from our representative system of government to achieve more seemingly rational political outcomes. By contrast, it seems to be generally accepted that the policy choices made by government—particularly those of the executive branch—should be based on sound thinking and—where it will make a difference—supported by rational analysis. It is not obvious whence this norm derives. Surely it is not the Constitution. Had our founding fathers foreseen the nature of our modern government, so intricately entwined with so many aspects of its citizens' lives, perhaps they would have laid down rules of procedure for government decision. They left no such instructions, however." Zeckhauser and Leebaert, *What Role for Government: Lessons from Policy Research* (Durham, N.C.: Duke University Press, 1983), pp. 10–11.

20. Woodrow Wilson, "A Study of Administration." For the imagery of perfection in each sphere, see Frank J. Goodnow, *Politics and Administration: A Study in Government* (New York: Russell and Russell, 1900), reprinted in Shafritz and Hyde, *Classics,* pp. 26–29.

21. Edward Banfield makes the distinction between substantive knowledge and administrative knowledge. See Banfield, "The Training of the Executive," *Public Policy: A Yearbook of the Graduate School of Public Administration*, vol. 10 (1960): 20–23.

22. E. Pendleton Herring is most insistent about this fact. See Herring, *Public Administration and the Public Interest* (New York: McGraw-Hill, 1936).

23. This problem continues today and is one of the reasons that public management is so difficult. See Erwin C. Hargrove and John C. Glidewell, eds., *Impossible Jobs in Public Management* (Lawrence: University of Kansas Press, 1990).

24. On the problem of "fickle mandates," see Martha Derthick, *Agency under Stress: The Social Security Administration in American Government* (Washington, D.C.: Brookings Institution, 1990), p. 4. See also Mark H. Moore, "Small Scale Statesmen: A Conception of Public Management," *Politiques et Management Public,* vol. 7, no. 2 (June 1989): 273–287.

25. According to Dwight Waldo, "It can be argued with some persuasiveness that the proper role of a bureaucracy is to act as a stabilizing force in the midst of vertiginous change, and that this is what it is doing when it seems to be unresponsive and stupid. In this view it has a balance wheel or gyroscopic function." It is significant, however, that Waldo goes on to reject this view in favor of increased responsiveness or leadership from public managers. See Waldo, "Public Administration in a Time of Revolution," *Public Administration Review,* 28 (July–August 1968), reprinted in Shafritz and Hyde, *Classics,* p. 367. Rufus Miles worked out a particular set of ideas about the extent to which career civil servants should adapt to the demands of incoming political executives in "Administrative Adaptability to Political Change," *Public Administration Review,* vol. 25, no. 3 (September 1965): 221–225. For a set of cases describing the responses of career civil servants to rather dramatic political change, see "Surviving at the EPA: David Tundermann," KSG Case #C16-84-588.0; "Surviving at the EPA: Mike Walsh," KSG Case #C16-84-589.0; "Surviving at the EPA: Mike Cook," KSG Case #C16-84-590.0; "Surviving at the EPA: Bill Hedeman," KSG Case #C16-84-591.0; "Surviving at the EPA: Gary Dietrich," KSG Case #C16-84-592.0; "Note on the EPA under Administrator Anne Gorsuch," KSG Case #N16-84-587.0 (all Cambridge, Mass.: Kennedy School of Government Case Program, 1984).

26. There is, now, a large literature that describes the techniques, gives representative examples of their application, assesses their impact on policymaking processes within and outside organizations, and offers critiques of their utility or appropriateness. For examples of early writings setting out the potential of these techniques, see Roland McKean, *Efficiency in Government through Systems Analysis* (New York: John Wiley, 1958); and E. S. Quade, *Analysis for Public Decisions* (New York: American Elsevier, 1975). For more contemporary treatments of the methods, see

Stokey and Zeckhauser *Primer;* Peter W. House, *The Art of Public Policy Analysis* (Thousand Oaks, Calif.: Sage, 1982); and David L. Weimar and Aidan R. Vining, *Policy Analysis: Concepts and Practice* (Englewood Cliffs, N.J.: Prentice-Hall, 1989). For doubts about the practical impact of such techniques on governmental decision making, see Laurence E. Lynn, Jr., ed., *Knowledge and Power: The Uncertain Connection* (Washington, D.C.: National Academy of Sciences, 1978); Arnold J. Meltsner, *Policy Analysts in the Bureaucracy* (Berkeley: University of California Press, 1976); Henry Aaron, *Politics and the Professors: The Great Society in Perspective* (Washington, D.C.: Brookings Institution, 1978); and Aaron Wildavsky, *Speaking Truth to Power: The Art and Craft of Policy Analysis* (Boston: Little, Brown, 1979). For a more recent evaluation of the influence of policy analysis, see Laurence E. Lynn's summary of two articles in "Policy Analysis in the Bureaucracy: How New? How Effective?" *Journal of Policy Analysis and Management,* vol. 8, no. 3. (Summer 1989): 375: "Over the long haul, the ideas of policy analysts appear to have counted for something, more or less, in the ordinary exercise of statecraft by ordinary as well as by the occasional extraordinary policymakers." For more radical critiques of policy analysis, see Peter Self, *Econocrats and the Policy Process: The Politics and Philosophy of Cost-Benefit Analysis* (Boulder, Colo.: Westview, 1975); John Forester, *Planning in the Face of Power* (Berkeley: University of California Press, 1989); and Charles E. Lindblom, *Inquiry and Change: The Troubled Attempt to Understand and Shape Society* (New Haven, Conn.: Yale University Press, 1990). For an idea of how policy analysis could support deliberative government, see Giandomenico Majone, "Policy Analysis and Public Deliberation," in Reich, *The Power of Public Ideas,* pp. 157–178.

27. See preceding note, particularly Lynn, Meltsner, Wildavsky, Forester, and Lindblom.

28. The literature on the utility of techniques of policy analysis and program evaluation is more limited than the literature on its successes. It consists mostly of examples of good pieces of policy analysis or program evaluation, not a demonstration that the work had much impact on policy-making processes. For an early example, see John P. Crecine, ed., *Research in Public Policy Analysis and Management* (Greenwich, Conn.: JAI Press, 1981). For a discussion of the sorts of ideas that become important in policy-making, and how techniques of policy analysis would have to be adapted to produce more powerful ideas, see Mark H. Moore, "What Sorts of Ideas Become Public Ideas?" in Reich, *The Power of Public Ideas,* pp. 55–84.

29. See David Osborne and Ted Gaebler, *Reinventing Government: How the Entrepreneurial Spirit Is Transforming the Public Sector from Schoolhouse to Statehouse, City Hall to the Pentagon* (Reading, Mass.: Addison-Wesley, 1992), pp. 166–194; and Michael Barzelay with Babak Armajani, *Breaking*

through Bureaucracy: A New Vision for Managing in Government (Berkeley: University of California Press, 1987), pp. 8–9.

30. Malcolm Sparrow, *Imposing Duties: Government's Changing Approach to Compliance* (Westport, Conn.: Praeger, 1994).

31. On the concept of a service encounter in the private sector, see John A. Czepiel, Michael R. Solomon, and Carol F. Surprenant, eds., *The Service Encounter: Managing Employee/Customer Interaction in Service Businesses* (Lexington, Mass.: D. C. Heath, 1985); and James L. Heskett, W. Earl Sasser, and Christopher W. L. Hart, *Service Breakthroughs: Breaking the Rules of the Game* (New York: Free Press, 1990).

32. For a discussion of the function and techniques of political management, see Chapters 4 and 5 of this book.

33. Graham T. Allison emphasizes the rigidities of public sector organizations, which come from their prior commitments and experiences. See Allison, *Essence of Decision: Explaining the Cuban Missile Crisis* (Boston: Little, Brown, 1971), pp. 67–100.

34. On the issue of oversight of public enterprises, see John D. Donahue, "The Architecture of Accountability," in *The Privatization Decision: Public Ends, Private Means* (New York: Basic Books, 1989), pp. 3–13.

35. This can be viewed as a principal and agent problem. See Pratt and Zeckhauser, *Principals and Agents.* For a discussion of some problems with this paradigm in the concrete circumstances of the public sector, see Fesler and Kettl, *The Politics of the Administrative Process,* pp. 319–321; and Mark H. Moore and Margaret J. Gates, *Inspectors-General: Junkyard Dogs or Man's Best Friend?* (New York: Russell Sage, 1986), Appendix A, pp. 95–115. For an even more recent critique of this idea, see John DiIulio, Jr., "Principled Agents: The Cultural Bases of Behavior in a Federal Government Bureaucracy," *Journal of Public Administration Research and Theory,* vol. 4, no. 3 (July 1994): 277–318.

36. James Q. Wilson offers what is commonly taken as a truism: "There is no liberal or conservative way to deliver the mail or issue a driver's license." See Wilson, *Bureaucracy: What Government Agencies Do and Why They Do It* (New York: Basic Books, 1989), p. 66. He could just as well have added (as others have done) "to pick up the garbage." In fact, it is becoming increasingly obvious that there *are* liberal and conservative ways to accomplish these tasks. The most obvious is whether or not the service is privatized. Generally speaking, liberals prefer public production; conservatives private.

More fundamentally, there might be real differences in how much of both services are provided; whether any public subsidy is provided in the delivery of the service, and if so, whether it is progressive or regressive; and whether and how public authority is used to mobilize citizens in the production of the activity. For example, the public can pay more or less to make it convenient for individual citizens to pick up their driver's license;

it can also decide to be more or less tough with respect to enforcing laws requiring people to have licenses to drive. Similarly, as will be discussed below, one can have quite different rules for the distribution of these public services, for example, where mailboxes will be placed, where registries of motor vehicles are located, and how much garbage collection occurs in what places.

What is probably really meant by these phrases is that there may be a relatively high degree of consensus on what constitutes effective service in these domains, and that there are many ways that managers can improve performance on all attributes of performance—including fairness. That I agree with. Nonetheless, there are often important value decisions to be made by public managers—even sanitation commissioners.

To claim that it is part of the sanitation manager's responsibility to imagine opportunities to create greater value for the public, I implicitly grant him, perhaps, more responsibility and initiative than is ordinarily assumed in the private sector. In this respect, I take for granted what I am trying to show. I think most people would not object to this language. Indeed, they think that it is part of a manager's job to ensure the production of value by encouraging workers to work hard and well in their jobs, perhaps even to invent new methods of achieving current objectives more effectively. Where they begin to get concerned is when managers stretch beyond the boundaries of their mandated missions. That is not obviously the case here. It is part of the concern about the librarian of Chapter 1.

37. I am indebted to my colleague William Hogan for identifying the central role of a "story" in justifying a public policy. By referring to a story, I do not mean to imply that it is false or made up for no purpose other than to rationalize the enterprise. I mean that there has to be an appeal made to citizens and their representatives as a collective consumer of collective aspirations and their accomplishment.

38. For historical references on the necessity of public health programs, see Stuart Galishoff, *Safeguarding the Public Health: Newark, 1895–1918* (Westport, Conn.: Greenwood Press, 1975).

39. Paul Berman, "The Study of Macro- and Micro-Implementation," *Public Policy,* vol. 26, no. 2 (Spring 1978): 157–184.

40. What things are worth establishing as "rights" in a liberal society is also the focus of much normative political theory. See, for example, Rawls, *Theory of Justice,* and Ronald M. Dworkin, *Taking Rights Seriously* (Cambridge, Mass.: Harvard University Press, 1978).

41. For an interesting catalog of government policy instruments that include several that make intensive use of authority as well as money, see Michael O'Hare, "A Typology of Governmental Action," *Journal of Policy Analysis and Management,* vol. 8, no. 4 (Fall 1989): 670–672.

42. On issues relating to smoking and government regulations, see Thomas C. Schelling, Nancy Rigotti, Michael Stoto, and Mark Kleiman, *Implementa-*

tion and Impact of a City's Regulation of Smoking in Public Places and the Workplace: The Experience of Cambridge, Massachusetts (Cambridge, Mass.: Harvard University, Kennedy School of Government Institute on Smoking Behavior, 1988). On issues relating to alcohol consumption and government regulations, see Mark H. Moore and Dean R. Gerstein, eds., *Alcohol and Public Policy: Beyond the Shadow of Prohibition* (Washington, D.C.: National Academy Press, 1981).

43. For a general discussion about the design and use of such campaigns, see Philip Kotler and Eduardo L. Roberto, *Social Marketing: Strategies for Changing Public Behavior* (New York: Free Press, 1989). For a discussion of efficacy, see Janet A. Weiss and Mary Tschirhart, "Public Information Campaigns as Policy Instruments," *Journal of Public Policy and Management,* vol. 13, no. 1 (1994): 82–119.

44. For a general discussion of the intrusiveness of criminal laws, see Herbert L. Packer, *The Limits of Criminal Sanction* (Stanford, Calif.: Stanford University Press, 1968).

45. From this perspective, courts could be viewed as the equivalent of the Office of Management and Budget, serving to eliminate fraud, waste, and abuse in the use of public authority!

46. Some important justifications for public intervention are presented in Stokey and Zeckhauser, *Primer,* pp. 291–319.

47. Ibid.

48. Ibid.

49. Rawls makes the distinction between "primary goods," which must be the concerns of justice, and natural goods in *Theory of Justice*, p. 62. He also cautions against doing what I am doing in this section: using his ideas about how to define justice at the broadest social level to also define justice in particular policy contexts. See pp. 9–10.

50. Zeckhauser and Leebaert, *Role for Government,* pp. 3–15.

51. Ibid.

52. Robert Stavins has developed these ideas extensively in the domain of environmental policy. See Stavins, *Project 88: Harnessing Market Forces to Protect Our Environment* (Washington, D.C.: U.S. Senate, 1988).

53. This idea, too, appears in Zeckhauser and Leebaert, *Role for Government,* pp. 3–15.

54. Dworkin, *Taking Rights Seriously,* pp. 82–100.

55. The concept of equity is central in Rawls, *Theory of Justice.* It is an important part of the "original position" that Rawls uses as the condition under which individuals could be expected to imagine what justice would require. And, in some respects, it is the most important goal of the concept of justice that he thinks would emerge from the "original position." See pp. 17–22, 60–75.

56. John Locke, *Two Treatises of Government* (New York: New American Library, 1960), second treatise, sections 87–89, pp. 366–369.

57. Ibid., section 131.
58. Ibid. Jeremy Bentham also agreed with this proposition. The work in which he developed his ideas of utilitarianism is entitled *The Theory of Legislation*. Its first sentence reads: "The public good ought to be the object of the legislator." Bentham then goes on to explain why the maximization of individual utility should be the proper goal of legislative action. See *The Theory of Legislation* (Dobbs Ferry, N.Y.: Oceana, 1975).
59. Ken Winston, "On Treating Like Cases Alike," *California Law Review,* vol. 62, no. 1 (1974): 1–39.
60. On the importance of "due process" as a feature of governmental operations, see Jerry L. Mashaw, *Bureaucratic Justice: Managing Social Security Disability Claims* (New Haven, Conn.: Yale University Press, 1983), pp. 21–34.
61. Doug Yates, *The Ungovernable City: The Politics of Urban Problems and Policy-Making* (Cambridge, Mass.: MIT Press, 1977).
62. For an in-depth discussion of this efficiency criterion, see Stokey and Zeckhauser, *Primer,* pp. 155–158.
63. Ibid., pp. 312–315.
64. This is a natural idea about distributional justice. For a discussion of the idea of need, its role in a theory of justice, and how it relates to governmental institutions, see Rawls, *Theory of Justice,* pp. 274–284. For an interesting empirical exploration of citizens' views of justice in contemporary America, see Jennifer L. Hochschild, *What's Fair: American Beliefs about Distributive Justice* (Cambridge, Mass.: Harvard University Press, 1981).
65. This is a principle of "horizontal equity": everyone gets treated the same by the public regardless of their status. For a discussion in the context of taxation, see Richard A. Musgrave and Peggy B. Musgrave, *Public Finance in Theory and Practice,* 5th ed. (New York: McGraw-Hill, 1989), pp. 218–219, 223–228. For a discussion in the context of law and justice, see Winston, "On Treating Like Cases Alike."
66. To many people, it is a little bit disappointing that the accounting systems of public sector organizations do not necessarily trigger political discussions about the cost-effectiveness of public sector organizations the way that they do in the private sector. Perhaps this difference occurs because the measurement systems for public sector organizations are weaker in revealing the value-producing capability of the organizations. But it may also signify that the political marketplace seems to be much less interested in "numbers" than in "stories" that seem to indicate something about how the organization is important. This bias, of course, also shows how behaviorally powerful systems of accountability tend to deal with publicity and press coverage more often than with the routine processes of oversight; moreover, "stories" are far more likely to get press attention than "numbers." For a case that reveals the startling power of the media as a device

for shaping both a manager's reputation and the performance of an important public sector organization, see Esther Scott, "Managing a Press 'Feeding Frenzy': Gregory Coler and the Florida Department of Health and Rehabilitative Services," KSG Case #C16-92-1135.0 (Cambridge, Mass.: Kennedy School of Government Case Program, 1992).

67. For a discussion of some of the desirable qualities of a political deliberative process, see Kelman, *Making Public Policy,* pp. 248–270; and Robert Reich, "Policy Making in a Democracy," in Reich, *The Power of Public Ideas,* pp. 123–156.

68. Allison, *Essence of Decision,* pp. 67–100. For examples of organizations whose continuity has been remarkable and important to their overall effectiveness (and difficulties!), see Herbert Kaufman, *The Forest Ranger* (Baltimore: Johns Hopkins University Press, 1960); and Arthur Maas, *Muddy Waters: The Army Engineers and the Nation's Rivers* (New York: Da Capo Press, 1974).

69. Hugh Heclo states succinctly: "Paradoxically, civil servants can provide some of their most valuable service [to political executives interested in change] by resisting." Heclo, *A Government of Strangers: Executive Politics in Washington* (Washington, D.C.: Brookings Institution, 1977), p. 176. He then goes on to explain how civil servants often have the substantive, administrative, and political knowledge that will allow them to keep their political executives out of trouble. What he does not discuss is to what extent the interests of civil servants lie in protecting the organizations they lead, and whether that is good or bad. Later, he offers an acutely observed picture of the collision between change-oriented political appointees and institutionally loyal civil servants: "The overall picture is one with a large number of supposed political controllers over the bureaucracy—transient, structurally divided, largely unknown to each other, and backed by a welter of individual patrons and supporters . . . They are too few and too temporary to actually seize control and operate the government machinery. Facing them are 'the others,' a spectrum of high-level bureaucrats . . . through whom executives must lead . . . These officials are not expected to have undivided loyalty to the minister of the day . . . On the contrary. Top bureaucrats gain more protection as they entrench themselves in particular bureaus and develop allegiances with outside power centers" (pp. 242–243).

70. Jay R. Galbraith discusses the useful role of "organizational slack" in enhancing the flexibility of organizations in *Designing Complex Organizations* (Reading, Mass.: Addison-Wesley, 1973).

71. Peters and Waterman, *In Search of Excellence,* pp. 121–125.

72. See the discussion of what constitutes managerial success in the Introduction to this book.

73. For a classic, empirical treatment of government's vulnerability to interest groups, see David Truman, *The Governmental Process: Political Interests*

and Public Opinion (New York: Knopf, 1951). For a more contemporary theoretical treatment of how the political process is vulnerable to the self-interest of both citizens and their representatives, see Morris P. Fiorina, *Congress: Keystone of the Washington Establishment* (New Haven, Conn.: Yale University Press, 1977).

74. Daniel Kahneman and Amos Tversky, *Extensional vs. Intuitive Reasoning: The Conjunction Fallacy in Probability Judgment* (Boston: Harvard Business School Press, 1983).

75. Giandomenico Majone, "Policy Analysis and Public Deliberation," in Reich, *The Power of Public Ideas.*

3. ORGANIZATIONAL STRATEGY
IN THE PUBLIC SECTOR

1. Robert A. Dahl observes: "In most societies, and particularly in democratic ones, ends are often in dispute; rarely are they clearly and unequivocally determined." Dahl, "The Science of Public Administration," *Public Administration Review,* 7, no. 1 (Winter 1947): 1–11. Reprinted in Jay M. Shafritz and Albert C. Hyde, eds., *Classics of Public Administration,* 2d ed. (Chicago: Dorsey Press, 1987), p. 184. James Q. Wilson makes a similar observation: "Government agencies, much more than business firms, are likely to have general, vague, or inconsistent goals about which clarity and agreement can only occasionally be obtained. Often any effort to clarify these will result either in the production of meaningless verbiage, or the exposure of deep disagreements." Wilson, *Bureaucracy: What Government Agencies Do and Why They Do It* (New York: Basic Books, 1989), pp. 25–26.

2. Martha Derthick thinks that frequent change is a permanent feature of American government, something that makes efficient administration problematic. "Democracy, which entails regular and frequent elections, fosters instability in policy guidance. The laws that agencies administer are subject to constant revision as officeholders change and incumbents seek to serve and satisfy a heterogeneous and ever-changing society." Derthick, *Agency under Stress: The Social Security Administration in American Government* (Washington, D.C.: Brookings Institution, 1990), p. 4.

3. William F. Willoughby emphasizes the importance of this accounting: "The popular will cannot be intelligently formulated nor expressed unless the public has adequate means for knowing currently how governmental affairs have been conducted in the past, what are present conditions, and what program for work in the future is under consideration. Of all means devised for meeting this requirement no single one approaches in completeness and effectiveness a budget if properly prepared." Willoughby, *The Movement for Budgetary Reform in the States* (New York: D. Appleton, for the Institute for Government Research, 1918), reprinted in Shafritz and Hyde, *Classics,* p. 33.

4. This case is based on "William D. Ruckelshaus and the Environmental Protection Agency," KSG Case #C14-74-27.0 (Cambridge, Mass.: Kennedy School of Government Case Program, 1974). The EPA as an agency has been closely monitored and analyzed in Marc K. Landy, Marc J. Roberts, and Stephen R. Thomas, *The Environmental Protection Agency: Asking the Wrong Questions from Nixon to Clinton* (New York: Oxford University Press, 1994).
5. For an interesting account of the mobilization of the *appearance* of widespread public support for environmental protection, see "Steven Cotton and Earth Day," KSG Case #C14-75-62.0 (Cambridge, Mass.: Kennedy School of Government Case Program, 1975).
6. Landy, Roberts, and Thomas, *The Environmental Protection Agency*, pp. 290–297.
7. This account is based on "Jerome Miller and the Department of Youth Services," KSG Cases #C14-76-101.0, #C14-76-102.0, and #C14-76-102.1 (Cambridge, Mass.: Kennedy School of Government Case Program, 1976). The Massachusetts experience with Miller's reforms was analyzed extensively shortly after they occurred in the following books: Lloyd E. Ohlin, Robert B. Coates, and Alden D. Miller, *Reforming Juvenile Corrections: The Massachusetts Experience* (Cambridge, Mass.: Ballinger, 1977); and Robert B. Coates, Alden D. Miller, and Lloyd E. Ohlin, *Diversity in a Youth Correctional System: Handling Delinquents in Massachusetts* (Cambridge, Mass.: Ballinger, 1978). This experience has even been evaluated more than a decade later in Barry Krisberg, James Austin, and Patricia Steele, *Unlocking Juvenile Corrections: Evaluating the Massachusetts Department of Youth Services* (San Francisco: National Council on Crime and Delinquency, 1989).
8. For a discussion of the strategic issues in juvenile justice, see Mark H. Moore with Thomas Bearrows, Jeffrey Bleich, Francis X. Hartmann, George L. Kelling, Michael Oshima, and Saul Weingart, *From Children to Citizens,* vol. 1, *The Mandate of the Juvenile Court* (New York: Springer-Verlag, 1987).
9. The vision of what the reform schools could accomplish was articulated by Governor George Briggs on opening the Lyman School for Boys in 1846: "Of the many and valuable institutions sustained in whole, or in part, from the public treasury, we may safely say that none is of more importance, or holds a more intimate connection with the future prosperity and moral integrity of the community, than one which promises to take neglected, wayward, wandering, idle and vicious boys, with perverse minds and corrupted hearts, and cleanse and purify and reform them, and thus send them forth in the erectness of manhood and in the beauty of virtue, educated and prepared to be industrious, useful and virtuous citizens" (quoted in "Jerome Miller and the Department of Youth Services," #C14-76-101.0, p. 1).

10. For a sociological theory that explains why institutions become warehouses, see Irving Goffman, *Asylums: Essays on the Social Situation of Mental Patients and Other Inmates* (Chicago: Aldine Publishing Company, 1970).

11. Coates, Miller, and Ohlin, *Diversity in a Youth Correctional System,* p. 186. See also Ellen Schall, "Principles for Juvenile Detention," in Francis X. Hartmann, ed., *From Children to Citizens,* vol. 2, *The Role of the Juvenile Court* (New York: Springer-Verlag, 1987), pp. 349–361.

12. Rosemary Sarri and Yeheskel Hashenfeld, eds., *Brought to Justice? Juveniles, the Courts, and the Law* (Ann Arbor: University of Michigan Press, 1976).

13. Moore et al., *The Mandate of the Juvenile Court.*

14. On the incoherence and the imprecision of legislative and political mandates, and the difficulties created for managers, see Erwin C. Hargrove and John C. Glidewell, eds., *Impossible Jobs in Public Management* (Lawrence: University Press of Kansas, 1990), pp. 16–20.

15. E. Pendleton Herring writes: "Upon the shoulders of the bureaucrat has been placed in large part the burden of reconciling group differences and making effective and workable the economic and social compromises arrived at through the legislative process . . . He is in a better position than the legislators to perform these duties." Herring, *Public Administration and the Public Interest,* reprinted in Shafritz and Hyde, *Classics,* p. 74. John Chubb, writing in a more contemporary context, agrees. "Congress and the President, or sometimes the courts, should establish the objectives of the intervention, and then turn over the job of accomplishing them to an administrative body . . . Politicians have neither the expertise to design policies in adequate detail nor the capacity to acquire expertise in every area in which they must act. The situations that policies address are subject to change, and politicians are not in a position to revise laws as needed." Chubb, "United States Energy Policy," in John Chubb and Paul Peterson, eds., *Can the Government Govern?* (Washington, D.C.: Brookings Institution, 1989), p. 59.

16. Herbert Kaufman, *The Administrative Behavior of Federal Bureau Chiefs* (Washington, D.C.: Brookings Institution, 1981), pp. 91–138.

17. For a discussion of the oversight that elected chief executives can give to executive branch agencies, see Richard Nathan, *The Administrative Presidency* (New York: Macmillan, 1986), and Robert Behn, *Governors on Governing* (Washington, D.C.: National Governors' Association, 1991). For a discussion of the oversight that appointed political officials can give, see Hugh M. Heclo, *A Government of Strangers: Executive Politics in Washington* (Washington, D.C.: Brookings Institution, 1977). For a discussion of how legislative oversight functions, see Joel D. Aberbach, *Keeping a Watchful Eye: The Politics of Congressional Oversight* (Washington, D.C.: Brookings Institution, 1990). For a discussion of how interest groups

constrain the discretion of public officials, see James Q. Wilson, ed., *The Politics of Regulation* (New York: Basic Books, 1980), pp. 372–382. And for a discussion of press oversight and its impact on public officials and policy-making, see Martin Linsky, *Impact: How the Press Affects Federal Policymaking* (New York: Norton, 1986).

18. Kaufman, *Federal Bureau Chiefs,* pp. 115–124. On the difficulty and risks of innovating in the public sector, see Mark H. Moore, *Accounting for Change: Reconciling the Demands for Accountability and Innovation in the Public Sector* (Washington, D.C.: Council for Excellence in Government, 1993).

19. Wilson states: "Political executives can change policy. They need not be either the captives of their agencies or the tools of congressional overseers" (*Bureaucracy,* p. 206).

20. Wilson observes, "[Congress] and the committees that comprise it do not speak with one voice, and neither Congress nor its committees have the means for exercising complete control over all bureaucratic agencies under all circumstances" (*Bureaucracy,* p. 238). He also notes the potential for agency managers to exploit the political conflict in Congress: "Sometimes a policy entrepreneur manages to mobilize a legislative majority in favor of a course of action that is against the interests of a client group, or that overrides a traditional interest-group conflict" (ibid., p. 249). Philip B. Heymann notes the skill that Caspar Weinberger used in exploiting such an opportunity when he led the Federal Trade Commission. See Heymann, *The Politics of Public Management* (New Haven, Conn.: Yale University Press, 1987), p. 21.

21. For a discussion of the problems that public sector executives encounter in creating room for innovation and experimentation, see Moore, *Accounting for Change.*

22. The allusion to "bankrupt" approaches is meant to be more than a metaphor. It is sometimes alleged that one of the important differences between managing in the private and public sector is that private sector companies can go bankrupt while public sector organizations cannot. That, alas, may no longer be true. Some city governments have literally gone bankrupt. Other agencies have suffered fates that in many respects are functionally equivalent to bankruptcies in the private sector. Some schools, prisons, and mental institutions have been taken over by courts, for example, owing to their repeated failures to protect the fundamental rights of their clients. Other agencies have been so severely criticized by the Congress, the press, or an incoming administration that their leaders have been forced to resign and their budgets severely cut. Such events can be viewed as the functional equivalent of bankruptcy in the private sector since they occur as a consequence of organizational failures and typically result in the firing of the heads of the organizations, as well as a radical restructuring of the organization's operations. Just like bankruptcies in the private sector, the public sector versions of bankruptcies often create a kind of crisis that allows a radical

restructuring of the organization to occur. Often that restructuring leads to a significant improvement in the performance of the organization. I thank Colyer Crum of the Harvard Business School for teaching me about bankruptcies in the private sector and suggesting the potential importance of this phenomenon in studying public sector organizations.

23. Many writers on management in the private sector consider defining an organization's overall purposes and character the key task of general management and leadership. Kenneth Andrews asserts: "The highest function of the executive is still seen as leading the continuous process of determining the nature of the enterprise, and setting, revising, and achieving its goals." Andrews, *The Concept of Corporate Strategy,* rev. ed. (Homewood, Ill.: R. D. Irwin, 1980), p. iii. John Kotter puts "setting basic goals, policies and strategies despite great uncertainties" at the top of his list of the "key challenges and dilemmas" facing general managers in the private sector. Kotter, *The General Managers* (New York: Free Press; London: Collier Macmillan, 1986), p. 122. Philip Selznick, writing about administrative leadership more generally, claims that "it is in the realm of policy—including the areas where policy-formulation and organization-building meet—that the distinctive quality of institutional leadership is found . . . It is the function of the leader-statesman . . . to define the ends of group existence, to design an enterprise distinctively adapted to these ends, and to see that the design becomes a living polity." Selznick, *Leadership in Administration: A Sociological Interpretation,* rev. ed. (Berkeley: University of California Press, 1984), p. 37.

24. Andrews describes what goes into the definition of a corporate strategy for a private sector enterprise. "A summary statement of strategy will characterize the product line and services offered or planned by the company, the markets and market segments for which products are now or will be designed, and the channels through which the markets will be reached. The means by which the operation is to be financed will be specified, as will the profit objectives and the emphasis to be placed on the safety of capital versus level of return . . . Major policy in control functions will be stated" (*The Concept of Corporate Strategy,* p. 21). Earlier in the text, he defines "strategy" as a "conscious purpose for the future"; "functional strategy" as a "strategy for functional areas"; "business strategy" as a "choice about products"; and "corporate strategy" as "an idea that embraces all including ideas about the organization and its constitution as well as more specific functional and business strategies" (pp. vi-vii).

25. For a general discussion of the similarities and differences between public and private sector management, see Graham T. Allison, "Public and Private Management: Are They Fundamentally Alike in All Unimportant Respects?" in Shafritz and Hyde, *Classics,* pp. 510–529. With respect to the specific question of goal setting, Allison finds important differences between the calculations made by Roy Chapin, president of American Motors

Corporation, and Doug Costle, head of the EPA: "Both Chapin and Costle had to establish objectives and priorities and to devise operational plans . . . In reshaping the strategy of AMC and concentrating on particular market segments . . . Chapin had to consult his board and arrange financing. But the control was substantially his. How much choice did Costle have at EPA as to the 'business it is or is to be in' or the kind of agency 'it is or is to be'? These major strategic choices emerged from the legislative process which mandated whether he should be in the business of controlling pesticides or toxic substances . . . The relative role of the President, other members of the administration (including White House staff, Congressional relations, and other agency heads), the EPA Administrator, Congressional Committee Chairmen and external groups in establishing the broad strategy of the agency constitutes an interesting question" (ibid., pp. 522–523).

26. Richard A. Brealey and Stewart C. Myers, *Principles of Corporate Finance,* 4th ed. (New York: McGraw-Hill, 1991), p. 22.

27. Andrews again: "Chief executives, presidents, chief operating officers and general managers are first and probably least pleasantly persons who are responsible for results obtained in the present as designated by plans made previously. Nothing that we will say shortly about the concern for the people in their organizations or later about their responsibility to society can gainsay this immediate truth. Achieving acceptable results against expectations of increased earnings per share and return on stockholders' investment requires them" (*The Concept of Corporate Strategy,* p. 5).

28. For a valuable general discussion of the role that program evaluation and benefit-cost analyses can play in improving the performance of nonprofit and public sector organizations, see Joseph S. Wholey, Mark A. Abrahamson, and Christopher Bellavita, *Performance and Credibility: Developing Excellence in Public and Nonprofit Organizations* (Lexington, Mass.: D. C. Heath, 1986).

29. See Chapter 2, n. 26.

30. See n. 24.

31. I am grateful to Dean John MacArthur of the Harvard Business School for emphasizing this point and for arguing that this fact implied a closer link between the problems of strategic management in the private and public sector than I had initially assumed.

32. For a basic introduction to this concept, see Andrews, *Corporate Strategy.* For a more recent development of the concept, see Michael E. Porter, *Competitive Strategy: Techniques for Analyzing Industries and Competitors* (New York: Free Press, 1980).

33. Porter, *Competitive Strategy.*

34. For evidence that having a coherent strategy improves the performance of private sector organizations, see Thomas J. Peters and Robert H. Waterman, Jr., *In Search of Excellence: Lessons from America's Best-Run Companies* (New York: Warner Books, 1982).

35. Porter comments: "The essence of formulating competitive strategy is relating a company to its environment . . . The key aspect of the firm's environment is the industry or industries in which it competes" (*Competitive Strategy,* p. 3).

36. Peters and Waterman found that a "focus on customers" was an important aspect of a private sector company's performance. See Peters and Waterman, *In Search of Excellence,* pp. 156–199. For a contemporary account of marketing and its role in business strategy, see Henry Assael, *Marketing Management: Strategy and Action* (Boston: Kent, 1985).

37. Porter, *Competitive Strategy,* pp. 156–188.

38. Ibid., pp. 3–33.

39. Ibid., pp. 47–71.

40. Ibid., pp. 88–108.

41. Ibid., pp. 361–367.

42. Selznick, *Leadership in Administration,* pp. 42–56.

43. I thank my colleague James Vaupel for this example. The firm described, I believe, was General Electric, circa 1970. For a list of other simple goal statements, see Terrence E. Deal and Allan A. Kennedy, *Corporate Cultures: The Rites and Rituals of Corporate Life* (Reading, Mass.: Addison-Wesley, 1982), pp. 23–25.

44. Finding the right level of abstraction to use in defining an organization's purpose is an important part of the art of developing an effective "strategy." It must be abstract enough to allow flexibility and future adjustments but concrete enough to challenge the organization's operations and ensure that managers can be held accountable. See the discussion of this point below in Chapters 3 and 7.

45. Porter, *Competitive Strategy,* pp. 129–155.

46. Ibid., pp. 40–41.

47. Ibid., pp. 361–367. See also D. F. Abell and J. S. Hammond, *Strategic Market Planning: Problems and Analytical Approaches* (Englewood Cliffs, N.J.: Prentice-Hall, 1979).

48. Ibid.

49. For an overview, see Richard B. Freeman and James L. Medoff, *What Do Unions Do* (New York: Basic Books, 1984); for managerial responses and implications for firm performance, see pp. 11–12 and 181–190.

50. For a discussion of "social regulation," its strategies, and its impacts, see Eugene Bardach and Robert A. Kagan, *Social Regulation: Strategies for Reform* (San Francisco: Institute for Contemporary Studies, 1982).

51. One kind of community claim on private industry is to require advance notice of plant closings. For a discussion of legislation in this domain, see C and R Associates, *Plant Location Legislation, Community Costs of Plant Closings: Bibliography and Survey of Literature* (Washington, D.C.: Federal Trade Commission, 1978).

52. One way to interpret these changes is to see the "constraints" as the claims

of a varied group of "stakeholders" who have interests in how a private sector company defines its strategy. This image of strategy is set out explicitly in R. E. Freeman, *Strategic Management: A Shareholder Approach* (Boston: Putnam, 1984).

53. For discussions of the phenomenon of corporate takeovers, see F. M. Scherer, "Corporate Takeovers: The Efficiency Arguments," *Journal of Economic Perspectives,* vol. 2, no. 1 (Winter 1988): 69–82; and John Pound, "Beyond Takeovers: Politics Comes to Corporate Control," *Harvard Business Review,* vol. 70, no. 2 (March–April 1992): 83–94.

54. The quotation is from Professor Malcolm Salter of the Harvard Business School in a personal communication. For a more formal development of this idea, see Joseph L. Bower, "The Managerial Estate" (Harvard Business School, photocopy, 1987).

55. The comfortable assumption that public sector organizations are natural monopolies is fast eroding. Perhaps the greatest threat to this assumption comes from the potential to privatize the production of many publicly financed services ranging from garbage collection, to libraries, to the operation of prisons. For a discussion of these trends, and an analytic framework to guide decisions about what sorts of things can best be privatized, see John D. Donahue, *The Privatization Decision: Public Ends, Private Means* (New York: Basic Books, 1989). But some public sector organizations are also threatened by two discoveries: first, that they are operating alongside a privately financed and privately produced sector that meets some of the needs that the public sector organization thought it was supposed to supply universally; and, second, that the publicly financed and publicly provided sector is losing "market share" in the overall development of the market. The police, in particular, have discovered that they are losing "market share" in the overall security industry. Malcolm Sparrow, Mark H. Moore, and David Kennedy, *Beyond 911: A New Era for Policing* (New York: Basic Books, 1990), pp. 47–50.

56. The assumption that public sector organizations have "coherent missions" rather than "bundles of product lines" may also be in error. For example, it is often observed that U.S. drug policy must focus at least part of its efforts on marijuana to maintain a suburban constituency for the efforts to deal with the more serious problems of inner city cocaine and heroin use. Similarly, it may be important for juvenile corrections systems to operate "boot camps" to give them the political leeway they need to also operate "community placements." In effect, in each case, operating one kind of program directed at one population earns a kind of credibility that can be used by the agency to deal with a different problem somewhere else. This is the kind of synergy across product lines that private sector managers have learned how to analyze and exploit.

57. This particular concept of strategy in the public sector grew out of discussions that started in the late seventies. Stephen Hitchener and Philip

Heymann, influenced by Joseph L. Bower, were among the leaders. Philip Heymann might have been the first person to draw the strategic triangle. Previous written discussions of this concept can be found in Heymann, *The Politics of Public Management,* pp. 12–24; and David Lax and James Sebenius, *The Manager as Negotiator: Bargaining for Cooperation and Competitive Gain* (New York: Free Press, 1986), pp. 264–267.

58. The sort of calculation suggested by the strategic triangle is hardly new. Selznick writes: "In defining the mission of the organization, leaders must take account of (1) the internal state of the polity—the strivings, inhibitions and competencies that exist within the organization; and (2) the external expectations that determine what must be sought or achieved if the organization is to survive" (*Leadership in Administration,* p. 67). Wilson describes the findings of Herbert Simon's classic study of the Economic Cooperation Administration, the agency established in 1948 to implement the Marshall Plan for the economic redevelopment of Europe: "The key factors that determined the survival of a given task definition was, first, how workable it was (could people, in fact, get the job done) and how strongly it was supported by external allies (other agencies and groups in Congress)" (*Bureaucracy,* p. 56). For a more elaborate schema of strategic planning in the public sector, see John M. Bryson, *Strategic Planning for Public and Nonprofit Organizations* (San Francisco: Jossey-Bass, 1988).

59. For a discussion of how a manager develops a new congruent vision for a public organization in a world in which an old strategy is beginning to fail, see Heymann's description of Caspar Weinberger's management of the Federal Trade Commission in *The Politics of Public Management,* pp. 19–24.

60. As such, this framework is designed to prevent one form of managerial failure—the failure to set purposes and goals for an organization. Selznick observes: "One type of [leadership] default is the failure to set goals. Once an organization becomes a 'going concern' with many forces working to keep it alive, the people who run it can readily escape the task of defining purposes. The evasion stems partly from the hard intellectual labor involved . . . In part, also, there is the wish to avoid conflicts with those in and out of the organization who would be threatened by a sharp definition of purpose . . . A critique of leadership . . . must include this emphasis on the leader's responsibility to define the mission of the enterprise. This view is not new. It is important because so much of administrative analysis takes the goal of the organization as given, whereas in many crucial instances this is precisely what is problematic" (*Leadership in Administration,* pp. 25–26).

61. For an interesting analysis of organizations that are in this position, see Marshall W. Meyer and Lynne G. Zucker, *Permanently Failing Organizations* (Thousand Oaks, Calif.: Sage Publications, 1989).

62. I am indebted to Martin Linsky for emphasizing the value of this particular way of formulating the different kinds of managerial challenges. It is closely linked to the idea of the "compass" that Richard N. Haass introduces in his recent book, *The Power to Persuade: How to Be Effective in Government, the Public Sector, or Any Unruly Organization* (Boston: Houghton Mifflin, 1994). Hugh Heclo, too, makes use of a similar conception in describing how successful political executives orient themselves to their jobs. See Heclo, *A Government of Strangers,* pp. 161–170.

63. Wilson describes how central the task of reconciling these conflicting demands are: "In the United States, high level government executives are pre-occupied with maintaining their agencies in a complex, conflict ridden, and unpredictable political environment" (*Bureaucracy,* p. 31).

64. For a discussion of what policy analysis is and how it can be helpful to public sector executives in determining whether a proposed use of public resources would be valuable or not, see Laurence E. Lynn, Jr., "Policy Analysis," in Frederick S. Lane, ed., *Current Issues in Public Administration,* 5th ed. (New York: St. Martin's Press, 1994). For a fuller discussion of the methodology, see Edith Stokey and Richard Zeckhauser, *A Primer for Policy Analysis* (New York: Norton, 1978), and Peter DeLeon, *The Foundations of Policy Analysis* (Homewood, Ill.: Dorsey, 1983). For a discussion of who does the analysis and how it is used in public sector organizations, see Arnold J. Meltsner, *Policy Analysts in the Bureaucracy* (Berkeley: University of California Press, 1976). For a discussion of how the techniques of program evaluation can be used to size up public sector performance, see Wholey, Abrahamson, and Bellavita, *Performance and Credibility.*

65. See, for example, the analysis and evaluation of the Social Security Administration's disability program by Jerry L. Mashaw, in *Bureaucratic Justice: Managing Social Security Disability Claims* (New Haven, Conn.: Yale University Press, 1983), esp. pp. 21–40.

66. For the methods to be used in this kind of analysis, see Heymann, *The Politics of Public Management;* Richard Neustadt and Ernest May, *Thinking in Time: The Uses of History for Decision Makers* (New York: Free Press, 1986), pp. 91–110, 212–231; and John M. Bryson, *Strategic Planning for Public and Nonprofit Organizations* (San Francisco: Jossey-Bass, 1988), pp. 93–116.

67. Robert B. Reich, "Introduction," in Reich, *The Power of Public Ideas* (Cambridge, Mass.: Ballinger, 1988), pp. 5–7.

68. Graham T. Allison, "Implementation Analysis—The 'Missing Chapter' in Conventional Analysis: A Teaching Enterprise," in *Benefit Cost and Policy Analysis: 1974* (Chicago: Aldine Publishing, 1975). See also Graham T. Allison and Mark H. Moore, special edition of *Public Policy,* vol. 26, no. 2; Mark H. Moore, "A Feasibility Estimate of a Policy Decision to Expand Methadone Maintenance," *Public Policy,* vol. 26, no. 2 (Spring 1978):

285–304; Richard Elmore, "Backward Mapping: Implementation Research and Policy Decisions," *Political Science Quarterly,* vol. 94, no. 4 (1980): 601–616; Gordon Chase, "Implementing a Human Services Program: How Hard Will It Be?" in *Public Policy,* vol. 27, no. 4 (Fall 1979): 385–436; Steven Kelman, "Using Implementation Research to Solve Implementation Problems: The Case of Energy Emergency Assistance," *Journal of Policy Analysis and Management,* vol. 4, no. 1 (1984): 75–91.

69. Herbert Kaufman, *Time, Chance, and Organizations: Natural Selection in a Perilous Environment* (Chatham, N.J.: Chatham House, 1985), pp. 46–53.

70. Meltsner, *Policy Analysts.*

71. On the role of political appointees, see Heclo, *Government of Strangers.* On the role of press offices, see Stephen Hess, *The Government/Press Connection: Press Officers and Offices* (Washington, D.C.: Brookings Institution, 1984).

72. For an overview of that tradition, see Shafritz and Hyde, *Classics in Public Administration,* particularly the quotations offered in n. 9 to Chapter 1. Of course, there are many different "traditions" to which I could be referring when I say that the distribution of thought and managerial attention suggested by the strategic triangle differs from the traditions of public administration. I could be referring to the historical origins of public administration or to the origins as they have been amended by contemporary writings. Equally important, I could be referring to the "academic" tradition or the "practitioner" tradition and implicitly recognizing that there are many ideas which are current in the contemporary academic discourse that are not yet current in practice.

What I *am* referring to is some combination of the original concepts of public administration and their strong echoes in the current thoughts and practices of public managers as I have encountered them in the Kennedy School's executive programs. The view that managers are accountable only for this efficient achievement of mandated objectives is immediately recognizable to practicing public officials. Indeed, they experience the challenge to look out to value and up to politics as a wider authorization for leadership than one they had previously enjoyed. They acknowledge, of course, that they have often made important judgments about public value and have engaged in political advocacy, but they experienced these as faintly illicit.

Moreover, it is also fair to say that although contemporary students of public administration well understand as a positive claim that the line between policy and administration cannot be well sustained, and that public officials are often involved in the political task of defining purpose and value, they remain a little uncertain about the implications of those realities for a normative theory of public administration. Indeed, I think Dwight Waldo captured this ambivalence exceptionally well in his essay entitled "Public Administration in a Time of Revolution" (*Public Administration Review,* 28 [July–August 1968]). It is worth quoting at length:

> Traditionally . . . we have had as theory or rationale for the bureaucracy . . . that it has no business making policy or engaging in politics. One expression of this is the idea of civil service neutrality . . . The duty of the civil servant is precisely to do his duty, and that is to follow instructions and (or) to carry out the law.
>
> Now this theory or ideology is far from silly. It can be argued cogently that by and large it has served us well, that it is still full of vitality, and that to abandon it is to open the gate to grave evils. On the other hand, all sorts of questions can be asked about it: Has it been more a useful myth than description of reality? Assuming that it *has been* a useful myth, is it *now* a useful myth? Didn't we, as a profession or discipline, decide some time ago that administration is perforce intimately involved in the political process? That is that we *have* and *should have* some role in making laws and deciding upon policies as well as simply carrying them out? That to conceive of ourselves as mere automata is demeaning and, under some circumstances, even irresponsible? If this is true, if this is what we believe, what are the implications for our behavior in a time of revolution?
>
> I'm going to take the position that we ought to respond more consciously, more *self-consciously,* to the revolutions of the day. But let me acknowledge that the case is far from being completely one-sided. The idea—fiction, ideology, call it what you will—of civil service neutrality has served its purposes, and real dangers *are* created by abandoning it. It can be argued . . . that the proper role of a bureaucracy is to act as a stabilizing force in the midst of vertiginous change, and that this is what it is doing when it seems to be unresponsive or stupid . . .
>
> Having admitted that this point of view has some force and validity, let me say that on balance I reject it. For reasons I have already partly suggested, I think it's unrealistic and wrong . . . Any institution that doesn't adjust to the rapidly changing milieu . . . will not be effective in terms of its purpose or assignment. Long range, it will not even survive. The public service, by intelligent and imaginative response . . . may serve not only its own "immediate" interest, but help society change and adjust in ways that maximize the potentials for "goods" and minimize the potentials for "bads."

In the end, I come out where Waldo does. Indeed, I am trying to write and think within the tradition he has developed. But one cannot help feeling the difficulty he experiences in striking out from what has been a comfortable position. It is *very* hard for both practitioners and scholars of public administration to abandon once and for all the comfortable images of politically neutral competence, particularly when it is by no means clear what the alternative would be. Consequently, many practitioners and many scholars almost unconsciously revert to this position when they are not pressed to remember that this stance is not possible. This book is largely an effort to work out an alternative stance for public managers.

73. The relationship between politics and administration was set out very early in the classic texts on public administration. Woodrow Wilson explained that "politics sets the tasks for administration." Wilson, "The Study of Administration," in Shafritz and Hyde, *Classics*, p. 18. Frank Goodnow echoed this understanding: "Politics has to do with policies or expressions of the state will. Administration has to do with the execution of these policies." Goodnow, *Politics and Administration: A Study in Government* (New York: Russell and Russell, 1900), reprinted in Shafritz and Hyde, *Classics*, p. 26.

74. Leonard White gives public administration this sharp focus on internal management: "Public administration is the management of men and materials in the accomplishment of the purposes of the state . . . The objective of public administration is the most efficient utilization of the resources at the disposal of officials and employees." White, *Introduction to the Study of Public Administration* (New York: Macmillan, 1926), reprinted in Shafritz and Hyde, *Classics*, pp. 56–57.

75. Luther Gulick identified the variety and importance of these techniques with the acronym PODSCORB. See Gulick, "Notes on the Theory of Organization," reprinted in Shafritz and Hyde, *Classics*, pp. 88–89.

76. For a discussion of the general idea of accountability and the particular role of inspectors general in holding managers to the legislated terms of accountability, see Mark H. Moore and Margaret J. Gates, *Inspectors-General: Junkyard Dogs or Man's Best Friend?* (New York: Russell Sage, 1986).

77. Heymann makes this point succinctly: "The manager cannot attempt to satisfy all those who can exercise influence over his organization . . . The manager's task is rather to articulate and then to execute desirable goals, the support for which will provide the money and physical resources, the popular approval and cooperation, the recruits and collaborators, and the authority the organization needs to carry out the goals" (*The Politics of Public Management*, p. 14).

78. Reich, "Policy Making in a Democracy," pp. 123–156.

79. This shift is described in Mark H. Moore, "Small Scale Statesmen: A Conception of Public Management," *Politiques et Management Public*, vol. 7, no. 2 (June 1989): 273–287. See also Herman Leonard, "Theory S and Theory T" (Kennedy School of Government, photocopy, 1984). Robert Behn also develops the idea of public manager as strategic leader in *Leadership Counts: Lessons for Public Managers from the Massachusetts Welfare, Training, and Employment Program* (Cambridge, Mass.: Harvard University Press, 1991), pp. 203–206. The implications of this change for the kinds of calculations that managers must make is captured superbly by Selznick: "As we ascend the echelons of administration, the analysis of decision-making becomes increasingly difficult, not simply because the decisions are more important or complex, but because a new

'logic' emerges. The logic of efficiency applies most clearly to subordinate units, usually having rather clearly defined operating responsibilities, limited discretion, set communication channels, and a sure position in the command structure. The logic of efficiency loses its force, however, as we approach the top level of the pyramid. Problems at this level are more resistant to the ordinary approaches of management experts. Mechanical metaphors—the organization as a 'smooth running machine'—suggest an overemphasis on neat organization and on efficient techniques of administration. It is probable that these emphases induce in the analyst a trained incapacity to observe the inter-relationship of policy and administration, with the result that the really critical experience of organizational leadership is largely overlooked" (*Leadership in Administration,* p. 3).

80. This is not quite true. The one institutional change I am recommending is that overseers' expectations about the amount and character of initiative they expect from public managers change a little to give them scope for the strategic calculations I propose. In effect, the "institution" I am trying to influence is the prevailing norms and expectations we have about the style of public managers. I am not suggesting any important changes in the structures of accountability or the requirements for reporting. Indeed, if anything, I am urging public managers to *embrace* accountability to their political overseers even more closely than they now do.

81. This account once again is based on the Kennedy School Case "William Ruckelshaus and the EPA." My interpretation is importantly influenced by Joseph L. Bower.

82. "William Ruckelshaus and the EPA," p. 3.

83. "Design for Environmental Protection," KSG Case #C16-74-26.0 (Cambridge, Mass.: Kennedy School of Government Case Program, 1974, rev. 1977).

84. On the importance of using competitive pressures to encourage regulatory compliance, see Robert A. Leone, *Who Profits: Winners, Losers, and Governmental Regulation* (New York: Basic Books, 1986).

85. For a discussion of subsequent events and the continued search for a substantively valuable and politically and administratively feasible approach to environmental protection, see Mark K. Landry, Marc J. Thomas, and Stephen R. Thomas, *The Environmental Protection Agency: Asking the Wrong Questions* (New York: Oxford University Press, 1990).

86. Andrews, *Corporate Strategy,* p. 11.

87. See Coates, Miller, and Ohlin, *Diversity in a Youth Correctional System,* pp. 175–178; and Krisberg, Austin, and Steele, *Unlocking Juvenile Corrections.*

88. The development of this new framework is described in "Contracting for Human Services: The Case of DYS," KSG Case #C14-79-268.0 and #C14-79-269.0 (Cambridge, Mass.: Kennedy School of Government Case Program, 1979, rev. 1984).

89. Krisberg, Austin, and Steele, *Unlocking Juvenile Corrections.*
90. "Contracting for Human Services: The Case of DYS."
91. In this respect, they are similar to the managers that John Kotter described: "The general managers always started their jobs with some knowledge of the business involved and some sense of what needed to be done . . . but rarely did they have a very clear agenda in mind" (*The General Managers,* p. 60).
92. Many writers on leadership emphasize the importance of defining purposes and repeating them often enough that they become part of the external reputation and internal cultural identity of the organization. Chester I. Barnard, for example, writes: "Willingness to coöperate, except as a vague feeling or desire for association with others, cannot develop without an objective of coöperation. Unless there is such an objective, it cannot be known or anticipated what specific efforts will be required of individuals, nor in many cases, what satisfactions to them can be in prospect . . . The inculcation of belief in the real existence of a common purpose is an essential executive function." Barnard, *The Functions of the Executive* (Cambridge, Mass.: Harvard University Press, 1966), pp. 86–87. Laurence E. Lynn, Jr., writing particularly about public sector executives and the ways in which they can make their leadership felt, puts the "develop[ment] of strategic premises by which the intent and significance of organizational actions can be interpreted" at the top of his list of recommendations to public sector executives who wish to be "change agents." Lynn, *Managing Public Policy* (Boston: Little, Brown, 1987), pp. 270–271.
93. Recall Selznick's observation that one of the most common causes of leadership failure is the failure to define and establish purpose: "When institutional leadership fails, it is perhaps more often by default than by positive error or sin . . . The default is partly a failure of nerve, partly a failure of understanding. It takes nerve to hold to a cause; it takes understanding to recognize and deal with the basic sources of institutional vulnerability" (*Leadership in Administration,* p. 25).
94. For an interesting discussion of the utility of staying focused on a purpose as one shifts through the debris of everyday managerial activities, see Thomas J. Peters, "Leadership: Sad Tales and Silver Linings," *Harvard Business Review,* no. 79611 (1979): 164–172. Norton Long agrees: "To appraise the policies of an administration, a well-considered and constantly developing conception of the public interest is needed to distinguish the important from the trivial and the successes from the failures," in "Public Administration, Ethics, and Epistemology," *American Review of Public Administration,* vol. 18, no. 2 (June 1988): 111.
95. Selznick sees actions such as these as crucial to the "institutionalization" of an organization's purpose—with both good and bad consequences: "As a business, a college, or a government agency develops a distinctive clien-

tele, the enterprise gains the stability that comes with a secure source of support and easy channel of communication. At the same time, it loses flexibility. The process of institutionalization has set in" (*Leadership in Administration,* p. 7).

96. John Kotter states: "The agendas and networks the general managers develop . . . allow them to be . . . opportunistic on a daily basis, to react to the flow of people and events around them in an efficient way, yet to do so knowing that they are still contributing more or less systematically to a longer run plan" (*The General Managers,* p. 88).

97. For an extended discussion of this gaming, see Aaron Wildavsky, *The Politics of the Budgetary Process,* 4th ed. (Boston: Little, Brown, 1984). See also Robert N. Anthony and Regina Herzlinger, *Management Control in Nonprofit Organizations* (Homewood, Ill.: Irwin, 1975), pp. 249–258.

98. Terrence E. Deal, *Corporate Cultures: The Rites and Rituals of Corporate Life* (Reading, Mass.: Addison-Wesley, 1982), pp. 21–25.

99. Graham T. Allison makes this observation the heart of his depiction of organizational behavior. See Allison, *Essence of Decision: Explaining the Cuban Missile Crisis* (Boston, Mass.: Little, Brown, 1971), pp. 67–100.

100. Recall Barnard's admonition: "An objective purpose . . . is one that is *believed* . . . to be the determined purpose of the organization" (*Functions of the Executive,* p. 87). Wilson makes the point even more sharply: "The executives that not only maintain their organizations but transform them do more than merely acquire constituency support; they project a compelling vision of the tasks, culture and importance of their agencies. The greatest executives infuse their organizations with value and convince others that this value is not merely useful to the bureau, but essential to the polity" (*Bureaucracy,* p. 217).

101. I thank my colleague Ronald Heifetz for this observation. He reports that this is a common view among those associated with the Tavistock Institute.

102. For a discussion of these different kinds of innovation, see Mark H. Moore, William Spelman, and Malcolm Sparrow, "From Production Lines to Job Shops: Innovations in Policing," in Alan Altshuler and Robert Behn, eds., *Research on Innovations in State and Local Government* (Washington D.C.: Urban Institute, forthcoming).

103. Herbert Simon viewed higher and lower level goals for organizations in the same terms as I am suggesting here: "There is no essential difference between a 'purpose' and a 'process' but only a distinction of degree. A 'process' is an activity whose immediate purpose is at a low level in the hierarchy of means and ends, while a 'purpose' is a collection of activities whose orienting value or aim is at a higher level in the means-end hierarchy." Simon, "The Proverbs of Administration," in Shafritz and Hyde, *Classics,* p. 171.

104. On the value of some degree of ambiguity in defining organizational purposes, see Wilson, *Bureaucracy,* pp. 25–26. Note also Selznick's com-

ment: "The aims of a large organization are often very broad. A certain vagueness must be accepted because it is difficult to foresee whether specific goals will be realistic or wise" (*Leadership in Administration,* p. 66). He also notes: "A characteristic threat to the . . . adequate definition of institutional mission is an excessive or premature technological orientation. This posture is marked by a concentration on ways and means. The ends of actions are taken for granted . . . As we move to areas where self-determination becomes increasingly important—where 'initiative' must be exercised—the setting of goals loses its innocence" (p. 74).

105. For a discussion of the utility of such goal structures, see Max D. Richards, *Organization Goal Structures* (St. Paul, Minn.: West Publishing, 1978).

106. The irony, however, is that precisely because there is uncertainty about how to proceed, there will be intense pressures focused on such agencies to give detailed accounts of their efforts. The uncertainty will generate increased demands for accountability, which can be satisfied only by giving detailed reports. For an interesting account of how these pressures have weakened the performance of an organization, see Malcolm Weiss, John S. Carroll, Kent F. Hansen, and Constance Perin, *Making Progress in Cleaning Up DOE's Weapons Complex: Issues of Organization and Management* (Cambridge, Mass.: MIT Energy Laboratory, 1993). For a more general discussion of the tension between the demand for accountability and the need to innovate, see Moore, *Accounting for Change.*

107. Behn argues that most public organizations could benefit from innovative efforts. See Behn, "A Curmudgeon's View of Public Administration," *State and Local Government Review,* Spring 1987, 47, 54–61.

108. Heymann observes: "The manager can bring energy and insight to a political process that is stagnant and confused. But in doing so, the manager is no more, at best, than a partner of elected powers and a servant of those who choose them" (*Politics of Public Management,* p. 189).

109. Kaufman, *Federal Bureau Chiefs.* See also Wilson, *Bureaucracy,* p. 35.

4. MOBILIZING SUPPORT, LEGITIMACY, AND COPRODUCTION

1. This account is based on a case developed by Colin Diver: "Park Plaza" (Boston University, 1975), distributed by the Kennedy School as KSG Case #C16-75-707.0 (Cambridge, Mass.: Kennedy School of Government Case Program, 1975).

2. The account of the swine flu case draws from two different sources. One is a Kennedy School case supervised by J. Bradley O'Connor and Laurence E. Lynn, Jr., and entitled "Swine Flu (A)," KSG Case #C14-80-313.0 (Cambridge, Mass.: Kennedy School of Government Case Program, 1980). The other is an excellent book describing and analyzing these events: Richard E. Neustadt and Harvey Fineberg, *The Epidemic That*

Never Was: Policy-Making and the Swine Flu Affair (New York: Vintage, 1983).

3. Graham T. Allison observes: "Underlying . . . [the] sharpest distinctions between public and private management is a fundamental *constitutional difference.* In business, the functions of general management are centralized in a single individual: the Chief Executive Officer . . . In contrast, in the U.S. government, the functions of general management are constitutionally spread among competing institutions: the executive, two houses of Congress, and the courts . . . Thus, the general management functions concentrated in the CEO of a private business are by constitutional design spread . . . among a number of competing institutions and thus shared by a number of individuals whose ambitions are set against one another . . . Since most public services are actually delivered by state and local governments, with independent sources of authority, this means a further array of individuals at these levels." Allison, "Public and Private Management: Are They Fundamentally Alike in All Unimportant Respects?" in Jay M. Shafritz and Allbert C. Hyde, eds., *Classics of Public Administration,* 2d ed. (Chicago: Dorsey Press, 1987), p. 519. No wonder, then, that the task of assembling sufficient authority to act from those who share that authority would be an important managerial function. See also the discussion of "indirect management" in David Lax and James K. Sebenius, *The Manager as Negotiator: Bargaining for Cooperation and Competitive Gain* (New York: Free Press, 1986), pp. 323–324.

4. Note that for such public sector enterprises as tax collection, regulation, and enforcement, which rely on authority to oblige others to contribute to their goals, a great deal of the capacity they need to accomplish their goals inevitably lies outside the boundaries of their organization. Thus, political management, understood as the effort to mobilize public authority and legitimacy behind a purpose, may be particularly important for regulatory and enforcement agencies. Without the weight of public support to help them with their enforcement efforts, they cannot achieve the degree of compliance they need to achieve their goals. See Malcolm Sparrow, *Imposing Duties: Government's Changing Approach to Compliance* (Westport, Conn.: Praeger, 1994), for a discussion of the special problems faced by agencies that "impose obligations" rather than "deliver services."

5. Richard Neustadt's memorable quote captured this basic idea about public management for all time: "When one man shares authority with another, but does not gain or lose his job on the other's whims, his willingness to act on the urging of the other turns on whether he conceives the action right for him. The essence of a President's persuasive task is to convince such men that what the White House wants of them is what they ought to do for their own sake and on their own authority." Richard E. Neustadt, *Presidential Power and the Modern Presidents: The Politics of Leadership from Roosevelt to Reagan* (New York: Free Press, 1990), p. 30.

6. Herbert Kaufman, *The Administrative Behavior of Bureau Chiefs* (Washington, D.C.: Brookings Institution, 1981), pp. 45–78.

7. Gordon Chase and Elizabeth C. Reveal, *How to Manage in the Public Sector* (Reading, Mass.: Addison-Wesley, 1983), pp. 64–75. For an interesting case in which public managers try to negotiate the routine terms of their accountability, see "The Executive Branch and the Legislature: Opening the Lines of Communication in Minnesota," KSG Case #C16-90-991.0 (Cambridge, Mass.: Kennedy School of Government Case Program, 1990). On the ways in which inspectors general seek to hold public managers accountable in routine operations, see Mark H. Moore and Margaret J. Gates, *Inspectors-General: Junkyard Dogs or Man's Best Friend?* (New York: Russell Sage, 1986).

8. For a discussion of this problem, see Mark H. Moore, *Accounting for Change: Reconciling the Tensions between Accountability and Innovation* (Washington, D.C.: Council for Excellence in Government, 1993), pp. 137–148.

9. Recall E. Pendleton Herring's observation: "Upon the shoulders of the bureaucrat has been placed in large part the burden of reconciling group differences and making effective and workable the economic and social compromises arrived at through the legislative process." Herring, "Public Administration and the Public Interest," in Jay M. Shafritz and Albert C. Hyde, eds., *Classics of Public Administration,* 2d ed. (Chicago: Dorsey Press, 1987), p. 74.

10. Neustadt observes that this situation will arise often: "Almost every policy entangles many agencies; almost every program calls for interagency collaboration" (*Presidential Power and the Modern Presidents,* p. 34).

11. For an example of such systems operating at the presidential level, see Laurence E. Lynn, Jr., and David DeF. Whitman, *The President as Policymaker: Jimmy Carter and Welfare Reform* (Philadelphia: Temple University Press, 1981). For a proposal about how to design such systems, see Laurence E. Lynn, Jr., and John M. Seidl, "Bottom-Line Management for Public Agencies," *Harvard Business Review,* vol. 55, no. 1 (1977).

12. Richard Neustadt reminds us that even presidents cannot always reliably control their subordinate bureaucracies: *Presidential Power and the Modern Presidents,* pp. 29–32. Lynn and Whitman tell a harrowing story of the failure of presidential leadership in the coordination of the development of a welfare policy: *The President as Policymaker,* pp. 265–268.

13. Philip B. Heymann, *The Politics of Public Management* (New Haven, Conn.: Yale University Press, 1987), p. 148.

14. For a discussion of how "incoherent authority" made success in Nixon's "war on drugs" quite difficult to achieve, see Mark H. Moore, "Reorganization Plan #2 Reviewed," *Public Policy,* vol. 26, no. 2 (Spring 1978): 249.

15. Martin Linsky, *Impact: How the Press Affects Federal Policymaking* (New York: Norton, 1986), pp. 60–88. See also E. E. Schattschneider, *The Semi-*

sovereign People: A Realist's View of Democracy in America (Hinsdale, Ill.: Dryden, 1960), p. 7.

16. Often, in these situations, public managers reach for public information campaigns as a means of achieving their intended results. For a discussion of such campaigns, see Janet A. Weiss and Mary Tschirhat, "Public Information Campaigns as Policy Instruments," *Journal of Policy Analysis and Management,* vol. 13, no. 1 (1994): 82–119.

17. Michael O'Hare, "A Typology of Governmental Action," *Journal of Policy Analysis and Management,* vol. 8, no. 4 (Fall 1989): 670–673.

18. Hugh Heclo, *A Government of Strangers: Executive Politics in Washington* (Washington, D.C.: Brookings Institution, 1977), pp. 158–190.

19. Philip Heymann observes that political appointees have at least three important roles: advocates of the president's positions; mediators between the executive and the legislative branches or the executive and the judicial branches; and nonpolitical experts, professionals, or quasi-judicial officers. Heymann, *The Politics of Public Management,* p. 120.

20. Joel D. Aberbach, *Keeping a Watchful Eye: The Politics of Congressional Oversight* (Washington, D.C.: Brookings Institution, 1990), and David Mayhew, *Congress: The Electoral Connection* (New Haven, Conn.: Yale University Press, 1974).

21. Chase and Reveal, *How to Manage in the Public Sector.*

22. Heymann, *The Politics of Public Management,* pp. 150–151.

23. Ibid., p. 151.

24. For a general discussion of the role that the press plays in policy-making, see Gary Orren, "Thinking about the Press and Government," in Linsky, *Impact,* pp. 12–20.

25. Linsky, *Impact,* pp. 87–118.

26. Ibid., p. 118.

27. Ibid., pp. 112–118.

28. For two interesting cases describing successful proactive press strategies, see "Selling the Reorganization of the Post Office," KSG Case #C14-84-610.0 (Cambridge, Mass.: Kennedy School of Government Case Program, 1984), and "Please Be Patient: The Seattle Solid Waste Utility Meets the Press," KSG Case #C16-91-1058.0 (Cambridge, Mass.: Kennedy School of Government Case Program, 1991).

29. For a discussion of how interest groups form, see James Q. Wilson, *Political Organizations* (New York: Basic Books, 1973). For a classic discussion of their impact on the political process, see David B. Truman, *The Governmental Process: Political Interests and Public Opinion* (New York: Knopf, 1951).

30. These are the kinds of interest groups discussed in Truman, *The Governmental Process,* and also in James Q. Wilson, ed., *The Politics of Regulation* (New York: Basic Books, 1980).

31. These are the kinds of interest groups that Wilson treats in *Political*

Organizations and *The Politics of Regulation,* pp. 385–386. For an interesting discussion of the formation and maintenance of such organizations, see Charles McCarry, *Citizen Nader* (New York: Saturday Review Press, 1972); and Osha Gray Davidson, *Under Fire: The NRA and the Battle for Gun Control* (New York: Henry Holt, 1993).

32. On latent groups, see Truman, *The Governmental Process,* p. 34.

33. Ibid. See also Raymond Bauer, Ithiel De Sola Pool, and Lewis Anthony Dexter, *Business and Public Policy: The Politics of Foreign Trade* (Chicago: Aldine-Atherton, 1972); and Charles Edward Lindblom, *The Policy-Making Process* (Englewood Cliffs, N.J.: Prentice-Hall, 1980).

34. Mancur Olson sets out an economic theory to explain the limited conditions under which interest groups can form. See Olson, *The Logic of Collective Action: Public Goods and the Theory of Groups* (Cambridge, Mass.: Harvard University Press, 1965). James Q. Wilson offers a theory that suggests a wider set of possibilities for interest group formation, including the idea that groups might be organized around "purposive incentives," i.e., the shared aspirations of individuals in the group to achieve some public purpose (Wilson, *Political Organizations*).

35. Jeffrey M. Berry, *The Interest Group Society,* 2d ed. (Glenview, Ill.: Scott Foresman, 1989).

36. Ibid., pp. 100–105. For a diatribe against interest groups, see Jonathan Rauch, *Demosclerosis: The Silent Killer of American Government* (New York: Random House, 1994).

37. Allison gives an example of the difficulty that a subordinate closely allied to an interest group can give to a public manager who is trying to shape the strategy of his organization. See Allison, "Public and Private Management," p. 523.

38. Recall Philip Selznick's observation: "As a . . . government agency develops a distinctive clientele, the enterprise gains the stability that comes with a secure source of support, an easy channel of communication." Selznick, *Leadership in Administration: A Sociological Interpretation,* rev. ed. (Berkeley: University of California Press, 1984), p. 7.

39. The circumstances under which courts may overrule agency decisions is the central subject of administrative law. For an overview, see Richard Stewart, "The Reformation of American Administrative Law," *Harvard Law Review,* vol. 88, no. 8 (June 1975): 1669–1813.

40. Robert C. Wood, ed., *Remedial Law: When Courts Become Administrators* (Amherst: University of Massachusetts Press, 1990).

41. On the theory, see Stewart, "The Reformation of American Administrative Law." On the practice, see Robert Katzmann, *Regulating Bureaucracy* (Cambridge, Mass.: MIT Press, 1980).

42. Daniel J. Meador, *The President, the Attorney General, and the Department of Justice* (Charlottesville: University of Virginia, White Burkett Miller Center of Public Affairs, 1980), pp. 36–39.

43. Heymann makes the same point in *The Politics of Public Management,* pp. 74–75.
44. Roger Porter, *Presidential Decisionmaking: The Economic Policy Board* (Cambridge: Cambridge University Press, 1980).
45. Neustadt, *Presidential Power and the Modern Presidents,* p. 30.
46. Ibid., pp. 150–151.
47. See, for example, "Les Aspin and the MX," KSG Case #C14-83-568.0 (Cambridge, Mass.: Kennedy School of Government Case Program, 1983).
48. Herbert Kaufman identifies some important process values such as "representativeness," "nonpartisan competence," and "executive leadership." See Kaufman, "Emerging Conflicts in the Doctrines of Public Administration," *American Political Science Review,* vol. 50, no. 4 (December 1956): 1057–1073. Other values are captured in the intuitions that form the backdrop of administrative law. See Jerry L. Mashaw, *Due Process in the Administrative State* (New Haven, Conn.: Yale University Press, 1985), pp. 172–182.
49. For some cases that describe situations in which managers seek to design a policy management process to maximize the legitimacy of the choices they have to make, see "The Recission of the Passive Restraints Standard," KSG Case #C16-82-455.0 (Cambridge, Mass.: Kennedy School of Government Case Program, 1982), and "Controlling Acid Rain, 1986," KSG Case #C15-86-699.0 (Cambridge, Mass.: Kennedy School of Government Case Program, 1986).
50. Charles E. Lindblom, "The Science of 'Muddling Through,'" *Public Administration Review,* 19 (Spring 1959): 79–88, reprinted in Shafritz and Hyde, *Classics,* pp. 268–269.
51. Mark H. Moore, "What Makes Ideas Powerful?" in Robert B. Reich, ed., *The Power of Public Ideas* (Cambridge, Mass.: Ballinger, 1988), pp. 55–83.
52. Ibid., pp. 55–57. For a more extended discussion of this idea, see Mark H. Moore and Dean L. Gerstein, *Alcohol and Public Policy: Beyond the Shadow of Prohibition* (Washington, D.C.: National Academy Press, 1981).
53. Moore, "What Makes Ideas Powerful?" pp. 57–60.
54. Moore and Gerstein, *Alcohol and Public Policy.*
55. Richard E. Neustadt and Ernest R. May, *Thinking in Time: The Uses of History for Decision Makers* (New York: Free Press, 1986), pp. 34–36.
56. Ibid., pp. 34–57.
57. Robert Martinson, "What Works? Questions and Answers about Prison Reform," *Public Interest,* 35 (1974): 22–54.
58. James Q. Wilson, ed., *Urban Renewal: The Record and the Controversy* (Cambridge, Mass.: MIT Press, 1966).
59. Erwin C. Hargrove and John Glidewell, eds., *Impossible Jobs in Public Management* (Lawrence: University Press of Kansas, 1990).
60. I base this statement on years of teaching practicing senior public sector executives in the Kennedy School's executive programs.

61. Recall James Q. Wilson's remark: "The executives that not only maintain their organizations but transform them do more than merely acquire constituency support; they project a compelling vision of the tasks, culture and importance of their agencies. The greatest executives infuse their organizations with value and convince others that this role is not merely useful to the bureau but essential to the polity." Wilson, *Bureaucracy: What Government Agencies Do and Why They Do It* (New York: Basic Books, 1989), p. 217. For accounts of executives who accomplished a great deal by engaging politics, see Jameson W. Doig and Erwin C. Hargrove, *Leadership and Innovation: A Biographical Perspective on Entrepreneurs in Government* (Baltimore: Johns Hopkins University Press, 1987). Herbert Kaufman, too, observed that public managers spent a quarter to a third of their time engaged in political management, more if one included their external "intelligence gathering" activities as part of political management, which I would be inclined to do. Kaufman, *The Administrative Behavior of Bureau Chiefs,* pp. 77–78. I note finally that there seems to have been an increasing tendency for public organizations to develop specialized offices to deal with external relations such as legislatures, the press, and other groups with whom the organizations must maintain a liaison. This trend has been documented for press offices. See Stephen Hess, *The Government/Press Connection: Press Officers and Their Offices* (Washington: Brookings Institution, 1984), pp. 1–3.

62. Karl Deutsch once observed that power was the ability of one individual to impose his preferred patterns on the world; hence it was the "ability to afford not to learn." Mahoney, having lost some of his power, was presented with the opportunity to revise his views of what constitutes public value. Deutsch, *The Nerves of Government: Models of Political Communication and Control* (New York: Free Press, 1966), p. 111.

5. ADVOCACY, NEGOTIATION, AND LEADERSHIP

1. The importance of this kind of political management was recognized early by Woodrow Wilson: "In order to make any advance at all, we must instruct and persuade a multitudinous monarch called public opinion—a much less feasible undertaking than to influence a single monarch called a king." Wilson, "The Study of Administration," in Jay M. Shafritz and Albert C. Hyde, eds., *Classics of Public Administration,* 2d ed. (Chicago: Dorsey Press, 1987), p. 16. Laurence E. Lynn, Jr., made the same point more recently: "Though [public executives] are given formal responsibility for countless tasks of real consequence, [they] . . . face continual frustration in their attempts to assemble the power and resources to accomplish them." Lynn, *Managing the Public's Business: The Job of the Government Executive* (New York: Basic Books, 1981), p. 158.

2. Woodrow Wilson also saw the importance of making the form of political management fit the requirements of democracy: "If we would employ it [the science of administration], we must Americanize it . . . It must learn our constitutions by heart; must get the bureaucratic fever out of its veins; must inhale much free American air" ("The Study of Administration," p. 13). More recently Robert Reich has observed: "Democracy is noisy, intrusive, frustrating, time consuming, unpredictable, and chaotic. But it is also the best system of government yet devised for ensuring that government is accountable to its citizens." Reich, *Public Management in a Democratic Society* (Englewood Cliffs, N.J.: Prentice-Hall, 1990), p. 4. He then goes on to recommend a particular way of interacting with this environment to preserve the values of democracy. He calls it the development of a "deliberative relationship" in which "[managers] bring to [their] job certain ideals and values and even some specific ideas of what [they] think should be done. But [they] nonetheless look to the public, and to its many intermediaries as a source of guidance. [Their] relationship is deliberative in the sense that [they] are honest and direct about [their] values and tentative goals, but [they] also listen carefully to how the public responds to [their] agendas and are willing to make adjustments accordingly" (p. 7).

3. For an excellent discussion of how principles of bureaucratic responsibility constrain the practices of public managers, see John P. Burke, *Bureaucratic Responsibility* (Baltimore: Johns Hopkins University Press, 1986). For a discussion of "virtue" and "virtu" in the conduct of public sector executives, see Mark H. Moore and Malcolm K. Sparrow, *Ethics in Government: The Moral Challenge of Public Leadership* (Englewood Cliffs, N.J.: Prentice-Hall, 1990).

4. For a description of the relationships between elected chief executives and the people they appoint to their cabinets in the ordinary workings of cabinets, see Roger Porter, *Presidential Decisionmaking: The Economic Policy Board* (Cambridge: Cambridge University Press, 1980), pp. 11–25. Richard E. Neustadt offers an absorbing story of the relationships among political principals, staffs, and cabinet secretaries and a brief historical perspective on these relationships in *Presidential Power and the Modern Presidents: The Politics of Leadership from Roosevelt to Reagan* (New York: Free Press, 1990), pp. 91–99, 193–194.

5. On difficulties that stubborn personalities can cause in negotiations, see Roger Fisher and William Ury, *Getting to Yes: Negotiating Agreement without Giving In,* 2d ed. (Boston: Houghton Mifflin, 1991), pp. 18–19, 29–32.

6. Fisher and Ury emphasize the importance of continuing communication in negotiations in *Getting to Yes,* pp. 32–36. Unfortunately, in many circumstances, people with common interests are prevented from talking to one another directly by legal rules designed to protect the integrity of the governmental process. Thus, for example, Mahoney may not have been

legally able to speak directly and privately to the developers without some legal or political risk to his subsequent decision on the plan.

7. On incentives to negotiate, see Howard Raiffa, *The Art and Science of Negotation* (Cambridge, Mass.: Harvard University Press, 1982). On the crucial importance of what bargainers think they can obtain for themselves without negotiating, see David A. Lax and James K. Sebenius, *The Manager as Negotiator: Bargaining for Cooperation and Competitive Gain* (New York: Free Press, 1986), pp. 46–62.

8. Richard E. Neustadt, *Presidential Power and the Modern Presidents: The Politics of Leadership from Roosevelt to Carter* (New York: Wiley and Sons, 1980), p. 90.

9. Roger B. Porter, "Economic Advice to the President: From Eisenhower to Reagan," *Political Science Quarterly,* vol. 8, no. 3 (Fall 1983): 403–426.

10. Richard G. Darman, "Policy Development Note #4: Propositions for Discussion on Recent Progress and Remaining Problems in the Design of Policy Development Systems" (Kennedy School of Government, photocopy, 1980).

11. For an excellent discussion of what goes into the design of cabinet-level policy-making systems, see Roger B. Porter, *Presidential Decisionmaking* (Cambridge: Cambridge University Press, 1980).

12. Neustadt describes similar difficulties in relations between presidents and their cabinet members in *Presidential Power and the Modern Presidents: From Roosevelt to Reagan,* pp. 32–37.

13. Martin Linsky, *Impact: How the Press Affects Federal Policymaking* (New York: Norton, 1986), pp. 40–68.

14. For evidence that this was the governor's calculation, see the description of his position in Colin S. Diver, "Park Plaza," KSG Case #C16-75-707.0 (Cambridge, Mass.: Kennedy School of Government Case Program, 1975).

15. In describing and analyzing Sencer's actions, I am again relying on Richard E. Neustadt and Harvey Fineberg, *The Epidemic That Never Was: Policy-Making and the Swine Flu Affair* (New York: Vintage, 1983); and J. Bradley O'Connor and Laurence E. Lynn, Jr., "Swine Flu (A)," KSG Case #C14-80-313.0 (Cambridge, Mass.: Kennedy School of Government Case Program, 1980). My description here is, at best, a superficial summary of Neustadt and Fineberg's detailed, subtle analysis. Anyone who wants to understand the full story should read their account of the events in the case.

16. The memorandum is reproduced in its entirety in Neustadt and Fineberg, *The Epidemic That Never Was,* pp. 198–206.

17. Ibid., p. 41.

18. As Neustadt and Fineberg report, "Institutional protection could not override the ethic of preventive medicine" (ibid., p. 25).

19. In O'Connor and Lynn's memorable phrase in "Swine Flu," "By close of business on Monday, swine flu policymaking outbreaks had occurred in numerous parts of Washington" (p. 9).

20. Neustadt and Fineberg, *The Epidemic That Never Was,* p. 35.
21. O'Connor and Lynn, "Swine Flu," p. 17.
22. Ibid., p. 15.
23. Ibid., p. 22.
24. Neustadt and Fineberg, *The Epidemic That Never Was,* p. 195.
25. Ibid., p. 95.
26. Ibid., p. 91.
27. Ibid., pp. 116–137.
28. Howard Raiffa, *Decision Analysis* (Reading, Mass.: Addison-Wesley, 1968).
29. Ibid., pp. 116–122.
30. Ibid., p. 117.
31. Ibid., pp. 118–122.
32. Ibid., pp. 122–126.
33. For an example of this style, see the description of the "jungle fighter" in Michael Maccoby, *The Gamesman: The New Corporate Leaders* (New York: Simon and Schuster, 1976), pp. 76–85.
34. Robert Reich observes pointedly: "If [managers] circumvent or subvert the system of accountability, [they] may not be able to discover what the public wants or needs in the first place. Effectiveness is a virtue only if [managers] are effective at accomplishing something of public value. [Managers'] own judgments about what the public wants may be wrong." Reich, *Public Management in a Democratic Society,* p. 5.
35. For a dramatic case of effective entrepreneurship that arguably produced some harms over the long run, see Robert Caro's account of Robert Moses and his influence on the development of New York City. Robert Caro, *The Power Broker: Robert Moses and the Fall of New York* (New York: Knopf, 1974).
36. Karl W. Deutsch, *The Nerves of Government: Models of Political Communication and Control* (New York: Free Press, 1966), p. 111.
37. This is the view taken by both Carl J. Friedrich and Herman Finer in their classic essays about the responsibilities of managers in the government. See Friedrich, "Public Policy and the Nature of Administrative Responsibility," in E. S. Mason and C. J. Friedrich, eds., *Public Policy, 1940* (Cambridge, Mass.: Harvard University Press, 1940), and Finer, "Administrative Responsibility in Democratic Government," *Public Administration Review,* 1 (1941): 335–350. This theme is echoed and illustrated in Reich, *Public Management in a Democratic Society,* and in Moore and Sparrow, *Ethics in Government.*
38. For an excellent discussion of this point, see Reich, *Public Management in a Democratic Society,* pp. 1–9.
39. I think the phrase "entrepreneurial advocacy" was first offered as an account of a coherent set of ideas about political management by Robert Reich. These techniques are set out generally in Philip B. Heymann, *The*

Politics of Public Management (New Haven, Conn.: Yale University Press, 1987), p. 144. For another version, see Morton H. Halperin, Peter Clapp, and Arnold Kanter, *Bureaucratic Politics and Foreign Policy* (Washington, D.C.: Brookings Institution, 1974). For an example of a quintessential entrepreneurial advocate, see Caro, *The Power Broker.* For a critique, see Reich, *Public Management in a Democratic Society,* pp. 60–63.

40. In setting out the techniques of entrepreneurial advocacy, I am relying heavily on conversations I have had over many years with Philip B. Heymann, Graham T. Allison, Robert Blackwell, and Richard Haas, among others. Any virtues in my discussion belong to them. Any failures are mine.

41. I am indebted to Philip B. Heymann for developing this point and much of the analysis I present here.

42. I thank Philip B. Heymann for this particular formulation.

43. Lynn makes this point powerfully and succinctly in *Managing the Public's Business,* pp. 158–159. Lax and Sebenius also describe the problem and the role that negotation plays as a technique for solving the problem in *The Manager as Negotiator,* pp. 314–338.

44. Graham T. Allison calls these routes to authoritative decisions "action channels." Allison, *Essence of Decision: Conceptual Models and the Cuban Missile Crisis* (Boston: Little, Brown, 1971), pp. 169–170.

45. On the idea of legitimacy and its various sources, see Heymann, *The Politics of Public Management,* pp. 74–89.

46. There appear to be some important exceptions to this rule. "Independent" regulatory agencies, for example, are thought to be independent of politics. So are "public authorities" of various kinds. Yet, on inspection, it becomes apparent that the political influence over these agencies is merely attenuated, not eliminated. They typically have to seek yearly appropriations from legislatures; their heads are appointed by elected politicians; and any time the legislature chooses, the agencies may be eliminated. So, the basic point remains true though there are some fine distinctions to be made. On the role of commissions, see Marver H. Bernstein, *Regulating Business by Independent Commission* (Westport, Conn.: Greenwood Press, 1977). For a discussion of public authorities, see Jameson Doig, "'If I See a Murderous Fellow Sharpening a Knife Cleverly . . .': The Wilsonian Dichotomy and the Public Authority Tradition" (Princeton University, photocopy, 1983).

47. Heymann devotes special attention to the legislature in ibid., pp. 109–124.

48. For a general discussion of how the courts become involved in public policy-making and an assessment of their capacity in this role, see Donald L. Horowitz, *The Courts and Social Policy* (Washington, D.C.: Brookings Institution, 1977).

49. An interesting example of this shows up in "Ellen Schall and the Department of Juvenile Justice," KSG Case #C16-87-793.0 (Cambridge, Mass.:

Kennedy School of Government Case Program, 1987). Reich also discusses an interesting example in *Public Management in a Democratic Society,* pp. 76–89.

50. This concept of channels may be what Heymann has in mind when he discusses the "configuration" of resources in political settings. See Heymann, *The Politics of Public Management,* pp. 156–158.

51. Hugh Heclo, "Issue Networks and the Executive Establishment," in Anthony King, ed. *The New American Political System* (Washington, D.C.: American Enterprise Institute, 1978), pp. 87–124.

52. This group could include "latent" interest groups. See David Truman, *The Governmental Process: Political Interests and Public Opinion* (New York: Knopf, 1951), p. 34.

53. I am relying here on the distinction that Allison makes between a player's "stakes" and "stands." See Allison, *Essence of Decision,* pp. 167–168. This is roughly analogous to the distinction that negotiation analysts make between a negotiator's "interests" and "positions." See Lax and Sebenius, *The Manager as Negotiator,* pp. 68–70.

54. Richard E. Neustadt and Ernest R. May suggest two different methods for doing this. One is to "inspect issue history"; the other is to "place people." See Neustadt and May, *Thinking in Time: The Uses of History for Decision Makers* (New York: Free Press, 1986), pp. 91–110 and 157–180, respectively.

55. Allison, *Essence of Decision,* p. 168.

56. Neustadt and May, *Thinking in Time,* pp. 34–57.

57. Heymann implicitly makes this distinction by dividing tactics that work within the existing "setting" for decision-making from those that seek to "reshape the political environment." See Heymann, *The Politics of Public Management,* pp. 145–189.

58. This is the point of Reich's criticisms of entrepreneurial advocacy. See Reich, *Public Management in a Democratic Society,* pp. 5–6. For an interesting example of a legislator who deliberately decided to take the harder course on a controversial subject to develop a more enduring mandate, see "Senator Scott Heidepriem and the South Dakota Anti-Abortion Bill," KSG Case #C16-93-1213.0 (Cambridge, Mass.: Kennedy School of Government Case Program, 1993).

59. As E. E. Schattschneider writes, "The first proposition is that the outcome of all conflict is determined by the scope of its contagion. The number of people involved in any conflict determines what happens; every change in the number of participants affects the results." Schattschneider, "The Contagiousness of Conflict," in *The Semisovereign People: A Realist's View of Democracy in America* (Hinsdale, Ill.: Dryden, 1960), p. 2.

60. Heymann, *The Politics of Public Management,* p. 137.

61. The events are described in "Les Aspin and the MX Missile," KSG Case #C14-83-568.0 (Cambridge, Mass.: Kennedy School of Government Case

Program, 1983). An interesting discussion of the case appears in Heymann's *Politics of Public Management,* pp. 125–163.

62. The events are described in "The Case of the Segregated Schools," KSG Case #C14-83-531.0 (Cambridge, Mass.: Kennedy School of Government Case Program, 1983). Linsky offers a trenchant analysis in *Impact,* pp. 95–104.

63. Linsky, *Impact,* pp. 88–118; see also Leon V. Sigal, "What the News Means Depends on How the News Gets Made," in *Reporters and Officials* (Lexington, Mass.: D. C. Heath, 1973), pp. 1–6.

64. Linsky, *Impact,* pp. 119–147.

65. Neustadt and May, *Thinking in Time,* pp. 48–57.

66. Heymann presents and develops the concept of "play" in a given setting in *The Politics of Public Management,* p. 165.

67. An interesting example is civil rights. See "Voting Rights Act of 1965," KSG Case #C14-80-307.0 (Cambridge, Mass.: Kennedy School of Government Case Program, 1980).

68. Richard Haass, "Ripeness and the Settlement of International Disputes," *Survival,* vol. 30, no. 3 (May–June 1988): 232–249.

69. I thank Phil Heymann for this observation. For an interesting case that illustrates the point, see Ron Beaulieu, "Section 103 of the Internal Revenue Code," KSG Case #C94-75-58.0 (Cambridge, Mass.: Kennedy School of Government Case Program, 1975).

70. Isaiah Berlin, *The Hedgehog and the Fox: An Essay on Tolstoy's View of History* (New York: Simon and Schuster, 1966).

71. Nancy Altman developed several cases on "commissions" at the Kennedy School. See "Les Aspin and the MX Missile," KSG Case #C14-83-568.0; "National Commission on Social Security Reform," KSG Case #C94-83-554.0 (Cambridge, Mass.: Kennedy School of Government Case Program, 1983); and "The Sawhill Commission: Weighing a State Takeover of LILCO," KSG Case #C15-86-718.0 (Cambridge, Mass.: Kennedy School of Government Case Program, 1986).

72. Beaulieu, "Section 103 of the Internal Revenue Code."

73. Dennis W. Banas and Robert C. Trojanowicz, *Uniform Crime Reporting and Community Policing: A Historical Perspective,* Community Policing Series, no. 5 (East Lansing: Michigan State University, National Neighborhood Foot Patrol Center, 1985).

74. "Hunger in America," KSG Case #C14-75-85.0 (Cambridge, Mass.: Kennedy School of Government Case Program, 1975).

75. John J. DiIulio, Jr., *No Escape: The Future of American Corrections* (New York: Basic Books, 1991), pp. 103–147.

76. Lisbeth Schorr (with Daniel Schorr), *Within Our Reach: Breaking the Cycle of Disadvantage* (New York: Anchor Press/Doubleday, 1988), pp. 184–192.

77. John P. Kotter, *The General Managers* (New York: Free Press, 1986),

p. 88. Hugh Heclo observes that this is also important for public managers: "Much of what political executives do to help themselves can be put under the general rubric of building personal networks." Heclo, *A Government of Strangers: Executive Policies in Washington* (Washington, D.C.: Brookings Institution, 1975), p. 158.

78. Reich is the most vocal critic; see *Public Management in a Democratic Society.*

79. The concepts of "policy management" as I develop them in this section are based on written work and extensive personal conversations with colleagues at the Kennedy School and elsewhere. The key documents include: Porter, *Presidential Decisionmaking;* Laurence E. Lynn, Jr., and John M. Seidl, "Bottom-Line Management for Public Agencies," *Harvard Business Review,* vol. 55, no. 1 (1977); Laurence E. Lynn, Jr., and David DeF. Whitman, *The President as Policymaker: Jimmy Carter and Welfare Reform* (Philadelphia: Temple University Press, 1981); Richard Darman, "Note on Policy Development #4." I have also benefited from a year-long faculty seminar on this subject in which Francis Bator, Hale Champion, Richard E. Neustadt, and Robert Zoellick, among others, participated. Other materials covering some of the same basic ideas include important works such as Alexander George, "The Case for Multiple Advocacy in Making Foreign Policy," *American Political Science Review,* 66 (September 1972): 751–785, on multiple advocacy; James W. Fessler and Donald F. Kettl, *The Politics of the Administrative Process* (Chatham, N.J.: Chatham House, 1991), pp. 208–238, on budgeting systems; and John M. Bryson, *Strategic Planning for Public and Nonprofit Organizations* (San Francisco: Jossey-Bass, 1988), on strategic planning systems in the public sector.

80. This technique has often been described as "managing" or "designing" the "process of policy development," a typical task facing managers in the government. Some cases that present this problem in a provocative way include: "The Recission of the Passive Restraints Standard," KSG Case #C16-82-455.0 (Cambridge, Mass.: Kennedy School of Government Case Program, 1982); "Ruckelshaus and Acid Rain," KSG Case #C16-86-658.0 (Cambridge, Mass.: Kennedy School of Government Case Program, 1986); "NHTSA and the Corporate Average Fuel Economy Standards," KSG Case #C15-86-672.0 (Cambridge, Mass.: Kennedy School of Government Case Program, 1986); "The Press and the Neutron Bomb," KSG Case #C14-84-607.0 (Cambridge, Mass.: Kennedy School of Government Case Program, 1984); "Ronald Reagan and Tax Exemptions for Racist Schools," KSG Case #C15-84-609.0 (Cambridge, Mass.: Kennedy School of Government Case Program, 1984); "Groundwater Regulation in Arizona," KSG Case #C16-91-1066.0 (Cambridge, Mass.: Kennedy School of Government Case Program, 1991).

81. This task is often described as "managing" or "designing" a "policy management system." It is closely related to the subject of designing strategic

planning systems and to the use of budgeting processes for strategic planning purposes. For a discussion of what goes into the design, development, and operations of such systems at the presidential level, see Porter, *Presidential Decisionmaking.* See also *A Presidency for the 1980's: A Report by a Panel of the National Academy of Public Administration* (Washington, D.C.: National Academy of Public Administration, n.d.). For some cases describing this problem, see Greg Mills, "PPB and the Surgeon General," HBS Case 9-375-111 (Boston: Harvard Business School, 1974); Regina Herzlinger and Arva Clark, "Zero-Based Budgeting in the Public Health Service," HBS Case 9-178-080 (Boston: Harvard Business School, 1977); Mark Moore, "Joan Claybrook and the National Highway Traffic Safety Administration," KSG Case #C95-81-370.0 (Cambridge, Mass.: Kennedy School of Government Case Program, 1981); David Kennedy, "Managing EPA," KSG Case #C16-87-729.0 (Cambridge, Mass.: Kennedy School of Government Case Program, 1987).

82. Recall the discussion in Chapter 4 emphasizing the role of both process and substance in producing a decision felt to be legitimate and persuasive. See also Heymann, *The Politics of Public Management,* pp. 74–89; and Edith Stokey and Richard Zeckhauser, *A Primer for Policy Analysis* (New York: Norton, 1978), pp. 283–286.

83. What goes into developing the legal standing of public policy decisions is the principal focus of administrative law. See Jerry L. Mashaw, *Due Process in the Administrative State* (New Haven, Conn.: Yale University Press, 1985), pp. 172–221.

84. I am explicitly adopting here the "rational actor" model of government as a normative ideal. Porter, too, seems inclined to adopt this position, for the criteria he uses to evaluate the performance of Ford's Economic Policy Board do focus on these kinds of factors. See Porter, *Presidential Decisionmaking,* pp. 184–189. For an alternative view, see Charles E. Lindblom, "The Science of Muddling Through," reprinted in Shafritz and Hyde, *Classics,* pp. 263–275, and Lindblom, *Inquiry and Change: The Troubled Attempt to Understand and Shape Society* (New Haven, Conn.: Yale University Press, 1990), pp. 257–302. Lindblom's critiques of this rational actor model shifted analysis toward models of deliberation and social learning. See the section "Public Deliberation, Social Learning, and Leadership," below.

85. For a discussion of how substantive expertise, social science, and policy analysis are and are not used in influencing public policy decisions, see Chapter 2, n. 26.

86. I am indebted to Hale Champion for emphasizing this point in many private conversations.

87. On the importance of structures of authority, see Jerry L. Mechling, "Analysis and Implementation: Sanitation Policies in New York City," *Public Policy,* vol. 26, no. 2 (Spring 1978): 278–283. On the importance of

deadlines to governmental decision-making, see Allison, *Essence of Decision,* p. 168.

88. John E. Chubb and Paul E. Peterson, eds., *Can the Government Govern?* (Washington, D.C.: Brookings Institution, 1989), pp. 20–37.

89. See n. 71.

90. Personal communication, March 9, 1995.

91. Stokey and Zeckhauser, *Primer,* pp. 5–6.

92. For a long list of references on this point, see Chapter 2, n. 26. See specifically Laurence E. Lynn, Jr., ed., *Knowledge and Power: The Uncertain Connection* (Washington, D.C.: National Academy of Sciences, 1978). For a critique, see Mark H. Moore, "Social Science v. Policy Analysis: Some Fundamental Differences," in Daniel Callahan and Bruce Jenning, eds., *Ethics: The Social Sciences and Policy Analysis* (New York: Plenum Publishing, 1983); and Lindblom, *Inquiry and Change.*

93. Moore, "Social Science v. Policy Analysis."

94. On the importance of estimating feasibility, see Graham T. Allison, "Implementation Analysis: 'The Missing Chapter' in Conventional Analysis," in *Benefit-Cost and Policy Analysis: 1974* (Chicago: Aldine Publishing, 1975), pp. 369–391.

95. Neustadt and Fineberg, *The Epidemic That Never Was,* pp. 232–236.

96. For a discussion of this relationship, see Arnold J. Meltsner, *Policy Analysts in the Bureaucracy* (Berkeley: University of California Press, 1976). See also Moore, "Social Science v. Policy Analysis." For a more sustained and radical critique of the potential for social science to contribute to public problem solving, see Lindblom, *Inquiry and Change.* For an idea of what the relationship could be, see Giandomenico Majone, "Policy Analysis and Public Deliberation," in Robert B. Reich, ed., *The Power of Public Ideas* (Cambridge, Mass.: Ballinger, 1988), pp. 157–178.

97. Raiffa, *Decision Analysis.*

98. It is precisely this subject that Neustadt and Fineberg focus their "reflections" on to great profit in *The Epidemic That Never Was,* pp. 116–137.

99. Lynn and Seidl, "Bottom Line Management." See also John M. Bryson, "Initiation of Strategic Planning by Governments," *Public Administration Review,* vol. 48, no. 6 (November–December 1988): 995–1004; James W. Fessler and Donald F. Kettl, "Budgeting," in *The Politics of the Administrative Process* (Chatham, N.J.: Chatham House, 1991), pp. 208–238; and Peter A. Pyhrr, "The Zero-Base Approach to Government Budgeting," in Shafritz and Hyde, *Classics,* pp. 495–505.

100. Policy management systems are closely related to strategic planning systems and budgeting systems used for strategic planning purposes. For key documents in this field, see note 81.

101. Allen Schick, "The Road to PPB: The Stages of Budget Reform," *Public Administration Review,* 26 (December 1966): 243–258, reprinted in Shafritz and Hyde, *Classics,* pp. 299–318. See also Fessler and Kettl,

"Budgeting," pp. 208–238; and Pyhrr, "The Zero-Base Approach," pp. 495–505.

102. Pyhrr, "The Zero-Base Approach." For some cases describing these budgeting systems, see Mills, "PPB and the Surgeon General," and Herzlinger and Clark, "Zero-Based Budgeting in the Public Health Service."

103. Darman is particularly critical of the fixed calendar features of both the budget systems and the more flexible systems proposed by Lynn and Seidl in "Bottom Line Management." In his view, the fixed calendar systems are too inflexible to deal with many of the problems (and opportunities!) that pop up in government. See Darman, "Policy Development Note #4," p. 4.

104. I had a particularly vivid personal experience with this difficulty. Roscoe Egger, then commissioner of the IRS, had asked his key staff and line subordinates to develop a strategic plan for the IRS. What he received from them was a document that closely resembled their budget submission. It identified all the major programs and activities of the organization and explained why they were important. He expressed dissatisfaction with this product because he thought a strategic plan should identify the relatively small number of areas in which innovations and investments could be expected to improve operations in the future—not describe everything that the organization was currently doing.

105. For cases describing policy management systems in regulatory agencies, see Moore, "Joan Claybrook and the National Highway Traffic Safety Administration," and Kennedy, "Managing EPA."

106. Porter, *Presidential Decisionmaking,* pp. 229–252.

107. Ibid., pp. 235–241.

108. On the dangers of viewing presidents in this way, see Laurence E. Lynn, Jr., and David DeF. Whitman, "The Perils of Policymaking," in *The President as Policymaker,* pp. 3–15.

109. Porter, *Presidential Decisionmaking,* pp. 231–235.

110. Ibid., pp. 241–247. This approach to decision-making has long been associated with Alexander L. George. See George, "The Case for Multiple Advocacy in Making Foreign Policy," *American Political Science Review,* 66 (September 1972): 751–785.

111. Porter, *Presidential Decisionmaking,* p. 177.

112. Darman, "Policy Development Note #4."

113. This is implicit in the separation he makes in his scheme for decisions that have "strategic" importance. Ibid., p. 3.

114. Heymann observes that "a strategy is a goal and plan giving coherence to an organization's activities. If it is something new and different, it represents an effort to bring about change, and change always fosters opposition." Heymann, *The Politics of Public Management,* p. 19.

115. Participation in that group could be used as a way of testing and building the capacity of those individuals who might become the key line managers

of the newly reoriented organization. Even in this case, however, most
decisions should be made on the basis of recommendations developed
through line rather than staff operations.

116. This focus is apparent in the emphasis that Darman gives to the function
of "relating issues to one another and to overall strategy." The point was
underscored in a meeting with Darman and Elliot Richardson, who was
the client of some of the systems that Darman developed in the Departments of State and Justice.

117. Hale Champion has expressed this view.

118. Lax and Sebenius, *The Manager as Negotiator,* pp. 29–45.

119. This is the ordinary assumption in economic analysis and was carried over
into both "game theory" and negotiation analysis. For an introduction to
game theory, see R. Duncan Luce and Howard Raiffa, *Games and Decisions* (New York: Wiley and Sons, 1967), pp. 3–6. For an introduction to
negotiation analysis, see Raiffa, *The Art and Science of Negotiation.*

120. On the idea of self-interest and politics, see John Ferejohn and Charles
Shipan, "Congressional Influence on Bureaucracy," and Morris P. Fiorina,
"Comment: The Problems with PPT," both in *Journal of Law, Economics,
and Organization,* vol. 6 (1990): 1–20 and 255–263, respectively.

121. Steven Kelman, *Making Public Policy: A Hopeful View of American Government* (New York: Basic Books, 1987), pp. 286–296. See also Gary Orren, "Beyond Self-Interest," and Steven Kelman, "Why Public Ideas Matter," in Reich, *The Power of Public Ideas,* pp. 13–30 and 31–54,
respectively.

122. Robert B. Reich, "Policy-Making in a Democracy," in Reich, *The Power
of Public Ideas,* pp. 123–156.

123. For some examples of situations where arguments about public interest
and duty were influential in building effective capacity to act, see Neustadt,
Presidential Power and the Modern Presidents: Roosevelt to Carter.

124. To analyze the outcomes of negotiating situations, analysts had to look at
the strategies of players in "reduced form." See Luce and Raiffa, *Games
and Decisions,* pp. 47–53.

125. Ibid., pp. 56–154.

126. Raiffa, *The Art and Science of Negotiation;* Lax and Sebenius, *The Manager as Negotiator.*

127. Lax and Sebenius, *The Manager as Negotiator,* pp. 70–74.

128. Neustadt, *Presidential Power and the Modern Presidents: Roosevelt to
Reagan,* pp. 50–90.

129. Lax and Sebenius, *The Manager as Negotiator,* pp. 246–254.

130. Ibid.

131. Ibid., pp. 226–237.

132. Ibid., p. 111.

133. Ibid., p. 11.

134. Ibid., pp. 84–86.

135. I believe that Roger Fisher and William Ury coined the phrase. See Fisher and Ury, *Getting to Yes,* pp. 97–106.
136. Lax and Sebenius, *The Manager as Negotiator,* pp. 29–45.
137. Thomas C. Schelling, *The Strategy of Conflict* (Cambridge, Mass.: Harvard University Press, 1960).
138. Fisher and Ury lay out the elements of "principled negotiation" in *Getting to Yes.*
139. Lax and Sebenius, *The Manager as Negotiator,* pp. 29–45.
140. Fisher and Ury take a different view and urge that parties to a negotiation adopt a principled stand. In their analysis, that will allow more negotiations to reach a satisfactory settlement, and reaching some agreement is generally better than having no agreement, which is a common outcome when people play too aggressively. See Fisher and Ury, *Getting to Yes.*
141. Lax and Sebenius, *The Manager as Negotiator,* pp. 218–230. See also James K. Sebenius, "Negotiation Arithmetic: Adding and Subtracting Issues and Parties," *International Organization,* vol. 37, no. 2 (Spring 1983): 281–316.
142. Lax and Sebenius, *The Manager as Negotiator,* pp. 46–62.
143. Lax and Sebenius recognize this criticism; ibid., pp. 237–241.
144. Recall the discussion of citizens in Chapter 2. The suggestion here is that something other than negotiation is necessary to develop and encourage expression of the values of "citizens," rather than "clients," whether "beneficiaries" or "obligatees."
145. These ideas are set out in Robert B. Reich, "Policy Making in a Democracy," and Ronald A. Heifetz and Riley M. Sinder, "Political Leadership: Managing the Public's Problem Solving," both in Reich, *The Power of Public Ideas,* pp. 137–147 and 179–203, respectively. See also Reich, *Public Management in a Democratic Society,* p. 175; and Ronald A. Heifetz, *Leadership without Easy Answers* (Cambridge, Mass.: Harvard University Press, 1994), pp. 125–149.
146. Heifetz, *Leadership,* pp. 235–236.
147. Heifetz makes an important distinction between "technical" and "adaptive" work; the first occurs when people in positions of authority know the answers; the second when answers are yet to be found, or when the solution involves adapting to a painful reality that cannot be changed. See Heifetz and Sinder, "Political Leadership," pp. 185–191; and Heifetz, *Leadership,* pp. 73–76.
148. Heifetz calls this creating an appropriate "holding environment." See Heifetz, *Leadership,* pp. 103–113.
149. Reich, "Policy Making in a Democracy," pp. 144–147.
150. Heifetz uses this idea of "adapting to a problematic reality" as key to his definition of leadership in *Leadership,* pp. 22–27.
151. See Robert B. Reich, "Public Administration and Public Deliberation: An Interpretive Essay," *Yale Law Journal,* vol. 94 (June 1985): 1617–1641; and

Arthur Applbaum, "Failure in the Marketplace of Ideas" (Kennedy School of Government, unpublished manuscript, 1993).

152. Reich, "Policy Making in a Democracy," pp. 144–147.

153. The events are described in Henry Lee and Esther Scott, "Managing Environmental Risk: The Case of Asarco," KSG Case #C16-88-847 (Cambridge, Mass.: Kennedy School of Government Case Program, 1988). The case is analyzed in Reich, "Policy Making in a Democracy," pp. 147–150, and in Heifetz, *Leadership,* pp. 88–100. I am simply repeating their analysis.

154. David L. Kirp, *Learning by Heart: AIDS and Schoolchildren in America's Communities* (New Brunswick, N.J.: Rutgers University Press, 1989), pp. 276–293.

155. Heifetz, *Leadership.* A different approach to "government learning" is usefully summarized in Lloyd Etheredge, "Government Learning: An Overview," in Samuel L. Long, ed., *The Handbook of Political Behavior,* vol. 2 (New York: Plenum Press, 1981), pp. 73–161. This article focuses more on how individual officials in high positions learn than on how citizens learn, but it is an extremely useful summary of some related ideas.

156. Heifetz, *Leadership,* pp. 194–201.

157. See n. 151.

158. Heifetz, *Leadership,* pp. 235–249.

159. Heifetz and Sinder, "Political Leadership," pp. 187–191.

160. Heifetz, *Leadership,* pp. 241–246.

161. The events are described in "Cancer and Environmental Hazards in Woburn, Massachusetts," KSG Cases #C16-86-659.0, #C16-86-660.0, #C16-86-660.1 (Cambridge, Mass.: Kennedy School of Government Case Program, 1986). The analysis presented here is mine.

162. The concept of "social marketing" is introduced and developed in Philip Kotler and Eduardo Roberto, *Social Marketing: Strategies for Changing Public Behavior* (New York: Free Press, 1989). See also Philip Kotler, "Social Marketing of Health Behavior," in L. W. Frederiksen, L. J. Solomon, and K. A. Brehany, eds., *Marketing Health Behavior* (New York: Plenum Press, 1984). For an excellent article reviewing the concepts of public sector marketing, the proper criteria for evaluating these campaigns, and the reported experience of one hundred media campaign efforts, see Janet A. Weiss and Mary Tschirhart, "Public Information Campaigns as Policy Instruments," *Journal of Policy Analysis and Management,* vol. 13, no. 1 (1994): 82–119. For some cases describing successful "strategic communication campaigns," see "Selling the Reorganization of the Post Office," KSG Case #C14-84-610.0 (Cambridge, Mass.: Kennedy School of Government Case Program, 1984), and "Please Be Patient: The Seattle Solid Waste Utility Meets the Press," KSG Case #C16-91-1058.0 (Cambridge, Mass.: Kennedy School of Government Case Program, 1991).

163. For criticisms of public information campaigns as propaganda, see Jacques Ellul, *Propaganda: The Formation of Men's Attitudes* (New York: Vintage,

1965), and Benjamin Ginsberg, *The Captive Public: How Mass Opinion Promotes State Power* (New York: Basic Books, 1986). For alternative, more hopeful views, see Walter Lippman, *Public Opinion* (New York: Free Press, 1981); Martin Linsky, "The Media and Public Deliberation," in Reich, *The Power of Public Ideas,* pp. 205–227; and Weiss and Tschirhart, "Public Information Campaigns as Policy Instruments."

164. R. Craig Lefebvre and June Flora, "Social Marketing and Public Health Intervention," *Health Education Quarterly,* vol. 15, no. 3 (Fall 1988): 300–301.

165. Even the police have begun surveying their clients: the general population, those who call for service, even those they arrest! See, for example, Frank Small and Associates, *Community Policing Initiatives in the Australian Capital Territory: 1992 Update* (Sydney, Australia: Frank Small Associates, 1992).

166. For a review of one hundred media campaign efforts, see Weiss and Tschirhart, "Public Information Campaigns as Policy Instruments." The public health field seems particularly interested and sophisticated in the development and use of these techniques. This may be because so many of their interventions depend on mobilizing large numbers of individuals to make important behavioral changes.

167. The events are described in Robert D. Behn, *Producing Results: How Public Managers Can Create a Culture of Performance* (Durham, N.C.: Governor's Center, Duke University, 1994). For a discussion of the theory of motivating people to want to pay their taxes, see Mark H. Moore, "On the Office of Taxpayer and the Social Process of Taxpaying," in Philip Sawicki, ed., *Income Tax Compliance* (Reston, Va.: American Bar Association, 1983).

168. Behn, *Producing Results,* chap. 3, pp. 7-9.

169. Ibid., pp. 19–21.

170. Ibid., chap. 4, pp. 9–17.

171. Ibid., chap. 5, pp. 3–6.

6. REENGINEERING PUBLIC SECTOR PRODUCTION

1. The distinction between leadership and management captures a great deal of attention. See, for example, John Kotter, *A Force for Change: How Leadership Differs from Management* (New York: Free Press; London: Collier Macmillan, 1990). For an argument that this distinction is not a useful one, see James Krantz and Thomas N. Gilmore, "The Splitting of Leadership and Management as a Social Defense," *Human Relations,* vol. 43, no. 2 (February 1990): 183–204.

2. This account is based on four cases written up by Esther Scott: "Managing the Boston Housing Authority: Note on Federal Public Housing Policy (1937–1980)," KSG Case #N16-85-626 (Cambridge, Mass.: Kennedy

School of Government Case Program, 1985); "The Boston Public Housing Authority (A)," KSG Case #C16-83-563 (Cambridge, Mass.: Kennedy School of Government Case Program, 1983); "The Boston Public Housing Authority (B)," KSG Case #C16-83-564 (Cambridge, Mass.: Kennedy School of Government Case Program, 1983); and "Managing the Boston Housing Authority: The Receivership Begins," KSG Case #C16-85-627 (Cambridge, Mass.: Kennedy School of Government Case Program, 1985). I have also benefited from personal conversations with Harry Spence, who was, for a while, my colleague at the Kennedy School.

3. Scott, "Boston Public Housing (A)," p. 1.
4. See the discussion of bankruptcy in the public sector in Chapters 2 and 3.
5. Scott, "Boston Public Housing (A)," p. 1.
6. "Voices from the Projects," *Boston Magazine,* vol. 73 (December 1981): 170, quoted in Scott, "Managing the Boston Housing Authority," p. 2.
7. Scott, "Managing the Boston Housing Authority," p. 3.
8. Ibid., p. 14.
9. Ibid., p. 13.
10. This account is based on Zachary Tumin, "Lee P. Brown and the Houston Police Department: Part A" and "Lee P. Brown and the Houston Police Department: Part B" (unpublished drafts, Kennedy School of Government, 1989).
11. Tumin, "Brown and the HPD: Part A," p. 8.
12. Ibid., p. 6.
13. Ibid., p. 8.
14. Ibid., p. 11.
15. Ibid.
16. Ibid.
17. Ibid.
18. Ibid., p. 14.
19. Ibid., p. 16.
20. Ibid., p. 19.
21. Ibid., p. 20.
22. Houston Police Department, *Assessment of the Department: Problems and Issues, September 1982* (Houston: Houston Police Department, 1982), p. ii.
23. Ibid.
24. Ibid., p. 61.
25. Ibid., pp. 64–65.
26. Ibid., p. 62.
27. Ibid., pp. 62–63.
28. See Robert C. Wood, *Remedial Law: When Courts Become Administrators* (Amherst: University of Massachusetts Press, 1990). Herbert Kaufman also found that public organizations did, sometimes, die. See Kaufman, *Are Government Organizations Immortal?* (Washington, D.C.: Brookings Institution, 1976), pp. 68–70.

29. See Chapter 2 for a theoretical discussion of this point. For a compelling introduction to organizations that impose obligations, see Malcolm Sparrow, *Imposing Duties: Government's Changing Approach to Compliance* (Westport, Conn.: Praeger, 1994).

30. How much public authorities can oblige their tenants to do has become an important issue as public housing projects have become centers of drug dealing and gang activity. For a discussion of how public housing authorities can use their power to drive these activities out of their projects, see Deborah Lamm Weisel, *Tackling Drug Problems in Public Housing: A Guide for Police* (Washington, D.C.: Police Executive Research Forum, 1990).

31. Herman Goldstein has offered the classic description of the variety of functions police must perform. See generally Goldstein, *Policing a Free Society* (Cambridge, Mass.: Ballinger, 1977).

32. For a discussion of the difficulties that public managers confront in finding the room to innovate, see Moore, *Accounting for Change: Reconciling the Demands for Accountability and Innovation in the Public Sector* (Washington, D.C.: Council for Excellence in Government, 1993), pp. 106–107. See also James Q. Wilson, *Bureaucracy: What Government Agencies Do and Why They Do It* (New York: Basic Books, 1989), pp. 218–232.

33. Herman B. Leonard, "Theory S vs. Theory T" (Kennedy School of Government, photocopy, 1984). See also Robert D. Behn, *Leadership Counts: Lessons for Public Managers from the Massachusetts Welfare, Training, and Employment Program* (Cambridge, Mass.: Harvard University Press, 1991), pp. 203–206.

34. Even the U.S. Mint might have to be strategically managed. In a discussion with a high-level official at the U.S. Bureau of Engraving and Printing, I learned that she was facing an important question about whether and how she should go into the business of serving coin collectors and competing with private companies such as the Franklin Mint in producing metal collectibles. In short, she found herself in the same position as the librarian of Chapter 1: heading a public organization that turned out to have a capability for producing things other than what its conventional mission required.

35. It is surprisingly difficult to measure or assess the overall operational performance of public sector organizations. The General Accounting Office (GAO) faced this task when it sought to produce "general management reviews" of federal departments. In the end, it found that all it could do was combine audits of management systems with rudimentary forms of program evaluations for a limited number of the programs operated by a particular department. The GAO could not assess productivity gains in core programs that had remained constant over a long period of time; nor could it assess the organization's ability to adapt to changing political expectations. For examples of these reports, see U.S. General Accounting

Office, *Increasing the Department of Housing and Urban Development's Effectiveness through Improved Management,* vols. 1 and 2 (Washington, D.C.: GAO, 1984); and U.S. General Accounting Office, *Social Security Administration: Stable Leadership and Better Management Needed to Improve Effectiveness* (Washington, D.C.: GAO, 1987).

36. Here I am following Laurence E. Lynn, Jr., who observed: "Translating public mandates into operating results requires governmental organizations and their leaders to understand and pay continuing attention to the technologies of product and service delivery." See Lynn, *Managing Public Policy* (Boston: Little, Brown, 1987), pp. 70–71. For a private sector analogy, see Michael Hammer, *Re-Engineering the Corporation: A Manifesto for Business Revolution* (New York: HarperBusiness, 1993).

37. Herbert Kaufmann presents an elegant account of one organization that has neatly adapted to its environment. See Kaufmann, *The Forest Ranger* (Baltimore: Johns Hopkins University Press, 1960). For an equally good account of an organization adapting to change, see Martha Derthick, *Agency under Stress: The Social Security Administration in American Government* (Washington, D.C.: Brookings Institution, 1990).

38. This is the only kind of innovation that James Q. Wilson thinks is worth calling an innovation. See Wilson, *Bureaucracy,* p. 225.

39. For a discussion of this problem as well as some cases that present concrete examples of public sector managers facing the challenge of innovating, see Moore, *Accounting for Change.*

40. Terrence E. Deal and Allan A. Kennedy, *Corporate Cultures: The Rites and Rituals of Corporate Life* (Reading, Mass.: Addison-Wesley, 1982), p. 23.

41. Max D. Richards, *Organizational Goal Structures* (St. Paul, Minn.: West Publishing, 1978), pp. 1–35.

42. Ibid., pp. 6–7.

43. Kenneth Andrews, for example, observes: "While long-range plans may be couched in relatively general terms, operating plans will often take the form of relatively detailed budgets. These can meet the need for the establishment of standards against which short-term performance can be judged." Andrews, *The Concept of Corporate Strategy* (Homewood, Ill.: Irwin, 1987), p. 111.

44. This seems to be the view of Herbert Simon: "There is no essential difference between a 'purpose' and a 'process' but only a distinction of degree. A 'process' is an activity whose immediate purpose is at a low level in the hierarchy of means and ends, while a 'purpose' is a collection of activities whose orienting value or aim is at a high level in the means-end hierarchy." Simon, "The Proverbs of Administration," reprinted in Jay M. Shafritz and Albert C. Hyde, eds., *Classics of Public Administration,* 2d ed. (Chicago: Dorsey Press, 1987), p. 171.

45. Richards, *Organizational Goal Structures,* pp. 89–109.

46. For a discussion of the goals of the public housing policy of the federal government, see Eugene J. Meehan, *The Quality of Federal Policymaking* (Columbia: University of Missouri Press, 1979).

47. For a description of the evolution of this strategic concept, see Malcolm K. Sparrow, Mark H. Moore, and David M. Kennedy, *Beyond 911: A New Era for Policing* (New York: Basic Books, 1990), pp. 30–57. See also George L. Kelling and Mark H. Moore, "The Evolving Strategy of Policing," *Perspectives on Policing,* no. 4 (Washington, D.C.: National Institute of Justice, and Cambridge, Mass.: Kennedy School of Government, 1988).

48. George L. Kelling et al., *The Kansas City Preventative Patrol Experiment: A Summary Report* (Washington, D.C.: Police Foundation, 1974).

49. William G. Spelman and Dale K. Brown, *Calling the Police: Citizen Reporting of Serious Crime* (Washington, D.C.: National Institute of Justice, 1984).

50. Peter W. Greenwood, Jan M. Chaiken, and Joan Petersilia, *The Criminal Investigation Process* (Lexington, Mass.: D. C. Heath, 1977); John Eck, *Solving Crimes: The Investigation of Burglary and Robbery* (Washington, D.C.: Police Executive Research Forum, 1984).

51. Sparrow, Moore, and Kennedy, *Beyond 911,* pp. 95–125. For a discussion of the evidence on the effectiveness of alternative strategies of policing such as "community policing" or "problem-solving policing," see Mark H. Moore, "Community and Problem-Solving Policing," in Michael Tonry and Norval Morris, eds., *Modern Policing* (Chicago: University of Chicago Press, 1992), pp. 99–158. See also Dennis Rosenbaum, *The Challenge of Community Policing* (Thousand Oaks, Calif.: Sage, 1994).

52. For a general view of the capacity of communities to defend themselves, see Dennis P. Rosenbaum, ed., *Community Crime Prevention: Does It Work?* (Thousand Oaks, Calif.: Sage, 1986).

53. Mark H. Moore and Robert Trojanowicz, "Policing and the Fear of Crime," *Perspectives on Policing,* no. 3 (Washington, D.C.: National Institute of Justice and Kennedy School of Government, 1988).

54. Ibid.

55. James Q. Wilson and George L. Kelling, "Police and Neighborhood Safety: Broken Windows," *Atlantic Monthly,* March 1982, 29–38.

56. Anthony M. Pate, Mary Ann Wycoff, Wesley G. Skogan, and Lawrence W. Sherman, *Reducing Fear of Crime in Houston and Newark: A Summary Report* (Washington, D.C.: Police Foundation, 1986).

57. John E. Boydstun, Michael E. Sherry, and Nicholas P. Moelter, *Patrol Staff in San Diego: One- or Two-Officer Units* (Washington, D.C.: Police Foundation, 1977), Table 18, p. 28.

58. Mark H. Moore and Darrel W. Stephens, *Beyond Command and Control: The Strategic Management of Police Departments* (Washington, D.C.: Police Executive Research Forum, 1991).

59. Herman Goldstein, *Problem-Oriented Policing* (New York: McGraw-Hill, 1990), pp. 32–34.

60. Lawrence W. Sherman, P. R. Garten, and M. E. Burger, "Hot Spots of Predatory Crime: Routing Activities in the Criminology of Place," *Criminology,* vol. 21 (February 1989): 27–55.
61. Goldstein, *Problem-Oriented Policing,* pp. 32–49.
62. Sparrow, Moore, and Kennedy, *Beyond 911,* pp. 97–104.
63. For a general discussion of these techniques, see Goldstein, *Problem-Oriented Policing.* For a description of how these techniques work in practice, see John E. Eck, William Spelman, Diane Hill, Darrel W. Stephens, John R. Stedman, and Gerard R. Murphy, *Problem-Solving: Problem Oriented Policing in Newport News* (Washington, D.C.: Police Executive Research Forum, 1987).
64. This operation is the subject of a videotape produced by the Santa Ana, California, Police Department as a training film.
65. The logic that links desired products to particular production processes and administrative systems is illustrated in Mark H. Moore, "A Feasibility Estimate of a Policy Decision to Expand Methadone Maintenance," *Public Policy,* vol. 26, no. 2 (Spring 1978): 285–304.
66. I am indebted to my colleague Robert Leone for emphasizing this point. It is further developed in the context of private sector service enterprises by James L. Heskett, W. Earl Sasser, and Christopher W. L. Hart, *Service Breakthroughs: Breaking the Rules of the Game* (New York: Free Press, 1990).
67. Scott, "Managing the Boston Housing Authority," p. 11.
68. Michael T. Farmer, *Survey of Police Operational and Administrative Practices* (Washington, D.C.: Police Executive Research Forum, 1978).
69. Philadelphia Police Study Task Force, *Philadelphia and Its Police: Toward a New Relationship* (Philadelphia: Philadelphia Police Study Task Force, 1987), p. 129.
70. For a discussion of the importance of legal institutions' being able to account for their use of legal authority to show that authority has been used properly, see Kenneth Culp Davis, *Discretionary Justice: A Preliminary Inquiry* (Baton Rouge: Louisiana State University Press, 1969).
71. For a discussion of the importance of reducing discretion in the administration of justice, see James Vorenberg, "Narrowing the Discretion of Criminal Justice Officials," *Duke Law Journal,* vol. 1976, no. 4 (1976): 651–697.
72. For a vivid factual account of the varied circumstances officers encounter, see Jonathan Rubinstein, *City Police* (New York: Farrar, Straus, and Giroux, 1973). For a fictional account, see Joseph Wambaugh, *The Blue Knight* (Boston: Little, Brown, 1972).
73. Sparrow, Moore, and Kennedy, *Beyond 911.* See also Mark H. Moore, William Spelman, and Malcolm Sparrow, "Police Innovation: From Production Lines to Job Shops," in Alan Altshuler and Robert Behn, eds., *Research on Innovations in State and Local Government* (Washington, D.C.: Urban Institute, forthcoming).

74. Claude Lévi-Strauss, *The Savage Mind* (Chicago: University of Chicago Press, 1966), pp. 16–36.

75. For a glimpse into the culture of the Houston Police Department at the time, and in particular its attitudes toward the use of deadly force and the role of women, see Kenneth Winston, "A Policewoman's (Non)Use of Deadly Force," KSG Case #C16-91-1040 (Cambridge, Mass.: Kennedy School of Government Case Program, 1991).

76. This attitude is not limited to Houston. See Mark H. Moore, "Police Accountability, Police Culture, and the 'Dirty Deal,'" *Governing,* vol. 4, no. 11 (August 1991): 9.

77. Robert M. Fogelson, *Big City Police: An Urban Institute Study* (Cambridge, Mass.: Harvard University Press, 1977).

78. Sparrow, Moore, and Kennedy, *Beyond 911,* pp. 50–54. For a more extended description, see Arthur Niederhoffer, *Behind the Shield: The Police in Urban Society* (Garden City, N.J.: Doubleday, 1967).

79. Sparrow, Moore, and Kennedy, *Beyond 911,* pp. 54–57.

80. Wesley G. Skogan, *Disorder and Decline: Crime and the Spiral of Decay in American Neighborhoods* (New York: Free Press, 1990), pp. 113–114.

81. Leonard, "Theory S and Theory T." See also Behn, *Leadership Counts,* pp. 203–206.

82. For a discussion of why formalization and traditional bureaucratic forms suit police departments so well, see Mark H. Moore, "Policing: Deregulating or Redefining Accountability," in John DiIulio, Jr., ed., *Deregulating the Public Service: Can Government Be Improved* (Washington: D.C.: Brookings Institution, 1994), pp. 198–235.

83. Fogelson, *Big City Police.*

84. For a discussion of the impact of the Unified Crime Reports on policing, see Dennis W. Banas and Robert C. Trojanowicz, "Uniform Crime Reporting and Community Policing: A Historical Perspective," *Community Policing Series,* no. 5 (Ann Arbor: Michigan State University, National Foot Patrol Center, 1985). See also George L. Kelling and James K. Stewart, "The Evolution of Contemporary Policing," in William Geller, ed., *Local Government Police Management,* 3d ed. (Washington, D.C.: International City Management Association, 1991), pp. 3–21.

85. For a discussion of the measurement of police performance, see Geoffrey Alpert and Mark H. Moore, "Measuring Police Performance in the New Paradigm of Policing," in John DiIulio, Jr., ed., *Performance Measures for the Criminal Justice System,* Discussion Papers from the Bureau of Justice Statistics-Princeton Project (Washington, D.C.: U.S. Department of Justice, 1993).

86. Wesley Skogan, "Dimensions of the 'Dark Figure' of Unreported Crime," *Crime and Delinquency,* vol. 23 (January 1977): 41–50.

87. Chester I. Barnard, *The Functions of the Executive* (Cambridge, Mass.: Harvard University Press, 1966), pp. 167–171.

88. Wilson, *Bureaucracy,* pp. 230–232.

89. Moore, *Accounting for Change,* pp. 119–122.

90. For a vivid example of how the press penalizes public managers for inno- vative efforts, see Esther Scott, "Managing a Press 'Feeding Frenzy': Gre- gory Coler and the Florida Department of Health and Rehabilitative Services," KSG Case #C16-92-1135.0 (Cambridge, Mass.: Kennedy School of Government Case Program, 1992).

91. For an interesting example of this phenomenon, see David M. Kennedy, "Fighting Fear in Baltimore County," KSG Case #C16-90-938.0 (Cam- bridge, Mass.: Kennedy School of Government Case Program, 1990).

92. Moore, Spelman, and Sparrow, "Police Innovation: From Production Lines to Job Shops."

93. For an excellent discussion of what it means to be "learning" organizations and what it takes to produce them, see Chris Argyris and Donald Schon, *Organizational Learning: A Theory of Action Perspective* (Reading, Mass.: Addison-Wesley, 1978).

94. Peter M. Senge, *The Fifth Discipline: The Art and Practice of the Learning Organization* (New York: Doubleday, 1990), p. 188.

95. Rosabeth Moss Kanter, *When Giants Learn to Dance: Mastering the Chal- lenge of Strategy, Management, and Careers in the 1990's* (New York: Simon and Schuster, 1989), pp. 152–155.

96. Thomas J. Peters and Robert H. Waterman, *In Search of Excellence: Lessons from America's Best-Run Companies* (New York: Warner, 1982), pp. 284–285.

97. Lee P. Brown, "Community Policing: A Practical Guide," *Perspectives on Policing,* no. 12 (Washington, D.C.: National Institute of Justice, and Cambridge, Mass.: Kennedy School of Government, 1989).

98. Jay Galbraith, *Designing Complex Organizations* (Reading, Mass.: Ad- dison-Wesley, 1973), pp. 15–16.

7. IMPLEMENTING STRATEGY

1. Richard F. Vancil, *Implementing Strategy: The Role of Top Management* (Boston: Division of Research, Harvard Business School, 1982), available from HBS Case Services.

2. President Harry S. Truman learned that not even presidents can command events. He vented some of his irritation by imagining how frustrated General Eisenhower would become as president. "He'll just sit behind this desk and say, 'Do this and do that,' and you know what will happen? Nothing." Quoted in Richard E. Neustadt, *Presidential Power and the Modern Presidents: The Politics of Leadership from Roosevelt to Reagan* (New York: Free Press, 1990), p. 10.

3. Laurence E. Lynn, Jr., and John M. Seidl, "Bottom-Line Management for Public Agencies," *Harvard Business Review,* vol. 55, no. 1 (1977). See also

Thomas North Gilmore, *Making a Leadership Change: How Organizations and Leaders Can Handle Leadership Transitions Successfully* (San Francisco: Jossey-Bass, 1988).
4. For a general description of what public managers do, see Herbert Kaufman, *The Administrative Behavior of Federal Bureau Chiefs* (Washington, D.C.: Brookings Institution, 1981).
5. Thomas J. Peters, "Leadership: Sad Tales in Silver Linings," *Harvard Business Review,* no. 79611 (1979): 164–172.
6. In describing Spence's interventions and their consequences, I am relying primarily on Esther Scott, "Managing the Boston Housing Authority: The Receivership Begins," KSG Case #C16-85-627 (Cambridge, Mass.: Kennedy School of Government Case Program, 1985); and Esther Scott, "The Boston Public Housing Authority (B)," KSG Case #C16-83-564 (Cambridge, Mass.: Kennedy School of Government Case Program, 1983).
7. Scott, "Managing the Boston Housing Authority," p. 32.
8. Scott, "Boston Public Housing (B)," p. 1.
9. Ibid., p. 3.
10. Ibid., p. 7.
11. For a general discussion of procurement issues, see Steven Kelman, *The Fear of Discretion and the Quality of Government Performance* (Washington, D.C.: AEI Press, 1990).
12. Scott, "Boston Public Housing (B)," p. 8.
13. Ibid., p. 9.
14. Ibid., p. 10.
15. Ibid., p. 6.
16. Ibid., p. 10.
17. Ibid., p. 15.
18. Ibid., p. 16.
19. Ibid.
20. Ibid., p. 17.
21. Ibid.
22. Ibid., p. 18.
23. Ibid.
24. Ibid., p. 20.
25. Ibid., p. 21.
26. Ibid.
27. Ibid., p. 22.
28. Ibid., p. 23.
29. Ibid., p. 25.
30. Ibid.
31. Robert N. Anthony and Regina Herzlinger, *Management Control in Nonprofit Organizations* (Homewood, Ill.: Irwin, 1975), pp. 17–18.
32. Scott, "Boston Public Housing (B)," p. 26.
33. Ibid.

34. Ibid.
35. Ibid.
36. Ibid., p. 27.
37. Ibid.
38. Ibid.
39. Ibid., p. 30.
40. Ibid.
41. Ibid.
42. Ibid., p. 34.
43. The account of the thoughts, actions, and consequences of Brown's inter-ventions is based on Zachary Tumin, "Lee P. Brown and the Houston Police Department: Part A" and "Lee P. Brown and the Houston Police Department: Part B" (unpublished drafts, Kennedy School of Government, 1989).
44. Tumin, "Brown and the HPD: Part A," p. 29.
45. Ibid.
46. Ibid.
47. Ibid.
48. Tumin, "Brown and the HPD: Part B," p. 5.
49. Houston Police Department, *Assessment of the Department: Problems and Issues, September 1982* (Houston: Houston Police Department, 1982), pp. 64–65.
50. Ibid., p. 65.
51. Ibid.
52. Ibid., p. 67.
53. Ibid.
54. Ibid.
55. Tumin, "Brown and the HPD: Part B," p. 9.
56. Ibid.
57. Ibid., p. 11.
58. Ibid., p. 12.
59. Ibid.
60. Lee P. Brown, *Plan of Action, April 1983* (Houston: Houston Police Department, 1983), p. 1.
61. Ibid.
62. Ibid., pp. 4–8.
63. Wilson believes this situation is one in which executives can make a big difference in the performance of their organizations. See Wilson, *Bureaucracy,* p. 217.
64. This argument is developed further in Mark H. Moore, "Police Leadership: The Impossible Dream?" in Erwin C. Hargrove and John C. Glidewell, eds., *Impossible Jobs in Public Management* (Lawrence: University of Kansas Press, 1991).
65. Brown, *Plan of Action,* p. 8.

66. Malcolm K. Sparrow, Mark H. Moore, and David M. Kennedy, *Beyond 911: A New Era for Policing* (New York: Basic Books, 1990), pp. 96–97.
67. Herman Goldstein, *Problem-Oriented Policing* (Philadelphia: Temple University Press, 1990).
68. Tumin, "Brown and the HPD: Part B," p. 17.
69. Ibid., p. 19.
70. Ibid., p. 22.
71. Ibid., p. 20.
72. Ibid., p. 21.
73. Ibid.
74. The management literature comes from both the private and public sectors. The private sector management literature includes classics such as Chester Barnard, *The Functions of the Executive* (Cambridge, Mass.: Harvard University Press, 1938); Peter F. Drucker, *Management: Tasks, Responsibilities, Practices* (New York: Harper and Row, 1973); Michael E. Porter, *Competitive Strategy: Techniques for Analyzing Industries and Competitors* (New York: Free Press, 1980); and Thomas J. Peters and Robert H. Waterman, *In Search of Excellence: Lessons from America's Best-Run Companies* (New York: Warner, 1982). The public management literature includes: Laurence E. Lynn, Jr., *Managing the Public's Business: The Job of the Government Executive* (New York: Basic Books, 1981); Gordon Chase and Elizabeth C. Reveal, *How to Manage in the Public Sector* (Reading, Mass.: Addison-Wesley, 1983); Jameson Doig and Erwin C. Hargrove, *Leadership and Innovation: A Biographical Perspective on Entrepreneurs in Government* (Baltimore: Johns Hopkins University Press, 1987); Laurence E. Lynn, *Managing Public Policy* (Boston: Little, Brown, 1987); Philip B. Heymann, *The Politics of Public Management* (New Haven, Conn.: Yale University Press, 1987); Steven Kelman, *Procurement and Public Management: The Fear of Discretion and the Quality of Government Performance* (Washington, D.C.: AEI Press, 1990); Erwin C. Hargrove and John C. Glidewell, eds., *Impossible Jobs in Public Management* (Lawrence: University of Kansas Press, 1991); Robert D. Behn, *Leadership Counts: Lessons for Public Managers from the Massachusetts Welfare, Training, and Employment Program* (Cambridge, Mass.: Harvard University Press, 1991); Martin A. Levin and Mary Bryna Sanger, *Making Government Work: How Entrepreneurial Executives Turn Bright Ideas into Real Results* (San Francisco: Jossey-Bass, 1994); and Richard N. Haass, *The Power to Persuade: How to Be Effective in Government, the Public Sector, or Any Unruly Organization* (Boston: Houghton Mifflin, 1994).
75. James Q. Wilson, for example, observes that many public sector executives focus a great deal of their attention on establishing their autonomy. Indeed, in a challenge to prevailing economic theories of bureaucracy, he thinks public executives often prefer autonomy to growth. See Wilson,

Bureaucracy, pp. 179–195. In his view, this need derives from their interest in meeting their special responsibilities to maintain their organizations at the lowest possible cost. As he observes, "To a government executive, an increase in the autonomy of his or her agency lowers the cost of organizational maintenance by minimizing the number of stakeholders and bureaucratic rivals and maximizing the opportunity for agency operators to develop a cohesive sense of mission" (p. 183). Note that Wilson offers this as a positive statement, not a normative one. He assumes that, on average, executives' principal interests lie in keeping things on an even keel and not doing any heavy lifting. If, however, an executive wants to change the course of an agency and is willing to do a great deal of work to accomplish this objective, one of the important paths he or she can take is to embrace those elements of the external environment that are demanding change.

76. For an example of an executive who was particularly skillful in insulating his organization from external accountability and demands for change, see the description of Hyman Rickover provided by Eugene Lewis: "Admiral Hyman Rickover: Technological Entrepreneurship in the U.S. Navy," in James W. Doig and Erwin C. Hargrove, eds., *Leadership and Innovation: Entrepreneurs in Government* (Baltimore: Johns Hopkins University Press, 1990).

77. For an illustrative account of conflicting pressures applied on the organization and its managers, see Gary E. Miller and Ira Iscoe, "A State Mental Health Commissioner and the Politics of Mental Illness," in Hargrove and Glidewell, *Impossible Jobs in Public Management.* John Chubb and Terry Moe think that conflicting political demands are the principal causes of school failure in the United States. See Chubb and Moe, *Politics, Markets, and America's Schools* (Washington, D.C.: Brookings Institution, 1990).

78. Rickover stands as an example at the opposite edge. See Lewis, "Admiral Hyman Rickover," pp. 84–87.

79. This mechanism was also key to Patrick Murphy's success in controlling corruption in the New York City Police Department in the era of the Knapp Commission. Without the Knapp Commission's continuing existence, Murphy could neither have taken the aggressive internal actions he did to control corruption, nor have expected his actions to have had the same effect. See "The Knapp Commission and Patrick Murphy," KSG Case #C14-77-181.0 (Cambridge, Mass.: Kennedy School of Government Case Program, 1977).

80. In this respect, they exploited one of the strategies Hargrove and Doig identified as being available to public sector entrepreneurs. They observed that political "fragmentation ... yields opportunities for initiative in building political coalitions that are not as readily available in a coherent and tightly run governmental system; and those possibilities attract men and women interested in this kind of entrepreneurial activity." Doig and Hargrove, *Leadership and Innovation: A Biographical Perspective,* p. 9.

81. Selznick, Wilson, and other theorists have long understood the importance of external, political environments in *establishing* and *institutionalizing* organizational purposes. Thus, for example, Selznick observes:
"As a business, a college, or a government agency develops a distinctive
clientele, the enterprise gains the stability that comes from a secure
source of support, and easy channel of communication." Philip Selznick,
Leadership in Administration: A Sociological Interpretation, rev. ed.
(Berkeley: University of California Press, 1984), p. 7. What is less commonly recognized is that these same external pressures are key to *dis-
establishing* or *changing* organizational purposes as well. Indeed, they
may be the only solvent that can dissolve past commitments. So, if executives wish to change their organization's purpose or mission, they
will have to embrace external accountability to do so. That is the interesting lesson of these cases in which the executives are seeking change
rather than continuity.

82. For an analysis of real public sector bankruptcies, see Robert C. Wood,
Remedial Law: When Courts Become Administrators (Amherst: University of Massachusetts Press, 1990).

83. The classic example is David Lilienthal at the Tennessee Valley Authority.
For an insightful analysis, see Erwin C. Hargrove, "David Lilienthal and
the Tennessee Valley Authority," in James W. Doig and Erwin C. Hargrove, *Leadership and Innovation: Entrepreneurs in Government* (Baltimore: Johns Hopkins University Press, 1990), pp. 25–60.

84. For a measure of the disaster that comes from being too "autonomous,"
see Robert Caro, *The Power Broker: Robert Moses and the Fall of New
York* (New York: Knopf, 1974).

85. Woodrow Wilson described the crucial importance of maintaining constant contact with the popular will: "The idea for us is a civil service
cultured and self-sufficient enough to act with sense and vigor, and yet so
intimately connected with the popular thought, by means of elections and
constant public counsel, as to find arbitrariness or class spirit quite out of
the question." Wilson, "The Study of Administration," in Jay M. Shafritz
and Albert C. Hyde, eds., *Classics of Public Administration,* 2d ed. (Chicago: Dorsey Press, 1987), p. 22.

86. Rosabeth Moss Kanter gives the external environment of an organization
an important role to play in stimulating organizational innovation and
improvement in the private sector: "The external world surrounding an
organization and poking and prodding it in numerous ways is obviously
important in stimulating change." Kanter, *The Change Masters: Innovation and Entrepreneurship in the American Corporation* (New York: Simon and Schuster, 1983), p. 280.

87. Ronald A. Heifetz gives a particularly vivid account of the pressures on
leaders to fulfill the expectations of their followers rather than to confront
employees with the challenge of doing the adaptive work they do not want

to do. See Heifetz, *Leadership without Easy Answers* (Cambridge, Mass.: Harvard University Press, 1994), pp. 69–73.

88. Robert Behn's work suggests that the creation of external demands on organizations may be important even in situations where the politics surrounding an organization are quiescent and where managers seek "program" innovations as well as "strategic" innovations. The idea appears in Behn, "A Curmudgeon's View of Public Administration," *State and Local Government Review,* Spring 1987, 47, 54–61. He then presents a compelling example in Behn, *Leadership Counts.*

89. Thomas Gilmore identifies subordinates as some of the most powerful instruments for making important strategic changes in organizations, particularly when organizations are going through leadership changes. See Gilmore, *Making a Leadership Change: How Organizations and Leaders Can Handle Leadership Transitions Successfully* (San Francisco: Jossey-Bass, 1988).

90. John Kotter believes this is one of the things that make managers successful. See Kotter, *The General Managers* (New York: Free Press; London: Collier Macmillan, 1986).

91. Alfred D. Chandler long ago observed the crucial connection between the selection of an organizational strategy and a consistent organizational structure. See Chandler, *Strategy and Structure: Chapters in the History of the Industrial Enterprise* (Cambridge, Mass.: MIT Press, 1962).

92. For a clear exposition of these different organizational logics, and a thorough discussion of the uses that managers may make of organizational structure to shape organizational activity and purpose, see Henry Mintzberg, *The Structuring of Organizations: A Synthesis of the Research* (Englewood Cliffs, N.J.: Prentice-Hall, 1979), pp. 108–115.

93. This link between the embrace of external accountability and the ability to demand a high degree of internal accountability is, again, most vivid in Patrick Murphy's efforts to control police corruption in New York City. See n. 79.

94. Behn describes a similar process used by Chet Atkins to manage the implementation of "Employment Training Choices" in the Massachusetts Welfare Department. See Behn, *Leadership Counts,* pp. 49–82.

95. On the role of budgeting in the management control process in nonprofit organizations, see Anthony and Herzlinger, *Management Control in Nonprofit Organizations,* pp. 227–258. For a discussion of budgeting in the public sector, see Allen Schick, "The Road to PPB: The Stages of Budget Reform," *Public Administration Review,* vol. 26 (December 1966): 243–258.

96. For another example of a manager facing a similar trade-off and making a different choice, see "The MBTA: The Budget Process (A)," KSG Case #C16-79-249.0, and "The MBTA: The Budget Process (B)," KSG Case #C16-79-250.0 (both Cambridge, Mass.: Kennedy School of Government Case Program, 1979).

97. Richard G. Darman, "Policy Development Note #4: Propositions for Discussion on Recent Progress and Remaining Problems in the Design of Policy Development Systems" (Kennedy School of Government, photocopy, 1980).

98. John M. Bryson, *Strategic Planning for Public and Nonprofit Organizations* (San Francisco: Jossey-Bass, 1988), p. 7.

99. This happened a little bit later as the political support for Brown's program collapsed in Houston following the defeat of Mayor Kathryn Whitmire in November 1991.

100. Kaufmann, *Federal Bureau Chiefs,* pp. 77–78.

101. For a discussion of innovating in the private sector, see Kanter, *The Change Masters;* and Donald K. Clifford and Richard Cavanagh, *The Winning Performance: How America's High-Growth Midsize Companies Succeed* (New York: Bantam, 1985).

102. For a discussion of the distinction between a significant "program innovation," on the one hand, and a "strategic innovation," on the other, see Mark H. Moore, "Gordon Chase and Public Sector Innovation," paper presented at the ninth annual meeting of the Association for Public Policy Analysis and Management, Seattle, Washington, October 30, 1987.

103. Malcolm Sparrow discusses the impact that innovations have in tilting organizations toward new purposes and in unfreezing them more generally. See Sparrow, "Implementing Community Policing," *Perspectives on Policing,* no. 9 (Washington, D.C.: National Institute of Justice, and Cambridge, Mass.: Kennedy School of Government, 1988).

104. Moore, "Gordon Chase and Public Sector Innovation."

105. Sparrow, "Implementing Community Policing."

106. Wilson gives a definition of an organization's core technology, explains why it is so difficult to change, and suggests the conditions under which it can be changed. See Wilson, *Bureaucracy,* pp. 221–232.

107. In this conviction, Brown joined many other police managers. See Sparrow, Moore, and Kennedy, *Beyond 911.*

108. Lee P. Brown, "Community Policing: A Practical Guide for Police Officials," *Perspectives on Policing,* no. 12 (Washington, D.C.: National Institute of Justice, and Cambridge, Mass.: Kennedy School of Government, 1989).

109. For an account of the problems faced in this effort, see David M. Kennedy, "Computer-Aided Police Dispatching in Houston, Texas," KSG Case #C16-90-985.0 (Cambridge, Mass.: Kennedy School of Government Case Program, 1990).

110. The role of clients in coproducing governmental results is discussed in David Osborne and Ted Gaebler, *Reinventing Government: How the Entrepreneurial Spirit Is Transforming the Public Sector from Schoolhouse to Statehouse, City Hall to the Pentagon* (Reading, Mass.: Addison-Wesley, 1992), pp. 49–75.

111. Ibid.

112. Henry Mintzberg, *Structure in Fives: Designing Effective Organizations* (Englewood Cliffs, N.J.: Prentice-Hall, 1993), pp. 53–54; 95.

113. Michael Barzelay with Babak Armajani, *Breaking through Bureaucracy: A New Vision for Managing in Government* (Berkeley: University of California Press, 1992), pp. 3–5.

114. Ibid.

115. The phrases for the private sector were developed in Peters and Waterman, *In Search of Excellence.* These themes are adapted for public sector use in Osborne and Gaebler, *Reinventing Government.*

116. Anthony and Herzlinger, *Management Control in Nonprofit Organizations.*

117. On the role of external environments in encouraging innovation, and the design of innovative organizations, see Kanter, *The Change Masters,* and Peter M. Senge, *The Fifth Discipline: The Art and Practice of the Learning Organization* (New York: Doubleday, 1990).

118. On the distinction between leadership and management, see John Kotter, *A Force for Change: How Leadership Differs from Management* (New York: Free Press; London: Collier Macmillan, 1990). For an interpretation of this distinction as a defensive device, see James Krantz and Thomas N. Gilmore, "The Splitting of Leadership and Management as a Social Defense," *Human Relations,* vol. 43, no. 2 (February 1990): 183–204. For an interesting definition of leadership as the challenge of helping groups and organizations do "adaptive work" and the difficulty of exercising this kind of leadership from positions of authority, see Heifetz, *Leadership without Easy Answers.*

119. According to Heifetz, managing the "pace of learning" is an important requirement for leadership. See Heifetz, *Leadership without Easy Answers,* pp. 241–246.

120. "Partners," too, are an important component of what Heifetz prescribes for effective leadership. Ibid., pp. 268–273.

121. Edward Banfield develops the difference between the "administrative" work of the manager and the "substantive" work of the organization. He also observes that the first should be subordinated to the second, and that many of the calculations made will be guided by "art" rather than "science," and particularly not the "science" of administration. See Banfield, "The Training of the Executive," *Public Policy,* vol. 10 (1960): 16–43.

122. Kanter also noted the importance of improvisation by top-level managers in the organizations she observed. "It may be more accurate to speak of a series of smaller decisions made over time than a single dramatic strategic decision . . . There may be key meetings at which a critical piece of what later became 'the' strategy was formulated, a plan or mission statement generated that articulated a commitment, or an important 'go-ahead' direction issued." Kanter, *The Change Masters,* p. 295. The improvisational

nature of much managerial activity is also captured by Behn in his concept of "groping"; see *Leadership Counts,* pp. 127–150. For an interesting case describing just this sort of process, which eventually developed into an overall strategy, see "Ellen Schall and the Department of Juvenile Justice," KSG Case #C16-87-793.0 (Cambridge, Mass.: Kennedy School of Government Case Program, 1987).

123. On the importance of maintaining momentum, consider Gordon Chase's actions in developing a large scale methadone maintenance program in New York City in the early seventies. See "Methadone Maintenance," KSG Case #C14-76-65.0 (Cambridge, Mass.: Kennedy School of Government Case Program, 1976).

CONCLUSION

1. Malcolm Sparrow and I set out these conflicting images in Mark H. Moore and Malcolm K. Sparrow, *Ethics in Government: The Moral Challenges of Public Leadership* (Englewood Cliffs, N.J.: Prentice-Hall, 1990), p. 21.

2. Herbert Kaufman, in his classic discussion of three core values that citizens seek to have expressed in the processes of government, describes this idea as the "pursuit of non-partisan competence." See Kaufman, "Emerging Conflicts in the Doctrines of Public Administration," *American Political Science Review,* vol. 50, no. 4 (December 1956): 1057–1073.

3. For an account, read Telford Taylor, *The Anatomy of the Nuremberg Trials: A Personal Memoir* (New York: Knopf, 1992). John P. Burke recognizes the Nuremberg principles as establishing an obligation for public officials to act on moral convictions against the demands of office, but he thinks this is quite a narrow exception. See Burke, *Bureaucratic Responsibility* (Baltimore: Johns Hopkins University, Press, 1986), pp. 167–178.

4. This principle was reaffirmed by the U.S. Army in its handling of the Lieutenant William Calley, Jr., case in Vietnam. See Robert Anthony Calaff, "Battling Evil from Within: Laws of War, Obedience, and U.S. Army Basic Training since My Lai" (A.B. Honors Thesis, Harvard University, 1985).

5. For a discussion of obligations to blow the whistle, see Sissela Bok, "Blowing the Whistle," in Joel Fleishman, Lance Liebman, and Mark H. Moore, eds., *Public Duties: The Moral Obligations of Government Officials* (Cambridge, Mass.: Harvard University Press, 1981), pp. 204–220. See also Edward Weisband and Thomas M. Franck, *Resignation in Protest* (New York: Grossman Publishers, 1975).

6. John F. Kennedy, *Profiles in Courage* (New York: Harper Perennial, 1956).

7. Burke expresses skepticism of this view in *Bureaucratic Responsibility,* pp. 162–164.

8. This statement reflects the value that Kaufman describes as "the pursuit of representativeness" in "Emerging Conflicts."

9. This view is commonly espoused by public officials whom I have taught over the last decade in the Kennedy School's executive programs.

10. Albert O. Hirshman describes the choices open to members of an enterprise in his classic book *Exit, Voice, and Loyalty* (Cambridge, Mass.: Harvard University Press, 1970).

11. Burke, for example, observes: "Bureaucratic officials generally face clear, pre-defined statements of or expectations about the role they are to play ... When expectations and obligations are unclear, bureaucrats can appeal for clarification to authorities like the legislature or superiors in the organizational hierarchy. Moreover, not only can an appeal to higher authority be made, but the other parties to that appeal often possess a better perspective for making political choices." Burke, *Bureaucratic Responsibility*, p. 163. This conflicts with the views of Pendleton Herring described earlier: "Upon the shoulders of the bureaucrat has been placed in large part the burden of reconciling group differences and making effective and workable the economic and social compromises arrived at through the legislative process. He is in a better position than legislators to perform these duties. His daily occupation brings him into direct contact with the situation the law is intended to meet." Herring, "Public Administration and the Public Interest," in Jay M. Shafritz and Albert C. Hyde, eds., *Classics of Public Administration*, 2d ed. (Chicago: Dorsey Press, 1987), p. 74.

12. Charles E. Lindblom, *The Policy-Making Process*, 2d ed. (Englewood Cliffs, N.J.: Prentice-Hall, 1980), p. 5: "Moreover, a policy sometimes is formed from a political compromise among policy-makers, none of whom had in mind quite the problem to which the agreed policy responds. Sometimes, as we have just noted, policies spring from new opportunities, not from 'problems' at all."

13. Laurence E. Lynn, Jr., makes this point strongly and eloquently in *Managing Public Policy* (Boston: Little, Brown, 1987), pp. 46–49.

14. Derek Bok, *The Cost of Talent: How Executives and Professionals Are Paid and How It Affects America* (New York: Free Press and Maxwell Macmillan International), p. 208.

15. Ibid.

16. For a set of cases that show public managers responding to this painful circumstance in quite different ways, see the set of cases entitled "Surviving at the EPA": "Surviving at the EPA: David Tundermann," KSG Case #C16-84-588.0; "Surviving at the EPA: Mike Walsh," KSG Case #C16-84-589.0; "Surviving at the EPA: Mike Cook," KSG Case #C16-84-590.0; "Surviving at the EPA: Bill Hedeman," KSG Case #C16-84-591.0; "Surviving at the EPA: Gary Dietrich," KSG Case #C16-84-592.0; "Note on the EPA under Administrator Anne Gorsuch," KSG Case #N16-84-587.0 (all Cambridge, Mass.: Kennedy School of Government Case Program, 1984).

17. For images of managers who have grown cynical, see Michael Maccoby, *The Gamesman: The New Corporate Leaders* (New York: Simon and Schuster, 1976).

18. See, for example, Robert Caro, *The Power Broker: Robert Moses and the Fall of New York* (New York: Knopf, 1974); and Eugene Lew, "Admiral Hyman Rickover: Technological Entrepreneurship in the U.S. Navy," in James W. Doig and Erwin C. Hargrove, eds., *Leadership and Innovation: Entrepreneurs in Government* (Baltimore: Johns Hopkins University Press, 1990), pp. 84–87.

19. In proposing this view, I am trying to respond to Woodrow Wilson's injunction set more than a century ago: "We have enthroned public opinion; and it is forbidden us to hope during its reign for any quick schooling of the sovereign in executive expertness . . . In order for us to make any advance at all we must instruct a multitudinous monarch called public opinion . . . [The people] can agree upon nothing simple: advance must be made by a compounding of differences, by a trimming of plans and a suppression of too straightforward principles. There will be a succession of resolves running through a course of years, a ripping fire of commands running through a whole gamut of modifications." Jay M. Shafritz and Albert C. Hyde, eds., *Classics of Public Administration*, 2d ed. (Chicago: Dorsey Press, 1987), reprint Wilson's "Study of Administration"; see pp. 13, 16.

20. In endorsing this position, I am aligning myself with the third core value that Kaufman identifies in public concerns about governmental enterprises: "the pursuit of executive leadership" (see "Emerging Conflicts"). I am also aligning myself with Robert Behn's idea of the "leadership meta-strategy." See Behn, *Leadership Counts: Lessons for Public Managers from the Massachusetts Welfare, Training, and Employment Program* (Cambridge, Mass.: Harvard University Press, 1991), pp. 203–208.

21. Shifting to "after-the-fact" accountability has the additional virtue of being consistent with a principle that managers of the firms celebrated by Thomas J. Peters and Robert H. Waterman seem to follow: the principle of "ready, fire, aim." The virtue they see in following this principle is that it gives organizations a "bias for action," which tends to increase not only the speed with which things happen but also the reliability with which ideas are carried out. The organization comes to think of itself as an enterprise that can accomplish things. See Peters and Waterman, *In Search of Excellence: Lessons from America's Best-Run Companies* (New York: Warner, 1982), pp. 119–155. I would add to this point that it is often easier to "aim" after one has "fired"—at least a tracer bullet. The reason is that managers know a great deal more about the feasibility and value of imagined efforts once they have tried them than they can know in advance. In the public sector, the more typical process is "ready, ready, ready, aim; nope, back to ready." The public sector places a great deal of pressure on

public officials to delay action until they have been fully authorized. This delay is supposed to guard society from the risks of both technical and moral failures; consultation is necessary to improve and to justify public action. No doubt, this often occurs. But this strategy takes its toll in organizations that move very slowly, that lose their confidence in their ability to act at all, and that place greater emphasis on trying to guess what will happen in advance through the techniques of policy analysis and planning than on learning and reporting what they have accomplished through the techniques of program evaluation.

22. See, for example, William F. Willoughby, *The Movement for Budgetary Reforms in the States* (New York: D. Appleton, for the Institute for Government Research, 1918), pp. 1–8, reprinted in Shafritz and Hyde, *Classics,* pp. 33–37.

23. Carol H. Weiss, "Purposes of Evaluation," reprinted in Shafritz and Hyde, *Classics,* pp. 474–483.

24. See Chapter 3.

25. Mark H. Moore, "Realms of Obligations and Virtues," in Joel L. Fleishman, Lance Liebman, and Mark H. Moore, eds., *Public Duties: The Moral Obligations of Government Officials* (Cambridge, Mass.: Harvard University Press, 1981). See also Moore and Sparrow, *Ethics in Government.*

26. For an account of the subjective experience of managing in the public sector, see Donald Rumsfeld, "A Politician Turned Executive Surveys Both Worlds," *Fortune,* vol. 100, no. 5 (September 10, 1979): 89–94; and Michael Blumenthal, "Candid Reflections of a Businessman in Washington," *Fortune,* vol. 98, no. 1 (January 29, 1979): 36–49.

27. For a discussion of the extent of public officials' rights to privacy, see Dennis F. Thompson, "The Private Lives of Public Officials," in Joel L. Fleishman, Lance Liebman, and Mark H. Moore, eds., *Public Duties: The Moral Obligations of Government Officials* (Cambridge, Mass.: Harvard University Press, 1981), pp. 221–247.

28. For a discussion of the moral problems faced by public officials who share a cause, and commit to a group of colleagues, but then begin to have doubts, see Michael Walzer, "Political Solidarity and Personal Honor," in Michael Walzer, *Obligations: Essays on Disobedience, War, and Citizenship* (Cambridge, Mass.: Harvard University Press, 1970), pp. 190–202.

29. For a vivid account of how the claims of one's colleagues can become compelling and ultimately corrupting, see Thomas Powers, *The Man Who Kept the Secrets: Richard Helms and the CIA* (New York: Knopf, 1979).

30. They must strike a balance between their interest in exercising power and their need to learn. Karl W. Deutsch described the dilemma: "In simple language, to have power means not to have to give in, and to force the environment or the other person to do so. Power in this narrow sense is the priority of output over intake, the ability to talk instead of listen. In a sense, it is the ability to afford not to learn." Deutsch, *The Nerves of*

Government: Models of Political Communication and Control (New York: Free Press, 1966), p. 11.

31. In this conclusion I am following Donald A. Schon, who observed: "In order to achieve such outcomes as these, professionals engaged in the political contention of the policy-making process would have to be capable of inquiry within an adversarial setting. They would have to be capable of advocating and acting on their own views of reality while at the same time subjecting them to reflection, of taking an adversarial stance toward their opponent's views while at the same time trying to understand them." Schon, *The Reflective Practitioner: How Professionals Think in Action* (New York: Basic Books, 1983), p. 350.

32. "Leadership is a razor's edge because one has to oversee a sustained period of social disequilibrium during which people confront the contradictions in their lives and communities and adjust their values and behavior to accommodate new realities." Ronald A. Heifetz, *Leadership without Easy Answers* (Cambridge, Mass.: Harvard University Press, 1994), pp. 126–128.

33. Ibid., pp. 163–165.

34. Ibid., pp. 235–237.

35. Ibid., pp. 268–271.

36. Max Weber, "Politics as a Vocation," in H. H. Gerth and C. Wright Mills, eds., *From Max Weber: Essays in Sociology* (New York: Oxford University Press, 1946), p. 115.

37. Ibid.

38. Ibid.

INDEX

Administrative systems, 390n121; defined, 226–227, 321n10; in BHA, 227–228; changes in, 291, 313n13

Affirmative action, 69

AIDS, 181

Allison, Graham, 1, 354n99, 356n3, 365n44, 366n53

Amenities, vs. rights, 41, 44–45, 46

Authority: as a resource, 29, 41–43, 50, 118, 125, 210, 222–223; in liberal democracy, 47, 153, 265; and politics, 48, 328n6; and wide consultations, 165

Authorizing environment, 120, 121, 125, 126, 128, 153, 213, 300, 305, 387n81; dynamics of, 130–132

Authorizing process, 48–50, 118

Bales, John P., 207, 257, 260–261, 262, 266, 270, 277, 278

Bankruptcy: in public sector, 193–194, 207, 208, 209, 240, 275, 342n22; in private sector, 342n22

Barnard, Chester, 233, 353n92, 354n100

BATNA (best alternative to a negotiated agreement), 176, 178

Benefit-cost analysis, 22, 34, 35–36, 41–43, 49, 55, 73, 77–78, 344n28

BHA. *See* Boston Housing Authority

Bond, Pappy, 201–202, 203

Boston Housing Authority (BHA), 193–200, 213, 220, 293, 303; financial resources of, 195–196, 281; management team of, 196; organizational structure of, 197, 198, 229, 230, 288; policies and procedures of, 197, 199–200, 207–208, 234, 285; as service agency, 208, 209; mission of, 214–216; production processes of, 220–222, 232, 282; administrative systems in, 227–228; innovation in, 235–236, 250, 282–283, 284–286; bankruptcy of, 240; reorganizing of, 242, 254–255, 287; and legislature, 243, 245, 247; stabilization program of, 244–245, 255; and Boston Police Department, 246; and selection of tenants, 247–250; Supportive Services Program of, 250; and community organization, 250–253; and routine maintenance, 253–254, 255; and judicial management, 312n10

Boston Redevelopment Authority (BRA), 108, 136, 155, 175, 176, 182, 296

Brown, Lee, 193, 203–207, 208, 210, 224, 255–273; and consultation with community, 209, 256–257, 259, 266; and mission of HPD, 214, 216, 219; and innovation, 234, 236, 237–238, 267–273, 283, 284, 286, 287, 288, 289, 290, 291, 303, 304; opposition to, 255–256; and assessment report of HPD, 257–260; leadership of, 270; and political management, 273, 274; and organizational staffing, 276–277; and internal accountability, 278–281; managerial style of, 281; gaining additional resources, 281–282; and risk, 302. *See also* Houston Police Department

Building and Construction Trades Council, 241

Bulger, William, 245

Bureaucrats, 21, 314n22, 321n10, 323n19, 357n9, 392n11; mindset of, 17–18; as civil servants, 19, 313n15, 338n69; public attitude toward, 19, 20; and politics, 33, 295, 324n23; vs. legislators, 341n15

Bureau of Biologics, 111, 117, 143

Caldwell, Harry, 202–203

Campos Torres, Joe, 202

Cannon, James, 144

Capital: financial, 86, 114–115, 236; political, 86, 236

Carson, Rachel, 79

Cases, use of, 6, 7

Cavanaugh, James, 142, 143, 144

CDC. *See* Center for Disease Control

Center for Disease Control (CDC), 110–111, 117, 131, 133–134, 143, 144, 145, 164, 293; Advisory Council on Immunization Programs of, 111, 140, 147

Chamberlain, Neville, 129

Cheney, Richard, 144

Chief executives, elected, 2, 5, 17, 119, 170

Citizens: view of bureaucrats, 19; contribution to public objectives, 29, 164; as a collective consumer, 29–31, 39, 335n37; and government, 37, 183–185, 196, 208, 330n13; view of value, 39, 40, 373n144; acting through politics, 44, 48; aspirations of, 52, 55, 70, 72, 211, 214–215; and the media, 122; and decision-making, 167, 179; and public deliberation, 180–181, 182–183; and police, 217–219, 226, 230, 259, 266, 268, 270, 286, 287. *See also* Clients; Customers

Civil service, 19, 338n69, 350n72. *See also* Bureaucrats

Civil Service Commissions, 119

Clients, 36–38, 40, 54, 70, 220, 375n165; and welfare departments, 37; satisfaction of, 187, 208, 210, 216; cooperation of, 209, 287, 290, 292

Cohen, Howard, 241, 246

Competitors, 66, 67, 70

Consumers. *See* Clients; Customers

Cooper, Theodore, 117, 119, 140, 142, 143, 144, 152, 160

Coproduction: and political management, 117–118, 121, 126, 211; organizing for, 287–290

Corporate strategy, 65-66, 345n44, 378n43, 390n122; and distinctive competence, 67; in diversified conglomerates, 67–68; and portfolios of businesses, 68; as sustainable deal, 68–70; and public sector, 70; and utility of framework, 72–73; pollution control as, 77–78; humanizing treatment as, 84–85; definition of, 343n24

Cost-effectiveness analysis. *See* Benefit-cost analysis

Council of Large Public Housing Authorities (CLPHA), 244

Courts, 125–126, 154, 336n45, 342n22, 359n39, 365n48; and judges, 2–3

Customers: satisfaction of, as criterion of value, 36–38, 54; acting through markets, 44; importance of, 65–66, 67

Darman, Richard, 170–171, 371n103, 372n116

DART. *See* Directed Area Responsibility Teams

DCA. *See* Massachusetts Department of Community Affairs

DDT, banning of, 79, 91

Decentralization, 4, 171, 235, 251–252, 253, 267, 268, 287; of budget processes, 280; geographic, 287, 288–289, 290, 291

Decision-making: equity in, 6; collective, 36, 178-179; political, 54–55, 140, 141, 143-144, 151–162, 164; political management of, 117–118; and press, 120–121; and combining interests, 126–128; and legitimacy, 127, 152–153; and policy management, 163, 169, 296–297; ingredients in quality, 163–164; dealing with

Individual preferences, as basis of public value, 46–47, 166

Initiative, 19, 34, 282-285, 293–294, 299, 323n19, 386n80

Innovation, 5, 6, 12, 55, 63, 267–271, 290; role in operational management, 17, 20, 211–213, 233, 267; administrative, 95, 234, 286; policy or program, 95, 233–234, 267–273, 282–284; strategic, 95, 98, 210, 234–235; authorizing, 115–116; political risks of, 233; in private sector, 387n86

Institutional reform, 84–89; vs. improved management, 3–4, 62, 85

Institutional structures, 3, 80, 85, 86

Institutions, 60–62; legislative, 5; private, vs. public bureaucracies, 43; capital value of, 50–52; and citizens' desires, 53

Interagency coordination, 116–117

Interest groups, 30, 31, 37, 54, 122–125, 129, 358n29, 359n34

Internal Revenue System (IRS), 158

Interventions: managerial, into organizations, 1, 6, 10, 11, 55; governmental, into markets, 43–48, 49, 55, 77, 336n45

Jackson, Ira, 187–188

James, Tim, 201

Johnson, B. K., 203, 207, 257, 260, 261, 268

Johnson, Spencer, 144

Kaufman, Herbert, 282, 360n48, 361n61, 378n37, 391n2, 392n8, 393n20

Kennedy School of Government (Harvard University), 4, 7, 8, 70, 78; Case Program of, 6; executive programs of, 313n16, 323n19, 349n72, 360n60, 392n9

Kirp, David, 181

Koby, Thomas, 271–272

Kotter, John, 161–162, 353n91, 354n96

Kramer, Al, 137, 138, 296

Lax, David, 177

Leadership, 93, 180, 182–183, 323n19, 327n3, 353n92, 395n32; in public sector, 18, 62–63, 139, 148, 149–150, 153, 290–291, 293–309, 314n22; and political management, 23; means vs. ends in, 62–63; in private sector, 63–64; and conflict, 116;

federal, 141–146; vs. management, 390n118. *See also* Public managers

Legislative mandates, 6, 8, 17, 30, 31–33, 42, 105, 106, 124; for youth services, 60, 61–62; uncertain, 62–63, 146; on pollution, 82; and legitimacy, 113, 114; and public managers, 119, 247

Linde, Edward, 108

Literature: economics, 5; on public administration, 5, 6; organizational theory, 5; political science, 5; on administrative law, 6; on private sector management, 6; management, 385n74

Lupu, Nancy Altman, 165

Lynn, James, 142, 143, 144

Mahoney, Miles, 115, 116, 131, 361n62; and Park Plaza, 105–110, 112, 114, 128; and political executives, 119, 120; and the media, 121; and interest groups, 122, 124; and courts, 125; and conventional wisdom, 129; authorizing environment of, 130, 132; and political management, 135–136, 146, 148; initiatives of, 135–139; as entrepreneurial advocate, 151, 152, 153, 154, 155, 157, 159, 160; as policy manager, 164, 166, 167, 168, 172, 296, 299; and negotiation, 173–174, 175, 177, 178, 362n6; and public deliberation, 181–182; and supporters, 308. *See also* Park Plaza project

Management, private, 28, 35, 65–70, 317n48, 327n3, 334n36; and regulatory agencies, 45; and customers, 53–54, 65–66, 345n36; defining goals in, 63–64, 343n23; and competitors, 66, 345n35

Marketing, public sector, 23, 150, 185–189, 374n162

Markets: power of, 43; preference for, 47; and individual desires, 52, 66, 330n12; defense of, 328n8

Massachusetts Department of Community Affairs (DCA), 105–106, 116, 131, 146, 152, 168, 175, 293; and redevelopment, 112, 155, 174. *See also* Park Plaza

Massachusetts Department of Public Health (DPH), 184, 185

Massachusetts Department of Revenue, 187–188

Massachusetts Department of Youth Services (DYS), 58, 60–62, 84–89, 293; alternative strategies for, 95–96
Mathews, David, 140, 142, 143, 144, 152
Matthews, Byron, 241
McAdoo, Myra, 251
McGee, Thomas, 60
McKeehan, John, 257, 260, 261
Media, 5, 87, 120–122, 139, 157, 159, 188, 214, 337n66, 375n166
Meyer, Harry M., 117, 143
Miller, Jerome, 57–58, 60–62, 63, 70, 76, 84-89, 275; operational focus of, 91–92; strategies of, 94, 98, 99–100, 102, 122, 299; and deinstitutionalization, 296; and risk, 302, 303, 304. *See also* Massachusetts Department of Youth Services
Mitchell, Thomas, 257, 260, 261
Mosher, Frederick C., 322n10
Municipal sanitation, 38–52
Muskie, Edmund, 58, 79, 303

National Highway Traffic Safety Administration, 169
National Rifle Association, 123
Negotiations, 5, 136–138, 172–179, 362n6, 373n140; and political management, 23, 150; tactics in, 176–178, 189; creating vs. claiming value in, 177; criticisms of, 178–179. *See also* BATNA
Newman, Leslie, 248, 250, 254
Nixon, Richard, 58, 77, 79, 94, 303
Nuremberg trials, 294

Obligations, 29, 30–31, 37, 41, 42, 53
Office for Juvenile Justice and Delinquency Prevention (OJJDP), 87–88
Office of Management and Budget (OMB), 80, 142, 143, 144, 152, 336n45
OJJDP. *See* Office for Juvenile Justice and Delinquency Prevention
OMB. *See* Office of Management and Budget
O'Neill, Paul, 142, 143, 144
Operational management, 59, 62, 80–83, 84–85, 107; defined, 193; function of, 207–213; strategic view of, 210–211; techniques of, 224, 239–292; and engineering programs, 284–287

Organizational capacity, 94; as capital asset, 50–52
Organizational goals, 22–23, 70–76, 104, 347n60, 353n95, 354n103, 371n114; and hierarchies, 213–214, 378n44
Organizational mission, 89–92, 213–219
Organizations, public: behavior of, 2; administration of, 8; and politics, 8, 23, 84, 273-274; cumulative experience of, 51; adaptability of, 52; task environment of, 55; and budget process, 168–169, 279–280, 339n3, 371n104; functional, 287–288, 289
Outputs and outcomes, 40
Overseers, 2, 3, 22, 116, 189, 196, 299–300, 305; and public managers, 70, 72; political, 79, 81, 98, 99; legislative, 119–120, 153; courts as, 125; satisfaction of, 209, 210; and production process, 220, 222; and responsive organizations, 274–276, 282. *See also* Authorizing environment

Park Plaza project, 107–110, 111, 135-139; approval of, 112, 121, 154, 296; rejection of, 114, 129, 130, 132, 146, 151, 152, 153, 155, 159, 164, 176, 177, 181; and legislature, 119, 124; legality of, 120, 125; and interest groups, 122; decision on, 126, 128, 132–133, 155, 156, 160; players in, 152, 155; options in, 158, 182; evaluation of, 166, 175-176. *See also* Massachusetts Department of Community Affairs
Persian Gulf War, financing of, 318n5
Philadelphia Police Study Task Force, 222
Policy: and administration, 21; as stories, 40, 54, 57, 211, 335n37, 337n66
Policy analysis, 33, 34-35, 38, 55, 165–166, 167, 348n64
Policy development: managing, 23, 150, 162–172, 368n80, 392n12; wide consultation in, 163, 164–165; and quality decisions, 163–164
Policy management systems, 81, 168–172, 189, 368n79, 370n100; ad hocracy in, 169; centralized, 169–170, 229, 232, 287–288, 291; multiple advocacy in, 169-170; functions of, 171; criticisms of, 172

Political management, 2, 12, 23, 38, 105–110, 111–126, 356n4; importance of, 113–115, 189, 210–211, 273; and accountability, 115, 274-275; and innovation, 115–116, 232-235; challenge of, 132–134; hazards of, 146; techniques of, 148–151, 164–165, 179, 183, 189; and democracy, 362n2. *See also* Entrepreneurial advocacy; Ethics; Leadership

Political mandates. *See* Legislative mandates

Politics, 5, 30, 214, 358n19; and public enterprises, 20, 63, 89, 342n19, 348n63, 365n46; and public value, 22, 32, 38, 48–49, 50, 54, 62, 77; and strategic management, 23, 105; and use of public resources, 32, 54, 105, 106; vs. administration, 32, 320n10, 341n15, 342n20, 351n73; of environmental legislation, 58–59; and level of abstraction, 96–99

Pollution: air, 80, 82, 91; water, 80, 82

Pollution control, 58–59, 76-83, 184–185, 300; as corporate strategy, 77–78; operational feasibility of, 78, 80-83, 89, 91

Porter, Roger, 126, 169–170, 171

Practical reasoning, 1, 13–15

Private enterprise, 47, 69, 114; and value, 28, 43, 64–65; and profitability, 35

Production processes: redesigning, 219–226; in public housing, 220–222; in community order, 222–226

Program evaluation, 22, 36, 38, 55, 73, 161, 344n28, 377n35; vs. policy analysis, 34–35, 394n21. *See also* Outputs and outcomes

Public administration: as an institution, 4; classic tradition of, 74–75, 349n72; definition of, 351n74

Public deliberation, 23, 150, 179, 180–182, 189

Public ideas, and conventional wisdom, 128–130, 131

Public management, 3, 7; philosophy of, 1, 5; in a democracy, 5, 17, 30–31, 34, 135, 149, 294, 303, 308, 329n11, 339n2; success in, 9–10, 11; strategic, 20–21, 23, 94–102, 105, 189, 273–290; aim of, 28-31, 70–76

Public managers, 1, 2–3, 6, 7, 56, 321n10, 356n5, 358n16, 361n61; and judges, 3; and private sector, 3; performance of, 3, 273–290, 291, 293, 395n31; and politics, 5, 19, 38, 135, 350n72, 351n77, 355n108; and political mandates, 6, 8; and public organizations, 6; town librarians as, 6, 13–23, 70, 75, 293, 300, 318n1, 377n34; and tests, 9–12; and volunteers, 14–15, 319n7; sanitation commissioners as, 27–28, 31, 38–52, 293, 300; vs. private sector managers, 31, 56, 343n25, 344n27, 346n55, 356n3; and substantive knowledge, 32, 323n17; and citizens' desires, 52; and discretion, 62–63; statements of purpose of, 89–94; and legal oversight committees, 119; and virtue, 133, 149, 297–299; powers of, 152, 394n30; and reengineering organizations, 211–212, 290–292; and accountability, 273–276, 278–281, 298, 300–302, 351n76, 352n80, 355n106, 364n34, 388n93, 393n21; ethical challenges of, 294–305; as explorers, 299–305; psychological challenges of, 305–309; and partners, 307-308, 390n120; temperament of, 308-309; autonomy of, 385n75. *See also* Policy development

Public officials, 19, 21, 119, 123, 152, 295–296, 392n9. *See also* Public managers

Public policy: study of, 7; implementation of, 8, 78–83, 85–88

Public resources, 17, 19, 32, 74, 222–223; use of, 6, 29, 50, 53, 54, 57, 89, 113, 125, 167, 208, 210, 281, 319n9

Public value, 43, 46, 70; as aim of public managers, 1, 7, 10, 15, 18, 19, 20, 21, 28, 39, 77, 101, 114, 132, 159, 173, 209, 301, 354n100; different standards for, 31–38; techniques for assessing, 33–36; definition of, 52–55, 57, 64, 73, 189; managerial view of, 52–56; creation of, 57, 76, 89, 102, 106, 177, 189, 210, 211, 238, 264–265, 287, 327n5, 335n36; and political forces, 100–101, 143, 166; claiming, 177; search for, 299, 305

Reagan, Ronald, 158, 165, 244